A Voice Still Heard

A Voice Still Heard
Selected Essays of Irving Howe

❧

Edited by Nina Howe

with the assistance of

Nicholas Howe Bukowski

❧

Foreword by Morris Dickstein

Yale UNIVERSITY PRESS

New Haven and London

Published with assistance from the Louis Stern Memorial Fund.

Yale University Press books may be purchased in quantity for educational,
business, or promotional use. For information, please e-mail sales.press@yale
.edu (U.S. office) or sales@yaleup.co.uk (U.K. office).

Designed by Nancy Ovedovitz and set in Quadraat type by Newgen North
America, Austin, Texas. Printed in the United States of America.

ISBN: 978-0-300-20366-0 (cloth)

Library of Congress Control Number: 2014934706
A catalogue record for this book is available from the British Library.
This paper meets the requirements of ANSI/NISO Z39.48−1992
(Permanence of Paper).

10 9 8 7 6 5 4 3 2 1

For Irving's Grandchildren

Anastasia and Nicholas Howe Bukowski

and to the memory

of their Uncle Nick

Contents

The 1970s

The 1980s

The 1990s

Personal Reflections

Foreword

MORRIS DICKSTEIN

I N ANY CONSIDERATION of the man of letters, political critic, or the public intellectual in the second half of the twentieth century, it would be hard to find a more exemplary or embattled figure than Irving Howe. Since Howe's death in 1993 at the age of seventy-two, his work and even his personal aura have had a vigorous afterlife. Literary criticism, though less topical than political writing, also fades with time. Once off the scene, the writer can no longer bring old ideas up to date or lend them coherence by sheer force of personality. Irving Howe, on the other hand, remains a real presence, not simply among those who knew him well. He remains one of my intellectual heroes, as Orwell was for him. His views were always strikingly formulated, and he is as frequently cited as any other critic of the period. Looking at writers and issues in a wide context, sharpening his arguments to make them hard to ignore, he could turn a book review into a general essay, laying down a challenge to any future writer on the subject.

Howe's death was followed by many memorial tributes, along with attacks by prominent neoconservatives who saw him still as a thorn in their side—too smart a writer, too biting a critic to be easily set aside. More comment followed when his son, Nicholas Howe, brought out his last and most literary work, *A Critic's Notebook*. With his sharp-tongued humor and debater's edge, Howe played a central role in an excellent documentary about four New York intellectuals, Joseph Dorman's *Arguing the World*. A leading professional journal, *American Jewish History*, devoted a whole issue to a not altogether friendly reconsideration of Howe's masterpiece, *World of Our Fathers*, which lies like a lion across the path of historians of Jewish immigrant life. There have been two well-researched intellectual biographies, one by a militant conservative, Edward Alexander (1998), who is critical of Howe's politics, early and late, the other by a sympathetic liberal, Gerald Sorin (2002). John Rodden, a leading Orwell scholar, has edited several engrossing volumes taking the measure of Howe's influential legacy.

I suspect I'm not the only writer who still hears his voice echoing in my head, wondering at times what he might have thought of this book or that political twist or turn. *Dissent*, the social democratic journal he founded with Lewis Coser in 1954, remains intellectually robust at sixty—an ecumenical magazine of the beleaguered left, as flexible in its social criticism as he became in his lifelong commitment to socialism. Howe and Coser knew from their own experience how much the left had suffered from sectarianism, dogmatism, an insistence on ideological purity. *Dissent* was conceived as a broad-gauged alternative. In his cogent reflections on it after twenty-five years, Howe wrote that "we had to learn to work piecemeal, to treat socialist thought as inherently problematic, and to move pragmatically from question to question." He knew this kind of "steady work" could be boring; it was certainly not the best way to fire up the troops.

Howe saw himself as a perpetual dissenter, but there were always others ready to follow where he led. His socialism seemed an anomaly in the 1950s as American power grew and intellectuals grew more complacent and self-satisfied. Yet he also felt shunted aside by the young leftists of the 1960s, and responded with a barrage of criticism so intemperate that it might have permanently alienated him from those who shared his deepest aims. Like Edmund Burke's attack on the French Revolution when it was still in its infancy, Howe's assault on the New Left was telling but premature, only to be borne out, at least in part, when the movement violently imploded four or five years later. By making his peace with the aging radicals of the sixties generation in his last decade, though he didn't always approve of where they stood, Howe insured that the magazine would not only survive but flourish, even as the world's political agenda dramatically shifted.

Today, in the face of an intransigent conservatism energized by unlimited money, grass-roots support, and a vast media presence, liberals feel thwarted, reduced to defending old gains rather than enacting new programs. As in the 1950s, this makes an inclusive journal, committed to both democracy and social change, all the more valuable. Howe and his fellow dissenters have served as a model for intellectuals who combine hopes for greater economic equality with a stubborn faith in democracy, who criticize their country for falling short of its ideals but refuse to see it as the root of evil in the world. For political writers like Richard Rorty, Michael Walzer, Todd Gitlin, George Packer, and Paul Berman, as well as a brace of younger writers in *Dissent*, he vindicated the figure of the activist thinker who somehow escaped the clutches of what Orwell called the "smelly little orthodoxies" of the twentieth century, very much as his old antagonist, the protean Ralph Ellison, became the unlikely model for a generation of black intellectuals who had outgrown the ideologies on which they cut their teeth, including black nationalism and Marxism.

The changing fortunes of Howe as a literary critic tell a similar story. The rise of theory, including deconstruction, academic feminism, ideological critique, and postmodernism, isolated him even more dramatically than the waves of conservatism and radical leftism. His style as a critic was marked by the vehement clarity of someone schooled in political argument, who had also learned his craft in the late 1940s as a rebellious protégé of Dwight Macdonald and an anonymous book reviewer for *Time* magazine. Even in his longest literary essays Howe remained a working journalist who made certain to give a clear, vigorous account of a writer's career, a book's texture and style, a character's human density, and a work's compelling claim on the reader. He invariably quoted well, a cardinal test of a good critic as well but also a generous gift to the reader. This approach went out of fashion in academic criticism after 1970 as theory and method came to the fore.

Howe saw this happening even earlier. In a stinging attack on Leslie Fiedler's *Love and Death in the American Novel*, he anticipated what would later be called "the hermeneutics of suspicion," the critic's search for a buried subtext that could reveal the writer's unconscious motives or be used to arraign the work itself. "Like a mass-culture imitation of a psychoanalyst, Fiedler refuses on principle to honor the 'surface' events, characters, statements and meanings of a novel. . . . He engages not in formal description or historical placement or critical evaluation, but in a relentless and joyless exposure. The work of literature comes before him as if it were a defendant without defense, or an enemy intent on deceiving him so that he will not see through its moral claims and coverings." Writing in 1960, Howe had little inkling of how fashionable this adversarial posture would become for later academic critics. Even earlier, in his landmark essay "This Age of Conformity" (1954), he foresaw how a concern with theory and method could displace an immediate response to a writer's work. "Learned young critics who have never troubled to open a novel by Turgenev can rattle off reams of Kenneth Burke."

They would not suppose that literature "is concerned with anything so gauche as human experience."

Beginning with his first major work, *Politics and the Novel* (1957), Howe made his reputation as a social and political critic of literature, not a strictly aesthetic one. The academic exegesis of the day he found narrow and dull, marred by a lack of both "literary tact," an indefinable feeling for a literary work, and an "interest in represented experience," the human element. But in trying to connect intimately with the literary text and make sense of it to a broader public, he cast his lot, surprisingly, with the formal critics, both New and old, whose approach was already going out of style. After a period of "painful soul-searching" around 1948, he reacted sharply against his own sectarian background and the Marxist criticism it had fostered. He felt a growing delight in literature itself, apart from its ideological tendency. Fiedler's imperious psychoanalytic method, he says, "disregards the work of literature as something 'made,' a construct of mind and imagination through the medium of language, requiring attention on its own terms and according to its own structure." We rightly think of Howe as a historical critic, yet he always grounds his commentary in a writer's language and style, the emotional patterns revealed in the work, and the unique or familiar ways the writer remakes the world.

Howe's range of subjects remains little short of astonishing, even on literature alone. Nina Howe's excellent selection gives full play to broad general essays, reviews of individual works, and overviews of a writer's full corpus. Who would have expected him to respond so warmly to that minor masterpiece, Sarah Orne Jewett's *The Country of the Pointed Firs*, or to the poetry of Edwin Arlington Robinson? When he liked a book, no one was better at "selling" it—at laying out its way of seeing, and carrying his readers along. His review of the paperback edition of Henry Roth's *Call It Sleep* singlehandedly revived a great novel that had languished, nearly forgotten, for thirty years. By the 1980s, as this selection makes clear, he found himself intrigued by other work—from Japan, from Israel—that added to his lifelong project of self-education.

For many years the clarity of Howe's prose, along with this focus on the individual author, the individual work, made him seem like an old-fashioned figure on the critical scene, more the journalist and omnivorous reviewer than the full-fledged critic. Yet on writer after writer as different as T. E. Lawrence, Sholom Aleichem, Louis-Ferdinand Céline, Ignazio Silone, George Orwell, I. B. Singer, Edith Wharton, Isaac Babel, and Theodore Dreiser, his essays were often the first place the general reader might turn for critical illumination. As a sometime radical with a deep, abiding sense of privacy, Howe did not reveal much of himself in these essays. Yet his grasp of these writers was so immediate, so personal, so determined to find the living pulse of their work—and to articulate something almost unsayable in his own visceral response—that we come to feel we know him intimately. His sharp, relentless, often scathingly funny voice is no doubt indebted to his political writing but also reenacts his probing, jabbing way of reading. Even his longtime antagonist Philip Roth acknowledged that Howe was a real *reader*, one of the chosen, whose criticism could cut to the quick.

Like Lionel Trilling, Howe took every literary work, as he took many political issues, as a moral challenge, a set of embodied convictions on how to live. This led him into sweeping polemics in which he would play the provocateur, evoke passionate controversy, but at times go badly astray. It was the outraged moralist in him that led him to attack James Baldwin and Ralph Ellison for betraying the legacy of rage in the work of their mentor, Richard Wright, and to revile Roth in *Portnoy's Complaint* for putting his talent "to the service of a creative vision deeply marred by vulgarity." The same puritanical streak led him to travesty the "new sensibility" of the 1960s as a toxic dose of primitive innocence, a form of moral anarchy, and to wonder "whether this outlook is compatible with a high order of culture or a complex civilization." Despite a lifetime's work fighting for social justice, Howe, like other Jewish writers (including Freud and Trilling), found himself caught up in a tragic vision that stressed an almost insoluble moral tension, an irreconcilable conflict.

In a brief essay on Isaac Babel, he picks up Trilling's cue that Babel, riding with the Red Cossacks through territory dotted with his fellow Jews, "was captivated by the vision of two ways of being, the way of violence and the way of peace, and he was torn between them." But typically, Howe, speaking out of his own sense of the conflicts between politics and art, gives a historical coloring to Trilling's timeless observation, seeing the soldiers' brutality in political terms: "Babel understood with absolute sureness the problem that has obsessed all modern novelists who deal with politics: the problem of action in both its heroic necessity and its ugly self-contamination." In other words, though radical goals may be admirable, the means at hand to realize them could easily prove offensive, unpalatable. In one story Babel's protagonist, part journalist, part combatant, is bitterly berated by a Russian soldier for riding through battle without cartridges in his revolver. "Crouching beneath the crown of death," the writer ends up "begging fate for the simplest ability—the ability to kill a man." In another story he meets an old Jew who feels as abused by the Revolution as by the feudal Polish landowners who are fighting against it, who longs for something "unattainable," a "sweet Revolution," the "International of good people." Characteristically, Howe shows how this tension is enacted in Babel's famously laconic style, where it becomes a tremendous source of energy. He finds something similar in the speed and intensity of Bernard Malamud's stories, so different from the drab Depression tales of Jewish life: "The place is familiar, but the tone, the tempo, the treatment are all new." Taking up John Berryman's comparison of Babel with Stephen Crane, he writes that "in both writers there is an obsessive concern with compression and explosion, a kinesthetic ferocity of control, a readiness to wrench language in order to gain nervous immediacy. Both use language to inflict a wound."

This is no casual insight, no imposed melodrama, but a remark dredged up from deep inside the critic's own psyche. Trilling and Howe, both conflicted Jews, respond strongly to the ambivalence about Jews, about violence, about revolution that makes Babel's *Red Cavalry* so starkly effective yet would one day make the author one of Stalin's victims. This personal identification gives power to Howe's essays, which are often obliquely autobiographical. In a memoir of one of his mentors, *Partisan Review* editor Philip Rahv, with whom he later quarreled, Howe describes how Rahv turned cautious in the conservative climate of the 1950s, provoking others (including Howe) to write the provocative critical essays Rahv himself might have written. By holding back, Rahv lost his "elan, his nervousness": "He could still turn out a lively piece full of the old fire and scorn, but he had made an estimate—politically mistaken, morally unheroic—that this wasn't the time to take chances. And by not taking chances (they didn't turn out to be such big chances either), he allowed his energy to dribble away, his voice to lose its forcefulness." Howe himself, at Rahv's urging, wrote the polemical essay "This Age of Conformity," one of the key dissenting texts of the decade, which Rahv then published in his magazine. In Howe's account, Rahv's cunning and timidity did him in; as Howe sees it, personal authenticity, keeping faith with one's convictions, is inseparable from political and moral daring. Rahv's flaw, his failure of nerve, gives Howe's portrait of him its tragic cast at the same time it justifies Howe's own zeal for controversy, his take-no-prisoners approach to public argument, his lifelong persistence as a political campaigner, and the peculiar nervous intensity of his own style.

Howe's personal voice, his refusal to rest or desist, brought him back into fashion as a critic in the same way that he became the political conscience for many in the younger generation. Just as he lived to witness the end of the Reagan revolution and the fall of the Soviet Union, he saw the beginning of a tectonic shift in the world of literature and criticism. Thanks mainly to the humiliation of the left in the culture wars of the late eighties and early nineties, a new fascination with the public intellectual challenged the long dominance of theory, with its arcane professional languages. In an obituary tribute to Trilling written many years earlier, Howe recalled asking Trilling whether he wasn't terrified of the new methodologists who were taking over the field. (Trilling responded puckishly that he was terrified of everything.) By the time Howe died the theorists had more or less had their day, and Howe himself became an important model for young literary scholars like David Bromwich and Ilan Stavans who were as interested in politics as in culture, and were eager to write for larger audiences without intellectual compromise. For me he had always been such a model, ever since I began reading him as an undergraduate around 1960. When I published my first piece in *Partisan Review* in 1962, I got a complimentary note from Howe, always on the lookout for young talent. He invited me to write for *Dissent*, something I didn't actually get to do until twenty-five years later. I didn't meet him until the early seventies, and disliked the fire-breathing pieces he wrote in the interim about politics and the arts in the uninhibited climate of the 1960s. It amazed me that he could write a sympathetic essay on Berkeley's Free Speech movement one year, then publish his furious onslaught against the New Left barely a year later. When Philip Rahv criticized him for setting up "anti-Communism as the supreme test of political rectitude on the Left," when Raymond Williams attacked the "rancor" of his tone, its sense of "unjustified superiority," I completely agreed, though Rahv had scarcely earned the right to attack him from the left and Williams's position boiled down to the hoary dictum "No enemies on the Left."

Howe escaped from politics, as he had done since the fifties, through his invaluable work on Yiddish literature, editing a series of anthologies, with superb introductions, that brought this largely invisible body of work into the American mainstream. Toward the end of the decade he also wrote two seminal essays summing up the culture of modernism and the world and style of the New York intellectuals, essays that showed not only his wide purview and bold synthesizing powers but his rueful sense, perhaps premature, that these chapters of cultural history were more or less over. Just as Howe saw himself as a latecomer to Yiddish literature, which paradoxically made him a pioneer in its dissemination to an English-speaking audience, he felt a sense of belatedness in both modernist culture and the fractious circle of the New York writers. Caught between vigorous engagement and an elegiac sense of farewell, he became the boldly assertive chronicler who brought each subject into focus, as he had done with the work of many individual writers. Yet he also believed that cultures could flourish brilliantly in their moment of decline, as I. B. Singer, Chaim Grade, and Jacob Glatstein had shown in the waning days of Yiddish literature, as Southern writers and Jewish-American writers had done when their cultural roots were (in his view) already disintegrating.

Not long after I met Howe I joined his department, the doctoral program in English at the City University of New York, and very soon the wariness between us dissolved. In the face of rising neoconservative influence, he had turned left again in the early 1970s, bringing his *Dissent* colleagues along with him. In a little-known but momentous essay from 1971, "What's the Trouble?," he took the malaise of the young more seriously as a "crisis of civilization." Previously, he had debunked their rebellion as a matter of style, a set of deliberate provocations. He resented their reducing "differences of opinion to grades of moral rectitude." Behind their deep alienation, he now saw a more metaphysical question: "How shall we live?" It was a crisis of meaning, marked by "residual sentiments of religion and vague but powerful yearnings toward transcendence," something he had rarely acknowledged earlier.

As an old Marxist, Howe must have felt uncomfortable about such ruminations, which may explain why he did not reprint this essay, but it was striking that he found himself thinking along these lines, among the most eloquent lines he had ever written. "Who, looking upon the experience of our century, does not feel repeated surges of nausea, a deep persuasion that the very course of civilization has gone wrong?" He suggested that "we live at a moment when problems beyond the reach of politics—problems that *should* be beyond the reach of politics—have come to seem especially urgent and disturbing." This recognition would eventually lead him to grapple with the Holocaust and its literature, as in his review of a Warsaw ghetto memoir, published only days before his death in 1993. He could even forgive the young their utopianism, their cherished innocence. "We have learned that the effort to force men into utopia leads to barbarism, but we also know that to live without utopia is to risk the death of imagination."

As his colleague at the City University, twenty years younger, I had a certain awe of him and kept my distance. He tended to be abrupt and impatient with everyone, which often made me feel I was keeping him from more important business, indeed, from getting his work done. The publication of *World of Our Fathers* in 1976 made him a household name in a way he never expected to become, and it also increased demands on his time. He had little small talk, and our conversations were swift, amusing, and often practical—a student to be examined, a wrinkle in a writer's work to be ironed out. (I remember one phone call in which he questioned me about the shifting names of the protagonists in Delmore Schwartz's mesmerizing stories.) I admired his political probity, literary intelligence, and scorching wit, and felt he was someone I would never really know well but was glad to have on my side. I came to know him better through his writing, which never failed to engage me, and through his public appearances, where he was always a master of argument, than through our snatches of conversation, which often seemed truncated. I find today that I annotated almost every page of his 1982 memoir, A Margin of Hope, agreeing and disagreeing more vigorously than I ever did when he was in the room. Yet when he died I felt a gap in my life that has never really been filled.

On an impulse, Howe retired from active teaching in 1986, but continued writing, editing, and lecturing until his death. In his reviews he often praised his subjects for staying the course, getting the work done, even in the face of defeat, discouragement, aging, and illness. "The years of my life coincided with the years of socialist defeat," he wrote near the end of his memoir. He says of Edmund Wilson that "his career took on a heroic shape, the curve of the writer who attains magisterial lucidity in middle age and then, in the years of decline, struggles ferociously to keep his powers." In describing his flawed heroes, Howe often enriched the portrait by projecting his own fears. The illnesses of his last years often left him depressed, and more than once I heard him wonder whether the world really needed another book from him. But he enormously admired Norman Thomas, the perennial Socialist candidate, for sticking to his political mission, and even for his eloquent style in debate ("he knew more, he talked faster, and—miracle of American miracles!—he came out with comely sentences and coherent paragraphs"). He described Thomas as "the only truly great man I have ever met." Howe reserved his contempt for the former radicals from his City College days who had grown up poor but turned comfortable and conservative, losing their feeling for the world they left behind and enjoying their new access to wealth and power. Another hero of his, a figure of genuine moral authority, was the Italian novelist Ignazio Silone, "the least bitter of ex-Communists, the most reflective of radical democrats," whose later books were nonetheless weakened by "his exhausting struggle with his own beliefs, the struggle of a socialist who has abandoned his dogmas yet wishes to preserve his animating values," something Howe himself experienced as well. Those who claimed to be exempt from such "crises of belief," he wrote, "were mere fools passing through the twentieth century without experiencing it."

It's hard not to see the touches of self-reflection in Howe's portraits of Wilson and Silone. Howe had begun redefining his socialism as early as the 1950s, transforming it from historical dogma to moral critique—"the name of our desire," as he called it, using Tolstoy's phrase. Eventually it became a more forceful extension of liberalism, an unwavering commitment to the labor movement and the welfare state, and a branch of the left wing of the Democratic Party. The very word, socialism, became a mantra for persistence and determination; it was his link to the radical past even as he was adapting it to the needs of the present. In the introduction to his 1966 collection of political essays, Steady Work, he described himself as "a man of the left, in dialogue with himself, asking which of his earlier ideas should be preserved, which modified, which discarded." This tentativeness was on view not so much in the essays themselves, which are never less than emphatic, but in the unresolved conflicts between them. This was especially the case with his essays on the New Left, marred by his impatience with a generation he clearly hoped would follow his political lead. Howe could be polemical, at times even infuriating, without losing his grasp of the complexity of the subject. Echoing Trilling's well-known critique of liberalism in The Liberal Imagination, he described a commitment to socialism in the mid-twentieth century as "a capacity for living with doubt, revaluation and crisis," yet also called it "an abiding ideal." Socialism for him became a politics of conscience rather than a specific program or a set of goals; he came to admire figures who put their conscience, as well as their powers of observation, before their theories and ideas.

Howe saw Orwell, like Silone, as a writer trying to live by a consistent set of values after they had lost their ideological underpinnings. Howe's stirring 1968 essay on Orwell can also be read as a self-portrait. He describes Orwell as someone who kept his head, "wrote with his bones," through the worst political episodes of the twentieth century: "the Depression, Hitlerism, Franco's victory in Spain, Stalinism, the collapse of bourgeois England in the thirties." Howe writes that "for a whole generation—mine—Orwell was an intellectual hero." He saw in Orwell many of the qualities he aspired to or regretted in himself. Like his other heroes, including Wilson, Orwell was an irascible, even "pugnacious" man, whose essays are rightly admired for their "blunt clarity of speech and ruthless determination to see what looms in front of one's nose." He notes, without really complaining, that Orwell "is reckless, he is ferociously polemical," even when arguing for a moderate position. In the face of those who see him as some kind of secular saint, he doubts that Orwell "was particularly virtuous or good." Although Orwell "could be mean in polemics," he sometimes befriended those he had criticized, for he was driven not by personal animus but "by a passion to clarify ideas, correct errors, persuade readers, straighten things out in the world and in his mind." He admires Orwell's "peculiar sandpapery humor" and the "charged lucidity" of his prose, which nicely describes his own. Like Howe, Orwell "rejected the rituals of Good Form" and "turned away from the pretentiousness of the 'literary.'" He notes that Orwell "had a horror of exposing his private life," a theme that surfaces repeatedly in Howe's pieces (on Joyce, for example, and on Salinger) but also sets parameters for his own memoir. Finally, Howe examines the formal features of Orwell's essays, especially their superb endings. Beginning with Orwell as a moral exemplar though a less than perfect man, in fact a difficult man, he ends by scanning Orwell's great essays for lessons on how to write. In Howe's final work, A Critic's Notebook, he is still searching and still learning.

The best responses to Howe's work were as attentive to his style as he was to the language of those he reviewed. A few reviewers took due note of his remarkable growth as a writer. Early on, in 1964, Ted Solotaroff observed how the critic and the socialist intellectual converged in him, not only in his sense of cultural crisis but in "his crisp, meticulous prose, his skill at literary description, his grasp of the relevant issue quite equal to any serious book or audience. He is almost always telling you something sound and worthwhile and he is almost always as clear as glass." In Howe's earlier work this could be a defect. His literary essays sometimes read like position papers, and one could almost discern a shadowy list of points, the skeleton of the argument, behind the merely efficient surface of the writing. This is even truer of political essays like "New Styles in 'Leftism,'" the description of a type that elides individual difference, an inventory of bullet points, each of them like a jab to the ribs or an uppercut to the jaw. But as Howe's politics and even his temperament lost their sharp edges, his feeling for the aesthetic, his exhilaration with the language, blossomed. Rereading the large body of Orwell's essays, he is surprised to find that "the sheer *pleasure* of it cannot be overstated . . . Orwell was an even better writer than I had supposed." In his review of Howe's 1973 collection The Critical Point, Roger Sale made a similar discovery about Howe himself—that "he seems to have grown over the years, and his prose is sharper, the insights more precise and flexible." He concluded that Howe "seems to be trusting his human and literary instincts more than he once did."

By attending to the touch and feel of a text, he became more of a genuine essayist. As Howe mellowed, the nuances, reservations, and exceptions that complicated his case became as important as the argument. He came to love the New York City Ballet, where he learned to appreciate Balanchine's dancers for their eloquence of the body, an eloquence beyond language. He soon found himself increasingly valuing literature as a source of "ease and pleasure," not simply of moral critique, "for me the equivalent of those paintings of Vuillard and Bonnard I had come to love." From the gifted historian Richard Hofstadter, from Trilling, he "learned about a life of the mind that can keep some distance from competitiveness and clamor." The felicity of his own prose, once merely workmanlike, burgeoned along with its complex powers of description. Struck by phrases like Howe's description of the "high radiance" of Frost's greatest poetry, Roger Sale remarked that "only the best critics are generous enough to find the right words for their authors." This laconic verbal precision, itself very literary, contrasts with the tedious elaboration that disfigures academic writing, in which every point must be spelled out, every remark illustrated by five examples. Howe later paid tribute to the deeply troubled Delmore Schwartz as "a wondrous talker, a first-rate literary intelligence—the sort who can light up the work of a poet or novelist with a single quick phrase." For a true critic this is a talent as basic as breathing.

Howe never became as fluent a writer as Trilling or Alfred Kazin, or as direct and uncluttered as Orwell and Wilson, those masters of the plain style. Working rapidly, he developed a better ear for his subjects' prose than for his own. He had one gift absolutely essential to a critic—the power of discrimination, the gift for striking the right note, and for getting under the writer's (and the reader's) skin. His literary judgment, his intuition, could create a benchmark, a point of reference for serious readers, even those who disagreed with him. It could reach the writers themselves, as his well-known attacks touched a nerve in Ellison and Roth, galvanizing Ellison to an eloquent defense and moving Roth in a subtly new direction, toward novels of greater historical scope and moral urgency.

As a writer himself Howe acknowledged that his talent for metaphor was limited. I've always been struck by a certain clumsiness in his account of his "reconquest of Jewishness" in *A Margin of Hope*. But "Jewish Quandaries," the chapter in which this odd, soldierly phrase appears, is a penetrating essay (with illustrations from his own life) on the struggle of Jewish intellectuals with their ethnic background; it is also a frank analysis of how his own feelings had changed over the years. Speaking for many cosmopolitan radicals who once disdained merely tribal loyalties, he writes ruefully that "we had tried to 'make' our lives through acts of decision, 'programs' that thwarted the deeper, more intuitive parts of our own being." Embarrassed by the immigrant poverty and parochialism of his early years, indoctrinated by the universalism of his later Marxist faith, with its trust in collective movements and contempt for bourgeois individualism, Howe never found it easy to talk about himself. It went against the grain. Yet his memoir, if rarely intimate, showed how well he could think about himself, trusting his human and literary instincts as he had increasingly done in his criticism. As early as 1946, in an essay for *Commentary* called "The Lost Young Intellectual," and in later essays like "Strangers" in 1974, he channeled his own story into composite portraits of his generation, the twice-alienated children of Yiddish-speaking immigrants who confounded their parents by pulling up their roots and turning into intellectuals. In *World of Our Fathers* he projected this deeply felt experience onto a broad historical canvas, rich with feeling and detail.

As with all the best critics, his work has a strong personal stamp. His tone was inimitable, unmistakable, and he himself comes through on every page—awkward, funny, impatient, at moments ruthless, yet with an uncanny ability to get to the heart of the matter, to highlight what really counts. More than a decade younger than Trilling, Rahv, and their generation, he always felt like a latecomer, a brash young man among the grownups, but as a critic and cultural historian he was distinctly an original, a writer with sweeping powers of synthesis, whose political savvy, humane moral outlook, and keen feeling for art ultimately enabled him to find his own voice.

Introduction:
A Voice Still Heard

NINA HOWE

ALTHOUGH MY FATHER, Irving Howe, died over twenty years ago, hardly a month goes by without at least one "Irving Howe sighting." Family and friends will mention that they have spotted references to his work or ideas in newspapers, magazines, books, interviews, and other media. These references might be about his work in literary or social criticism or in Jewish history. In spite of the passage of time since his death, my father's voice remains strong and his observations and comments continue to be current, relevant, and important. His work is still a source of inspiration and guidance. This book was assembled to represent and to revisit the breadth and depth of his work as an engaged and engaging scholar who spoke to multiple audiences on many topics.

The pieces in this collection are drawn from the multiple domains in which my father worked across the several decades when he was an active writer and critic. Choosing the pieces to include in the present volume was initially a daunting task given the vast number of reviews, essays, and pieces of criticism that my father published during his forty-five-year career. To help choose which pieces to include, I enlisted the assistance of several individuals who proposed a range of suggestions that formed the starting point for the volume. There were some obvious pieces as well as some that my father had selected himself in previous books of collected essays (*Celebrations and Attacks; The Critical Point; Steady Work; The Decline of the New; Selected Writings 1950–1990*). Yet, I also wanted to include pieces that would enrich the reader's sense of his accomplishments and ideas from a variety of print sources and decided to include some pieces that had not been part of previous collections of his work. Also, a decision was made to focus on essays and not chapters from some of his books, although there were some tempting choices that we might have included from books (e.g., *Politics and the Novel; World of Our Fathers*).

Clearly, an organizational scheme was required to make sense of the body of work for the reader, since it ranged over so many topics and over so many decades. Initially, a thematic approach appeared to make sense, and I attempted to separate the possible selections into literary, political, and social commentary pieces but quickly abandoned this scheme. As I read over the body of my father's work, especially the pieces published during my childhood and adolescence in the 1950s and 1960s, I came to realize that literary and political themes were deeply intertwined in all of his writing. For example, in "This Age of Conformity" and "What's the Trouble?," the intersection of politics and literature is so strong that trying to separate the pieces thematically would have been an impossible venture. Given that my father wrote a book titled *Politics and the Novel* (1957), perhaps the notion of a thematic organizational scheme was naïve on my part. Fortunately, in reviewing previous books of his collected works (*Celebrations and Attacks; Selected Writings 1950–1990*), it was apparent that my father resolved the organizational issue by using a chronological approach. Given that this was his decision, I decided to follow his direction.

The temporal approach also allows the reader to understand the chronological development of my father's work and the contemporary ideas and issues that were of interest to him at any point in time. There were periods when the political themes appeared to dominate his thinking and writing and he produced a number of books (e.g., *Essential Works of Socialism; Basic Writings of Trotsky*). The literary themes were always present too, but often more apparent in book reviews and longer essays, although he did write full-length books on Sherwood Anderson, William Faulkner, and Thomas Hardy. It is clear that my father favored the longer essay form of writing, which allowed him to explore his ideas in more depth, and he perfected it in his political and social commentary and in his literary pieces. Accordingly, I have included a number of longer essays in addition to some shorter pieces.

Each of the decades includes at least one major political or social commentary piece, which serves as the framework for my father's contemporary ideas and perceptions regarding the world scene. Thus, we selected the following as representative of each decade: "This Age of Conformity" (1950s), "New Styles in 'Leftism'" (1960s), "What's the Trouble?" (1970s), "Reaganism: The Spirit of the Times" (1980s), and "Two Cheers for Utopia" (1990s). There are a number of other important political pieces that focus on socialism, and place my father as a leading political and social thinker of the late twentieth century. The piece on George Orwell ("As the Bones Know") provides an historical and political critique of Orwell's work that every student of history should read, along with a "Tribune of Socialism," about Norman Thomas. My father's early love of politics and socialism was his major preoccupation during his college years and a driving force throughout his life. Although he never wavered in his political beliefs and remained steady in his vision of democratic socialism, his recognition of what was realistic is apparent in many of his later writings ("Why Has Socialism Failed in America?"; "Two Cheers for Utopia").

It is well known that my father's founding of Dissent with Lewis Coser in 1954 was just one expression of his belief in democratic socialism. Considering that Dissent served as an outlet for much of his own political writing, it is not surprising that several essays in the present collection originally appeared in this magazine. Although my father was joined by other co-editors in later years (Michael Walzer and Mitchell Cohen), it was clear that he was the main pillar at Dissent in producing a lively and important "little magazine," as he called it. He was proud to publish a number of European writers for the first time in English (e.g., Ignazio Silone) as well as important American writers such as Norman Mailer. I would be remiss not to note the importance of Dissent in my father's life work. His introduction to Twenty-five Years of Dissent is included in the present volume, where he articulates a broad social and political context and vision for the magazine. This piece is a fitting reminder of my father's work as Dissent celebrates its sixtieth anniversary in 2014.

Several pieces of social criticism are included here, and the present volume would be incomplete without them. One is the essay on "The New York Intellectuals," which was recommended by all those involved in the selection process. Given its broad expanse and focus, this piece is considered by many individuals to be one of my father's seminal essays. The essay titled "Strangers" is in some ways a companion piece to "The New York Intellectuals," but it is a more personal account of how young Jewish American students growing up in the immigrant slums of New York in the 1920s and 1930s came to terms with American literature. How does one make sense of Ralph Waldo Emerson or Robert Frost when their experiences were so distant from that of the urban immigrant? My father explores these ideas in a relaxed and insightful way.

Each decade is also represented by a number of literary pieces, which include short but always crisp book reviews and longer essays. Book reviews were the mainstay of much of my father's writing. Across the five decades of his career, he wrote hundreds of book reviews. In fact, he started by writing anonymous book reviews for *Time* magazine sometime around 1950, which was a good source of income for a beginning writer. At the same time that he was toiling away within the Luce empire, he was also publishing book reviews in a number of other magazines such as *Partisan Review*. By the time my father started teaching at Brandeis University in 1953 (having barely set foot in graduate school!) he had given up writing for *Time* magazine. Some of his early book reviews from the 1950s, 60s, and 70s were reprinted in *Celebrations and Attacks* (1979), and later my father chose them for *Selected Writings 1950–1990* (e.g., his outstanding review of Doris Lessing's *The Golden Notebook*). As I read my father's essays included in *Celebrations and Attacks*, I realized that he had recommended so many of the same books to me over the years. For this reason, some selections for the current volume were guided by my personal memories of his recommendations and love of these books. One example is his review of Sarah Orne Jewett's *The Country of the Pointed Firs*, a minor but wonderful gem of a novel about a part of the country that later in his life my father came to love. The range of books and authors covered in my father's reviews was quite striking, including leading contemporary authors such as Doris Lessing and Philip Roth, as well as lesser-known authors including Henry Roth (*Call It Sleep*) and the Israeli writer Yaakov Shabtai (*Past Continuous*). His reviews celebrated and attacked various authors, to paraphrase my father's title; he could be scathing in his criticisms, but he could also be generous, as apparent in our selections in the present volume.

Although my father favored nineteenth- and twentieth-century American, European, and Russian literature, he was willing to move beyond this comfort zone into new territory. Once when I was visiting my father, a package of Japanese novels by various authors arrived unannounced from Robert Silvers, editor of the *New York Review of Books*. His first reaction was to send them back, but curiosity soon overtook him and he began to read the books. The review of *The Samurai* by Shusaku Endo reveals his attempts to understand the mind of the Japanese author and the literary themes of this body of work, which he indicated was not an easy, comfortable, or always successful process for him. Nevertheless, the book review is a compelling piece and reveals the breadth of my father's reading and literary understanding.

Beyond the book reviews, there are a number of longer literary essays on topics that captured my father's attention, such as "The City in Literature" and "Writing and the Holocaust." These are serious and deeply thoughtful literary essays, which illuminate his perceptive and brilliant mind and are free of jargon and flashy, self-involved, or narrow ideas. Nor are they confined by heavily scripted theoretical stances. My father once told me "write clearly and simply," to which I would add "write with grace, insight, intelligence, humor, and passion"; these essays are a model of such writing. My father's literary preferences were personal and never guided by the fashions of the day, as evidenced by his thoughtful essay on the American poet Edwin Arlington Robinson ("A Grave and Solitary Voice") or his assessment that Arnold Bennett was sometimes a better writer than Virginia Woolf ("Mr. Bennett and Mrs. Woolf"). Reading the latter piece spurred me to take Bennett's books out of the library for a personal reassessment of these two authors, a journey which I hope that others will also take in the coming years.

Yiddish was my father's first language and became a major theme in his professional work, as is evident in the collections of Yiddish stories, essays, and poetry co-edited by the likes of Eliezer Greenberg and Ruth Wisse. The present volume would not be complete without some selections of Yiddish literature. The introduction to the The Best of Sholom Aleichem is an exchange of letters between my father and Ruth Wisse, which brings to light a number of the important themes of Yiddish literature in an engaging way. His interest in Jewish American writers is also recalled in the book review of stories by Bernard Malamud.

In the last few years of his life, my father returned to literature, one of his first loves. As described by my late and beloved brother, Nicholas, in the preface to my father's book A Critic's Notebook, published posthumously, my father felt that he still had a number of things to say about literature that were best suited to the short essay. His choice of topics was certainly eclectic, but they were ideas that gave him joy and allowed him to reflect on the nature of literature and writing. Thus, there were pieces about some of his favorite authors (Dickens, Tolstoy), particular facets of writing or style (characters, farce, tone in fiction), and some questions that puzzled him such as the fads and fashions of literary preferences, for example, why Walter Scott fell out of the canon. It was a pleasure to reread this book. The choice of which pieces to include from this book in the present volume was not easy, but with the assistance of others I selected three pieces that reflect my father's eclectic and delightful interests, ideas, and thoughts ("Mr. Bennett and Mrs. Woolf"; "Dickens: Three Notes"; "Tolstoy: Did Anna Have to Die?"). In the piece about Dickens, my father explores ideas about "absolute goodness and the limits of fiction," the role of minor characters, and "Becoming Dostoevsky" in Dickens's late work. In the piece about Tolstoy, my father grapples with the central question about the fate of Anna Karenina given societal norms, Tolstoy's personal views, and the fact that she is a character in a novel.

Although my father was immersed in literary criticism, his deep interest in politics and social history remained to the end. As one of the anonymous reviewers of this collection noted, in one of his last political essays, "Two Cheers for Utopia," my father provided an "autumnal" and highly nuanced perspective of his former Communist adversaries. His nearly last book review (*The Road Leads Far Away: Antek and Warsaw Resistance*) was a fascinating review of the history of the Warsaw ghetto rebellion that, of course, included a review of the book but also provided an insightful historical account of those events. It was published two days before his death on May 5, 1993.

The final section of this volume includes two pieces that my father wrote in a more personal voice, which seemed a fitting way to end the book. He was a private person, but these pieces provide a glimpse into the world in which he grew up and some of his formative early experiences. The first piece is an excerpt from my father's intellectual autobiography, *A Margin of Hope*, about the death of his father; it is a deeply poignant, conflicted, and touching piece. The second piece is an interview conducted by the Canadian social democrat Stephen Lewis, for a CBC radio program that took place when my father was visiting me in Toronto. I was present at the interview and was struck at how comfortable and relaxed my father was while talking to Lewis about his life and political views. These two pieces provide some insight into different aspects of his life, ideas, and work.

Although the pieces in this book cover topics from different domains of thought and inquiry, the voice that runs through each of them is the same. Regardless of whether my father was writing about politics, social issues, a novel, or a moment from Jewish history, his voice emerged from his deep interest in the lives of ordinary people and their individual joys and struggles. He cared about people, how they lived, and how they dealt with the circumstances of their experiences. Across the breadth of these pieces, there is just one voice, a voice that is still heard. It is the voice I recall from my childhood with my father.

I am indebted to a number of people for their assistance in compiling this volume. First, I thank Ilana Weiner Howe for urging me over several years to embark on the project and for her thoughtful suggestions for pieces, particularly of the literary kind. I am also very grateful to David Bromwich for his enthusiasm about the project, for his critical and thoughtful suggestions, and for his guidance throughout the publication process. Brian Morton and Mark Levinson made recommendations that sometimes coincided with those of David Bromwich, but they also brought forth important suggestions of their own. I am very grateful for their willingness to participate and for their excellent recommendations. Together, these four individuals helped to establish the core of the final selections. I would also like to thank Eric Brandt, my editor at Yale University Press, his assistant Erica Hanson, my agent Georges Borchardt, and his assistant, Rachel Brooke, for their help with the publication process.

Three other individuals also provided invaluable recommendations that have made the book complete. I thank my husband, William Bukowski, for his recommendations and for remembering the Antek book review. His love, support, and patience during this project has been a source of inspiration for me. Finally, I thank my two children for their interest in this project and the opportunity to come to know their grandfather better through his writing. My daughter Ana's deep interest in literature was an invaluable help in selecting pieces from A Critic's Notebook, and her perceptive choices were most appreciated. My son, Nick, was an incredible assistant throughout all stages of this project, researching and reading all of the recommendations, especially the political and social commentary pieces, which fed into his interests in politics and history. Nick provided invaluable advice concerning the various recommendations and together we sorted through the lengthy list to compile the final selections. I could not have completed the project without him. Were my father still alive, I know that he would be very proud of his grandchildren and would have dedicated this book to them. Since he cannot do so, I take the liberty of dedicating this book to Anastasia and Nicholas Howe Bukowski.

On a personal note, this has been an incredible journey for me. I have read more of my father's work than I had ever in the past, particularly the work published in my childhood and adolescence. It has given me a greater appreciation for my father's public work and for the brilliance of his fine and critical mind, for his sense of humor sprinkled throughout his writing, for his crisp and sparkling prose, for the range and depth of his interests and knowledge, and for his passion for literature, politics, social history, and above all, ideas. As the twentieth anniversary of his death has passed, I miss him more than I can say, but it is clear that many others miss his voice too. My hope is that this collection will bring his presence back to the fore for both older and new readers of Irving Howe. It seems fitting to end this introduction with my father's own words from his seminal piece, "The New York Intellectuals." Although he did not specifically write about himself in the piece, I think that the words he used to describe the driving ambition of the New York intellectuals, a group of which he was part, are most fitting:

"What drove them, and sometimes drove them crazy, was not, however, the quest for money, nor even a chance to 'mix' with White House residents; it was finally a gnawing ambition to write something, even three pages, that might live." We believe that Irving Howe's voice still lives!

Montreal, Canada
August 2013

The 1950s

This Age of Conformity
{1954}

INTELLECTUALS HAVE ALWAYS been partial to grandiose ideas about themselves, whether of a heroic or a masochistic kind, but surely no one has ever had a more grandiose idea about the destiny of modern intellectuals than the brilliant economist Joseph Schumpeter. Though he desired nothing so much as to be realistic and hard-boiled, Schumpeter had somehow absorbed all those romantic notions about the revolutionary potential and critical independence of the intellectuals which have now and again swept through the radical and bohemian worlds. Marx, said Schumpeter, was wrong in supposing that capitalism would break down from inherent economic contradictions; it would break down, instead, from an inability to claim people through ties of loyalty and value. "Unlike any other type of society, capitalism inevitably . . . creates, educates and subsidizes a vested interest in social unrest." The intellectuals, bristling with neurotic aspirations and deranged by fantasies of utopia made possible by the very society they would destroy, become agents of discontent who infect rich and poor, high and low. In drawing this picture Schumpeter hardly meant to praise the intellectuals, yet until a few years ago many of them would have accepted it as both truth and tribute, though a few of the more realistic ones might have smiled a doubt as to their capacity to do all that.

Schumpeter's picture of the intellectuals is not, of course, without historical validity, but at the moment it seems spectacularly, even comically wrong. And wrong for a reason that Schumpeter, with his elaborate sense of irony, would have appreciated: he who had insisted that capitalism is "a form or method of economic change and not only never is but never can be stationary" had failed sufficiently to consider those new developments in our society which have changed the whole position and status of the intellectuals. Far from creating and subsidizing unrest, capitalism in its most recent stage has found an honored place for the intellectuals; and the intellectuals, far from thinking of themselves as a desperate "opposition," have been enjoying a return to the bosom of the nation. Were Archibald MacLeish again tempted to play Cato and chastise the Irresponsibles, he could hardly find a victim. We have all, even the handful who still try to retain a glower of criticism, become responsible and moderate.

2

In 1932 not many American intellectuals saw any hope for the revival of capitalism. Few of them could support this feeling with any well-grounded theory of society; many held to a highly simplified idea of what capitalism was; and almost all were committed to a vision of the *crisis* of capitalism which was merely a vulgarized model of the class struggle in Europe. Suddenly, with the appearance of the New Deal, the intellectuals saw fresh hope: capitalism was not to be exhausted by the naive specifications they had assigned it, and consequently the "European" policies of the Roosevelt administration might help dissolve their "Europeanized" sense of crisis. So that the more American society became Europeanized, adopting measures that had been common practice on the Continent for decades, the more the American intellectuals began to believe in . . . American uniqueness. Somehow, the major capitalist power in the world would evade the troubles afflicting capitalism as a world economy.

The two central policies of the New Deal, social legislation and state intervention in economic life, were not unrelated, but they were separable as to time; in Europe they had not always appeared together. Here, in America, it was the simultaneous introduction of these two policies that aroused the enthusiasm, as it dulled the criticism, of the intellectuals. Had the drive toward bureaucratic state regulation of a capitalist economy appeared by itself, so that one could see the state becoming a major buyer and hence indirect controller of industry, and industries on the verge of collapse being systematically subsidized by the state, and the whole of economic life being rationalized according to the long-run needs, if

not the immediate tastes, of corporate economy—had all this appeared in isolation, the intellectuals would have reacted critically, they would have recognized
the trend toward "state capitalism" as the danger it was. But their desire for the
genuine social reforms that came with this trend made them blind or indifferent to the danger. Still, one may suppose that their enthusiasm would have mellowed had not the New Deal been gradually transformed into a permanent war
economy; for whatever the theoretical attractions of the Keynesian formula for
salvaging capitalism, it has thus far "worked" only in times of war or preparation
for war. And it was in the war economy, itself closely related to the trend toward
statification, that the intellectuals came into their own.

Statification, war economy, the growth of a mass society and mass culture—
all these are aspects of the same historical process. The kind of society that has
been emerging in the West, a society in which bureaucratic controls are imposed
upon (but not fundamentally against) an interplay of private interests, has need
for intellectuals in a way the earlier, "traditional" capitalism never did. It is a society in which ideology plays an unprecedented part: as social relations become
more abstract and elusive, the human object is bound to the state with ideological
slogans and abstractions—and for this chore intellectuals are indispensable; no
one else can do the job as well. Because industrialism grants large quantities of
leisure time without any creative sense of how to employ it, there springs up a
vast new industry that must be staffed by intellectuals and quasi-intellectuals: the
industry of mass culture. And because the state subsidizes mass education and
our uneasy prosperity allows additional millions to gain a "higher" education,
many new jobs suddenly become available in the academy: some fall to intellectuals. Bohemia gradually disappears as a setting for our intellectual life, and what
remains of it seems willed or fake. Looking upon the prosperous ruins of Green-
wich Village, one sometimes feels that a full-time bohemian career has become
as arduous, if not as expensive, as acquiring a Ph.D.

Bohemia, said Flaubert, was "the fatherland of my breed." If so, his breed, at
least in America, is becoming extinct. The most exciting periods of American intellectual life tend to coincide with the rise of bohemia, with the tragic yet liberating
rhythm of the break from the small town into the literary roominess of the city, or
from the provincial immigrant family into the centers of intellectual experiment.
Given the nature of contemporary life, bohemia flourishes in the city—but that
has not always been so. Concord too was a kind of bohemia, sedate, subversive,
and transcendental all at once. Today, however, the idea of bohemia, which was
a strategy for bringing artists and writers together in their struggle with and for
the world—this idea has become disreputable, being rather nastily associated

with kinds of exhibitionism that have only an incidental relationship to bohemia. Nonetheless, it is the disintegration of bohemia that is a major cause for the way intellectuals feel, as distinct from and far more important than what they say or think. Those feelings of loneliness one finds among so many American intellectuals, feelings of damp dispirited isolation which undercut the ideology of liberal optimism, are partly due to the breakup of bohemia. Where young writers would once face the world together, they now sink into suburbs, country homes, and college towns. And the price they pay for this rise in social status is to be measured in more than an increase in rent.

It is not my purpose to berate anyone, for the pressures of conformism are at work upon all of us, to say nothing of the need to earn one's bread; and all of us bend under the terrible weight of our time—though some take pleasure in learning to enjoy it. Nor do I wish to indulge in the sort of good-natured condescension with which Malcolm Cowley recently described the younger writers as lugubrious and timid longhairs huddling in chill academies and poring over the gnostic texts of Henry James—by contrast, no doubt, to Cowley's own career of risk-taking. Some intellectuals, to be sure, have "sold out" and we can all point to examples, probably the same examples. But far more prevalent and far more insidious is that slow attrition which destroys one's ability to stand firm and alone: the temptations of an improved standard of living combined with guilt over the historical tragedy that has made possible our prosperity; one's sense of being swamped by the rubbish of a reactionary period together with the loss of those earlier certainties that had the advantage, at least, of making resistance easy. Nor, in saying these things, do I look forward to any sort of material or intellectual asceticism. Our world is to be neither flatly accepted nor rejected: it must be engaged, resisted, and—who knows, perhaps still—transformed.

All of life, my older friends often tell me, is a conspiracy against that ideal of independence with which a young intellectual begins; but if so, wisdom consists not in premature surrender but in learning when to evade, when to stave off, and when to oppose head-on. Conformity, as Arthur Koestler said some years ago, "is often a form of betrayal which can be carried out with a clear conscience." Gradually we make our peace with the world, and not by anything as exciting as a secret pact; nowadays Lucifer is a very patient and reasonable fellow with a gift for indulging one's most legitimate desires; and we learn, if we learn anything at all, that betrayal may consist in a chain of small compromises, even while we also learn that in this age one cannot survive without compromise. What is most alarming is not that a number of intellectuals have abandoned the posture of iconoclasm: let the zeitgeist give them a jog and they will again be radical, all too radical. What is most alarming is that the whole idea of the intellectual vocation—the idea of a life dedicated to values that cannot possibly be realized by a commercial civilization—has gradually lost its allure. And it is this, rather than the abandonment of a particular program, which constitutes our rout.

In a recent number of *Perspectives* Lionel Trilling addressed himself to some of these problems; his perspective is sharply different from mine. Trilling believes that "there is an unmistakable improvement in the American cultural situation of today over that of, say, thirty years ago," while to me it seems that any comparison between the buoyant free-spirited cultural life of 1923 with the dreariness of 1953, or between their literary achievements, must lead to the conclusion that Trilling is indulging in a pleasant fantasy. More important, however, is his analysis of how this "improvement" has occurred:

> In many civilizations there comes a point at which wealth shows a tendency to submit itself, in some degree, to the rule of mind and imagination, to apologize for its existence by a show of taste and sensitivity. In America the signs of this submission have for some time been visible. . . . Intellect has associated itself with power, perhaps as never before in history, and is now conceded to be in itself a kind of power.

Such stately terms as "wealth" and "intellect" hardly make for sharp distinctions, yet the drift of Trilling's remarks is clear enough—and, I think, disastrous.

It is perfectly true that in the government bureaucracy and institutional staff, in the mass-culture industries and the academy, intellectuals have been welcomed and absorbed as never before. It is true, again, that "wealth" has become far more indulgent in its treatment of intellectuals, and for good reasons: it needs them more than ever, they are tamer than ever, and its own position is more comfortable and expansive than it has been for a long time. But if "wealth" has made a mild bow toward "intellect" (sometimes while picking its pocket), then "intellect" has engaged in some undignified prostrations before "wealth." Thirty years ago "wealth" was on the defensive, and twenty years ago it was frightened, hesitant, apologetic. "Intellect" was self-confident, aggressive, secure in its belief or, if you wish, delusions. Today the ideology of American capitalism, with its claim to a unique and immaculate destiny, is trumpeted through every medium of communication: official propaganda, institutional advertising, and the scholarly writings of people who, until a few years ago, were its major opponents. Marx-baiting, that least risky of occupations, has become a favorite sport in the academic journals; a whining genteel chauvinism is widespread among intellectuals;

and the bemoaning of their own fears and timidities a constant theme among professors. Is this to be taken as evidence that "wealth" has subordinated itself to "intellect"? Or is the evidence to be found in the careers of such writers as Max Eastman and James Burnham? To be sure, culture has acquired a more honorific status, as restrained ostentation has replaced conspicuous consumption: wealthy people collect more pictures or at least more modern ones, they endow foundations with large sums—but all this is possible because "intellect" no longer pretends to challenge "wealth."

What has actually been taking place is the absorption of large numbers of intellectuals, previously independent, into the world of government bureaucracy and public committees; into the constantly growing industries of pseudo culture; into the adult-education business, which subsists on regulated culture-anxiety. This process of bureaucratic absorption does not proceed without check: the Eisenhower administration has recently dismissed a good many intellectuals from government posts. Yet it seems likely that such stupidity will prove temporary and that one way or another, in one administration or another, the intellectuals will drift back into the government: they must, they are indispensable.

Some years ago C. Wright Mills wrote an article in which he labeled the intellectuals as "powerless people." He meant, of course, that they felt incapable of translating their ideas into action and that their consequent frustration had become a major motif in their behavior. His description was accurate enough; yet we might remember that the truly powerless people are those intellectuals— the new realists—who attach themselves to the seats of power, where they surrender their freedom of expression without gaining any significance as political figures. For it is crucial to the history of the American intellectuals in the past few decades—as well as to the relationship between "wealth" and "intellect"—that whenever they become absorbed into the accredited institutions of society they not only lose their traditional rebelliousness but to one extent or another *they cease to function as intellectuals.* The institutional world needs intellectuals *because* they are intellectuals but it does not want them *as* intellectuals. It beckons to them because of what they are but it will not allow them, at least within its sphere of articulation, to either remain or entirely cease being what they are. It needs them for their knowledge, their talent, their inclinations and passions; it insists that they retain a measure of these endowments, which it means to employ for its own ends, and without which the intellectuals would be of no use to it whatever. A simplified but useful equation suggests itself: the relation of the institutional world to the intellectuals is like the relation of middlebrow culture to serious culture. The one battens on the other, absorbs and raids it with increasing frequency and skill, subsidizes and encourages it enough to make further raids possible—at times the parasite will support its victim. Surely this relationship must be one reason for the high incidence of neurosis that is supposed to prevail among intellectuals. A total estrangement from the sources of power and prestige, even a blind unreasoning rejection of every aspect of our culture, would be far healthier, if only because it would permit a free discharge of aggression.

I do not mean to suggest that for intellectuals all institutions are equally dangerous or disadvantageous. Even during the New Deal, the life of those intellectuals who journeyed to Washington was far from happy. The independence possible to a professor of sociology is usually greater than that possible to a writer of television scripts, and a professor of English, since the world will not take his subject seriously, can generally enjoy more intellectual leeway than a professor of sociology. Philip Rieff, a sociologist, has caustically described a major tendency among his colleagues as a drift from "science" to "policy" in which "loyalty, not truth, provides the social condition by which the intellectual discovers his new environment." It is a drift "from the New School to the Rand Corporation."

There is, to be sure, a qualitative difference between the academy and the government bureau or the editorial staff. The university is still committed to the ideology of freedom, and many professors try hard and honestly to live by it. If the intellectual cannot subsist independently, off his work or his relatives, the academy is usually his best bet. But no one who has a live sense of what the literary life has been and might still be, in either Europe or this country, can accept the notion that the academy is the natural home of intellect. What seems so unfortunate is that the whole *idea* of independence is losing its traditional power. Scientists are bound with chains of official secrecy; sociologists compete for government research chores; foundations become indifferent to solitary writers and delight in "teams"; the possibility of living in decent poverty from moderately serious literary journalism becomes more and more remote. Compromises are no doubt necessary, but they had better be recognized for what they are.

Perhaps something should be said here about "alienation." Involved, primarily, is a matter of historical fact. During most of the bourgeois epoch, the European intellectuals grew increasingly alienated from the social community because the very ideals that had animated the bourgeois revolution were now being violated by bourgeois society; their "alienation" was prompted not by bohemian willfulness or socialist dogmatism but by a loyalty to Liberty, Fraternity, Equality, or to a vision of a preindustrial society that, by a trick of history, came pretty much to resemble Liberty, Fraternity, Equality. Just as it was the triumph of capitalism which largely caused this sense of estrangement, so it was the expansion of capitalism that allowed the intellectuals enough freedom to express it. As Philip Rahv has put it: "During the greater part of the bourgeois epoch . . . [writers] preferred alienation from the community to alienation from themselves." Precisely this choice made possible their strength and boldness, precisely this "lack of roots" gave them their speculative power. Almost always, the talk one hears these days about "the need for roots" veils a desire to compromise the tradition of intellectual independence, to seek in a nation or religion or party a substitute for the tenacity one should find in oneself. Isaac Rosenfeld's remark that "the ideal society . . . cannot afford to include many deeply rooted individuals" is not merely a clever mot but an important observation.

It may be that the issue is no longer relevant; that, with the partial submission of "wealth" to "intellect," the clash between a business civilization and the values of art is no longer as urgent as we once thought; but if so, we must discard a great deal, and mostly the best, of the literature, the criticism, and the speculative thought of the twentieth century. For to deny the historical fact of "alienation" (as if that would make it any the less real!) is to deny our heritage, both as burden and advantage, and also, I think, to deny our possible future as a community.

Much of what I have been describing here must be due to a feeling among intellectuals that the danger of Stalinism allows them little or no freedom in their relations with bourgeois society. This feeling seems to me only partly justified, and I do not suffer from any inclination to minimize the Stalinist threat. To be sure, it does limit our possibilities for action—if, that is, we still want to engage in any dissident politics—and sometimes it may force us into political alignments that are distasteful. But here a crucial distinction should be made: the danger of Stalinism may require temporary expedients in the area of *power* such as would have seemed compromising some years ago, but there is no reason, at least no good reason, why it should require compromise or conformity in the area of *ideas*, no reason why it should lead us to become partisans of bourgeois society, which is itself, we might remember, heavily responsible for the Stalinist victories.

3

"In the United States at this time liberalism is not only the dominant but even the sole intellectual tradition." This sentence of Lionel Trilling's contains a sharp insight into the political life of contemporary America. If I understand him correctly, he is saying that our society is at present so free from those pressures of conflicting classes and interests which make for sharply defined ideologies, that liberalism colors, or perhaps the word should be, bleaches all political tendencies. It becomes a loose shelter, a poncho rather than a program; to call oneself a liberal one doesn't really have to believe in anything. In such a moment of social slackness, the more extreme intellectual tendencies have a way, as soon as an effort is made to put them into practice, of sliding into and becoming barely distinguishable from the dominant liberalism. Both conservatism and radicalism can retain, at most, an intellectual recalcitrance, but neither is presently able to engage in a sustained practical politics of its own; which does not mean they will never be able to.

The point is enforced by looking at the recent effort to affirm a conservative ideology. Russell Kirk, who makes this effort with some earnestness, can hardly avoid the eccentricity of appealing to Providence as a putative force in American politics: an appeal that suggests both the intensity of his conservative desire and the desperation behind the intensity. Peter Viereck, a friskier sort of writer, calls himself a conservative, but surely this is nothing more than a mystifying pleasantry, for aside from the usual distinctions of temperament and talent it is hard to see how his conservatism differs from the liberalism of Arthur Schlesinger, Jr. For Viereck conservatism is a shuffling together of attractive formulas, without any effort to discover their relationship to deep *actual* clashes of interest: he fails, for example, even to consider that in America there is today neither opportunity nor need for conservatism (since the liberals do the necessary themselves) and that if an opportunity were to arise, conservatism could seize upon it only by acquiring a mass, perhaps reactionary dynamic, that is, by "going into the streets." And that, surely, Viereck doesn't want.

If conservatism is taken to mean, as in some "classical" sense it should be, a principled rejection of industrial economy and a yearning for an ordered, hierarchical society that is not centered on the city, then conservatism in America is best defended by a group of literary men whose seriousness is proportionate to their recognition that such a politics is now utterly hopeless and, in any but a utopian sense, meaningless. Such a conservatism, in America, goes back to Fenimore Cooper, who anticipates those implicit criticisms of our society which we honor in Faulkner; and in the hands of serious imaginative writers, but hardly in the hands of political writers obliged to deal with immediate relations of power, it can become a myth which, through abrasion, profoundly challenges modern experience. As for the "conservatism" of the late Senator Robert Taft, which consists of nothing but liberal economics and wounded nostalgia, it lacks intellectual content and, more important, when in power it merely continues those "statist" policies it had previously attacked.

This prevalence of liberalism yields, to be sure, some obvious and substantial benefits. It makes us properly skeptical of the excessive claims and fanaticisms that accompany ideologies. It makes implausible those "aristocratic" rantings against democracy which were fashionable in some literary circles a few years ago. And it allows for the hope that any revival of American radicalism will acknowledge not only its break from, but also its roots in, the liberal tradition.

At the same time, however, the dominance of liberalism contributes heavily to our intellectual conformity. Liberalism dominates, but without confidence or security; it knows that its victories at home are tied to disasters abroad; and for the élan it cannot summon, it substitutes a blend of complacence and anxiety. It makes for an atmosphere of blur in the realm of ideas, since it has a stake in seeing momentary concurrences as deep harmonies. In an age that suffers from incredible catastrophes it scoffs at theories of social apocalypse—as if any more evidence were needed; in an era convulsed by war, revolution and counterrevolution it discovers the virtues of "moderation." And when the dominant school of liberalism, the school of realpolitik, scores points in attacking "the ritualistic liberals," it also betrays a subterranean desire to retreat into the caves of bureaucratic caution. Liberalism as an ideology, as "the haunted air," has never been stronger in this country; but can as much be said of the appetite for freedom?

Sidney Hook discovers merit in the Smith Act: he was not for its passage but doubts the wisdom of its repeal.* Mary McCarthy, zooming to earth from never-never land, discovers in the American war economy no less than paradise: "Class barriers disappear or tend to become porous; the factory worker is an economic aristocrat in comparison to the middle-class clerk. . . . The America . . . of vast inequalities and dramatic contrasts is rapidly ceasing to exist." Daniel Boorstin—he cannot be charged with the self-deceptions peculiar to idealism—discovers that "the genius of American politics" consists not in the universal possibilities of democracy but in a uniquely fortunate geography which, obviously, cannot be exported. David Riesman is so disturbed by Veblen's rebelliousness toward American society that he explains it as a projection of father-hatred; and what complex is it, one wonders, which explains a writer's assumption that Veblen's view of America is so inconceivable as to require a home-brewed psychoanalysis? Irving

* The Smith Act, passed in 1940, was a loosely worded piece of legislation that made it unlawful to "conspire to advocate the overthrow of the government by force and violence."

Kristol writes an article minimizing the threat to civil liberties and shortly there-
after is chosen to be public spokesman for the American Committee for Cultural
Freedom. And in the committee itself, it is possible for serious intellectuals to
debate—none is *for* Senator McCarthy—whether the public activities of the Wis-
consin hooligan constitute a serious menace to freedom.

One likes to speculate: suppose Simone de Beauvoir and Bertrand Russell
didn't exist; would not many of the political writers for *Commentary* and the *New
Leader* have to invent them? It is all very well, and even necessary, to demonstrate
that Russell's description of America as subject to "a reign of terror" is malicious
and ignorant, or that Beauvoir's picture of America is a blend of Stalinist clichés
and second-rate literary fantasies; but this hardly disposes of the problem of civil
liberties or of the justified alarm many sober European intellectuals feel with regard to America. Between the willfulness of those who see only terror and the
indifference of those who see only health, there is need for simple truth: that intellectual freedom in the United States is under severe attack and that the intellectuals have, by and large, shown a painful lack of militancy in defending the rights
which are a precondition of their existence.*

It is in the pages of the influential magazine *Commentary* that liberalism is most
skillfully and systematically advanced as a strategy for adapting to the American
status quo. Until the last few months, when a shift in editorial temper seems
to have occurred, the magazine was more deeply preoccupied, or preoccupied
at deeper levels, with the dangers to freedom stemming from people like Freda
Kirchwey and Arthur Miller than the dangers from people like Senator McCarthy.
In March 1952 Irving Kristol, then an editor of *Commentary*, could write that "there
is one thing the American people know about Senator McCarthy: he, like them, is
unequivocally anti-Communist. About the spokesmen for American liberalism,
they feel they know no such thing. And with some justification." In September
1952, at the very moment when McCarthy had become a central issue in the presidential campaign, Elliot Cohen, the senior editor of *Commentary*, could write that
McCarthy "remains in the popular mind an unreliable, second-string blowhard;
his *only* support as a great national figure is from the fascinated fears of the intelligentsia" (emphasis mine). As if to blot out the memory of these performances,

---

* It must in honesty be noted that many of the intellectuals least alive to the problem of civil
liberties are former Stalinists or radicals; and this, more than the vast anti-Marxist literature
of recent years, constitutes a serious criticism of American radicalism. For the truth is that the
"old-fashioned liberals" like John Dewey and Alexander Meiklejohn, at whom it was once so
fashionable to sneer, have displayed a finer sensitivity to the need for defending domestic freedoms than the more "sophisticated" intellectuals who leapt from Marx to Machiavelli.

Nathan Glazer, still another editor, wrote an excellent analysis of McCarthy in the March 1953 issue; but at the end of his article, almost as if from another hand, there again appeared the magazine's earlier line: "All that Senator McCarthy can do on his own authority that someone equally unpleasant and not a Senator can't, is to haul people down to Washington for a grilling by his committee. It is a shame and an outrage that Senator McCarthy should remain in the Senate; yet I cannot see that it is an imminent danger to personal liberty in the United States." It is, I suppose, this sort of thing that is meant when people speak about the need for replacing the outworn formulas and clichés of liberalism and radicalism with *new ideas*.

4

To what does one conform? To institutions, obviously. To the dead images that rot in one's mind, unavoidably. And almost always, to the small grating necessities of day-to-day survival. In these senses it may be said that we are all conformists to one or another degree. When Sidney Hook writes, "I see no specific virtue in the attitude of conformity or non-conformity," he is right if he means that no human being can, or should, entirely accept or reject the moral and social modes of his time. And he is right in adding that there are occasions, such as the crisis of the Weimar republic, when the nonconformism of a Stefan George or an Oswald Spengler can have unhappy consequences.

But Professor Hook seems to me quite wrong in supposing that his remark applies significantly to present-day America. It would apply if we lived in a world where ideas could be weighed in free and delicate balance, without social pressures or contaminations, so that our choices would be made solely from a passion for truth. As it happens, however, there are tremendous pressures in America that make for intellectual conformism and consequently, in this tense and difficult age, there are very real virtues in preserving the attitude of critical skepticism and distance. Even some of the more extreme antics of the professional "bohemians" or literary anarchists take on a certain value which in cooler moments they might not have.*

What one conforms to most of all—despite and against one's intentions—is the zeitgeist, that vast insidious sum of pressures and fashions; one drifts along,

---

* It may be asked whether a Stalinist's "nonconformism" is valuable. No, it isn't; the Stalinist is anything but a nonconformist; he has merely shifted the object of his worship, as later, when he abandons Stalinism, he usually shifts it again.

anxious and compliant, upon the favored assumptions of the moment; and not a soul in the intellectual world can escape this. Only, some resist and some don't. Today the zeitgeist presses down upon us with a greater insistence than at any other moment of the century. In the 1930s many of those who hovered about the *New Masses* were mere camp followers of success; but the conformism of the party-line intellectual, at least before 1936, did sometimes bring him into conflict with established power: he had to risk something. Now, by contrast, established power and the dominant intellectual tendencies have come together in a harmony such as this country has not seen since the Gilded Age; and this, of course, makes the temptations of conformism all the more acute. The carrots, for once, are real.

Real even for literary men, who these days prefer to meditate upon symbolic vegetables. I would certainly not wish to suggest any direct correlation between our literary assumptions and the nature of our politics; but surely some of the recent literary trends and fashions owe something to the more general intellectual drift toward conformism. Not, of course, that liberalism dominates literary life, as it dominates the rest of the intellectual world. Whatever practical interest most literary men have in politics comes to little else than the usual liberalism, but their efforts at constructing literary ideologies—frequently as forced marches to discover values our society will not yield them—result in something quite different from liberalism. Through much of our writing, both creative and critical, there run a number of ideological motifs, the importance of which is hardly diminished by the failure of the men who employ them to be fully aware of their implications. Thus, a major charge that might be brought against some New Critics is not that they practice formal criticism but that they don't; not that they see the work of art as an object to be judged according to laws of its own realm but that, often unconsciously, they weave ideological assumptions into their writings.* Listening last summer to Cleanth Brooks lecture on Faulkner, I was struck by the deep hold

* This may be true of all critics, but is most perilous to those who suppose themselves free of ideological coloring. In a review of my Faulkner book—rather favorable, so that no ego wounds prompt what follows—Robert Daniel writes that "Because of Mr. Howe's connections with . . . the *Partisan Review*, one might expect his literary judgments to be shaped by political and social preconceptions, but that does not happen often." Daniel is surprised that a critic whose politics happen to be radical should try to keep his literary views distinct from his nonliterary ones. To be sure, this is sometimes very difficult, and perhaps no one entirely succeeds. But the one sure way of not succeeding is to write, as Daniel does, from no very pressing awareness that it is a problem for critics who appear in the *Sewanee Review* quite as much as for those who appear in *Partisan Review*.

that the term "orthodox" has acquired on his critical imagination, and not, by the way, on his alone. But "orthodox" is not, properly speaking, a critical term at all; it pertains to matters of religious or other belief rather than to literary judgment; and a habitual use of such terms can only result in the kind of "slanted" criticism Mr. Brooks has been so quick, and right, to condemn.

Together with "orthodox" there goes a cluster of terms which, in their sum, reveal an implicit ideological bias. The word "traditional" is especially tricky here, since it has legitimate uses in both literary and moral-ideological contexts. What happens, however, in much contemporary criticism is that these two contexts are taken to either be one or to be organically related, so that it becomes possible to assume that a sense of literary tradition necessarily involves and sanctions a "traditional" view of morality. There is a powerful inclination here—it is the doing of the impish zeitgeist—to forget that literary tradition can be fruitfully seen as a series of revolts, literary but sometimes more than literary, of generation against generation, age against age. The emphasis on "tradition" has other contemporary implications: it is used as a not very courageous means of countering the experimental and the modern; it can enclose the academic assumption—and this is the curse of the Ph.D. system—that the whole of the literary past is at every point equally relevant to a modern intelligence; and it frequently includes the provincial American need to be more genteel than the gentry, more English than the English. Basically, it has served as a means of asserting conservative or reactionary moral-ideological views not, as they should be asserted, in their own terms, but through the refining medium of literary talk.

In general, there has been a tendency among critics to subsume literature under their own moral musings, which makes for a conspicuously humorless kind of criticism.* Morality is assumed to be a sufficient container for the floods of experience, and poems or novels that gain their richness from the complexity with which they dramatize the incommensurability between man's existence and his conceptualizing, are thinned, pruned, and allegorized into moral fables. Writers who spent—in both senses of the word—their lives wrestling with terrible private demons are elevated into literary dons and deacons. It is as if Stendhal had never come forth, with his subversive wit, to testify how often life and literature

---

* Writing about *Wuthering Heights* Mark Schorer solemnly declares that "the theme of the moral magnificence of unmoral passion is an impossible theme to sustain, and the needs of her temperament to the contrary, all personal longing and reverie to the contrary, Emily Brontë teaches herself that this was indeed not at all what her material must mean as art." What is more, if Emily Brontë had lived a little longer she would have been offered a Chair in Moral Philosophy.

find the whole moral apparatus irrelevant or tedious, as if Lawrence had never written *The Man Who Died*, as if Nietzsche had never launched his great attack on the Christian impoverishment of the human psyche. One can only be relieved, therefore, at knowing a few critics personally: how pleasant the discrepancy between their writings and their lives!

But it is Original Sin that today commands the highest prestige in the literary world. Like nothing else, it allows literary men to enjoy a sense of profundity and depth—to relish a disenchantment which allows no further risk of becoming enchanted—as against the superficiality of *mere* rationalism. It allows them to appropriate to the "tradition" the greatest modern writers, precisely those whose values and allegiances are most ambiguous, complex, and enigmatic, while at the same time generously leaving, as Leslie Fiedler once suggested, Dreiser and Farrell as the proper idols for that remnant benighted enough to maintain a naturalist philosophy. To hold, as Dickens remarks in *Bleak House*, "a loose belief that if the world go wrong, it was, in some off-hand manner, never meant to go right," this becomes the essence of wisdom. (Liberals too have learned to cast a warm eye on "man's fallen nature," so that one gets the high comedy of Arthur Schlesinger, Jr. interrupting his quite worldly political articles with uneasy bows in the direction of Kierkegaard.) And with this latest dispensation come, of course, many facile references to the ideas supposedly held by Rousseau★ and Marx, that man is "perfectible" and that progress moves in a steady upward curve.

I say, facile references, because no one who has troubled to read Rousseau or Marx could write such things. Exactly what the "perfectibility of man" is supposed to mean, if anything at all, I cannot say; but it is not a phrase intrinsic to the kind of thought one finds in the mature Marx or, most of the time, in Rousseau. Marx did not base his argument for socialism on any view that one could isolate a constant called "human nature"; he would certainly have agreed with Ortega that man has not a nature, but a history. Nor did he have a very rosy view of the human beings who were his contemporaries or recent predecessors: see in *Capital* the chapter on the Working Day, a grisly catalogue of human bestiality. Nor did he hold to a naive theory of progress: he wrote that the victories of progress "seem bought by the loss of character. At the same pace that mankind masters nature, man seems to become enslaved to other men or to his own infamy."

★ Randall Jarrell, who usually avoids fashionable cant: "Most of us know, now, that Rousseau was wrong; that man, when you knock his chains off, sets up the death camps." Which chains were knocked off in Germany to permit the setting up of death camps? And which chains must be put up again to prevent a repetition of the death camps?

As for Rousseau, the use of even a finger's worth of historical imagination should suggest that the notion of "a state of nature," which modern literary people so enjoy attacking, was a political metaphor employed in a prerevolutionary situation, and not, therefore, to be understood outside its context. Rousseau explicitly declared that he did not suppose the "state of nature" to have existed in historical time; it was, he said, "a pure idea of reason" reached by abstraction from the observable state of society. As G. D. H. Cole remarks, "in political matters at any rate, the 'state of nature' is for [Rousseau] only a term of controversy . . . he means by 'nature' not the original state of a thing, nor even its reduction to the simplest terms; he is passing over to the conception of 'nature' as identical with the full development of [human] capacity. . . ." There are, to be sure, elements in Rousseau's thought which one may well find distasteful, but these are not the elements commonly referred to when he is used in literary talk as a straw man to be beaten with the cudgels of "orthodoxy."

What then is the significance of the turn to Original Sin among so many intellectuals? Surely not to inform us, at this late moment, that man is capable of evil. Or is it, as Cleanth Brooks writes, to suggest that man is a "limited" creature, limited in possibilities and capacities, and hence unable to achieve his salvation through social means? Yes, to be sure; but the problem of history is to determine, by action, how far those limits may go. Conservative critics like to say that "man's fallen nature" makes unrealistic the liberal-radical vision of the good society— apparently, when Eve bit the apple she predetermined, with one fatal crunch, that her progeny could work its way up to capitalism, and not a step further. But the liberal-radical vision of the good society does not depend upon a belief in the "unqualified goodness of man"; nor does it locate salvation in society: anyone in need of being saved had better engage in a private scrutiny. The liberal-radical claim is merely that the development of technology has now made possible—possible, not inevitable—a solution of those material problems that have burdened mankind for centuries. These problems solved, man is then on his own, to make of his self and his world what he can.

The literary prestige of Original Sin cannot be understood without reference to the current cultural situation; it cannot be understood except as a historical phenomenon reflecting, like the whole turn to religion and religiosity, the weariness of intellectuals in an age of defeat and their yearning to remove themselves from the bloodied arena of historical action and choice, which necessarily means, of secular action and choice. Much sarcasm and anger has been expended on the "failure of nerve" theory, usually by people who take it as a personal affront to be told that there is a connection between what happens in their minds and what happens in the world; but if one looks at the large-scale shifts among intellectuals during the past twenty-five years, it becomes impossible to put all of them down to a simultaneous, and thereby miraculous, discovery of Truth; some at least must be seen as a consequence of those historical pressures which make this an age of conformism. Like other efforts to explain major changes in belief, the "failure of nerve" theory does not tell us why certain people believed in the thirties what was only to become popular in the fifties and why others still believe in the fifties what was popular in the thirties; but it does tell us something more important: why a complex of beliefs is dominant at one time and subordinate at another.

5

I have tried to trace a rough pattern from social history through politics and finally into literary ideology, as a means of explaining the power of the conformist impulse in our time. But it is obvious that in each intellectual "world" there are impulses of this kind that cannot easily be shown to have their sources in social or historical pressures. Each intellectual world gives rise to its own patterns of obligation and preference. The literary world, being relatively free from the coarser kinds of social pressure, enjoys a considerable degree of detachment and autonomy. (Not as much as it likes to suppose, but a considerable degree.) That the general intellectual tendency is to acquiesce in what one no longer feels able to change or modify strongly encourages the internal patterns of conformism in the literary world and intensifies the yearning, common to all groups but especially to small and insecure groups, to draw together in a phalanx of solidarity. Then too, those groups that live by hostility to the dominant values of society—in this case, cultural values—find it extremely difficult to avoid an inner conservatism as a way of balancing their public role of opposition; anyone familiar with radical politics knows this phenomenon only too well. Finally, the literary world, while quite powerless in relation to, say, the worlds of business and politics, disposes of a measurable amount of power and patronage within its own domain; which makes, again, for predictable kinds of influence.

Whoever would examine the inner life of the literary world should turn first not to the magazines or the dignitaries or famous writers but to the graduate students, for like it or not the graduate school has become the main recruiting grounds for critics and sometimes even for writers. Here, in conversation with the depressed classes of the academy, one sees how the Ph.D. system—more powerful today than it has been for decades, since so few other choices are open to young literary men—grinds and batters personality into a mold of cautious routine. And what one finds among these young people, for all their intelligence and devotion and eagerness, is often appalling: a remarkable desire to be "critics," not as an accompaniment to the writing of poetry or the changing of the world or the study of man and God, but just critics—as if criticism were a *subject*, as if one could be a critic without having at least four nonliterary opinions, or as if criticism "in itself" could adequately engage an adult mind for more than a small part of its waking time. An equally astonishing indifference to the ideas that occupy the serious modern mind—Freud, Marx, Nietzsche, Frazer, Dewey are not great thinkers in their right, but reservoirs from which one dredges up "approaches to criticism"—together with a fabulous knowledge of what Ransom said about Winters with regard to what Winters had said about Eliot. And a curiously humble discipleship—but also arrogant to those beyond the circle—so that one meets not fresh minds in growth but apostles of Burke or Trilling or Winters or Leavis or Brooks or neo-Aristotle.

Very little of this is the fault of the graduate students themselves, for they, like the distinguished figures I have just listed, are the victims of an unhappy cultural moment. What we have today in the literary world is a gradual bureaucratization of opinion and taste; not a dictatorship, not a conspiracy, not a coup, not a Machiavellian plot to impose a mandatory "syllabus"; but the inevitable result of outer success and inner hardening. Fourth-rate exercises in exegesis are puffed in the magazines while so remarkable and provocative a work as Arnold Hauser's *Social History of Art* is hardly reviewed, its very title indicating the reason. Learned young critics who have never troubled to open a novel by Turgenev can rattle off reams of Kenneth Burke, which gives them, understandably, a sensation of having enlarged upon literature. Literature itself becomes a raw material which critics work up into schemes of structure and symbol; to suppose that it is concerned with anything so gauche as human experience or obsolete as human beings—"You mean," a student said to me, "that you're interested in the *characters* of novels!" Symbols clutter the literary landscape like the pots and pans a two-year-old strews over the kitchen floor; and what is wrong here is not merely the transparent absence of literary tact—the gift for saying when a pan is a pan and when a pan is a symbol—but far more important, a transparent lack of interest in represented experience. For Robert Wooster Stallman the fact that Stephen Crane looking at the sun felt moved to compare it to a wafer is not enough, the existence of suns and wafers and their possible conjunction is not sufficiently marvelous: both objects must be absorbed into Christian symbolism (an ancient theory of literature developed by the church fathers to prove that suns, moons, vulva, chairs, money, hair, pots, pans, and words are really crucifixes). Techniques for reading a novel that have at best a limited relevance are frozen into dogmas: one might suppose from glancing at the more imposing literary manuals that "point of view" is the crucial means of judging a novel. (Willa Cather, according to Caroline Gordon, was "astonishingly ignorant of her craft," for she refrained from "using a single consciousness as a prism of moral reflection." The very mistake Tolstoy made, too!) Criticism itself, far from being the reflection of a solitary mind upon a work of art and therefore, like the solitary mind, incomplete and subjective, comes increasingly to be regarded as a problem in mechanics, the tools, methods, and trade secrets of which can be picked up, usually during the summer, from the more experienced operatives. In the mind of Stanley Hyman, who serves the indispensable function of reducing fashionable literary notions, criticism seems to resemble Macy's on bargain day: *First floor, symbols; Second floor, myths (rituals to the rear on your right); Third floor, ambiguities and paradoxes; Fourth floor, word counting; Fifth floor, Miss Harrison's antiquities; Attic, Marxist remnants; Basement, Freud; Sub-basement, Jung. Watch your step, please.*

What is most disturbing, however, is that writing about literature and writers has become an industry. The preposterous academic requirement that professors write books they don't want to write and no one wants to read, together with the obtuse assumption that piling up more and more irrelevant information about an author's life helps us understand his work—this makes for a vast flood of books that have little to do with literature, criticism, or even scholarship. Would you care to know the contents of the cargo (including one elephant) carried by the vessel of which Hawthorne's father was captain in 1795? Robert Cantwell has an itemized list, no doubt as an aid to reading *The Scarlet Letter*. Jay Leyda knows what happened to Melville day by day and it is hardly his fault that most days nothing very much happened. Edgar Johnson does as much for Dickens and adds plot summaries too, no doubt because he is dealing with a little-read author. Another American scholar has published a full book on *Mardi*, which is astonishing not because he wrote the book but because he managed to finish reading *Mardi* at all.

I have obviously chosen extreme examples and it would be silly to contend that they adequately describe the American literary scene; but like the distorting mirrors in Coney Island they help bring into sharper contour the major features. Or as Donald Davie writes in the English journal, *Twentieth Century*:

> The professional poet has already disappeared from the literary scene, and the professional man of letters is following him into the grave. . . . It becomes more and more difficult, and will soon be impossible, for a man to make his living as a literary dilettante. . . . And instead of the professional

man of letters we have the professional critic, the young don writing in the
first place for other dons, and only incidentally for that supremely necessary
fiction, the common reader. In other words, an even greater proportion of
what is written about literature, and even of what literature is written, is
"academic." . . . Literary standards are now in academic hands; for the free-
lance man of letters, who once supplemented and corrected the don, is fast
disappearing from the literary scene. . . .

The pedant is as common as he ever was. And now that willy-nilly so
much writing about literature is in academic hands, his activities are more
dangerous than ever. But he has changed his habits. Twenty years ago he
was to be heard asserting that his business was with hard facts, that questions of value and technique were not his affair, and that criticism could
therefore be left to the impressionistic journalist. Now the pedant is proud
to call himself a critic; he prides himself on evaluation and analysis; he aims
to be penetrating, not informative. . . .

The pedant is a very adaptable creature, and can be as comfortable
with Mr. Eliot's "objective correlative," Mr. Empson's "ambiguities" and
Dr. Leavis's "complexities" as in the older suit of critical clothes that he has
now, for the most part, abandoned.

Davie has in mind the literary situation in England, but all one needs for apply-
ing his remarks to America is an ability to multiply.

6

All of the tendencies toward cultural conformism come to a head in the assumption that the avant-garde, as both concept and intellectual grouping, has
become obsolete or irrelevant. Yet the future quality of American culture, I would
maintain, largely depends on the survival, and the terms of survival, of precisely
the kind of dedicated group that the avant-garde has been.

The avant-garde first appeared on the American scene some twenty-five or
thirty years ago, as a response to the need for absorbing the meanings of the
cultural revolution that had taken place in Europe during the first two decades
of the century. The achievements of Joyce, Proust, Schoenberg, Bartók, Picasso,
Matisse, to mention only the obvious figures, signified one of the major turnings
in the cultural history of the West, a turning made all the more crucial by the fact
that it came not during the vigor of a society but during its crisis. To counter the
hostility which the work of such artists met among all the official spokesmen

of culture, to discover formal terms and modes through which to secure these achievements, to insist upon the continuity between their work and the accepted, because dead, artists of the past—this became the task of the avant-garde. Somewhat later a section of the avant-garde also became politically active, and not by accident; for precisely those aroused sensibilities that had responded to the innovations of the modern masters now responded to the crisis of modern society. Thus, in the early years of a magazine like *Partisan Review*—roughly between 1936 and 1941—these two radical impulses came together in an uneasy but fruitful union; and it was in those years that the magazine seemed most exciting and vital as a link between art and experience, between the critical consciousness and the political conscience, between the avant-garde of letters and the independent left of politics.

That union has since been dissolved, and there is no likelihood that it will soon be re-established. American radicalism exists only as an idea, and that barely; the literary avant-garde—it has become a stock comment for reviewers to make—is rapidly disintegrating, without function or spirit, and held together only by an inert nostalgia.

Had the purpose of the avant-garde been to establish the currency of certain names, to make the reading of *The Waste Land* and *Ulysses* respectable in the universities, there would be no further need for its continuance. But clearly this was not the central purpose of the avant-garde; it was only an unavoidable fringe of snobbery and fashion. The struggle for Joyce mattered only as it was a struggle for literary standards; the defense of Joyce was a defense not merely of modern innovation but of that traditional culture which was the source of modern innovation. And at its best it was a defense against those spokesmen for the genteel, the respectable, and the academic who had established a stranglehold over traditional culture. At the most serious level, the avant-garde was trying to face the problem of the quality of our culture, and when all is said and done, it faced that problem with a courage and honesty that no other group in society could match.

If the history of the avant-garde is seen in this way, there is every reason for believing that its survival is as necessary today as it was twenty-five years ago. To be sure, our immediate prospect is not nearly so exciting as it must then have seemed: we face no battle on behalf of great and difficult artists who are scorned by the official voices of culture. Today, in a sense, the danger is that the serious artists are not scorned enough. Philistinism has become very shrewd: it does not attack its enemies as much as it disarms them through reasonable cautions and moderate amendments. But this hardly makes the defense of those standards that animated the avant-garde during its best days any the less a critical obligation.

It has been urged in some circles that only the pressure of habit keeps serious writers from making "raids" upon the middlebrow world, that it is now possible to win substantial outposts in that world if we are ready to take risks. Perhaps. But surely no one desires a policy of highbrow isolation, and no one could oppose raids, provided that is what they really are. The precondition for successful raids, however, is that the serious writers themselves have a sense—not of belonging to an exclusive club—but of representing those cultural values which alone can sustain them while making their raids. Thus far the incursions of serious writers into the middlebrow world have not been remarkably successful: for every short-story writer who has survived the *New Yorker* one could point to a dozen whose work became trivial and frozen after they had begun to write for it. Nor do I advocate, in saying this, a policy of evading temptations. I advocate overcoming them. Writers today have no choice, often enough, but to write for magazines like the *New Yorker*—and worse, far worse. But what matters is the terms upon which the writer enters into such relationships, his willingness to understand with whom he is dealing, his readiness not to deceive himself that an unpleasant necessity is a desirable virtue.

It seems to me beyond dispute that, thus far at least, in the encounter between high and middle culture, the latter has come off by far the better. Every current of the zeitgeist, every imprint of social power, every assumption of contemporary American life favors the safe and comforting patterns of middlebrow feeling. And then too the gloomier Christian writers may have a point when they tell us that it is easier for a soul to fall than to rise.*

Precisely at the time that the highbrows seem inclined to abandon what is sometimes called their "proud isolation," the middlebrows have become more intransigent in their opposition to everything that is serious and creative in our culture (which does not, of course, prevent them from exploiting and contaminating, for purposes of mass gossip, everything that is serious and creative in our culture). What else is the meaning of the coarse attack launched by the *Saturday Review* against the highbrows, under the guise of discussing the Pound case? What, for that matter, is the meaning of the hostility with which the *Partisan Review*

* Thus Professor Gilbert Highet, the distinguished classicist, writing in *Harper's* finds André Gide "an abominably wicked man. His work seems to me to be either shallowly based symbolism, or else cheap cynicism made by inverting commonplaces or by grinning through them. . . . Gide had the curse of perpetual immaturity. But then I am always aware of the central fact about Gide—that he was a sexual pervert who kept proclaiming and justifying his perversion; and perhaps this blinds me to his merits . . . the garrulous, Pangloss-like, pimple-scratching, self-exposure of Gide." I don't mean to suggest that many fall so low, but then not many philistines are so well educated as Highet.

symposium on "Our Country and Our Culture" was received? It would take no straining of texts to see this symposium as a disconcerting sign of how far intellectuals have drifted in the direction of cultural adaptation, yet the middlebrows wrote of it with blunt enmity. And perhaps because they too sensed this drift in the symposium, the middlebrows, highly confident at the moment, became more aggressive, for they do not desire compromise, they know that none is possible. So genial a middlebrow as Elmer Davis, in a long review of the symposium, entitled with a characteristic smirk "The Care and Feeding of Intellectuals," ends up on a revealing note: "The highbrows seem to be getting around to recognizing what the middlebrows have known for the past thirty years. This is progress." It is also the best possible argument for the maintenance of the avant-garde, even if only as a kind of limited defense.

Much has been written about the improvement of cultural standards in America, though a major piece of evidence—the wide circulation of paperbound books—is still an unweighed and unanalyzed quantity. The basic relations of cultural power remain unchanged, however: the middlebrows continue to dominate. The most distinguished newspaper in this country retains as its music critic a mediocrity named Olin Downes; the literary critic for that newspaper is a philistine named Orville Prescott; the most widely read book reviewer in this country is a buffoon named Sterling North; the most powerful literary journal, read with admiration by many librarians and professors, remains the *Saturday Review*. Nothing here gives us cause for reassurance or relaxation; nothing gives us reason to dissolve that compact in behalf of critical intransigence known as the avant-garde.

No formal ideology or program is entirely adequate for coping with the problems that intellectuals face in the twentieth century. No easy certainties and no easy acceptance of uncertainty. All the forms of authority, the states and institutions and monster bureaucracies, that press in upon modern life—what have these shown us to warrant the surrender of independence?

The most glorious vision of the intellectual life is still that which is loosely called humanist: the idea of a mind committed yet dispassionate, ready to stand alone, curious, eager, skeptical. The banner of critical independence, ragged and torn though it may be, is still the best we have.

Review of The Country of the Pointed Firs by Sarah Orne Jewett

{1954}

SARAH ORNE JEWETT was a writer of deep pure feeling and a limited capacity for emotional expression: there is always, one senses, more behind the language than actually comes through it. In her best work she employed—it was an instinctive and inevitable choice—a tone of muted nostalgia. She knew that the Maine country she loved so well was slowly being pushed into a social impasse: it could not compete in the jungle warfare that was American life in the late nineteenth century. But even as this knowledge formed and limited her vision of things, she did not let it become the dominant content of her work, for she understood, or felt, that the obsolete also has its claim upon us. She was honest and tactful enough not to inflate her sense of passing and nostalgia with the urgencies of a heroism that could only have been willed; in her bare, linear stories about country people struggling to keep their farms alive, she made no false claims, for she saw that even when one or another figure in her Maine country might be heroic there was nothing distinctively heroic in the spectacle of a community in decline, a way of life gradually dying. But she knew—it was an enviable knowledge—that admiration and love can be extended to those who have neither the vocation nor the possibility for heroism. She paid a price, of course. In a country where literature has so often been given over to roaring and proclaiming and "promulging" it was nearly impossible for so exquisite an artist—exquisite precisely because she was, and knew she was, a minor figure—to be properly valued.

At first glance *The Country of the Pointed Firs* bears a certain structural resemblance to Mrs. Gaskell's *Cranford*. In both books a young woman who has tasted urban knowledge returns to a quaint, outmoded village which represents pre-industrial society, and there observes the manners of its inhabitants with a mixture of fondness and amusement. But charming as *Cranford* obviously is, it does not seem to me nearly so good as Miss Jewett's book. Too often Mrs. Gaskell is content to bask in the soft glow of eccentricity and oddity, so that her narrator leaves Cranford pretty much the person she was. But Miss Jewett's "I" registers the meaning of Deephaven with an increase of force and insight that is beautifully arranged: for her the experience of arriving and leaving becomes an education in mortality.

The people in *The Country of the Pointed Firs* are eccentrics, a little gnarled by the American weather and twisted by American loneliness; but it is not for a display of these deformities that Miss Jewett presents them. She is interested in reaching some human core beneath the crusted surface and like so many other American writers, like Anderson and Frost and Robinson, she knows the value and pathos of the buried life. That is why it is harmful, despite the fact that her stories are set in the same locale, to speak of her as a regional writer; for regional literature, by its very premise, implies a certain slackening of the human measure, a complacent readiness to accept the merely accidental and quaint.

Miss Jewett moves her light from one figure to another: the shy fisherman William who late in life returns to the interior country to claim his love; the jilted Miss Joanna Todd who in the immensity of her grief cuts herself off from humanity and lives alone on a coastal island; the touched sea captain who remembers journeys to places that never were; and most of all, Mrs. Almiry Todd, the central figure of the book, sharp-tongued, wise, witty, a somewhat greyed version of George Eliot's Mrs. Poyser. (As Mrs. Todd recalls her dead husband, "She might have been Antigone alone on the Theban plain. . . . An absolute, archaic grief possessed this countrywoman; she seemed like a renewal of some historic soul, with her sorrows and the remoteness of a daily life busied with rustic simplicities and the scents of primeval herbs.") The book is set in a dramatic present that is necessarily somewhat fragile, but it resounds with full echoes of the past: tradition lives as an element of experience, not a proposition of ideology. ("Conversation's got to have some root in the past," says an old lady, "or else you've got to explain every remark you make, and it wears a person out.")

The Country of the Pointed Firs gains organic structure from its relaxed loyalty to the rhythms of natural life. The world it memorializes is small and shrinking, and the dominant images of the book serve only to bound this world more stringently: images of the ranked firs and the water, which together suggest the enclosing force of everything beyond the social perimeter. But meanwhile a community survives, endowed with rare powers of implicit communication: to say in this world that someone has "real feelins" is to say everything.

Finally the book is a triumph of style, a precise and delicate style such as we seldom find in nineteenth-century American prose. The breakdown of distinctions between prose and verse which occurs under the sponsorship of romanticism and for a variety of reasons is particularly extreme in America, where it produces two such ambiguous figures of genius as Melville and Whitman—this breakdown hardly affected Miss Jewett. Very probably this is one reason she remained a minor figure while Melville and Whitman were, occasionally, major ones. But at the moment there is much to be gained from a study of her finely modulated prose, which never strains for effects beyond its reach and always achieves a secure pattern of rhythm. Listen to this sentence with its sly abrupt climax: "There was something quite charming in his appearance: it was a face thin and delicate with refinement, but worn into appealing lines, as if he had suffered from loneliness and misapprehension." Or to the lucid gravity of this sentence: "There was in the eyes a look of anticipation and joy, a far-off look that sought the horizon; one often sees it in seafaring families, inherited by girls and boys alike from men who spend their lives at sea, and are always watching for distant sails or the first loom of the land." Or to the wit of Mrs. Todd as she places her minister: "He seemed to know no remedies, but he had a great use of words."

The Country of the Pointed Firs is not a "great" book; it isn't *Moby Dick* or *Sister Carrie* or even *The Great Gatsby*. It cannot sustain profound exegesis or symbol hunting. But living as we do in a country where minor works are underrated because major ones are overrated, it is good to remember that we have writers like Miss Jewett calmly waiting for us to remember them.

The Stories of Bernard Malamud
{1958}

IT IS VERY HARD to describe the stories in *The Magic Barrel* with any sort of exactness—and not because they are so weird or exotic but because they are genuinely original. Part of the shock of pleasure in reading them comes from the discovery that one's initial response is mistaken. One reacts, first of all, to Malamud's painfully familiar setting: the Jewish immigrant neighborhood of the depression years. Here, predictably, are the Jewish grocery-man dragging in cases of milk each morning, the Jewish baker slowly expiring over his ovens. Somewhat later in time comes the Jewish graduate student fumbling his way through Rome, eager to grasp knowledge of the Gentile world yet perversely oppressed by a strange Jew, an archetypal *nudnik*, who in his unqualified shamelessness represents the claim that each Jew has on all others: the claim of trouble.

Malamud's stories bring back, for a page or two, memories of half-forgotten novels: the cramped, grey, weepy aura of "American Jewish" fiction. But then one learns that Malamud is not so easily "placed," and that if it is legitimate to admire the care with which he summons the Jewish immigrant world, an important reason is that he treats it as no writer before him—except perhaps Daniel Fuchs— has ever done.

For in each of Malamud's best stories something surprising happens: it is as if the speed of the movie reel were crazily increased, as if the characters leapt clear of the earth, as if a Chagall painting snapped into motion and its figures, long frozen in mid-air, began to dip and soar. The place is familiar; but the tone, the tempo, the treatment are all new.

In what way? Malamud, as it seems to me, moves not to surrealism or fantasy but to a realistic fable in which the life cycle is exhausted at double-time: a wink, a shrug, a collapse. Everything—action, dialogue, comment—is sped up, driven to a climax in which a gesture compresses and releases an essential meaning, and the characters, hurtling themselves across a dozen pages, rise to a fabulous sort of "Yiddish" articulateness of gesture and speech.

Now, in any obvious sense this is not realism at all: the stories seldom plot along accumulating incidents, and they frequently diverge from strict standards of probability in order to leap-frog to dramatic moments of revelation. Nonetheless, their essential economy, the psychological pattern to which they remain loyal, can be called "realistic": for they aim at verisimilitude in depth, they are closely responsive to a serious public morality, they wish ultimately to indicate that this is the way things *really* are. Malamud spurs the realistic story to a pace so feverish as to leave behind the usual stylizations of realism, but the moral and psychological intentions that are typical of realistic stories continue to operate in his work.

This is a procedure with obvious dangers. Partly they are inherent ones, since his stories usually involve gambling everything on one or two paragraphs; partly they seem the result of a manner that Malamud shares with a good many other recent American Jewish writers: a jazzed-up, slap-dash, knock-em-down-and-hit-em-again approach to language and action. In his inferior stories Malamud depends too much on hard and flashy climaxes, so that the most beautiful aspect of his novel The Assistant—its hum of contemplativeness, its quiet humane undertone—is not to be found here. And too often Malamud's stories seem excessively brilliant on the surface, a ruthless dash for effect, and then one has the feeling that one is being bullied and blinded by a virtuoso.

But these are incidental faults, and at his best Malamud has worked out for himself a kind of story that is spectacularly successful. In "The Loan," Kobotsky, an impoverished Jew, comes to his old friend Lieb, an aging and harassed baker, to ask for some money. Years ago they had quarreled, but still a spark of feeling survives. Among his other troubles Lieb now has a second wife, Bessie, who shares with him the tears of poverty and adds some salt of her own. Kobotsky begs for his loan on the ground that his wife is sick, but Bessie, who must make the final decision, remains unmoved; then Kobotsky tells the truth, his wife has been dead for five years and he wants the money to buy a long overdue stone for her grave. Bessie, who can identify with a wife in a grave more easily than with a wife in a hospital, begins to weaken. Gathering force and lyricism, the story now speeds along to its climax: through a device I shall not disclose, Malamud achieves another reversal, this time to show that Bessie's heart has again hardened and Lieb will not be able to help his friend. The last paragraph:

> Kobotsky and the baker embraced and sighed over their lost youth. They pressed mouths together and parted forever.

Now by any usual standard this ending is melodramatic and most improbable: Jews like Kobotsky and Lieb do not press mouths together. But in the story the ending works, since it embodies what Malamud could neither have represented through ordinary realism nor risked stating in his own right: the beauty of defeat as a kind of love. And the reason it works is that Malamud has prepared for surprise by leading us so surely from one moment of suppressed intensity to another that the burst of pressure which creates the final excitement also dissolves any lingering expectations of ordinary realism. It is for similar reasons that one does not find it disturbing that in the superb title story a matchmaker who has arranged for a meeting between a rabbinical student and his (apparently) sluttish daughter should watch them on the sly, chanting "prayers for the dead." Such incidents, in Malamud's stories, are not symbolic; they are synoptic.

At his best, then, Malamud has managed to bring together that sense of the power of external circumstance which so overwhelmed writers a few decades ago and the concern of more recent writers for the gratuitous sign that declares a man's humanity even as it is being crushed. The settings contribute an atmosphere of limitation, oppression, coercion: man is not free. The action and language preserve, through the renewing powers of imagination, the possibility of freedom.

Malamud is one of the very few American writers about whom it makes sense to say that his work has a distinctly "Jewish" tone. He writes as if the ethos of Yiddish literature, the quiver of *menshlichkeit*, had, through a miraculous salvage, become his possession. And he preserves this heritage with an easiness, a lack of self-consciousness, that makes most American Jewish writers seem local colorists exploiting accidental associations. Malamud can grind a character to the earth, but there is always a hard ironic pity, a wry affection better than wet gestures of love, which makes him seem a grandson of the Yiddish writers. How this has happened I cannot say, for my guess would be that Malamud does not have a close knowledge of Yiddish literature; but perhaps the moral is that for those who know why to wait, the magic barrel will reappear.

The 1960s

Doris Lessing:
No Compromise, No Happiness
{1963}

I N OUR TIME THE LIFE of cultivated people is marked by a fierce attachment to "personal values." I put the phrase in quote marks to point toward something more problematic than the usual web of involvements that appear when human beings live together in society. The condition I have in mind—perhaps new for us, though hardly unprecedented—can be observed in the cosmopolitan centers of the West and increasingly in the more advanced totalitarian countries.

"Personal relations" as the very substance and sufficient end of our existence; "personal relations" as a surrogate for transcendence through religion, fulfillment through work, satisfaction through community; "personal relations" as a fragile shelter for sensitive men, a bulwark against the nihilist void, an ideology of privacy to replace the lapsed ideologies of public action—all this has become a style of life in New York and Moscow, London and Warsaw, accepted by some intellectuals with a tiresome literalness and by others with a skeptical grin. Among ourselves the devotion to "personal relations" seems at times like a malaise eating away at personal life; in the Communist countries it can serve as a rallying call for marginal freedoms. But in both parts of the world, psychological man begins to replace social man.

It is a particular distinction of *The Golden Notebook*, a long and ambitious novel by the gifted English writer Doris Lessing, that while dealing with some of the materials favored by the novelists of sensibility, it escapes their constrictions of tone and outlook. Both Miss Lessing and her characters are deeply caught up with the cult of "personal relations," yet she is able to keep some critical distance from her material and to look upon it as merely the latest turn in the confusion of modern history. She yields her sympathies to those of her characters who fall back upon "personal relations" in order to get through their days, but she tries not to settle for the limitations of experience they must accept. She understands that the idea of "personal relations" has been shaped by the catastrophes of our time and, in the form we know it, is not to be taken as an absolute or uncontaminated value.

It is a further distinction of Miss Lessing's novel that its action is mainly carried by that rarity in modern fiction: a heroine, Anna Wulf, who is a mature intellectual woman. A writer with a sophisticated mind, sharp tongue and an abundance of emotional troubles, Anna Wulf is sufficiently representative of a certain kind of modern woman to persuade us that her troubles have a relevance beyond their immediate setting; she is also an intelligence keen enough to support the public combativeness and personal introspectiveness that Miss Lessing has given her. At the very least, Anna Wulf is someone who has measured the price for being what she chooses to be—"a free woman," she would say with pride and irony—and who is prepared, no matter how much she groans, to pay it.

Miss Lessing is radically different from other women writers who have dealt with the problems of their sex, first in that she grasps the connection between Anna Wulf's neuroses and the public disorders of the day, and second in that she has no use either for the quaverings of the feminist writers or the aggressions of those female novelists whose every sentence leads a charge in the war of the sexes. The feminine element in *The Golden Notebook* does not become a self-contained universe of being as in some of Virginia Woolf's novels, nor is the narrative voice established through minute gradations of the writer's sensibility, as in some of Elizabeth Bowen's.

Anna Wulf and her old friend Molly understand perfectly well that modern women do face crippling difficulties when they choose one or another role of freedom. But they do not fall back upon their charm, wit or headaches; they take their beatings, they ask no quarter, they spin and bear it. They are tough-minded, generous and battered—descriptives one is tempted to apply to the author herself, formerly close to the English Communist movement, a woman whose youth in southern Africa had shaken her into a sense of how brutal human beings can become, a novelist who has published extensively and taken the risks of her craft. One feels about Miss Lessing that she works from so complex and copious a fund of experience that among women writers her English predecessors seem pale and her American contemporaries parochial.

At the center of The Golden Notebook is a series of remarkable conversations between Anna Wulf and Molly. Meeting in one another's London homes, they talk again and again about "personal relations," but always with a muted irony, an impatience with the very topics they know to concern them most. They are alternately open and guarded, sometimes wounding but usually honest. Simply as precise and nuanced dialogue, this is the best writing in a novel that never stoops to verbal display and is always directed toward establishing a visible world.

When they discuss their failures in love, their problems as divorced women with children to raise, their disillusionments as former Communists who would still like to needle the Establishment, their inability to talk with the passionless and apolitical young, their contempt for the new gentility of intellectual London, their difficulties in reconciling the image they hold of a self-sufficient human being with the needs they feel as anything but self-sufficient women—when these conversations between Anna and Molly recur throughout the book, one turns to them with the delight of encountering something real and fresh. My own curiosity, as a masculine outsider, was enormous, for here, I felt, was the way intellectual women really talk to one another when they feel free and unobserved.

Though their interest in politics has lessened, both Anna and Molly feel themselves to be voices of a baffled generation, those people who gave their youth to radicalism and ended not knowing how to live. This could be, it so often has been, a sticky self-pitying kind of subject; but not in The Golden Notebook, for it is a virtue of these deeply interesting women that even while suffering neurotic torments they can still regard themselves as objects of laughter. And also, as figures of hope. History, they feel, has left them stranded, but on the beaches of disillusion there must still be other stranded ones, there must be men of strength, to help them.

For both women remain interested in men with a curiosity that is almost archaeological: as if there were so few good ones left that it is necessary to hunt for them amid the ruins. Both Anna and Molly, in a wry and pleasing way, are frank about their sexuality; both are ready to have affairs when their emotions are stirred. Yet, as they feel it, men somehow "fail" them. Their men do not "come through," and the more pliant they seem, the less dependable they prove. All this serves as a subject for jokes between Anna and Molly, jokes with an edge of desperation.

In temperament the two women are sharply different: Anna morose and burrowing, Molly cheerful and extrovert; but they share problems, needs, failures.
Both try hard to preserve their independence, which means not a refusal of relationships but a hard decision not to delude themselves when they do take up with
second-raters and even more, a strict watch, mostly within themselves, against
the mediocre, the resigned, the merely comfortable. At the end Molly does give in
to a marriage of convenience, though with a characteristic quip: "There's nothing
like knowing the exact dimensions of the bed you're going to fit yourself into."
Anna, reduced to hysteria by a disastrous affair with an American writer, still
keeps pushing ahead, deciding to go into Labour Party work and—a nice touch
of irony—to take a job as a marriage counsellor ("I'm very good at other people's
marriages"). She remains loyal to that refusal to compromise which had bound
the two women in friendship.

Refusal to compromise with what? It is not easy to say, since the answer depends at least as much upon Anna's visceral reactions as her conscious ideas.
Miss Lessing, with the patience of a true novelist, keeps returning to the problem,
not explicitly but through a series of narrative variations. Sick as Anna is, trapped
as she often finds herself in a pit of anxiety, she still commands a burning sense of
the possibilities of life. That this very restlessness of hers may itself be a function
of neurosis, she also knows; for she has undergone the inevitable analytic bout,
with a spiderish lady doctor she calls "Mother Sugar."

Yet she clings to her saving difference. She demands from her men the completion of her being. She demands that they provide those elements of strength and
assurance which she, as a woman, cannot. She wants in her men both intimacy
and power, closeness and self-sufficiency, hereness and thereness. Modernist in
sensibility, she is traditional in her desires. And no matter what she must settle
for at a given moment, she does not delude herself; she will not compromise with
the idea of compromise.

Anna is the kind of woman who would send D. H. Lawrence into a sputter of
rage: so much the worse for him. To be sure, many of the complaints he might
make of her would be accurate. She whines, she is a bit of a drag, she often drives
her men crazy. She does not inquire closely enough as to why she seems so gifted
at picking losers. In her steady groaning about her writer's block, she does not
ask herself whether it is caused by a deep contempt for the whole idea of the intellectual life—like many women of her sort, she has fitful passions for cooking and
domesticity—or whether it is caused by overweening ambition—at times one
suspects her of wanting to write a novel as good as The Golden Notebook. She is open
to almost every judgment except that of having died before her death.

In its structure *The Golden Notebook* is original but not entirely successful. Miss Lessing has wanted to show the relation between Anna's past and her present, as well as between both of these and her fantasies, but she has wanted to show them not simply through the usual juxtaposition of narrative strands which might, for her purposes, lack tension and the effect of simultaneity. She therefore hit upon the ingenious device of carrying her narrative line forward in the present while inserting long excerpts from several notebooks Anna keeps, each a different color and representing a distinct part of her life. The advantage of this scheme is that Miss Lessing can isolate the main elements of Anna's experience with a sharpness that might not be possible in a traditional kind of novel; the disadvantage, that she has had to force large chunks of narrative into a discursive context.

In a black notebook Anna returns to her youth, sketching a group of English radicals astray in a provisional African town and preying on each other's nerves. In a red notebook Anna looks back upon her political life, drawing a number of amusing vignettes of left-wing intellectual circles in the London of the fifties. In a yellow notebook she writes a fictional version of her own experience, focusing on a love affair which has, in the narrative present, already reached its end. And in a blue notebook she keeps an objective record of her daily life, which comes to a brilliant climax in a detailed account of a single day. Bit by bit she builds up the mosaic of anxiety: how she must face early in the morning the conflicting needs of her lively child and sleepy lover; how she copes with the irritations of work in a fellow-travelling publishing house; how she gives way to the compulsion of repeatedly washing her body for fear that her period causes her to have a bad smell; how she returns home at night to the nagging of her thoughts.

Finally there comes the golden notebook which is to record the reintegration of the various Annas who appear in the other notebooks. But as the love affair on which she stakes her hopes begins to crumble, the golden notebook turns into a record of collapse, and in pages of nightmarish power Anna is shown entering a psychotic episode, locking herself into her bedroom where she pastes alarming newspaper items on the walls and slowly tastes the progress from despair, in which she abandons herself to the vividness of remembering what she has lost, to desolation, in which the image of loss becomes dim but the pain, feeding on itself, lives on.

Doris Lessing is a natural writer: she has the prime novelistic gift of involving one so deeply in the desires and frustrations of her characters that one reads with a positive yearning to spend more time with them. Some of her failures, however, I found disturbing. The cumbersome structure of the novel allows for a rich interweaving of complexities but does not fully encourage the free flow of emotion which her story demands. She writes about Americans with the astigmatism peculiar to certain English leftists: she has no ear for American speech nor eye for American manners. More important, at the end of the book she fails to keep a sufficient distance from her heroine, so that Anna's hysteria comes dangerously close to taking over the narrative. Perhaps Miss Lessing faced an insoluble problem at this point: she achieves enormous intensity through surrendering herself to Anna's suffering, but the price she pays is a loss of the critical objectivity she had maintained in earlier pages. It is a feat of evocation, but not matched by steadiness of control. Still, *The Golden Notebook* moves with the beat of our time, and it is true.

Postscript

In the years since *The Golden Notebook* appeared, a number of friends have charged me with having overestimated the book, which they found claustrophobic, humorless, overwrought. Perhaps they are right; I have never reread it. But a reviewer of contemporary writing ought not to have his eye on "the ages"; his job is to respond honestly, immediately, and with an inner awareness that he cannot possibly command the objectivity of judgment which time may enable. I am speaking here not of commercial trash or the obviously meretricious, but of serious books to which one responds with a certain initial gratitude, even if also with an element of excess. What mattered about a novel like *The Golden Notebook* was that it touched a nerve of contemporary life, and that is why, I imagine, it stirred many readers when it first came out. I'm glad I was one of them.

Life Never Let Up:
Review of Call It Sleep
{1964}

THIRTY YEARS AGO a young New Yorker named Henry Roth published his first and thus far his only novel, Call It Sleep. It was a splendid book, one of the few genuinely distinguished novels written by a 20th-century American; and there were critics and readers who recognized this immediately. From the general public, however, the book never won any attention.

In its deepest impress, Call It Sleep was alien to the spirit of the times. The politically radical critics then dominating the New York literary scene had enough taste to honor Roth for composing an impressive work, but they did not really know what to make of it. They could not bend the novel to their polemical purposes, and some of them, one suspects, must have felt that the severe detachment with which Roth presented the inner life of a Jewish immigrant boy between the ages of 6 and 8 was an evasion of the social needs of the moment.

Time passed, thousands of cluttering novels came and went each year, and Call It Sleep faded from sight. So too did its author, about whom vague rumors arose that he became a hospital attendant in upstate New York and then a duck farmer in Maine. But if most books die and a very few live, some just survive precariously in a kind of underground existence. Copies of Call It Sleep became hard to find, but all through the 1940s and 1950s a number of serious critics, writing in such magazines as *Commentary* and *Partisan Review*, remained loyal to the book, and kept insisting that it was a neglected masterpiece which people ought to read and some publisher reprint.

In 1960 a small firm (Pageant Books, Inc., now Cooper Square Publishers) did put out the novel in hardcover, but to little effect. Now, with some accompanying flourishes, Avon has issued the novel in paperback and this time, one hopes, it will finally gain the public it deserves. As with all belated acts of justice, there is something bitter in the thought of the many years that have had to go by; still, it is an act of justice, and a welcome one.

Call It Sleep is one of those novels—there are not very many—which patiently enter and then wholly exhaust an experience. Taking fierce imaginative possession of its subject, the novel scrutinizes it with an almost unnerving intensity, yet also manages to preserve a sense of distance and dispassion. The central figure is David Schearl, an overwrought, phobic and dangerously imaginative little boy. He has come to New York with his east European Jewish parents, and now, in the years between 1911 and 1913, he is exposed, shock by shock, to the blows of slum life.

Everything is channeled through the child's perceptions. For considerable sections, David's uncorrected apprehensions of the world become the substance of the narrative, a mixture of stony realism and ecstatic phantasmagoria. Yet the book is not at all the kind of precious or narrowing study of a child's sensibility that such a description might suggest; for Henry Roth has taken pains to root it deeply in the external world, in the streets, the tenements, the other children David encounters. We are locked into the experience of a child, but are not limited to his grasp of it.

One of Roth's admirers, the English critic Walter Allen, has elsewhere described this aspect of *Call It Sleep* very well: "David recreates, transmutes, the world he lives in not into any simple fantasy of make-believe—we're a long way here either from Tom Sawyer or the young Studs Lonigan—but with the desperate, compulsive imagination of a poet. He is, indeed, for all the grotesque difference in milieu, much closer to the boy Wordsworth of 'The Prelude.'"

Call It Sleep yields a picture of brutality in the slums quite as oppressive as can be found in any 1930s novel—and because Henry Roth has neither political nor literary preconceptions to advance, neither revolutionary rhetoric nor fatalistic behaviorism, his picture is more authoritative than that of most slum novels. Through the transfiguring imagination of David, *Call It Sleep* also achieves an obbligato of lyricism such as few American novels can match. David Schearl, in his besieged and quavering presence, exemplifies the force of G. M. Doughty's epigram: "The Semites are like to a man sitting in a cloaca to the eyes, and whose brow touches heaven."

"*. . . a cloaca to the eyes.*" That is the world of Brownsville and the Lower East Side into which the child is thrust. Quarrelsome grown-ups, marauding toughs, experiments in voyeurism and precocious sex, dark tenements with rat-infested cellars and looming stairways, an overwhelming incident in which David's father, a milkman, whips two derelicts who have stolen a few bottles of milk, the oppressive comedy of Hebrew school where children cower before and learn to torment an enraged rabbi—all these comprise the outer life of the boy, described by Roth with deliberate and gritty detail.

One is reminded of Dickens's evocation of childhood terrors, and Roth certainly shares with Dickens the vision of an unmediated war between the child and society; but nothing in Dickens is so completely and gravely caught up, as is *Call It Sleep*, with the child's vision of the world as nightmare. Yet—and this seems to me a remarkable achievement—Roth never acquiesces in the child's delusions, never sentimentalizes or quivers over his David. In the economy of psychic life, the book makes abundantly clear, the outer world's vitality and toughness have their claims too.

"*. . . and whose brow touches heaven.*" For David heaven is his mother's lap, the warming banter of her faintly ironic voice. Genya Schearl, immigrant wife who speaks only Yiddish, a tall and pale beauty, fearful of her violent-tempered husband, yet glowing with feminine grace and chastened sexuality—this marvelous figure should some day be honored as one of the great women of American literature, a fit companion to Hawthorne's Hester Prynne. Genya brings radiance and dignity to every page on which she appears. We cannot help share David's craving for her, even as we recognize its morbid elements; we see her most powerfully through the eyes of the child, as the enclosing mother who provides total security, but we also sense what David has begun uneasily to sense, that she has a complex emotional and bodily life beyond the reach of the child.

As we would say in our contemporary glibness, it is a classical Oedipal situation: the troubled delicate boy, the passionate mother, the inflamed father whom the child looks upon as an agent of punishment and who, in turn, feels himself cut off from the household's circle of love. An Oedipal situation indeed—but in our mindless jargon we forget that this phrase refers to one of the most sustaining experiences a human being can know. Henry Roth, who seems to have been happily innocent of Freudian hypotheses, provides in *Call It Sleep* a recognizable "case," but far more important, an experience superbly alive and fluid. He writes:

"'It is summer,' she pointed to the window, 'the weather grows warm. Whom will you refresh with the icy lips the water lent you?'

"'Oh!' he lifted his smiling face.

"'You remember nothing,' she reproached him, and with a throaty chuckle, lifted him in her arms.

"Sinking his fingers in her hair, David kissed her brow. The faint familiar warmth and odor of her skin and hair.

"'There!' she laughed, nuzzling his cheek, 'but you've waited too long; the sweet chill has dulled. Lips for me,' she reminded him, 'must always be cool as the water that wet them.' She put him down."

Away from his mother, David is torn by fears; fears of the fingering sexuality he discovers in the street; fears—also hopes—that he is not really the child of his father, fears of the rabbi who curses a fate requiring him to teach the intractable young. At the climax of the book David runs away from home, fleeing the anger of his father who has caught him playing with a rosary and believes him implicated in an act of depravity.

There follows a brilliantly rendered flight through the streets, composed in a Joycean stream-of-consciousness that is broken with fragments of gutter talk, street noise and left-wing oratory. For David, in whose mind a scriptural passage about the fiery coal God put to the lips of Isaiah becomes linked to the terrifying flash of the live rail on a streetcar track, there is now an overmastering urge to sacrifice and cleanse himself. He thrusts the ladle of a milk can into the slot between the car tracks which carries the live rail, suffers a violent shock, and then, recovering, harbors a vision in which all guilts become assuaged and there may yet be a way of containing the terrors of the world.

The writing in *Call It Sleep* is consistently strong. When speaking in his own right, as disciplined narrator, Roth provides a series of powerful urban vignettes: slum kids fishing for pennies through the grate of a cellar, the ghastly little candy store in which David's Aunt Bertha, a red-haired gargoyle, bitterly trades with urchins, the freedom of tenement roofs on which David learns to climb.

Roth is even better at rendering varieties of speech. With a hard impersonality he records the patois of immigrant children several generations back, and because he never condescends to them or tries to exploit them as local color, he transforms their mutilated language into a kind of poetry:

"My ticher calls id Xmas, bod de kids call id Chrizmas. Id's a goyish holiday anyways. Wunst I hanged op a stockin' in Brooklyn. Bod mine fodder pud in eggshells wid terlit paper an' a piece f'om a ol' kendle. So he leffed w'en he seen me."

And here the rabbi curses his "scholars" with a brimstone eloquence:

"May your skull be dark! . . . and your eyes be dark and your fate be of such dearth and darkness that you will call a poppyseed the sun and a carroway the moon. . . . Away! Or I'll empty my bitter heart upon you."

But when Genya speaks, Roth transposes her Yiddish into a pure and glowing English, reflecting in prose the ultimate serenity of her character.

Intensely Jewish in tone and setting, *Call It Sleep* rises above all the dangers that beset the usual ghetto novel; it does not deliquesce into nostalgia, nor sentimentalize poverty and parochialism. The Jewish immigrant milieu happens to be its locale, quite as Dublin is Joyce's and Mississippi Faulkner's. A writer possessed by his materials, driven by a need to recapture the world of his youth, does not choose his setting: it chooses him. And to be drawn into Roth's trembling world, the reader need have no special knowledge about Jewish life, just as he need have no special knowledge about the South in order to enjoy Faulkner.

Call It Sleep ends without any explicit moral statement. A human experience scoured to its innermost qualities can take on a value of its own, beyond the convenience of gloss or judgment. At the end of a novel like *Call It Sleep*, one has lived through a completeness of rendered life, and all one need do is silently to acknowledge its truth.

New Styles in "Leftism"
{1965}

I PROPOSE TO DESCRIBE a political style or outlook before it has become hardened into an ideology or the property of an organization. This outlook is visible along limited portions of the political scene; for the sake of exposition I will make it seem more precise and structured than it really is.

There is a new radical mood in limited sectors of American society: on the campus, in sections of the civil rights movement. The number of people who express this mood is not very large, but that it should appear at all is cause for encouragement and satisfaction. Yet there is a segment or fringe among the newly blossoming young radicals that causes one disturbance—and not simply because they have ideas different from persons like me, who neither expect nor desire that younger generations of radicals should repeat our thoughts or our words. For this disturbing minority I have no simple name: sometimes it looks like kamikaze radicalism, sometimes like white Malcolmism, sometimes like black Maoism. But since none of these phrases will quite do, I have had to fall back upon the loose and not very accurate term "new leftists." Let me therefore stress as strongly as I can that I am not talking about all or the majority of the American young and not-so-young who have recently come to regard themselves as radicals.

The form I have felt obliged to use here—a composite portrait of the sort of "new leftist" who seems to me open to criticism—also creates some difficulties. It may seem to lump together problems, ideas, and moods that should be kept distinct. But my conviction is that this kind of "new leftism" is not a matter of organized political tendencies, at least not yet, and that there is no organization, certainly none of any importance, which expresses the kind of "new leftism" I am here discussing. So I would say that if some young radicals read this text and feel that much of it does not pertain to them, I will be delighted by such a response.

Some Background Conditions

A. The society we live in fails to elicit the idealism of the more rebellious and generous young. Even among those who play the game and accept the social masks necessary for gaining success, there is a widespread disenchantment. Certainly there is very little ardor, very little of the joy that comes from a conviction that the values of a society are good, and that it is therefore good to live by them. The intelligent young know that if they keep out of trouble, accept academic drudgery, and preserve a respectable "image," they can hope for successful careers, even if not personal gratification. But the price they must pay for this choice is a considerable quantity of inner adaptation to the prevalent norms: there is a limit to the social duplicity that anyone can sustain.

The society not only undercuts the possibilities of constructive participation; it also makes very difficult a coherent and thought-out political opposition. The small minority that does rebel tends to adopt a stance that seems to be political, sometimes even ideological, but often turns out to be little more than an effort to assert a personal style.

Personal style: that seems to me a key. Most of whatever rebellion we have had up to—and even into—the civil rights movement takes the form of a decision on how to live individually within this society, rather than how to change it collectively. A recurrent stress among the young has been upon differentiation of speech, dress, and appearance, by means of which a small elite can signify its special status; or the stress has been upon moral self-regeneration, a kind of Emersonianism with shock treatment. All through the fifties and sixties disaffiliation was a central impulse, in the beatnik style or the more sedate J. D. Salinger way, but disaffiliation nevertheless, as both a signal of nausea and a tacit recognition of impotence.

I say "recognition of impotence" because movements that are powerful, groups that are self-confident, do not opt out of society: they live and work within society in order to transform it.

Now, to a notable extent, all this has changed since and through the civil rights movement—*but not changed as much as may seem.* Some of the people involved in that movement show an inclination to make of their radicalism not a politics of common action, which would require the inclusion of saints, sinners, and ordinary folk, but, rather, a gesture of moral rectitude. And the paradox is that they often sincerely regard themselves as committed to politics—but a politics that asserts so unmodulated and total a dismissal of society, while also departing from Marxist expectations of social revolution, that little is left to them but the glory or burden of maintaining a distinct personal style.

By contrast, the radicalism of an earlier generation, despite numerous faults, had at least this advantage: it did not have to start *as if* from scratch; there were available movements, parties, agencies, and patterns of thought through which one could act. The radicals of the thirties certainly had their share of bohemianism, but their politics were not nearly so interwoven with and dependent upon tokens of style as is today's radicalism.

The great value of the present rebelliousness is that it requires a personal decision, not merely as to what one shall do but also as to what one shall be. It requires authenticity, a challenge to the self, or, as some young people like to say, an "existential" decision. And it makes more difficult the moral double-bookkeeping of the thirties, whereby in the name of a sanctified movement or unquestioned ideology, scoundrels and fools could be exalted as "leaders" and detestable conduct exonerated.

This is a real and very impressive strength, but with it there goes a significant weakness: the lack of clear-cut ideas, sometimes even a feeling that it is wrong—or, worse, "middle-class"—to think systematically, and as a corollary, the absence of a social channel or agency through which to act. At first it seemed as if the civil rights movement would provide such a channel; and no person of moral awareness can fail to be profoundly moved by the outpouring of idealism and the readiness to face danger which characterizes the vanguard of this movement. Yet at a certain point it turns out that the civil rights movement, through the intensity of its work, seems to dramatize . . . its own insufficiency. Indeed, it acts as a training school for experienced, gifted, courageous people who have learned how to lead, how to sacrifice, how to work, but have no place in which to enlarge upon their gifts. There may in time appear a new kind of "dropout"—the "dropout" trained by and profoundly attached to the civil rights movement who yet feels that it does not, and by its very nature cannot, come to grips with the central problems of modern society; the "dropout" who has been trained to a fine edge of frustration and despair.

B. These problems are exacerbated by an educational system that often seems inherently schizoid. It appeals to the life of the mind, yet justifies that appeal through crass utilitarianism. It invokes the traditions of freedom, yet processes students to bureaucratic cut. It speaks for the spirit, yet increasingly becomes an appendage of a spirit-squashing system.

C. The "new leftism" appears at a moment when the intellectual and academic worlds—and not they alone—are experiencing an intense and largely justifiable revulsion against the immediate American past. Many people are sick unto death of the whole structure of feeling—that mixture of chauvinism, hysteria, and demagogy—which was created during the Cold War years. Like children subjected to forced feeding, they regurgitate almost automatically. Their response is an inevitable consequence of overorganizing the propaganda resources of a modern state; the same sort of nausea exists among the young in the Communist world.

Unfortunately, revulsion seldom encourages nuances of thought or precise discriminations of politics. You cannot stand the deceits of official anti-Communism? Then respond with a rejection equally blatant. You have been raised to give credit to every American power move, no matter how reactionary or cynical? Then respond by castigating everything American. You are weary of Sidney Hook's messages in the *New York Times Magazine?* Then respond as if talk about Communist totalitarianism were simply irrelevant or a bogey to frighten infants.

Yet we should be clear in our minds that such a response is not at all the same as a commitment to Communism, even though it may lend itself to obvious exploitation. It is, rather, a spewing out of distasteful matter—in the course of which other values, such as the possibility of learning from the traumas and tragedies of recent history, may also be spewed out.

D. Generational clashes are recurrent in our society, perhaps in any society. But the present rupture between the young and their elders seems especially deep. This is a social phenomenon that goes beyond our immediate subject, indeed, it cuts through the whole of society; what it signifies is the society's failure to transmit with sufficient force its values to the young, or, perhaps more accurately, that the best of the young take the proclaimed values of their elders with a seriousness which leads them to be appalled by their violation in practice.

In rejecting the older generations, however, the young sometimes betray the conditioning mark of the very American culture they are so quick to denounce:

for ours is a culture that celebrates youthfulness as if it were a moral good in its own right. Like the regular Americans they wish so hard not to be, yet, through wishing, so very much are, they believe that the past is mere dust and ashes and that they can start afresh, immaculately.

There are, in addition, a few facts to be noted concerning the relationship between the radical young and those few older people who have remained radicals.

A generation is missing in the life of American radicalism, the generation that would now be in its mid-thirties, the generation that did not show up. The result is an inordinate difficulty in communication between the young radicals and those unfortunate enough to have reached — or, God help us, even gone beyond — the age of forty. Here, of course, our failure is very much in evidence too: a failure that should prompt us to speak with modesty, simply as people who have tried, and in their trying perhaps have learned something.

To the younger radicals it seems clear that a good many of the radicals of the thirties have grown tired, or dropped out, or, in some instances, sold out. They encounter teachers who, on ceremonial occasions, like to proclaim old socialist affiliations, but who really have little or no sympathy with any kind of rebelliousness today. They are quick—and quite right—to sense that announcements of old Young People's Socialist League ties can serve as a self-protective nostalgia or even as a cloak for acquiescence in the status quo. But it must also be said that there is a tendency among the "new leftists" toward much too quick a dismissal of those who may disagree with them—they are a little too fast on the draw with such terms as "fink" and "establishment."

All this may describe the conditions under which the new political outlook appears, but it does not yet tell us anything about the specific culture, so to say, in which it thrives. Let me therefore indicate some of the political and intellectual influences acting upon the "new leftism," by setting up two very rough categories.

Ideologues and Desperadoes

A. *Ideologues, White.* The disintegration of American radicalism these last few decades left a good many ideologues emotionally unemployed: people accustomed to grand theorizing who have had their theories shot out from under them; people still looking for some belated evidence that they were "right" all along; people with unexpended social energy and idealism of a sort, who desperately needed new arenas in which to function.

1. *The Remains of Stalinism.* The American Communist Party was broken first by McCarthyite and government persecution, and second by an inner crisis follow-

ing Khrushchev's revelations and the Hungarian revolution. Those who left out of disillusionment were heartsick people, their convictions and sometimes their lives shattered. But those who left the party or its supporting organizations because they feared government attack were often people who kept, semiprivately, their earlier convictions. Many of them had a good deal of political experience; some remained significantly placed in the network of what might be called conscience organizations. Naturally enough, they continued to keep in touch with one another, forming a kind of reserve apparatus based on common opinions, feelings, memories. As soon as some ferment began in the civil rights movement and the peace groups, these people were present, ready and eager; they needed no directives from the Communist Party to which, in any case, they no longer (or may never have) belonged; they were quite capable of working on their own *as if they were working together*, through a variety of groups and periodicals like the *National Guardian*. Organizational Stalinism declined, but a good part of its heritage remained: people who could offer political advice, raise money, write leaflets, sit patiently at meetings, put up in a pleasant New York apartment visitors from a distant state, who, by chance, had been recommended by an old friend.

2. *True Believers.* On the far left there remains a scatter of groups still convinced that Marxism-Leninism, in one or another version, is "correct." What has failed them, however, is the historical motor provided by Marxist theory: the proletariat, which has not shown the "revolutionary potential" or fulfilled the "historical mission" to which it was assigned. Though the veteran Marxists cannot, for fear of shattering their whole structure of belief, give up the *idea* of the proletariat, they can hardly act, day by day, as if the American working class were indeed satisfying Marxist expectations or were the actual center of revolutionary ferment. Thus, in somewhat schizoid fashion, they have clung to their traditional faith in the proletariat as the revolutionary class, while in practice searching for a new embodiment of it which might provide the social energy they desire. And in the Negro movement they sometimes think to have found it.

That this movement, with great creative flair, has worked out an indigenous strategy of its own; that it has developed nonviolent resistance into an enormously powerful weapon; that the Negro clergy, in apparent disregard of Leninist formulas, plays a leading and often militant role—all this does not sit well with the old Marxists. They must therefore develop new theories, by means of which the Negroes become the vanguard of the working class or perhaps the "true" (not yet "bought-off") working class. And, clustering around the Negro movement, they contribute a mite of wisdom here and there: scoffing at nonviolence, employing the shibboleth of "militancy" as if it were a magical device for satisfying the needs of the Negro poor, and so forth. They are experienced in "deepening the struggle," usually other people's struggles: which means to scorn the leadership of Dr. Martin Luther King, Jr. without considering that the "revolutionary" course they propose for the Negro movement could, if adopted, lead it into a cul-de-sac of isolation, exhaustion, and heroic blood. Understandably, they find allies in Negro nationalists who want not so much to deepen as to divert the struggle, and among young militants who dislike the idea that Negroes might, if successful in their struggle, come to share some of the American affluence and thus become "middle class."

3. *Authoritarian Leftists.* In figures like Isaac Deutscher and Paul Sweezy we find the true intellectual progenitors of at least part of the "new leftism"; the influence they exert has been indirect, since they are not involved in immediate struggles, but it has nevertheless been there.

Sweezy's *Monthly Review* is the main spokesman in this country for the view that authoritarianism is inherent or necessary in the so-called socialist countries; that what makes them "socialist" is simply the nationalization of the means of production; that democracy, while perhaps desirable in some long-range calculation, is not crucial for judging the socialist character of a society; that the claim that workers must be in a position to exercise political power if the state can in any sense be called "theirs" is a utopian fallacy. At times this technological determinism, put to the service of brutal dictatorship, has been given a more subtle reading by Sweezy, namely, that when the conditions supposedly causing the Communist dictatorship—economic backwardness and international insecurity—have been overcome, the Soviet regime would in some unspecified way democratize itself. In November 1957, after the Khrushchev revelations, *Monthly Review* printed a notably frank editorial:

> The conditions which produced the [Soviet] dictatorship have been overcome. . . . Our theory is being put to the crucial test of practise. And so far—let us face it frankly—there is precious little evidence to confirm it. In all that has happened since Stalin's death we can find nothing to indicate that the Communist Party or any of its competing factions, has changed in the slightest degree its view of the proper relation between the people and their leadership. . . . there is apparently no thought that the Soviet people will ever grow up enough to decide for itself who knows best and hence who should make and administer the policies which determine its fate.

And finally from Sweezy: "Forty years is too long for a dictatorship to remain temporary"—surely the understatement of the Christian Era!

One might suppose that if "our theory is being put to the crucial test" and "there is precious little evidence to confirm it," honest men would proceed to look for another theory, provided, that is, they continued to believe that freedom is desirable.

A good number of years have passed since the above passage appeared in the *Monthly Review*, the "precious little evidence" remains precious little, and Sweezy, once apparently dismayed over the lack of democracy in Russia, has moved not to Titoism or "revisionism." No, he has moved toward Maoist China, where presumably one does not have to worry about "the proper relation between the people and their leadership. . . ." Writing in December 1964 the *Monthly Review* editors declared with satisfaction that "there could be no question of the moral ascendency of Peking over Moscow in the underdeveloped world." They agreed with the Chinese that Khrushchev's fall was "a good thing" and they wrote further: "The Chinese possession of a nuclear potential does not increase the danger of nuclear war. Quite the contrary. The Chinese have solemnly pledged never to be the first to use nuclear weapons . . . and their revolutionary record of devotion to the cause of socialism and progress entitles them to full trust and confidence."

The logic is clear: begin with theoretical inquiry and concern over the perpetuation of dictatorship in Russia and end with "full trust and confidence" in China, where the dictatorship is more severe.

There is an aphorism by a recent Polish writer: "The dispensing of injustice is always in the right hands." And so is its defense.

B. Ideologues, Negro.

1. *Black Nationalism*. Here is a creed that speaks or appears to speak totally against compromise, against negotiating with "the white power structure," against the falsities of white liberals, indeed, against anything but an indulgence of verbal violence. Shortly before his tragic death Malcolm X spoke at a Trotskyist-sponsored meeting and listening to him I felt, as did others, that he was in a state of internal struggle, reaching out for an ideology he did not yet have. For the Negroes in his audience he offered the relief of articulating subterranean feelings of hatred, contempt, defiance, feelings that did not have to be held in check because there was a tacit compact that the talk about violence would remain talk. For both the Negroes and whites in the audience there was an apparent feeling that Malcolm and Malcolm alone among the Negro spokesmen was authentic because . . . well, because finally he spoke for nothing but his rage, for no proposal, no plan, no program, just a sheer outpouring of anger and pain. And that they could understand. The formidable sterility of his speech, so impressive in its relation to a

deep personal suffering, touched something in their hearts. For Malcolm, intransigent in words and nihilistic in reality, never invoked the possibility or temptations of immediate struggle; he never posed the problems, confusions, and risks of maneuver, compromise, retreat. Brilliantly Malcolm spoke for a rejection so complete it transformed him into an apolitical spectator, or in the language of his admirers, a "cop-out."

2. *Caricature.* If, nevertheless, there was something about Malcolm which commands our respect, that is because we know his life-struggle, his rise from the depths, his conquest of thought and speech. Leroi Jones, by contrast, stands as a burlesque double of whatever is significant in Malcolm.

In his success as both a New School lecturer and a prophet of "guerrilla warfare" in the United States; in his badgering of white liberal audiences; in his orgies of verbal violence committed, to be sure, not in Selma, Alabama, but Sheridan Square, New York; in his fantasies of an international race war in which the whites will be slaughtered, Jones speaks for a contemporary sensibility. But he speaks for it in a special way: as a distinctively American success, the pop-art guerrilla warrior.

He speaks at that center of revolutionary upsurge, the Village Vanguard. He explains that the murder of Negroes in the South does not arouse the kind of horror and indignation that the murder of white civil rights workers does. *He is absolutely right*; the point cannot be made too often. But Jones cannot stop there: it would be too sensible, too humane, and it would not yield pages in the *Village Voice*. Instead, responding to a question, "What about Goodman and Schwerner, the two white boys killed in Mississippi, don't you care about them?" Jones said, as quoted in the *Voice*: "Absolutely not. Those boys were just artifacts, artifacts, man. They weren't real. If they want to assuage their leaking consciences, that's their business. I won't mourn for them. I have my own dead to mourn for."

Is this not exactly the attitude Jones had a moment earlier condemned in regard to killings in the South, but the same attitude in reverse? And is it really impossible for the human heart to mourn for *both* Negro and white victims? Not, to be sure, for ordinary whites, since they, we all know, are "white devils"; but at least for those who have given their lives in the struggle?

The essential point about Jones's racist buffoonery has been made by George Dennison in a recent review of Jones's plays:

> Just as he mis-labels the victims *black*, he mis-labels the authority *white*. Certainly he knows, or should know, that the authority which in fact pertains is not the authority of race . . . but an authority of property and arms; and

certainly he knows, or should know, that the life-destroying evil inheres in the nature of the authority, not in the color of those who wield it. But if Jones wanted change, he would speak change. He speaks, instead, for the greatest possible rejection, a rejection so absolute, so confined to fantasy, that it amounts to nothing more than hands-off-the-status-quo. . . . Point by point his is an upside down version of the most genteel, middle-class, liberal position. And I think that the liberals see him as one of their own, albeit a Dropout. He addresses every word to them and is confined to their systems of values because he is in the business of denying no other values but those. That spurious anger, so resonant with career, can be trusted not to upset the applecart.

C. *Desperadoes, White.* In effect, I have already described this group, so let me here confine myself to a few remarks about one of its central battle cries, "alienation."

The trouble with the recurrent use of alienation as a mode of social analysis is that it includes almost everything, and thereby explains almost nothing. The term has become impossibly loose (like those other handy tags, "the establishment" and "the power structure"). As used by Marx, alienation had a rather precise reference: it pointed to the condition of the worker in the capitalist productive process, a condition in which "the worker's deed becomes an alien power . . . forcing him to develop some specialized dexterity at the cost of a world of productive impulses." This kind of analysis focuses upon the place of the proletarian within the social structure, and not upon the sediment of malaise among those outside it.

Since Marx wrote, the term has acquired an impossible load of signification. During most of the bourgeois era, the European intellectuals grew increasingly estranged from the social community because the very ideals that had animated the bourgeois revolution were now being violated by bourgeois society; their "alienation" was prompted not by bohemian willfulness but by a loyalty to Liberty, Fraternity, Equality, or to an induced vision of preindustrial society which, by a twist of history, came pretty much to resemble Liberty, Fraternity, Equality. Just as it was the triumph of capitalism which largely caused this sense of estrangement, so it was the expansion of capitalism which allowed the intellectuals enough freedom to release it. During the greater part of the bourgeois era, intellectuals preferred alienation from the community to alienation from themselves. Precisely this choice made possible their boldness and strength, precisely this "lack of roots" gave them their speculative power.

By now the term "alienation" frequently carries with it a curious reversal of moral and emotional stress. For where intellectuals had once used it as a banner of pride and self-assertion, today it tends to become a complaint, a token of self-pity, a rationale for a degree of estrangement from the society which connotes not an active rebellion against—nor even any active relation to—it, but, rather, a justification for marginality and withdrawal.

Somewhere amid the current talk about "alienation" an important reality is being touched upon or pointed to. There is, in our society, a profound estrange-ment from the sources of selfhood, the possibilities of human growth and social cohesion. But simply to proclaim this estrangement can be a way of preserving it. Alienation is not some metaphysical equivalent of the bubonic plague, which constitutes an irrevocable doom; it is the powerlessness deriving from human failure to act. It is neither a substitute for thought, nor a dissolvent of human will, nor even a roadblock in the way of useful work. To enter into the society which in part causes this estrangement and by establishing bonds with other men to trans-form the society is one way of partially overcoming alienation. Each time the civil rights movement brings previously mute Negroes into active political life, each time a trade union extends its power of decision within a factory, the boundaries of alienation are shrunk.

D. *Desperadoes, Negro*. A new kind of young Negro militant has appeared in the last few years, and he is a figure far more authentic and impressive than any of those I have thus far mentioned. He is fed up with white promises. He is proud to be estranged from white society. He has strong, if vague, "nationalist" inclina-tions. He is desperate—impatient with the tactics of gradualism, nonviolence, and passive resistance. He sees few, if any, allies upon whom he can count; few, if any, positive forces in society that might stir people into action. In effect, he decides that he must "go it alone," scornful of the white liberal and labor groups, as well as of those Negro leaders who choose to work with them. He seeks to substitute for a stagnant history his own desire and sacrifice.

Let me suggest a very limited comparison. This kind of young Negro militant, though not of course interested in any kind of individual terrorism, acts out of social and psychological motives somewhat like those of the late-nineteenth-century Russian terrorists, who also tried to substitute their intransigent will for the sluggishness of history. And the consequences will perhaps be similar; the best cadres exhausted in isolation and defeat.

Such a response may well be the inevitable result of an abrupt and painful coming-to-awareness on the part of young Negro militants who had previously suppressed their suffering simply in order to survive but now feel somewhat freer to release it. Their devotion is beyond doubt, as their heroism is beyond praise; yet what I'm here tempted to call kamikaze radicalism, or what Bayard Rustin calls the "no win" outlook, can become self-defeating in political life.

The "New Leftist"—A Sketch

We can now venture a portrait of the new leftist, not as one or another individual but as a composite type—with all the qualifications I stated at the outset.

A. Cultural Style. The "new leftist" appears, at times, as a figure embodying a style of speech, dress, work, and culture. Often, especially if white, the son of the middle class—and sometimes the son of middle-class parents nursing radical memories—he asserts his rebellion against the deceit and hollowness of American society. Very good; there is plenty to rebel against. But in the course of his rebellion he tends to reject not merely the middle-class ethos but a good many other things he too hastily associates with it: the intellectual heritage of the West, the tradition of liberalism at its most serious, the commitment to democracy as an indispensable part of civilized life. He tends to make style into the very substance of his revolt, and while he may, on one side of himself, engage in valuable activities in behalf of civil rights, student freedom, and so on, he nevertheless tacitly accepts the "givenness" of American society, has little hope or expectation of changing it, and thereby, in effect, settles for a mode of personal differentiation.

Primarily that means the wish to shock, the wish to assault the sensibilities of a world he cannot overcome. If he cannot change it, then at least he can outrage it. He searches in the limited repertoire of sensation and shock: for sick comics who will say "fuck" in nightclubs; for drugs that will vault him beyond the perimeters of the suburbs; for varieties, perversities, and publicities of sex so as perhaps to create an inner, private revolution that will accompany—or replace?—the outer, public revolution.

But the "new leftist" is frequently trapped in a symbiotic relationship with the very middle class he rejects, dependent upon it for his self-definition: quite as the professional anti-Communist of a few years ago was caught up with the Communist Party, which, had it not existed, he would have had to invent—as indeed at times he did invent. So that for all its humor and charm, the style of the "new leftist" tends to become a rigid antistyle, dependent for its survival on the enemy it is supposed to panic. *Epater le bourgeois*—in this case, perhaps *épater le père*—is to acquiesce in a basic assumption of at least the more sophisticated segments of the middle class: that values can be inferred from, or are resident in, the externals of dress, appearance, furnishings, and hairdos.

Shock as he will, disaffiliate as he may choose, the "new leftist" discovers after a while that nothing has greatly changed. The relations of power remain as before, the Man still hovers over the scene, the "power structure" is unshaken. A few old ladies in California may grow indignant, a DA occasionally arrest someone, a *Village Voice* reporter arrange an interview; but surely that is all small change. And soon the "new leftist" must recognize that even he has not been greatly transformed. For in his personal manner he is acting out the dilemmas of a utopian community, and just as Brook Farm had to remain subject to the laws of the market despite its internal ethic of cooperation, so must he remain subject to the impress of the dominant institutions despite his desire to be totally different.

Victimized by a lack of the historical sense, the "new leftist" does not realize that the desire to shock and create sensations has itself a long and largely disastrous history. The notion, as Meyer Schapiro has remarked, that opium is the revolution of the people has been luring powerless intellectuals and semi-intellectuals for a long time. But the damnable thing is that for an almost equally long time the more sophisticated and urban sectors of the middle class have refused to be shocked. They know the repertoire of sensationalism quite as well as the "new leftist"; and if he is to succeed in shocking them or even himself, he must keep raising the ante. The very rebel who believes himself devoted to an absolute of freedom and looks with contempt upon any mode of compromise is thereby caught up in the compulsiveness of his escalation: a compulsiveness inherently bad enough, but rendered still more difficult, and sometimes pathetic, by the fact that, alas, each year he gets a year older.

Let me amend this somewhat. To say that the urban middle class has become jaded and can no longer be shocked is not quite correct. No; a kind of complicity is set up between the outraged and/or amused urban middle class and the rebels of sensation. Their mutual dependency requires that each shock, to provide the pleasures of indignation, must be a little stronger (like a larger dose) than the previous one. For the point is not so much that the urban middle class can no longer be shocked as that it positively yearns for and comes to depend upon the titillating assaults of its cultural enemies. So that when a new sensation (be it literary violence, sexual fashion, intellectual outrage, high-toned pornography, or sadistic denunciation) is provided by the shock troops of culture, the sophisticated middle class responds with outrage, resistance, and anger—*for upon these initial responses its pleasure depends*. But then, a little later, it rolls over like a happy puppy on its back, moaning, "Oh, baby, *épatez* me again, harder this time, tell me what a sterile impotent louse I am and how you are so tough and virile, how you're planning to murder me, *épatez* me again. . . ."

Thus a fire-eating character like LeRoi Jones becomes an adjunct of middle-class amusement and, to take an enormous leap upward in talent and seriousness, a writer like Norman Mailer becomes enmeshed with popular journalism and publicity.

The whole problem was anticipated many years ago by Trotsky when, writing about the Russian poet Esenin, he remarked that the poet thought to frighten the bourgeoisie by making scenes but as it turned out, the bourgeoisie was delighted, it adored scenes.

One thing alone will not delight the bourgeoisie: a decrease in income, a loss in social power, a threat to its property.

There is another sense in which cultural style dominates the behavior of the "new leftists." Some of them display a tendency to regard political—and perhaps all of—life as a Hemingwayesque contest in courage and rectitude. People are constantly being tested for endurance, bravery, resistance to temptation, and if found inadequate, are denounced for having "copped out." Personal endurance thus becomes the substance of, and perhaps even a replacement for, political ideas.

Now this can be a valid and serious way of looking at things, especially in extreme situations: which is, of course, what Hemingway had in mind. Among civil rights workers in the deep South such a vision of life reflects the ordeal they must constantly face; they *are* under extreme pressure and their courage is constantly being tested. Yet their situation cannot be taken as a model for the political life of the country as a whole. If one wants to do more than create a tiny group of the heroic, the tested, and the martyred, their style of work will not suffice. If one wants to build a movement in which not everyone need give "the whole of their lives," then the suspicion and hostility such an outlook is bound to engender toward the somewhat less active and somewhat less committed can only be damaging. For in effect, if not intent, it is a strategy of exclusion, leaving no place for anyone but the vanguard of the scarred.

It is, at times, a strategy of exclusion in a still more troubling sense: it reduces differences of opinion to grades of moral rectitude. If, for example, you think Martin Luther King or Bayard Rustin wrong in regard to certain tactical matters; if you disagree with what Rustin proposed at the Democratic national convention in 1964 and what King did in Selma, then you call into question their loyalty and commitment: you charge them with "copping out" or "fooling with the power structure." This approach makes it impossible to build a movement and, in the long run, even to maintain a sect.

B. *Domestic Politics.* A division of opinion, still incipient and confused, has appeared among people in the radical, student, and civil rights movements. There are those who, in effect, want to "go it alone," refusing to have anything to do with "the Establishment," and those who look forward to creating a loose coalition of Negro, labor, liberal, and church groups in order to stretch the limits of the welfare state. To an inexperienced eye, this may suggest a division between the more and less radical; but it is not. Radicalism is not a quantity.

The "go it alone" tendency in the civil rights movement starts from a recognition that the obstacles to success are enormous. It sees no forces within the society that could provide a new social dynamic. It shares with the liberals the questionable assumption that everyone in our society, except perhaps the bottom-dog poor, is bound to it by ties of material satisfaction. The labor movement is mired in its own fat; the ministers are Sunday allies; the liberals are two-faced, unreliable, perhaps cowards. What remains is a strategy of lonely assault, which must necessarily lead to shock tactics and desperation.

For if the above estimate of the American situation is valid, if there is so little possibility of a new social dynamism arising from or within its major social segments, then the outlook of the Black Muslims has to be acknowledged as persuasive. For obviously an estimate which sees major reforms as unlikely makes a traditional revolutionary overthrow seem still more unlikely; and the talk among irresponsibles about "guerrilla warfare in America" is mere self-indulgence since guerrilla warfare can succeed only when a large portion or a majority of the population is profoundly disaffected, something certainly not true in the United States. Consequently—the logic of this argument moves inexorably—there is nothing left for American Negroes but the separatism of the Muslims.

Unless, of course, one turns to the tactic of shock, inducing such misadventures as the 1964 stall-ins at the World's Fair or the Triborough Bridge fiasco. Neither of these demonstrations had a precise objective, neither had any way of measuring achievement, accumulating allies, registering victory. Such methods, born of desperation, could only cut off the dedicated minority of civil rights activists from their white allies and, more important, from the mass of Negroes.

Now it is not our business to give advice to the civil rights movement on tactical issues or to rush into taking positions about its inner disputes. It is not the business of anyone except those directly engaged. But about some larger aspects of its problem we can speak.

One issue has been posed simply but conveniently by a *Village Voice* reporter, Jack Newfield, who writes that Dr. King's "basic goal is integration, and SNCC's is a revolution." Earlier Newfield had described this revolution as being not against capitalist society but "against Brotherhood Weeks, factories called colleges, desperation called success, and sex twice a week."

What the people who talk about integration vs. revolution don't see is that to achieve integration, even in the limited terms presumably favored by Dr. King, would indeed *be* a revolution, greater in consequence and impact than that effected by the rise of industrial unionism in the thirties.

Bayard Rustin puts the matter as follows:

> While most Negroes—in their hearts—unquestionably seek only to enjoy the fruits of American society as it now exists, their quest cannot objectively be satisfied within the framework of existing political and economic relations. The young Negro who would demonstrate his way into the labor market may be motivated by a thoroughly bourgeois ambition . . . but he will end up having to favor a great expansion of the public sector of the economy. . . .
>
> . . . the term revolutionary as I am using it, does not connote violence; it refers to the quantitative transformation of fundamental institutions, more or less rapidly, to the point where the social and economic structure . . . can no longer be said to be the same. . . . I fail to see how the [civil rights] movement can be victorious in the absence of radical programs for full employment, abolition of slums, the reconstruction of our educational system, new definitions of work and leisure. Adding up the cost of such programs, we can only conclude that we are talking about a refashioning of our political economy.

To this lucid analysis I would add only a word concerning the desire of Negroes "to enjoy the fruits of American society as it now exists." Certain intellectuals bemoan this desire because they don't want the Negro poor integrated into a "rotten middle-class society" and thereby end up with two cars, barbecue pits, and ulcers. Even more than wrong, these intellectuals seem to me snobbish. For Negroes should have just as much *right* to suburban pleasures as anyone else; they should be in a position just as much as the whites to choose the middle-class style of life. We need not approve, we can argue against that choice, but we are obliged to support their right to make it. And why not? I don't notice James Baldwin or LeRoi Jones taking vows of poverty. Nor should they. There is something a bit manipulative in the view that Negroes should be preserved from the temptations that, presumably, all the rest of us are entitled to. What's more, the Negroes themselves are far too experienced in the ways of the world to allow themselves to be cast in the role of sacrificial ascetic.

But let us return to "integration vs. revolution" and for the sake of the argument accept this formulation. Naturally enough—it's an old habit—we then opt
for revolution; there remains only the little detail of who is going to make it.

Clearly, the vast majority of whites are in the grip of the Establishment. The
liberals? Establishment. The churches? Establishment. The unions? Establishment. Intellectuals? Establishment.

But not only the whites, also the Negroes. Wilkins, Young, Powell, King,
Farmer? The black Establishment. Rustin? He sold out to it.

Where then does that leave us? Well, some students . . . but can we be so sure of
them? May they not in time decide to go back to graduate school, perhaps after discovering that "the people," in refusing to heed the revolutionary missions from
the campus, are a rather hopeless quantity? What is left, then, is a handful . . . and
where that handful must end is in despair, exhaustion, burning themselves out
in the all-too-characteristic rhythm of American radicalism, which too often has
tried to compensate for its powerlessness in reality by ferocity in words.

At this point I hear a voice crying out: "No, not just a vanguard of the desperate!
We are going to organize the poor, the millions beneath the floor of society, those
who have been mute and unrepresented for too long . . . and it is they who will
form the basis of a new movement, beyond the pale of Establishment politics."

Good. The poor need to be organized, and more power to those who try. Every such effort, big or small, deserves the approval and support of socialists and
liberals. But some problems remain. I leave aside the fact that twentieth-century
history indicates a high rate of failure in previous efforts of this kind; that the
unstructured, atomized, and often demoralized "underclass" has been the most
resistant to organization. History need not always repeat itself, and perhaps this
time the effort will succeed. No, the questions I would raise have to do not with
failure but with success.

Imagine a campaign to organize the poor in a large city, undertaken by young
people who will have no truck with the Establishment. Through hard work and
devotion, they build up a group of, let's say, 150 people in a slum of mixed racial composition—a notable achievement. What happens next? The municipal
"power structure" begins to pay some attention and decides either to smash the
group as a dangerous nuisance or to lure away some of its leading members. If
the local organization of the poor must now face attack, it would seem to have
no choice but quickly to find some allies—in the unions, among churchmen,
perhaps even in the American Jewish Congress, "establishmentarian" as all of
these may seem. Suppose, however, the "power structure" decides to offer various inducements—jobs, improved housing—to some of the Negro members,

and various other organizations, like the reform wing of the Democrats and certain trade unions, also enter the picture. What will the uncompromising, anti-Establishment leaders of the poor do now? Does not the reality of the situation require them to enter negotiations, formally or informally, and thereby become involved in the socioeconomic life of the city? Can they remain exempt from it? And if so, how long do you suppose their followers will stay with them? For that matter, why should they? The goods and services that, with enough pressure, the "power structure" can be made to provide, the poor need, want, and deserve. Can one seriously suppose they will be exempt from such "temptations"? There is only one way to be certain the poor will remain beyond the temptations of our society, and that is to keep them hopelessly poor.

Nor is this quite a new problem. It was faced, in somewhat different form, years ago when revolutionists led trade unions and discovered that they had to sign agreements which in practice signified acquiescence in the bargaining arrangements between capital and labor within the confines of the status quo. Had these revolutionists, in the name of principle, refused to sign such agreements with the employers, they would have been sabotaging the functions of the union and would soon, deservedly, cease to be leaders.

The idea of coalition or realignment politics as advanced by socialists is not a rigid formula, or a plot to deliver our souls into the hands of the Establishment. It is meant as a strategy for energizing all those forces within the society that want to move forward toward an extension of the welfare state. In some places, such a loose coalition might take the form of politics outside the established institutions, like the Freedom Democratic Party of Mississippi—though that movement, if it is to succeed, must begin to find allies within the white community. In other places, as in Texas, there is a coalition of labor, liberal, intellectual, and minority groups (Negro, Mexican) within the Democratic Party—and by all accounts a pretty good coalition. Can one say, as if all wisdom were bunched into our fists, that such a development should not be supported simply because it grows up within the framework of a major party?

If we are serious in our wish to affect American political life, we must learn to see the reality as it is. We have to seek out and prod the forces that exist. And I think it is a gross error—the kind of deep-seated conservatism that often alloys ultraradicalism—to say that everything in the major sectors of American society is static, sated, "Establishment." Who, twenty-five or thirty years ago, could have foreseen that Catholic priests and nuns would be marching into Montgomery? Who could have foreseen the thoroughgoing ferment in the American churches of which this incident is merely a symptom? Instead of scoffing at such people as civil rights "tourists," we ought to be seeking them out and trying to get them to move a little further, up north too.

And a word about the labor movement. Its failures, ills, and decline have been documented in great detail by American socialists—perhaps because we ourselves have not quite understood what its nature and possibilities are, preferring instead to nag away when it did not conform to our preconceptions. Right now, to be sure, the unions look pretty sluggish and drab. Still, two leaders, named David MacDonald and James Carey, have recently been toppled by membership votes (and when something like that happens to a trade-union leader in Russia, China, Cuba, North Vietnam, or Zanzibar, please let me know).

Bayard Rustin says: "The labor movement, despite its obvious faults, has been the largest single organized force in this country pushing for progressive social legislation." That is true, but not enough. What seems the static quality of the trade unions may be a phase of rest between the enormous achievements of the past forty years and possible achievements of the future. If the civil rights movement succeeds, may it not also enter such a phase? And do you suppose that the struggles a few decades ago to organize unions were any the less difficult, bloody, and heroic than those in the South today? And if it's a revolution in the quality of American life that you want, then have not the industrial unions come closer to achieving that for millions of people than any other force in the country?

We are speaking here partly of speculations, partly of hopes. None of us has any certain answer or magic formula by which to overcome the painful isolation of the radical movement: if there were such a thing, someone would by now have discovered it. We are all groping to find a way out of our difficulties. I don't wish to draw a hard-and-fast line between "realigners" and "go-it-aloners." There is room for both disagreement and cooperation. You want to organize the poor? Splendid. We propose certain sorts of coalitions? An essential part of such a coalition ought to be drawn from the poor you propose to organize. And in turn, if you're to keep them organized, you will have to engage in coalitions. Right now—let's be candid—you don't have very many of the poor and we don't have much of a coalition. Disagreements of this kind are fraternal, and can be tested patiently in experience.

The true line of division between democratic socialists and left authoritarians concerns not tactics, but basic commitments, values, the vision of what a good society should be. It concerns:

C. *Politics and Freedom.* The "new leftists" feel little attachment to Russia. Precisely as it has turned away from the more extreme and terroristic version of totalitarianism, so have they begun to find it unsatisfactory as a model: too Victorian, even "bourgeois." Nor are they interested in distinguishing among kinds of anti-Communism, whether of the right or the left.

When they turn to politics, they have little concern for precise or complex thought. A few years ago the "new leftists" were likely to be drawn to Communist China, which then seemed bolder than Khrushchev's Russia. But though the Mao regime has kept the loyalty of a small group of students, most of the "new leftists" seem to find it too grim and repressive. They tend to look for their new heroes and models among the leaders of underdeveloped countries. Figures like Lumumba, Nasser, Sukarno, Babu, and above all Castro attract them, suggesting the possibility of a politics not yet bureaucratized and rationalized. But meanwhile they neglect to notice, or do not care, that totalitarian and authoritarian dictatorship can set in even before a society has become fully modernized. They have been drawn to charismatic figures like Lumumba and Castro out of a distaste for the mania of industrial production which the Soviet Union shares with the United States; but they fail to see that such leaders of the underdeveloped countries, who in their eyes represent spontaneity and anarchic freedom, are themselves—perhaps unavoidably—infused with the same mania for industrial production.

Let me specify a few more of the characteristic attitudes among the "new leftists":

1. An extreme, sometimes unwarranted, hostility toward liberalism. They see liberalism only in its current version, institutional, corporate, and debased; but avoiding history, they know very little about the elements of the liberal tradition, which should remain valuable for any democratic socialist. For the "new leftists," as I have here delimited them, liberalism means Clark Kerr, not John Dewey; Max Lerner, not John Stuart Mill; Pat Brown, not George Norris. And thereby they would cut off the resurgent American radicalism from what is, or should be, one of its sustaining sources: the tradition that has yielded us a heritage of civil freedoms, disinterested speculation, humane tolerance.

2. An impatience with the problems that concerned an older generation of radicals. Here the generational conflict breaks out with strong feelings on both sides, the older people feeling threatened in whatever they have been able to salvage from past experiences, the younger people feeling the need to shake off dogma and create their own terms of action.

Perhaps if we all try to restrain—not deny—our emotions, we can agree upon certain essentials. There are traditional radical topics which no one, except the historically minded, need trouble with. To be unconcerned with the dispute in the late twenties over the Anglo-Russian Trade Union Committee or the differences between Lenin and Rosa Luxemburg on the "national question"—well and good. These are not quite burning problems of the moment. But *some* of the issues hotly debated in the thirties do remain burning problems: in fact, it should be said for the anti-Stalinist left of the past several decades that it anticipated, in its own somewhat constricted way, a number of the problems (especially, the nature of Stalinism) which have since been widely debated by political scientists, sociologists, indeed, by all people concerned with politics. The nature of Stalinism and of post-Stalinist Communism is not an abstract or esoteric matter; the views one holds concerning these questions determine a large part of one's political conduct: and what is still more important, *they reflect one's fundamental moral values.*

No sensible radical over the age of thirty (something of a cutoff point, I'm told) wants young people merely to rehearse his ideas, or mimic her vocabulary, or look back upon his dusty old articles. On the contrary, what we find disturbing in some of the "new leftists" is that, while barely knowing it, they tend to repeat somewhat too casually the tags of the very past they believe themselves to be transcending. But we do insist that in regard to a few crucial issues, above all, those regarding totalitarian movements and societies, there should be no ambiguity, no evasiveness.

So that if some "new leftists" say that all the older radicals are equally acceptable or equally distasteful or equally inconsequential in their eyes; if they see no significant difference between, say, Norman Thomas and Paul Sweezy such as would require them to regard Thomas as a comrade and Sweezy as an opponent—then the sad truth is that they have not at all left behind them the old disputes, but, on the contrary, are still completely in their grip, though perhaps without being quite aware of what is happening to them. The issue of totalitarianism is neither academic nor merely historical; no one can seriously engage in politics without clearly and publicly defining an attitude toward it. I deliberately say "attitude" rather than "analysis," for while there can be a great many legitimate differences of analytic stress and nuance in discussing totalitarian society, morally there should be only a candid and sustained opposition to it.

3. A vicarious indulgence in violence, often merely theoretic and thereby all the more irresponsible. Not being a pacifist, I believe there may be times when violence is unavoidable; being a man of the twentieth century, I believe that a recognition of its necessity must come only after the most prolonged consideration, as an utterly last resort. To "advise" the Negro movement to adopt a policy encouraging or sanctioning violence, to sneer at Martin Luther King for his principled refusal of violence, is to take upon oneself a heavy responsibility—and if, as usually happens, taken lightly, it becomes sheer irresponsibility.

It is to be insensitive to the fact that the nonviolent strategy has arisen from Negro experience. It is to ignore the notable achievements that strategy has already brought. It is to evade the hard truth expressed by the Reverend Abernathy: "The whites have the guns." And it is to dismiss the striking moral advantage that nonviolence has yielded the Negro movement, as well as the turmoil, anxiety, and pain—perhaps even fundamental reconsideration—it has caused among whites in the North and the South.

There are situations in which Negroes will choose to defend themselves by arms against terrorist assault, as in the Louisiana towns where they have formed a club of "Elders" which patrols the streets peaceably but with the clear intent of retaliation in case of attack. The Negroes there seem to know what they are doing, and I would not fault them. Yet as a matter of general policy and upon a nationwide level, the Negro movement has chosen nonviolence: rightly, wisely, and heroically.

There are "revolutionaries" who deride this choice. They show a greater interest in ideological preconceptions than in the experience and needs of a living movement; and sometimes they are profoundly irresponsible, in that their true interest is not in helping to reach the goals chosen by the American Negroes, but is, rather, a social conflagration which would satisfy their apocalyptic yearnings even if meanwhile the Negroes were drowned in blood. The immediate consequence of such talk is a withdrawal from the ongoing struggles. And another consequence is to manufacture a cult out of figures like Malcolm X, who neither led nor won nor taught, and Robert Williams, the Negro leader who declared for violence and ended not with the Negroes in Selma, or at their strike in the hospitals of Westchester County, or on the picket line before the Atlanta Scripto plant (places where the kind of coalition we desire between Negro and labor was being foreshadowed), but by delivering shortwave broadcasts from Cuba.

4. *An unconsidered enmity toward something vaguely called the Establishment.* As the term "Establishment" was first used in England, it had the value of describing—which is to say, delimiting—a precise social group; as it has come to be used in the United States, it tends to be an all-purpose put-down. In England it refers to a caste of intellectuals with an Oxbridge education, closely related in values to the ruling class, and setting the cultural standards which largely dominate both the London literary world and the two leading universities.

Is there an Establishment in this, or any cognate, sense in the United States? Perhaps. There may now be in the process of formation, for the first time, such an intellectual caste; but if so, precise discriminations of analysis and clear boundaries of specification would be required as to what it signifies and how it operates.

As the term is currently employed, however, it is difficult to know who, besides those merrily using it as a thunderbolt of opprobrium, is *not* in the Establishment. And a reference that includes almost everyone tells us almost nothing.

5. *An equally unreflective belief in "the decline of the West"*—apparently without the knowledge that, more seriously held, this belief has itself been deeply ingrained in Western thought, frequently in the thought of reactionaries opposed to modern rationality, democracy, and sensibility.

The notion is so loose and baggy, it means little. Can it, however, be broken down? If war is a symptom of this decline, then it holds for the East as well. If totalitarianism is a sign, then it is not confined to the West. If economics is a criterion, then we must acknowledge, Marxist predictions aside, that there has been an astonishing recovery in Western Europe. If we turn to culture, then we must recognize that in the West there has just come to an end one of the greatest periods in human culture—that period of "modernism" represented by figures like Joyce, Stravinsky, Picasso. If improving the life of the workers is to count, then the West can say something in its own behalf. And if personal freedom matters, then, for all its grave imperfections, the West remains virtually alone as a place of hope. There remains, not least of all, the matter of racial prejudice, and here no judgment of the West can be too harsh—so long as we remember that even this blight is by no means confined to the West, and that the very judgments we make draw upon values nurtured by the West.

But is it not really childish to talk about "the West" as if it were some indivisible whole we must either accept or reject without amendment? There are innumerable strands in the Western tradition, and our task is to nourish those which encourage dignity and freedom. But to envisage some global apocalypse that will end in the destruction of the West is a sad fantasy, a token of surrender before the struggles of the moment.

6. *A crude, unqualified anti-Americanism, drawing from every possible source, even if one contradicts another: the aristocratic bias of Eliot and Ortega, Communist propaganda, the speculations of Tocqueville, the ressentiment of postwar Europe, and so on.*

7. *An increasing identification with that sector of the "third world" in which "radical" nationalism and Communist authoritarianism merge.* Consider this remarkable fact; In the past decade there have occurred major changes in the Communist world, and many of the intellectuals in Russia and Eastern Europe have reexamined their assumptions, often coming to the conclusion, masked only by the need for caution, that democratic values are primary in any serious effort at socialist reconstruction. Yet at the very same time most of the "new leftists" have identified not with the "revisionists" in Poland or dissident Milovan Djilas in Yugoslavia—or even Tito. They identify with the harder, more violent, more dictatorial segments of the

Communist world. And they carry this authoritarian bias into their consideration of the "third world," where they praise those rulers who choke off whatever weak impulses there may be toward democratic life.

About the problems of the underdeveloped countries, among the most thorny of our time, it is impossible to speak with any fullness here. Nor do I mean to suggest that an attack upon authoritarianism and a defense of democracy exhausts consideration of those problems; on the contrary, it is the merest beginning. But what matters in this context is not so much the problems themselves as the attitudes, reflecting a deeper political-moral bias, which the "new leftists" take toward such countries.

• Between the suppression of democratic rights and the justification or excuse the "new leftists" offer for such suppression there is often a very large distance, sometimes a complete lack of connection. Consider Cuba. It may well be true that United States policy became unjustifiably hostile toward the Castro regime at an early point in its history; but how is this supposed to have occasioned, or how is it supposed to justify, the suppression of democratic rights (including, and especially, those of all other left-wing tendencies) in Cuba? The apologists for Castro have an obligation to show what I think cannot be shown: the alleged close causal relation between United States pressure and the destruction of freedom in Cuba. Frequently, behind such rationales there is a tacit assumption that in times of national stress a people can be rallied more effectively by a dictatorship than by a democratic regime. But this notion—it was used to justify the suppression of political freedoms during the early Bolshevik years—is at the very least called into question by the experience of England and the United States during World War II. Furthermore, if Castro does indeed have the degree of mass support that his friends claim, one would think that the preservation of democratic liberties in Cuba would have been an enormously powerful symbol of self-confidence; would have won him greater support at home and certainly in other Latin-American countries; and would have significantly disarmed his opponents in the United States.

• We are all familiar with the "social context" argument: that for democracy to flourish there has first to be a certain level of economic development, a quantity of infrastructure, and a coherent national culture. As usually put forward in academic and certain authoritarian-left circles, it is a crudely deterministic notion, which I do not believe to be valid: for one thing, it fails to show how the suppression of even very limited political-social rights contributes, or is in fact caused by a wish, to solve these problems. (Who is prepared to maintain that Sukarno's suppression of the Indonesian Socialists and other dissident parties helped solve that country's economic or growth problems?) But for the sake of argument let us accept a version of this theory: let us grant what is certainly a bit more plausible, that a full or stable democratic society cannot be established in a country ridden by economic primitivism, illiteracy, disease, cultural disunion, and so on. The crucial question then becomes: can at least some measure of democratic rights be won or granted?—say, the right of workers to form unions or the right of dissidents within a single-party state to form factions and express their views? For if a richer socioeconomic development is a prerequisite of democracy, it must also be remembered that such democratic rights, as they enable the emergence of autonomous social groups, are also needed for socioeconomic development.

• Let us go even further and grant, again for the sake of argument, that in some underdeveloped countries authoritarian regimes may be necessary for a time. But even if this is true, which I do not believe it is, then it must be acknowledged as an unpleasant necessity, a price we are paying for historical crimes and mistakes of the past. In that case, radicals can hardly find their models in, and should certainly not become an uncritical cheering squad for, authoritarian dictators whose presence is a supposed unavoidability.

The "new leftists," searching for an ideology by which to rationalize their sentiments, can now find exactly what they need in a remarkable book recently translated from the French, *The Wretched of the Earth*. Its author, Frantz Fanon, is a Negro from Martinique who became active in the Algerian revolution. He articulates with notable power the views of those nationalist revolutionaries in the underdeveloped countries who are contemptuous of their native bourgeois leadership, who see their revolution being pushed beyond national limits and into their own social structure, who do not wish to merge with or become subservient to the Communists yet have no strong objection in principle to Communist methods and values.

Fanon tries to locate a new source of revolutionary energy: the peasants who, he says, "have nothing to lose and everything to gain." He deprecates the working class: in the Western countries it has been bought off, and in the underdeveloped nations it constitutes a tiny "aristocracy." What emerges is a curious version of Trotsky's theory of permanent revolution concerning national revolts in the backward countries which, to fulfill themselves, must become social revolutions. But with one major difference: Fanon assigns to the peasants and the urban declassed poor the vanguard role Trotsky had assigned to the workers.

What, however, has really happened in countries like Algeria? The peasantry contributes men and blood for an anticolonial war. Once the war is won, it tends to disperse, relapsing into local interests and seeking individual small-scale ownership of the land. It is too poor, too weak, too diffuse to remain or become the leading social force in a newly liberated country. The bourgeoisie, what there was of it, having been shattered and the working class pushed aside, what remains? Primarily the party of nationalism, led by men who are dedicated, uprooted, semieducated, and ruthless. The party rules, increasingly an independent force perched upon and above the weakened classes.

But Fanon is not taken in by his own propaganda. He recognizes the dangers of a preening dictator. He proposes, instead, that "the party should be the direct expression of the masses," and adds, "Only those underdeveloped countries led by revolutionary elites who have come up from the people can today *allow* the entry of the masses upon the scene of history" (emphasis added).

Fanon wants the masses to participate, yet throughout his book the single-party state remains an unquestioned assumption. But what if the masses do not wish to "participate"? And what if they are hostile to "the"—always "the"—party? Participation without choice is a burlesque of democracy; indeed, it is an essential element of a totalitarian or authoritarian society, for it means that the masses of people act out a charade of involvement but are denied the reality of decision.

The authoritarians find political tendencies and representative men with whom to identify in the Communist world; so do we. We identify with the people who have died for freedom, like Imre Nagy, or who rot in prison, like Djilas. We identify with the "revisionists," those political *marranos* who, forced to employ Communist jargon, yet spoke out for a socialism democratic in character and distinct from both Communism and capitalism. As it happens, our friends in the Communist world are not in power; but since when has that mattered to socialists?

In 1957, at the height of the Polish ferment, the young philosopher Leszek Kolakowski wrote a brief article entitled "What Is Socialism?" It consisted of a series of epigrammatic sentences describing what socialism is not (at the moment perhaps the more immediate concern), but tacitly indicating as well what socialism should be. The article was banned by the Gomulka regime but copies reached Western periodicals. Here are a few sentences.

Socialism is not
    A society in which a person who has committed no crime sits at home waiting for the police.
    A society in which one person is unhappy because he says what he thinks, and another happy because he does not say what is in his mind.
    A society in which a person lives better because he does not think at all.

A state whose neighbors curse geography.

A state which wants all its citizens to have the same opinions in philosophy, foreign policy, economics, literature, and ethics.

A state whose government defines its citizens' rights, but whose citizens do not define the government's rights.

A state in which there is private ownership of the means of production.

A state which considers itself solidly socialist because it has liquidated private ownership of the means of production.

A state which always knows the will of the people before it asks them.

A state in which the philosophers and writers always say the same as the generals and ministers, but always after them.

A state in which the returns of parliamentary elections are always predictable.

A state which does not like to see its citizens read back numbers of newspapers.

These negatives imply a positive, and that positive is a central lesson of contemporary history: the unity of socialism and democracy. To preserve democracy as a political mode without extending it into every crevice of social and economic life is to allow it to become increasingly sterile, formal, ceremonial. To nationalize an economy without enlarging democratic freedoms is to create a new kind of social exploitation. Radicals and liberals may properly and fraternally disagree about many other things; but upon this single axiom concerning the value of democracy, this conviction wrung from the tragedy of our age, politics must rest.

George Orwell: "As the Bones Know"
{1968}

G EORGE ORWELL WROTE with his bones. To read again his essays, together with previously uncollected journalism and unpublished letters,
is to encounter the bone-weariness, and bone-courage, of a writer who
lived through the Depression, Hitlerism, Franco's victory in Spain, Stalinism, the
collapse of bourgeois England in the thirties. Even when he wanted to pull back to
his novels and even when he lay sick with tuberculosis, Orwell kept summoning
those energies of combat and resources of irritation which made him so powerful
a fighter against the cant of his age. His bones would not let him rest.

For a whole generation—mine—Orwell was an intellectual hero. He stormed
against those English writers who were ready to yield to Hitler; he fought almost
single-handed against those who blinded themselves to the evils of Stalin. More
than any other English intellectual of our age, he embodied the values of personal
independence and a fiercely democratic radicalism. Yet, just because for years I
have intensely admired him, I hesitated to return to him. One learns to fear the
disappointment of lapsed enthusiasms.

I was wrong to hesitate. Reading through these four large volumes*—the
sheer *pleasure* of it cannot be overstated—has convinced me that Orwell was an

---

* *The Collected Essays, Journalism and Letters of George Orwell* (New York: Harcourt, Brace & World,
1968).

even better writer than I had supposed. He was neither a first-rank literary critic nor a major novelist, and certainly not an original political thinker; but he was, I now believe, the best English essayist since Hazlitt, perhaps since Dr. Johnson. He was the greatest moral force in English letters during the last several decades: craggy, fiercely polemical, sometimes mistaken, but an utterly free man. In his readiness to stand alone and take on all comers, he was a model for every writer of our age. And when my students ask, "Whom shall I read in order to write better?" I answer, "Orwell, the master of the plain style, that style which seems so easy to copy but is almost impossible to reach."

If you look through them casually, the earliest of Orwell's essays seem to share that blunt clarity of speech and ruthless determination to see what looms in front of one's nose that everyone admires in his later work. The first important essay came out in 1931, when Orwell was still in his late twenties, and is called "The Spike." It describes his experience as an unemployed wanderer on the roads of England, finding shelter in a "spike," or hostel, where the poor were given a bed and two or three meals but then required to move along. The piece makes one quiver with anger at the inhumanity of good works, but it is absolutely free of sentimentalism, and almost miraculously untainted by the sticky *loving* condescension of 1930s radicalism.

Any ordinary writer should be willing to give his right arm, or at least two fingers, to have written that piece. Yet a close inspection will show, I think, that it doesn't reach Orwell's highest level of social reportage. There is still an occasional clutter of unabsorbed detail, still a self-consciousness about his role as half-outsider barging in upon and thereby perhaps subtly betraying the lives of the men on the road. The discipline of the plain style—and that fierce control of self which forms its foundation—comes hard.

For Orwell, it also came quickly. In a piece called "Hop Picking," written a few months later but now published for the first time, Orwell describes some weeks spent as an agricultural worker in the hop fields. The prose is now keener:

> Straw is rotten stuff to sleep in (it is much more draughty than hay) and Ginger and I had only a blanket each, so we suffered agonies of cold for the first week. . . .
>
> Dick's Café in Billingsgate . . . was one of the very few places where you could get a cup of tea for 1d, and there were fires there, so that anyone who had a penny could warm himself for hours in the early morning. Only this last week the London County Council closed it on the ground that it was unhygienic.

In "Hop Picking" Orwell had already solved the problem of narrative distance: how to establish a simultaneous relationship with the men whose experience he shared and the readers to whom he makes the experience available. "Hop Picking" was a small effort in the kind of writing Orwell would undertake on a large scale a few years later, when he produced his classic report on the condition of English miners, The Road to Wigan Pier. What Orwell commanded, above all, was a natural respect for the workers. He saw and liked them as they were, not as he or a political party felt they should be. He didn't twist them into Marxist abstractions, nor did he cuddle them in the fashion of New Left Populism. He saw the workers neither as potential revolutionists nor savage innocents nor stupid clods. He saw them as ordinary suffering and confused human beings: rather like you and me, yet because of their circumstances radically different from you and me. When one thinks of the falseness that runs through so much current writing of this kind it becomes clear that Orwell was a master of the art of exposition.

Other sides of Orwell's talent soon begin to unfold. He develops quickly: the idea of *pressure* is decisive. His career can be understood only as a series of moral and intellectual crises, the painful confrontation of a man driven to plunge into every vortex of misery that he saw, yet a man with an obvious distaste for the corruptions of modern politics.

Even in casual bits of journalism, his voice begins to come through. As a literary critic he seldom had the patience to work his way deeply into a text, though he did have an oblique sort of literary penetration. He remarks, in an otherwise commonplace review, that George Moore enjoyed the advantage of "not having an over-developed sense of pity; hence he could resist the temptation to make his characters more sensitive than they would have been in real life." In "Bookshop Memories," never before printed in a book, Orwell shows the peculiar sandpapery humor that would emerge in his later writings:

> Seen in the mass, five or ten thousand at a time, books were boring and even slightly sickening. . . . The sweet smell of decaying paper appeals to me no longer. It is too closely associated in my mind with paranoiac customers and dead bluebottles.

In another early piece, not otherwise notable, there suddenly leaps out a sentence carrying Orwell's deepest view of life, his faith in the value and strength of common existence: "The fact to which we have got to cling, as to a life-belt, is that it is possible to be a normal decent person and yet to be fully alive."

Orwell's affectionate sense of English life, its oddities, paradoxes, and even outrages, comes through in an anecdote he tells:

... the other day I saw a man—Communist, I suppose—selling the *Daily Worker*, & I went up to him & said, "Have you the DW?"—He: "Yes, sir." Dear Old England!

There are even a few early poems, slightly this side of *Weltschmerz*, which I rather like:

> I know, not as in barren thought,
> But wordlessly, as the bones know,
> What quenching of my brain, what numbness,
> Wait in the dark grave where I go.

Orwell's first fully achieved piece of writing appears in 1936: "Shooting an Elephant," a mixture of reminiscence and reflection. The essay takes off from his experience as a minor British official in Burma who, in the half-jeering, half-respectful presence of a crowd of "natives," must destroy a maddened elephant; and then it moves on to larger issues of imperialism and the corruption of human nature by excessive power. For the first time, his characteristic fusion of personal and public themes is realized, and the essay as a form—vibrant, tight-packed, nervous—becomes a token of his meaning. The evocation of brutality is brought to climax through one of those symbolic moments he would employ brilliantly in his later pieces: "The elephant's mouth was wide and open—I could see far down into caverns of pale pink throat."

During these years, the late thirties, Orwell went through a rapid political development. He kept assaulting the deceits of Popular Frontism, and this brought him even more intellectual loneliness than it would have in America. He tried to find a tenable basis for his anti-Stalinist leftism, a task at which he encountered the same difficulties other intellectuals did—which, after all, were intrinsic to a world-wide crisis of socialist thought. For a while he fought in Spain with the militia of the POUM, a left-wing anti-Communist party, and suffered a throat wound; back in England he spoke some painful truths about the Stalinist terror launched against dissident leftists on the Loyalist side, and for this he was hated by the *New Statesman* and most of the Popular Front intellectuals. He published one of his most valuable and neglected books, *Homage to Catalonia*, the record of his experience in Spain. He went through a brief interval in which he put forward a semi-Trotskyist line, denying that the bourgeois West could successfully oppose Hitlerism and insisting that the prerequisite for destroying Fascism was a socialist revolution in England. But when the war broke out, he had the good sense—not all his co-thinkers did—to see that his earlier views on combating Fascism had been abstract, unreal, ultimatistic. He supported the war, yet remained a radical, steadily criticizing social privilege and snobbism. Here is a passage in his previously unpublished "War-Time Diary," breathing his ingrained plebeian distaste for the English upper classes:

> From a letter from Lady Oxford to the *Daily Telegraph*:
> "Since most London houses are deserted there is little entertaining . . . in any case, most people have to part with their cooks and live in hotels."
>
> Apparently nothing will ever teach these people that the other 99% of the population exists.

The high plateau of Orwell's career as essayist—and it is as essayist he is likely to be remembered best—begins around 1940. He had by then perfected his gritty style; he had settled into his combative manner (sometimes the object of an unattractive kind of self-imitation); and he had found his subjects: the distinctive nature of English life and its relation to the hope for socialism, a number of close examinations of popular culture, a series of literary studies on writers ranging from Dickens to Henry Miller, and continued social reportage on the life of the poor. His productivity during the next five or six years is amazing. He works for the BBC, he writes a weekly column for the socialist *Tribune*, he sends regular London Letters to *Partisan Review* in New York, he keeps returning to his fiction, and he still manages to produce such extraordinary essays as the appreciation of Dickens, the piquant investigation of boys' magazines, the half-defense of and half-assault on Kipling, the brilliant "Raffles and Miss Blandish," the discussion of Tolstoy's hatred for Shakespeare—to say nothing of such unknown gems, rescued from little magazines, as his moving essays on writers so thoroughly out of fashion as Smollett and Gissing.

We see him now in his mature public role. There is something irascible about Orwell, even pugnacious, which both conventional liberals and literary aesthetes find unnerving. He is constantly getting into fights, and by no means always with good judgment. He is reckless, he is ferociously polemical, and when arguing for a "moderate" opinion he is harsh and intransigent in tone.

My sense of Orwell, as it emerges from reading him in bulk, is rather different from that which became prevalent in the conservative fifties: the "social saint" one of his biographers called him, the "conscience of his generation" V. S. Pritchett declared him to be, or the notably good man Lionel Trilling saw in him. The more I read of Orwell, the more I doubt that he was particularly virtuous or good. Neither the selflessness nor the patience of the saint, certainly not the indifference to temporal passion that would seem a goal of sainthood, can be found in Orwell. He himself wrote in his essay on Gandhi: "No doubt alcohol, tobacco and so forth are things a saint must avoid, but sainthood is a thing that human beings must avoid."

As a "saint" Orwell would not trouble us, for by now we have learned how to put up with saints: we canonize them and are rid of them. Orwell, however, stirs us by his all too human, his truculent example. He stood in basic opposition to the modes and assumptions that have dominated English cultural life. He rejected the rituals of Good Form which had been so deeply ingrained among the English and took on a brief popularity among us in the fifties; he knew how empty, and often how filled with immoderate aggression the praise of moderation could be; he turned away from the pretentiousness of the "literary." He wasn't a Marxist or even a political revolutionary. He was something better: a revolutionary personality. He turned his back on his own caste; he tried to discover what was happening beyond the provincial limits of high-brow life. If he was a good man, it was mainly in the sense that he had measured his desperation and come to accept it as a mode of honor. And he possessed an impulse essential to a serious writer: he was prepared to take chances, even while continuing to respect the heritage of the past.

Both as writer and thinker, Orwell had serious faults. He liked to indulge himself in a pseudo-tough anti-intellectualism, some of it pretty damned nasty, as in his sneers at "pansy-pinks"—though later he was man enough to apologize to those he had hurt. He was less than clear-sighted or generous on the subject of the Jews, sharing something of the English impatience with what he regarded—in the 1940s!—as their need for special claims. He could be mean in polemics. During the war he was quite outrageous in attacking English anarchists and pacifists like Alex Comfort, Julian Symons, and George Woodcock for lending "objective" comfort to the Nazis. Yet it speaks well for Orwell that in a short time at least two of these men became his friends, and it isn't at all clear to me that in his angry and overstated denunciation, Orwell wasn't making a point against them and all other pacifists which must be seriously considered.

Meanwhile, one suddenly comes to a stop and notices that those of Orwell's letters reprinted in the few volumes of his collected prose are not, as letters, particularly interesting or distinguished. At first, this comes as a surprise, for one might have expected the same pungency, the same verbal thrust, as in the public writing. There is, however, nothing to be found of the qualities that make for great letter writing: nothing of the brilliant rumination of Keats in his letters, or the profound self-involvement of Joyce in his, or the creation of a dramatic persona such as T. E. Lawrence began in his. He seems to have poured all his energies into his published work and used his letters simply as a convenience for making appointments, conveying information, rehearsing opinion. Perhaps it's just as well, for he had a horror of exposing his private life and asked that no biography be written about him. In these days of instant self-revelation, there is something attractive about a writer who throws up so thick a screen of reticence.

One reason these uninteresting letters do finally hold our attention is that they put to rest the notion that Orwell's prose was an achievement easily come by. The standard critical formula is that he wrote in a "conversational" style, and he himself is partly responsible for this simplification. I think, however, that Yvor Winters was right in saying that human conversation is a sloppy form of communication and seldom a good model for prose. What we call colloquial or conversational prose is the result of cultivation, and can be written only by a disciplined refusal of the looseness of both the colloquial and the conversational. If you compare the charged lucidity of Orwell's prose in his best essays with the merely adequate and often flat writing of his letters, you see at once that the style for which he became famous was the result of artistry and hard work. It always is.

In an essay called "Why I Write," Orwell ends with a passage at once revealing and misleading:

> All writers are vain, selfish and lazy, and at the very bottom of their motives there lies a mystery. Writing a book is a horrible, exhausting struggle, like a long bout of some painful illness. . . . Good prose is like a window pane. I cannot say with certainty which of my motives are the strongest, but I know which of them deserve to be followed. And looking back through my work, I see that it is invariably where I lacked a *political* purpose that I wrote lifeless books and was betrayed into purple passages. . . .

Orwell is saying something of great importance here, but saying it in a perverse way. (After a time he relished a little too much his role of embattled iconoclast.) He does *not* mean what some literary people would gleefully suppose him to mean: that only tendentiousness, only propaganda, makes for good prose. He deliberately overstates the case, as a provocation to the literary people he liked to bait. But a loyal reader, prepared to brush aside his mannerisms, would take this passage to mean that, once a minimal craftsmanship has been reached, good writing is the result of being absorbed by an end greater than the mere production of good writing. A deliberate effort to achieve virtuosity or beauty or simplicity usually results in mannerism, which is often no more than a way of showing off.

In his best work Orwell seldom allowed himself to show off. He was driven by a passion to clarify ideas, correct errors, persuade readers, straighten things out in the world and in his mind. Hemingway speaks of "grace under pressure," and many of his critics have used this marvelous phrase to describe the excellence of his style. What I think you get in Orwell at his best is something different: "pressure under grace." He achieves a state of "grace" as a writer through having sloughed off the usual vanities of composition, and thereby he speaks not merely for himself but as a voice of moral urgency. His prose becomes a prose of pressure, the issue at stake being too important to allow him to slip into fancies or fanciness. Moral pressure makes for verbal compression, a search like Flaubert's for le mot juste, but not at all to achieve aesthetic nicety, rather to achieve a stripped speech. And the result turns out to be aesthetically pleasing: the Christians, with much more to be risked, understood all this when they spoke of "dying into life."

Good prose, says Orwell, should be "like a window pane." He is both right and wrong. Part of his limitation as a literary critic is that he shows little taste for the prose of virtuosity: one can't easily imagine him enjoying Sir Thomas Browne. If some windows should be clear and transparent, why may not others be stained and opaque? Like all critics who are also significant writers themselves, Orwell developed standards that were largely self-justifying: he liked the prose that's like a window pane because that's the kind of prose he wrote.

His style doesn't seem to change much from early essays to late, but closely watched it shows significant modulations. At the outset his effort to be clear at all costs does involve him in heavy costs: a certain affectation of bluntness, a tendency to make common sense into an absolute virtue. But by the end, as in the superb prose of "Such, Such Were the Joys," there has occurred a gradual increase of control and thereby suppleness.

"Pressure under grace" brings rewards. Orwell learns to mold the essay into a tense structure, learns to open with a strong thrust ("Dickens is one of those writers who are well worth stealing"), and above all, to end with an earned climax, a release of the tension that has been accumulating and can now be put to the service of lucidity. I think a useful critical study could be made of the way he ends his essays. Here is the last paragraph on Dickens:

When one reads any strongly individual piece of writing, one has the impression of seeing a face somewhere behind the page. It is not necessarily the actual face of the writer. . . . What one sees is the face that the writer ought to have. Well, in the case of Dickens I see a face that is not quite the face of Dickens' photographs, though it resembles it. It is the face of a man about forty, with a small beard and a high color. He is laughing, with a touch of anger in his laughter, but no triumph, no malignity. It is the face of a man who is always fighting against something, but who fights in the open and is not frightened, the face of a man who is *generously angry*—in other words, of a nineteenth-century liberal, a free intelligence, a type hated with equal hatred by all the smelly little orthodoxies which are now contending for our souls.

The passage is marvelous, but if a criticism is to be made, it is that Orwell has composed a set piece too easily lifted out of context and in the final sentence has allowed himself to turn away from his subject in order to take a smack at fanatics of left and right. Yet this self-indulgence, if it is one, works pretty well, mainly because Orwell has by now so thoroughly persuaded his readers that the qualities he admires in Dickens *are* indeed admirable.

Here is another Orwell ending, this time from the essay on Swift, "Politics vs. Literature," published some seven years after the one on Dickens. Orwell makes some important observations on the problem of "belief" in literature:

In so far as a writer is a propagandist, the most one can ask of him is that he shall genuinely believe in what he is saying, and that it shall not be something blazingly silly. Today . . . one can imagine a good book being written by a Catholic, a Communist, a Fascist, a Pacifist, an Anarchist, perhaps by an old-styled Liberal or an ordinary Conservative; one cannot imagine a good book being written by a spiritualist, a Buchmanite or a member of the Ku Klux Klan. The views that a writer holds must be compatible with sanity, in the medical sense, and with the power of continuous thought: beyond that what we ask of him is talent, which is probably another name for conviction. Swift did not possess ordinary wisdom, but he did possess a terrible intensity of vision. . . . The durability of *Gulliver's Travels* goes to show that, if the force of belief is behind it, a world-view which only just passes the test of sanity is sufficient to produce a great work of art.

What grips our attention here is the ferocity with which Orwell drives home his point—by reaction, we almost see old Tolstoy rising from his grave to thunder against this heresy. Rhetorically, the passage depends on the sudden drop of the last sentence, with its shocking reduction of the preceding argument—so that in the movement of his prose Orwell seems to be enacting the curve of his argument. It is a method he must have picked up from Swift himself.

And, finally, here is the ending of his great essay, "How the Poor Die":

The dread of hospitals probably still survives among the very poor and in
all of us it has only recently disappeared. It is a dark patch not far beneath
the surface of our minds. I have said earlier that, when I entered the ward at
the Hospital X, I was conscious of a strange feeling of familiarity. What the
scene reminded me of, of course, was the reeking, pain-filled hospitals of
the nineteenth century, which I had never seen but of which I had a traditional knowledge. And something, perhaps the black-clad doctor with his
frowsy black bag, or perhaps only the sickly smell, played the queer trick
of unearthing from my memory that poem of Tennyson's, "The Children's
Hour," which I had not thought of for twenty years. It happened that as
a child I had had it read aloud to me by a sick-nurse. . . . Seemingly I had
forgotten it. Even its name would probably have recalled nothing to me.
But the first glimpse of the ill-lit, murmurous room, with the beds so close
together, suddenly roused the train of thought to which it belonged, and in
the night that followed I found myself remembering the whole story and
atmosphere of the poem, with many of its lines complete.

This ending seems to me a triumph of composition. All that has been detailed
with such gruesome care about the terribleness of a French hospital is brought
to imaginative climax through the anecdote at the end. Proust could hardly have
done better.

Orwell died, in 1950, at the age of forty-six, stricken by tuberculosis. It is depressing to think that if he had lived, he would today be no more than sixty-five
years old. How much we have missed in these two decades! Imagine Orwell rip-
ping into one of Harold Wilson's mealy speeches, imagine him examining the
thought of Spiro Agnew, imagine him dissecting the ideology of Herbert Marcuse, imagine him casting a frosty eye on the current wave of irrationalism in
Western culture!

The loss seems enormous. . . . He was one of the few heroes of our younger
years who remains untarnished. Having to live in a rotten time was made just a
little more bearable by his presence.

The New York Intellectuals
{1969}

THE SOCIAL ROOTS of the New York writers are not hard to trace. With a few delightful exceptions—a tendril from Yale, a vine from Seattle—they stem from the world of the immigrant Jews, either workers or petty bourgeois.* They come at a moment in the development of immigrant Jewish culture when there is a strong drive not only to break out of the ghetto but also to leave behind the bonds of Jewishness entirely. Earlier generations had known such

---

* In placing this emphasis on the Jewish origins of the New York intellectuals. I am guilty of a certain—perhaps unavoidable—compression of realities. Were I writing a book rather than an essay, I would have to describe in some detail the relationship between the intellectuals who came on the scene in the thirties and those of earlier periods. There were significant ties between *Partisan Review* and the Dial, Politics and The Masses. But I choose here to bypass this historical connection because I wish to stress what has been distinctive.

A similar qualification has to be made concerning intellectuals associated with this milieu but not Jewish. I am working on the premise that in background and style there was something decidedly Jewish about the intellectuals who began to cohere as a group around *Partisan Review* in the late thirties—and one of the things that was "decidedly Jewish" was that most were of Jewish birth! Perhaps it ought to be said, then, that my use of the phrase "New York intellectuals" is simply a designation of convenience, a shorthand for what might awkwardly be spelled out as "the intellectuals of New York who began to appear in the thirties, most of whom were Jewish."

feelings, and through many works of fiction, especially those by Henry Roth, Michael Gold, and Daniel Fuchs, one can return to the classic pattern of a fierce attachment to the provincialism of origins as it becomes entangled with a fierce eagerness to plunge into the Gentile world of success, manners, freedom.

The New York intellectuals were the first group of Jewish writers to come out of the immigrant milieu who did not define themselves through a relationship, nostalgic or hostile, to memories of Jewishness. They were the first generation of Jewish writers for whom the recall of an immigrant childhood does not seem to have been completely overwhelming. That this severance from Jewish immigrant sources would later come to seem a little suspect is another matter. All I wish to stress here is that, precisely at the point in the thirties when the New York intellectuals began to form themselves into a loose cultural-political tendency, Jewishness as idea and sentiment played no significant role in their expectations—apart, to be sure, from a bitter awareness that no matter what their political or cultural desires, the sheer fact of their recent emergence had still to be regarded as an event within Jewish American life.

For decades the life of the East European Jews, in both the old country and the new, might be compared to a tightly gathered spring, trembling with unused force, which had been held in check until the climactic moment of settlement in America. Then the energies of generations came bursting out, with an ambition that would range from pure to coarse, and indeed would mix all these together, but finally—this ambition—would count for more as an absolute release than in any of its local manifestations. What made Sammy run was partly that his father and his father's father had been bound hand and foot. And in all the New York intellectuals there was a fraction of Sammy.

The youthful experiences described by Alfred Kazin in his autobiography are, apart from his distinctive outcroppings of temperament, more or less typical of the experiences of many New York intellectuals—except for the handful who involved themselves deeply in the radical movement. It is my impression, however, that Kazin's affectionate stress on the Jewish sources of his experience is mainly a feeling of retrospect, mainly a recognition that no matter how you might try to shake off your past, it would still cling to your speech, gestures, skin, and nose; it would still shape, with a thousand subtle movements, the way you did your work and raised your children. In the thirties, however, it was precisely the idea of discarding the past, breaking away from families, traditions, and memories which excited intellectuals.

The Jewish immigrant world branded upon its sons and daughters marks of separateness even while encouraging them to dreams of universalism. This subculture may have been formed to preserve ethnic continuity, but it was a continuity that would reach its triumph in self-disintegration. It taught its children both to conquer the Gentile world and to be conquered by it, both to leave an intellectual impress and to accept the dominant social norms. By the twenties and thirties the values dominating Jewish immigrant life were often secular, radical, and universalist, and if these were conveyed through a parochial vocabulary, they nonetheless carried some remnants of European culture. Even as they were moving out of a constricted immigrant milieu, the New York intellectuals were being prepared by it for the tasks they would set themselves. They were being prepared for the intellectual vocation as one of assertiveness, speculation, and freewheeling; for the strategic maneuvers of a vanguard, at this point almost a vanguard in the abstract, with no ranks following in the rear; and for the union of politics and culture, with the politics radical and the culture cosmopolitan. What made this goal all the more attractive was that the best living American critic, Edmund Wilson, had triumphantly reached it. The author of both *The Triple Thinkers* and *To the Finland Station*, he gave this view of the intellectual life a special authority.

That the literary avant-garde and the political left were not really comfortable partners would become clear with the passage of time; in Europe it already had. But during the years the New York intellectuals began to appear as writers and critics there was a feeling in the air that a union of the *advanced*—critical consciousness and political conscience—could be forged.

Throughout the thirties the New York intellectuals believed, somewhat naively, that this union was not only a desirable possibility but also a tie both natural and appropriate. Except, however, for the surrealists in Paris—and it is not clear how seriously this instance should be taken—the paths of political radicalism and cultural modernism have seldom met.

The history of the West in the last century offers many instances in which Jewish intellectuals played an important role in the development of political radicalism; but almost always this occurred when there were sizable movements, with the intellectuals serving as propagandists and functionaries of a party. In New York, by contrast, the intellectuals had no choice but to begin with a dissociation from the only significant radical movement in this country, the Communist Party. What for European writers like Koestler, Silone, and Malraux would be the end of the road was here a beginning. In a fairly short time, the New York writers found that the meeting of political and cultural ideas which had stirred them to excitement could also leave them stranded. Radicalism, in both its daily practice and ethical biases, proved inhospitable to certain aspects of modernism—and not always, I now think, mistakenly. Literary modernism often had a way of cavalierly dismissing the world of daily existence, a world that remained intensely absorbing to the New York writers. Literary modernism could sometimes align itself with reactionary movements, an embarrassing fact that required either tortuous explanations or complex dissociations. The New York writers discovered, as well, that their relationship to modernism as a purely literary phenomenon was less authoritative and more ambiguous than they had wished to feel. The great battles for Joyce, Eliot, and Proust had been fought in the twenties and mostly won; and now, while clashes with entrenched philistinism might still take place, they were mostly skirmishes or mopping-up operations (as in the polemics against the transfigured Van Wyck Brooks). The New York writers came at the end of the modernist experience, just as they came at what may yet have to be judged the end of the radical experience, and as they certainly came at the end of the immigrant Jewish experience. One shorthand way of describing their situation, a cause of both their feverish intensity and their recurrent instability, is to say that *they came late.*

During the thirties and forties their radicalism was anxious, problematic, and beginning to decay at the very moment it was adopted. They had no choice: the crisis of socialism was worldwide, profound, with no end in sight, and the only way to avoid that crisis was to bury oneself, as a few did, in left-wing sects. Some of the New York writers had gone through the "political school" of Stalinism, a training in coarseness from which not all recovered; some had even spent a short time in the organizational coils of the Communist Party. By 1936, when the anti-Stalinist *Partisan Review* was conceived, the central figures of that moment— Philip Rahv, William Phillips, Sidney Hook—had shed whatever sympathies they once felt for Stalinism, but the hope that they could find another ideological system, some cleansed version of Marxism associated perhaps with Trotsky or Rosa Luxemburg, was doomed to failure. Some gravitated for a year or two toward the Trotskyist group, but apart from admiration for Trotsky's personal qualities and dialectical prowess, they found little satisfaction there; no version of orthodox Marxism could retain a hold on intellectuals who had gone through the trauma of abandoning the Leninist weltanschauung and had experienced the depth to which the politics of this century, notably the rise of totalitarianism, called into question Marxist categories. From now on, the comforts of system would have to be relinquished.

Though sometimes brilliant in expression and often a stimulus to cultural speculation, the radicalism of the New York intellectuals during the thirties was not a deeply grounded experience. It lacked roots in a popular movement which might bring them into relationship with the complexities of power and stringencies of organization. From a doctrine it became a style, and from a style a memory. It was symptomatic that the *Marxist Quarterly*, started in 1937 and probably the most distinguished Marxist journal ever published in this country, could survive no more than a year. The differences among its founders, some like James Burnham holding to a revolutionary Marxist line and others like Sidney Hook and Lewis Corey moving toward versions of liberalism and social democracy, proved too severe for collaboration. And even the radicalism of the *Partisan Review* editors and writers during its vivid early years—how deeply did it cut, except as a tool enabling them to break away from Marxism?

2

Yet if the radicalism of the New York intellectuals seems to have been without much political foundation or ideological strength, it certainly played an important role in their own development. For the New York writers, and even, I suspect, those among them who would later turn sour on the whole idea of radicalism (including the few who in the mid-sixties would try to erase the memory of having turned sour), the thirties represented a time of intensity and fervor, a reality or illusion of engagement, a youth tensed with conviction; so that even Dwight Macdonald, who at each point in his life made a specialty out of mocking his previous beliefs, could not help displaying tender feelings upon remembering his years, God help us, as a "revolutionist." The radicalism of the thirties gave the New York intellectuals their distinctive style: a flair for polemic, a taste for the grand generalization, an impatience with what they regarded (often parochially) as parochial scholarship, an internationalist perspective, and a tacit belief in the unity—even if a unity beyond immediate reach—of intellectual work.

By comparison with competing schools of thought, the radicalism of the anti-Stalinist left, as it was then being advanced in *Partisan Review*, seemed cogent, fertile, alive; it could stir good minds to argument, it could gain the attention of writers abroad, it seemed to offer a combination of system and independence. With time the anti-Stalinist intellectuals came to enjoy advantages somewhat like those which have enabled old radicals to flourish in the trade unions; they could talk faster than anyone else, they were quicker on their feet.

Yet in fairness I should add that this radicalism did achieve something of substantial value in the history of American culture. It helped destroy Stalinism as a force in our intellectual life, and also those varieties of populist sentimentality which the Communist movement of the late thirties exploited with notable skill.

If certain sorts of manipulative softheadedness have been all but banished from serious American writing, and the kinds of rhetoric once associated with Archibald MacLeish and Van Wyck Brooks cast into permanent disrepute, at least some credit for this ought to go to the New York writers.

It has recently become fashionable, especially in the pages of the *New York Review of Books*, to sneer at the achievements of the anti-Stalinist left by muttering darkly about "the Cold War." But we ought to have enough respect for the past to avoid telescoping several decades. The major battle against Stalinism as a force within intellectual life, and in truth a powerful force, occurred before anyone heard of the Cold War; it occurred in the late thirties and early forties. In our own moment we see "the old crap," as Marx once called it, rise to the surface with unnerving ease; there is something dizzying in an encounter with Stalin's theory of "social Fascism," particularly when it comes from the lips of young people who may not even be quite sure when Stalin lived. Still, I think there will not and probably cannot be repeated in our intellectual life the ghastly large-scale infatuation with a totalitarian regime which disgraced the thirties.

A little credit is due. Whatever judgments one may have about Sidney Hook's later political writings, and mine have been very critical, it is a matter of decency to recall the liberating role he played in the thirties as spokesman for a democratic radicalism and a fierce opponent of all the rationalizations for totalitarianism a good many intellectuals allowed themselves. One reason people have recently felt free to look down their noses at "anti-Communism" as if it were a mass voodoo infecting everyone from far right to democratic left is precisely the toughness with which the New York intellectuals fought against Stalinism. Neither they nor anybody else could reestablish socialism as a viable politics in the United States; but for a time they did help to salvage the honor of the socialist idea—which meant primarily to place it in the sharpest opposition to all totalitarian systems. What many intellectuals now say they take for granted had first to be won through bitter and exhausting struggle.

I should not like to give the impression that Stalinism was the beginning and end of whatever was detestable in American intellectual life during the thirties. Like the decades to come, perhaps like all decades, this was a "low dishonest" time. No one who grew up in, or lived through, these years should wish for a replay of their ideological melodramas. Nostalgia for the thirties is a sentiment possible only to the very young or the very old, those who have not known and those who no longer remember. Whatever distinction can be assigned to the New York intellectuals during those years lies mainly in their persistence as a small minority, in its readiness to defend unpopular positions against apologists for the Moscow trials and Popular-Front culture. Some historians, with the selectivity of retrospect, have recently begun to place the New York intellectuals at the center of cultural life in the thirties—but this is both a comic misapprehension and a soiling honor. On the contrary; their best hours were spent on the margin, in opposition.

Later, in the forties and fifties, most of the New York intellectuals would abandon the effort to find a renewed basis for a socialist politics—to their serious discredit, I believe. Some would vulgarize anti-Stalinism into a politics barely distinguishable from reaction. Yet for almost all New York intellectuals the radical years proved a decisive moment in their lives. And for a very few, the decisive moment.

I have been speaking here as if the New York intellectuals were mainly political people, but in reality this was true for only a few of them, writers like Hook, Macdonald, and perhaps Rahv. Most were literary men with no experience in any political movement; they had come to radical politics through the pressures of conscience and a flair for the dramatic; and even in later years, when they abandoned any direct political involvement, they would in some sense remain "political." They would respond with eagerness to historical changes, even if these promised renewed favor for the very ideas they had largely discarded. They would continue to structure their cultural responses through a sharp, perhaps excessively sharp, kind of categorization, in itself a sign that political styles and habits persisted. But for the most part, the contributions of the New York intellectuals were not to political thought. Given the brief span of time during which they fancied themselves agents of a renewed Marxism, there was little they could have done. Sidney Hook wrote one or two excellent books on the sources of Marxism, Harold Rosenberg one or two penetrating essays on the dramatics of Marxism; and not much more. The real contribution of the New York writers was toward creating a new, and for this country almost exotic, style of work. They thought of themselves as cultural radicals even after they had begun to wonder whether there was much point in remaining political radicals. But what could this mean? Cultural radicalism was a notion extremely hard to define and perhaps impossible to defend, as Richard Chase would discover in the late fifties when against the main drift of New York opinion he put forward the idea of a radicalism without immediate political ends but oriented toward criticism of a meretricious culture.

Chase was seriously trying to preserve a major impetus of New York intellectual life: the exploration and defense of literary modernism. He failed to see, however, that this was a task largely fulfilled and, in any case, taking on a far more ambiguous and less militant character in the fifties than it would have had twenty or thirty years earlier. The New York writers had done useful work in behalf of modernist literature. Without fully realizing it, they were continuing a cultural movement that had begun in the United States during the mid-nineteenth century: the return to Europe, not as provincials knocking humbly at the doors of the great, but as equals in an enterprise which by its very nature had to be international. We see this at work in Howells's reception of Ibsen and Tolstoy; in Van Wyck Brooks's use of European models to assault the timidities of American literature; in the responsiveness of the *Little Review* and the *Dial* to European experiments and, somewhat paradoxically, in the later fixation of the New Critics, despite an ideology of cultural provincialism, on modernist writing from abroad.

3

The New York critics helped complete this process of internationalizing American culture (also, by the way, Americanizing international culture). They gave a touch of glamour to that style which the Russians and Poles now call "cosmopolitan." *Partisan Review* was the first journal in which it was not merely respectable but a matter of pride to print one of Eliot's *Four Quartets* side by side with Marxist criticism. And not only did the magazine break down the polar rigidities of the hard-line Marxists and the hard-line nativists; it also sanctioned the idea, perhaps the most powerful cultural idea of the last half-century, that there existed an all but incomparable generation of modern masters, some of them still alive, who in this terrible age represented the highest possibilities of the imagination. On a more restricted scale, *Partisan Review* helped win attention and respect for a generation of European writers—Silone, Orwell, Malraux, Koestler, Victor Serge— who were not quite of the first rank as novelists but had suffered the failure of socialism.

If the *Partisan* critics came too late for a direct encounter with new work from the modern masters, they did serve the valuable end of placing that work in a cultural context more vital and urgent than could be provided by any other school of American criticism. For young people up to and through World War II, the *Partisan* critics helped to mold a new sensibility, a mixture of rootless radicalism and a desanctified admiration for writers like Joyce, Eliot, and Kafka. I can recall that even in my orthodox Marxist phase I felt that the central literary expression of the time was a poem by a St. Louis writer called "The Waste Land."

In truth, however, the New York critics were then performing no more than an auxiliary service. They were following upon the work of earlier, more fortunate critics. And even in the task of cultural consolidation, which soon had the unhappy result of overconsolidating the modern masters in the academy, the New York critics found important allies among their occasional opponents in the New Criticism. As it turned out, the commitment to literary modernism proved insufficient either as a binding literary purpose or as a theme that might inform the writings of the New York critics. By now modernism was entering its period of decline; the old excitements had paled and the old achievements been registered. Modernism had become successful; it was no longer a literature of opposition, and thereby had begun a metamorphosis signifying ultimate death. The problem was no longer to fight for modernism; the problem was now to consider why the fight had so easily ended in triumph. And as time went on, modernism surfaced an increasing portion of its limitations and ambiguities, so that among some critics earlier passions of advocacy gave way to increasing anxieties of judgment. Yet the moment had certainly not come when a cool and objective reconsideration could be undertaken of works that had formed the sensibility of our time. The New York critics, like many others, were trapped in a dilemma from which no escape could be found, but which lent itself to brilliant improvisation; it was too late for unobstructed enthusiasm, it was too soon for unobstructed valuation, and meanwhile the literary work that was being published, though sometimes distinguished, was composed in the heavy shadows of the modernists. At almost every point this work betrayed the marks of *having come after*.

Except for Harold Rosenberg, who would make "the tradition of the new" a signature of his criticism, the New York writers slowly began to release those sentiments of uneasiness they had been harboring about the modernist poets and novelists. One instance was the notorious Pound case,* in which literary and moral values, if not jammed into a head-on collision, were certainly entangled beyond easy separation. Essays on writers like D. H. Lawrence—what to make of his call for "blood consciousness," what one's true response might be to his notions of the leader cult—began to appear. A book by John Harrison, *The Reactionaries*, which contains a full-scale attack on the politics of several modernist writers, is mostly a compilation of views that had already been gathering force over the last few decades. And then, as modernism stumbled into its late period, those recent years in which its early energies evidently reached a point of exhaustion, the New York critics became still more discomfited. There was a notable essay by Lionel Trilling in which he acknowledged mixed feelings toward the

---

* In 1948 Ezra Pound, who had spent the war years as a propagandist for Mussolini and whose writings contained strongly anti-Semitic passages, was awarded the prestigious Bollingen Prize. The committee voting for this award contained a number of ranking American poets. After the award was announced, there occurred a harsh dispute as to its appropriateness.

modernist writers he had long praised and taught. There was a cutting attack by
Philip Rahv on Jean Genet, that perverse genius in whose fiction the composi-
tional resources of modernism seem all but severed from its moral—one might
even say, its human—interests.

For the New York intellectuals in the thirties and forties there was still another
focus of interest, never quite as strong as radical politics or literary modernism
but seeming, for a brief time, to promise a valuable new line of discussion. In the
essays of writers like Clement Greenberg and Dwight Macdonald, more or less
influenced by the German neo-Marxist school of Adorno-Horkheimer, there were
beginnings at a theory of "mass culture," that mass-produced pseudo-art characteristic of industrialized urban society, together with its paralyzed audiences,
its inaccessible sources, its parasitic relation to high culture. More insight than
system, this slender body of work was nevertheless a contribution to the study of
that hazy area where culture and society meet. It was attacked by writers like Edward Shils as being haughtily elitist, on the ground that it assumed a condescension to the tastes and experiences of the masses. It was attacked by writers like
Harold Rosenberg, who charged that only people taking a surreptitious pleasure
in dipping their noses into trash would study the "content" (he had no objection
to sociological investigations) of mass culture. Even at its most penetrating, the
criticism of mass culture was beset by uncertainty and improvisation; perhaps all
necessary for a beginning.

Then, almost as if by common decision, the whole subject was dropped. For
years hardly a word could be found in the advanced journals about what a little
earlier had been called a crucial problem of the modern era. One reason was that
the theory advanced by Greenberg and Macdonald turned out to be static: it could
be stated but apparently not developed. It suffered from weaknesses parallel to
those of Hannah Arendt's theory of totalitarianism: by positing a cul-de-sac, a
virtual end of days, for twentieth-century man and his culture, it proposed a suf-
focating relationship between high or minority culture and the ever-multiplying
mass culture.

In the absence of more complex speculations, there was little point in continuing to write about mass culture. Besides, hostility toward the commercial pseudo-
arts was hard to maintain with unyielding intensity, mostly because it was hard to
remain all that interested in them—only in Macdonald's essays did both hostility
and interest survive intact. Some felt that the whole matter had been inflated and
that writers should stick to their business, which was literature, and intellectuals
to theirs, which was ideas. Others felt that the movies and TV were beginning

to show more ingenuity and resourcefulness than the severe notions advanced by Greenberg and Macdonald allowed for, though no one could have anticipated that glorious infatuation with trash which Marshall McLuhan would make acceptable. And still others felt that the multiplication of insights, even if pleasing as an exercise, failed to yield significant results: a critic who contributes a nuance to Dostoevsky criticism is working within a structured tradition, while one who throws off a clever observation about Little Orphan Annie is simply showing that he can do what he has done.

There was another and more political reason for the collapse of mass-culture criticism. One incentive toward this kind of writing was the feeling that industrial society had reached a point of affluent stasis where major events could now be registered much more vividly in culture than in economics. While aware of the dangers of reductionism here, I think the criticism of mass culture did serve, as some of its critics charged, conveniently to replace the criticism of bourgeois society. If you couldn't stir the proletariat to action, you could denounce Madison Avenue in comfort. Once, however, it began to be felt among intellectuals in the fifties that there was no longer so overwhelming a need for political criticism, and once it began to seem in the sixties that there were new openings for political criticism, the appetite for cultural surrogates became less keen.

Greenberg now said little more about mass culture; Macdonald made no serious effort to extend his theory or test it against new events; and in recent years, younger writers have seemed to feel that the whole approach of these men was heavy and humorless. Susan Sontag has proposed a cheerfully eclectic view which undercuts just about everything written from the Greenberg-Macdonald position. Now everyone is to do "his thing," high, middle, or low; the old puritan habit of interpretation and judgment, so inimical to sensuousness, gives way to a programmed receptivity; and we are enlightened by lengthy studies of the Beatles.

By the end of World War II, the New York writers had reached a point of severe intellectual crisis, though they themselves often felt they were entering a phase of enlarged influence. Perhaps there was a relation between inner crisis and external influence. Everything that had kept them going—the idea of socialism, the advocacy of literary modernism, the assault on mass culture, a special brand of literary criticism—was judged to be irrelevant to the postwar years. But as a group, just at the time their internal disintegration had seriously begun, the New York writers could be readily identified. The leading critics were Rahv, Phillips, Trilling, Rosenberg, Lionel Abel, and Kazin. The main political theorist was Hook. Writers of poetry and fiction related to the New York milieu were Delmore Schwartz,

Saul Bellow, Paul Goodman, and Isaac Rosenfeld. And the recognized scholar, and also inspiring moral force, was Meyer Schapiro.

4

A sharp turn occurs, or is completed, soon after World War II. The intellectuals now go racing or stumbling from idea to idea, notion to notion, hope to hope, fashion to fashion. This instability often derives from a genuine eagerness to capture all that seems new — or threatening — in experience, sometimes from a mere desire to please a bitch goddess named Novelty. The abandonment of ideology can be liberating: a number of talents, thrown back on their own resources, begin to grow. The surrender of "commitment" can be damaging: some writers find themselves rattling about in a gray freedom. The culture opens up, with both temptation and generosity, and together with intellectual anxieties there are public rewards, often deserved. A period of dispersion; extreme oscillations in thought; and a turn in politics toward an increasingly conservative kind of liberalism — reflective, subtle, acquiescent.

The postwar years were marked by a sustained discussion of the new political and intellectual problems raised by the totalitarian state. Nothing in received political systems, neither Marxist nor liberal, adequately prepared one for the frightful mixture of terror and ideology, the capacity to sweep along the plebeian masses and organize a warfare state, and above all the readiness to destroy entire peoples, which characterized totalitarianism. Still less was anyone prepared — who had heeded the warning voices of the Russian socialist Julian Martov or the English liberal Bertrand Russell? — for the transformation of the revolutionary Bolshevik state, through either a "necessary" degeneration or an internal counterrevolution, into one of the major totalitarian powers. Marxist theories of fascism — the "last stage" of capitalism, with the economy stratified to organize a permanent war machine and mass terror employed to put down rebellious workers — came to seem, if not entirely mistaken, then certainly insufficient. The quasi- or pseudo-Leninist notion that "bourgeois democracy" was merely a veiled form of capitalist domination, little different in principle from its open dictatorship, proved to be a moral and political disaster. The assumption that socialism was an ordained "next step," or that nationalization of industry constituted a sufficient basis for working-class rule, was as great a disaster. No wonder intellectual certainties were shattered and these years marked by frenetic improvisation. At every point, with the growth of Communist power in Europe and with the manufacture of the Bomb at home, apocalypse seemed the fate of tomorrow.

So much foolishness has been written about the New York intellectuals and their anti-Communism, either by those who have signed a separate peace with the authoritarian idea or those who lack the courage to defend what is defensible in their own past, that I want here to be both blunt and unyielding.

Given the enormous growth of Russian power after the war and the real possibility of a Communist takeover in Europe, the intellectuals—and not they alone—had to reconsider their political responses.* An old-style Marxist declaration of rectitude, a plague repeated on both their houses? Or the difficult position of making foreign-policy proposals for the United States, while maintaining criticism of its social order, so as to block totalitarian expansion without resort to war? Most intellectuals decided they had to choose the second course, and they were right.

Like anticapitalism, anti-Communism was a tricky politics, all too open to easy distortion. Like anticapitalism, anti-Communism could be put to the service of ideological racketeering and reaction. Just as ideologues of the fanatic right insisted that by some ineluctable logic anti-capitalism led to a Stalinist terror, so ideologues of the authoritarian left, commandeering the same logic, declared that anti-Communism led to the politics of Dulles and Rusk. But there is no "anticapitalism" or "anti-Communism" in the abstract; these take on political flesh only when linked with a larger body of programs and values, so that it becomes clear what kind of "anticapitalism" or "anti-Communism" we are dealing with. It is absurd, and indeed disreputable, for intellectuals in the sixties to write as if there were a unified "anti-Communism" which can be used to enclose the views of everyone from William Buckley to Michael Harrington.

There were difficulties. A position could be worked out for conditional support of the West when it defended Berlin or introduced the Marshall Plan or provided economic help to underdeveloped countries; but in the course of daily politics, in the effort to influence the foreign policy of what remained a capitalist power,

---

* Some recent historians, under New Left inspiration, have argued that in countries like France and Italy the possibility of a Communist seizure of power was really quite small. Perhaps; counterfactuals are hard to dispose of. What matters is the political consequences these historians would retrospectively have us draw, if they were at all specific on this point. Was it erroneous, or reactionary, to believe that resistance had to be created in Europe against further Communist expansion? What attitude, for example, would they have had intellectuals, or anyone else, take during the Berlin crisis? Should the city, in the name of peace, have been yielded to the East Germans? Did the possibility of Communist victories in Western Europe require an extraordinary politics? And to what extent are later reconsiderations of Communist power in postwar Europe made possible by the fact that it was, in fact, successfully contained?

intellectuals could lose their independence and slip into vulgarities of analysis and speech.

Painful choices had to be faced. When the Hungarian revolution broke out in 1956, most intellectuals sympathized strongly with the rebels, yet feared that active intervention by the West might provoke a world war. For a rational and humane mind, anti-Communism could not be the sole motive—it could be only one of several—in political behavior and policy; and even those intellectuals who had by now swung a considerable distance to the right did not advocate military intervention in Hungary. There was simply no way out—as there was none in Czechoslovakia.

It became clear, furthermore, that United States military intervention in underdeveloped countries could help local reactionaries in the short run, and the Communists in the long run. These difficulties were inherent in postwar politics, and they ruled out—though for that very reason, also made tempting—a simplistic moralism. These difficulties were also exacerbated by the spread among intellectuals of a crude sort of anti-Communism, often ready to justify whatever the United States might do at home and abroad. For a hard-line group within the American Committee for Cultural Freedom, all that seemed to matter in any strongly felt way was a sour hatred of the Stalinists, historically justifiable but more and more a political liability even in the fight against Stalinism. The dangers in such a politics now seem all too obvious, but I should note, for whatever we may mean by the record, that in the early fifties they were already being pointed out by a mostly unheeded minority of intellectuals around *Dissent*. Yet, with all these qualifications registered, the criticism to be launched against the New York intellectuals in the postwar years is not that they were strongly anti-Communist but, rather, that many of them, through disorientation or insensibility, allowed their anti-Communism to become something cheap and illiberal.

Nor is the main point of *moral* criticism that the intellectuals abandoned socialism. We have no reason to suppose that the declaration of a socialist opinion induces a greater humaneness than does acquiescence in liberalism. It could be argued (I would) that in the ease with which ideas of socialism were now brushed aside there was something shabby. It was undignified, at the very least, for people who had made so much of their Marxist credentials now to put to rest so impatiently the radicalism of their youth. Still, it might be said by some of the New York writers that reality itself had forced them to conclude socialism was no longer viable or had become irrelevant to the American scene, and that while this conclusion might be open to political argument, it was not to moral attack.

Let us grant that for a moment. What cannot be granted is that the shift in ideologies required or warranted the surrender of critical independence which was prevalent during the fifties. In the trauma—or relief—of ideological ricochet, all too many intellectuals joined the American celebration. It was possible, to cite but one of many instances, for Mary McCarthy to write: "Class barriers disappear or tend to become porous [in the U.S.]; the factory worker is an economic aristocrat in comparison with the middle-class clerk. . . . *The America . . . of vast inequalities and dramatic contrasts is rapidly ceasing to exist*" (emphasis added). Because the New York writers all but surrendered their critical perspective on American society—*that is* why they were open to attack.

It was the growth of McCarthyism which brought most sharply into question the role of the intellectuals. Here, presumably, all men of good will could agree; here the interests of the intellectuals were beyond dispute and directly at stake. The record is not glorious. In New York circles it was often said that Bertrand Russell exaggerated wildly in describing the United States as "subject to a reign of terror" and that Simone de Beauvoir retailed Stalinist clichés in her reportage from America. Yet it should not be forgotten that, if not "a reign of terror," McCarthyism was frightful and disgusting, and that a number of Communists and fellow-travelers, not always carefully specified, suffered serious harm.

A magazine like *Partisan Review* was of course opposed to McCarthy's campaign, but it failed to take the lead on the issue of freedom which might once again have imbued the intellectuals with fighting spirit. Unlike some of its New York counterparts, it did print sharp attacks on the drift toward conservatism, and it did not try to minimize the badness of the situation in the name of anti-Communism. But the magazine failed to speak out with enough force and persistence, or to break past the hedgings of those intellectuals who led the American Committee for Cultural Freedom.

Commentary, under Elliot Cohen's editorship, was still more inclined to minimize the threat of McCarthyism. In September 1952, at the very moment McCarthy became a central issue in the presidential campaign, Cohen could write: "McCarthy remains in the popular mind an unreliable, second-string blowhard; his only support as a great national figure is from the fascinated fears of the intelligentsia"—a mode of argument all too close to that of the anti-anti-Communists who kept repeating that Communism was a serious problem only in the minds of anti-Communists.

In the American Committee for Cultural Freedom the increasingly conformist and conservative impulses of the New York intellectuals, or at least of a good number of them, found formal expression. I quote at length from Michael

Harrington in a 1955 issue of *Dissent*, because it says precisely what needs to be said:

> In practice the ACCF has fallen behind Sidney Hook's views on civil liber-
> ties. Without implying any "conspiracy" theory of history ... one may safely
> say that it is Hook who has molded the decisive ACCF policies. His *Heresy*
> *Yes, Conspiracy No* articles were widely circulated by the Committee, which
> meant that in effect it endorsed his systematic, explicit efforts to minimize
> the threat to civil liberties and to attack those European intellectuals who,
> whatever their own political or intellectual deficiencies, took a dim view of
> American developments. Under the guidance of Hook and the leadership of
> Irving Kristol . . . the American Committee cast its weight not so much in
> defense of those civil liberties which were steadily being nibbled away, but
> rather against those few remaining fellow-travelers who tried to exploit the
> civil-liberties issue.
>
> At times this had an almost comic aspect. When Irving Kristol was ex-
> ecutive secretary of the ACCF, one learned to expect from him silence on
> those issues that were agitating the whole intellectual and academic world,
> and enraged communiqués on the outrages performed by people like Ar-
> thur Miller and Bertrand Russell in exaggerating the dangers to civil liber-
> ties in the U.S.
>
> Inevitably this led to more serious problems. In an article by Kristol,
> which first appeared in *Commentary* and was later circulated under the ACCF
> imprimatur, one could read such astonishing and appalling statements as
> "there is one thing the American people know about Senator McCarthy;
> he, like them, is unequivocally anti-Communist. About the spokesmen for
> American liberalism, they feel they know no such thing. And with some
> justification." This in the name of defending cultural freedom!

Harrington then proceeded to list several instances in which the ACCF had "acted within the United States in defense of freedom." But

> these activities do not absorb the main attention or interest of the Commit-
> tee; its leadership is too jaded, too imbued with the sourness of indiscrimi-
> nate anti-Stalinism to give itself to an active struggle against the dominant
> trend of contemporary intellectual life in America. What it *really* cares about
> is a struggle against fellow-travelers and "neutralists"—that is, against
> many European intellectuals. . . .

One of the crippling assumptions of the Committee has been that it would not intervene in cases where Stalinists or accused Stalinists were involved. It has rested this position on the academic argument . . . that Stalinists, being enemies of democracy, have no "right" to democratic privileges. . . . But the actual problem is not the metaphysical one of whether enemies of democracy (as the Stalinists clearly are) have a "right" to democratic privileges. What matters is that the drive against cultural freedom and civil liberties takes on the guise of anti-Stalinism.

Years later came the revelations that the Congress for Cultural Freedom, which had its headquarters in Paris and with which the American Committee was for a time affiliated, had received secret funds from the CIA. Some of the people, it turned out, with whom one had sincerely disagreed were not free men at all; they were accomplices of an intelligence service. What a sad denouement! And yet not the heart of the matter, as the malicious *Ramparts* journalists have tried to make out. Most of the intellectuals who belonged to the ACCF seem not to have had any knowledge of the CIA connection—on this, as on anything else, I would completely accept the word of Dwight Macdonald. It is also true, however, that these intellectuals seem not to have inquired very closely into the Congress's sources of support. That a few, deceiving their closest associates, established connections with the CIA was not nearly so important, however, as that a majority within the Committee acquiesced in a politics of acquiescence. We Americans have a strong taste for conspiracy theories, supposing that if you scratch a trouble you'll find a villain. But history is far more complicated; and squalid as the CIA tie was, it should not be used to smear honest people who had nothing to do with secret services even as they remain open to criticism for what they did say and do.

At the same time, the retrospective defenses offered by some New York intellectuals strike me as decidedly lame. Meetings and magazines sponsored by the Congress, Daniel Bell has said, kept their intellectual freedom and contained criticism of U.S. policy—true but hardly to the point, since the issue at stake is not the opinions the Congress tolerated but the larger problem of good faith in intellectual life. The leadership of the Congress did not give its own supporters the opportunity to choose whether they wished to belong to a CIA-financed group. Another defense, this one offered by Sidney Hook, is that private backing was hard to find during the years it was essential to publish journals like *Preuves* and *Encounter* in Europe. Simply as a matter of fact, I do not believe this. For the Congress to have raised its funds openly, from nongovernmental sources, would have meant discomfort, scrounging, penny-pinching: all the irksome things editors of little magazines have always had to do. By the postwar years, however, leading figures of both the Congress and the Committee no longer thought or behaved in that tradition.

Dwight Macdonald did. His magazine Politics was the one significant effort during the late forties to return to radicalism. Enlivened by Macdonald's ingratiating personality and his table-hopping mind, Politics brought together sophisticated muckraking with tortuous revaluations of Marxist ideology. Macdonald could not long keep in balance the competing interests which finally tore apart his magazine: lively commentary on current affairs and unavoidable if depressing retrospects on the failure of the left. As always with Macdonald, honesty won out (one almost adds, alas) and the "inside" political discussion reached its climax with his essay "The Root Is Man," in which he arrived at a kind of anarcho-pacifism based on an absolutist morality. This essay was in many ways the most poignant and authentic expression of the plight of those few intellectuals—Nicola Chiaromonte, Paul Goodman, Macdonald—who wished to dissociate themselves from the postwar turn to realpolitik but could not find ways of transforming sentiments of rectitude and visions of utopia into a workable politics. It was also a perfect leftist rationale for a kind of internal emigration of spirit and mind, with some odd shadings of similarity to the Salinger cult of the late fifties.*

The overwhelming intellectual drift, however, was toward the right. Arthur Schlesinger, Jr., with moony glances at Kierkegaard, wrote essays in which he maintained that American society had all but taken care of its economic problems and could now concentrate on raising its cultural level. The "end of ideology" became a favorite shield for intellectuals in retreat, though it was never entirely clear whether this phrase meant the end of "our" ideology (partly true) or that all ideologies were soon to disintegrate (not true) or that the time had come to abandon the nostalgia for ideology (at least debatable). And in the mid-fifties, as if to codify things, there appeared in Partisan Review a symposium, "Our Country and Our Culture," in which all but three or four of the thirty participants clearly moved away from their earlier radical views. The rapprochement with "America

---

* It is not clear whether Macdonald still adheres to "The Root Is Man." In a BBC broadcast he said about the student uprising at Columbia: "I don't approve of their methods, but Columbia will be a better place afterwards." Perhaps it will, perhaps it won't; but I don't see how the author of "The Root Is Man" could say this, since the one thing he kept insisting was that means could not be separated from ends, as the Marxists too readily separated them. He would surely have felt that if the means used by the students were objectionable, then their ends would be contaminated as well—and thereby the consequences of their action. But in the swinging sixties not many people troubled to remember their own lessons.

the Beautiful," as Mary McCarthy now called it in a tone not wholly ironic, seemed almost complete.

5

In these years there also began that series of gyrations in opinion, interest, and outlook—so frenetic, so unserious—which would mark our intellectual life. In place of the avant-garde idea we now had the *style of fashion*, though to suggest a mere replacement may be too simple, since fashion has often shadowed the avant-garde as a kind of dandified double. Some intellectuals turned to a weekend of religion, some to a semester of existentialism, some to a holiday of Jewishness without faith or knowledge, some to a season of genteel conservatism. Leslie Fiedler, no doubt by design, seemed to go through more of such episodes than anyone else: even his admirers could not always be certain whether he was davenning or doing a rain dance.

These twists and turns were lively, and they could all seem harmless if only one could learn to look upon intellectual life as a variety of play, like potsy or king of the hill. What struck one as troubling, however, was not this or that fashion (tomorrow morning would bring another), but the dynamic of fashion itself, the ruthlessness with which, to remain in fashion, fashion had to keep devouring itself.

It would be unfair to give the impression that the fifteen years after the war were without significant growth or achievement among the New York writers. The attempt of recent New Left ideologues to present the forties and fifties as if they were no more than a time of intellectual sterility and reaction is an oversimplification. Together with the turn toward conservative acquiescence, there were serious and valuable achievements. Hannah Arendt's book on totalitarianism may now seem open to many criticisms, but it certainly must rank as a major piece of work which, at the very least, made impossible—I mean, implausible—those theories of totalitarianism which, before and after she wrote, tended to reduce fascism and Stalinism to a matter of class rule or economic interest. Daniel Bell's writing contributed to the rightward turn of these years, but some of it, such as his excellent little book *Work and Its Discontents*, constitutes a permanent contribution, and one that is valuable for radicals too. The stress upon complexity of thought which characterized intellectual life during these years could be used as a rationale for conservatism, and perhaps even arose from the turn toward conservatism; but in truth, the lapsed radicalism of earlier years *had* proved to be simplistic, the world of late capitalism *was* perplexing, and for serious people complexity is a positive

value. Even the few intellectuals who resisted the dominant temper of the fifties
underwent during these years significant changes in their political outlooks and
styles of thought: e.g., those around *Dissent* who cut whatever ties of sentiment
still held them to the Bolshevik tradition and made the indissoluble connection
between democracy and socialism a crux of their thought. Much that happened
during these years is to be deplored and dismissed, but not all was waste; the
increasing sophistication and complication of mind was a genuine gain, and it
would be absurd, at this late date, to forgo it.

In literary criticism there were equivalent achievements. The very instability
that might make a shambles out of political thought could have the effect of mag-
nifying the powers required for criticism. Floundering in life and uncertainty in
thought could make for an increased responsiveness to art. In the criticism of
men like Trilling, Rahv, Richard Chase, and F. W. Dupee there was now a more
authoritative relation to the literary text and a richer awareness of the cultural
past than was likely to be found in their earlier work. And a useful tension was
also set up between the New York critics, whose instinctive response to literature
was through a social-moral contextualism, and the New Critics, whose formalism proved of great value to those who opposed it.

Meanwhile, the world seemed to be opening up, with all its charms, seduc-
tions, and falsities. In the thirties the life of the New York writers had been confined: the little magazine as island, the radical sect as cave. Partly they were re-
capitulating the pattern of immigrant Jewish experience: an ingathering of the
flock in order to break out into the world and taste the Gentile fruits of status and
success. Once it became clear that waiting for the revolution might turn out to
be steady work and that the United States would neither veer to fascism nor sink
into depression, the intellectuals had little choice but to live within (which didn't
necessarily mean, become partisans of) the existing society.

There was money to be had from publishers, no great amounts, but more than
in the past. There were jobs in the universities, even for those without degrees.
Some writers began to discover that publishing a story in the *New Yorker* or *Esquire*
was not a sure ticket to Satan; others to see that the academy, while perhaps less
exciting than the Village, wasn't invariably a graveyard for intellect and might even
provide the only harbor in which serious people could do their own writing and
perform honorable work. This dispersion involved losses, but usually there was
nothing sinister about it. Writers ought to know something about the world; they
ought to test their notions against the reality of the country in which they live.

Worldly involvements would, of course, bring risks, and one of these was power, really a very trifling kind of power, but still enough to raise the fear of corruption. That power corrupts everyone knows by now, but we ought also to recognize that powerlessness, if not corrupting, can be damaging—as in the case of Paul Goodman, a courageous writer who stuck to his anarchist beliefs through years in which he was mocked and all but excluded from the New York journals, yet who could also come to seem an example of asphyxiating righteousness.

What brought about these changes? Partly ideological adaptation, a feeling that capitalist society was here to stay and there wasn't much point in maintaining a radical position. Partly the sly workings of prosperity. But also a loosening of the society itself, the start of that process which only now is in full swing—I mean the remarkable absorptiveness of modern society, its readiness to abandon traditional precepts for a moment of excitement, its growing permissiveness toward social criticism, perhaps out of indifference, or security, or even tolerance.

In the sixties well-placed young professors and radical students would denounce the "success," sometimes the "sellout," of the New York writers. Their attitude reminds one a little of George Orwell's remark about wartime France: only a Pétain could afford the luxury of asceticism, ordinary people had to live by the necessities of materialism. But really, when you come to think of it, what did this "success" of the intellectuals amount to? A decent or a good job, a chance to earn extra money by working hard, and in the case of a few, like Trilling and Kazin, some fame beyond New York—rewards most European intellectuals would take for granted, so paltry would they seem. For the New York writers who lived through the thirties expecting never to have a job at all, a regular paycheck might be remarkable; but in the American scale of things it was very modest indeed. And what the "leftist" prigs of the sixties, sons of psychiatrists and manufacturers, failed to understand—or perhaps understood only too well—was that the "success" with which they kept scaring themselves was simply one of the possibilities of adult life, a possibility, like failure, heavy with moral risks and disappointment. Could they imagine that they too might have to face the common lot? I mean the whole business: debts, overwork, varicose veins, alimony, drinking, quarrels, hemorrhoids, depletion, the recognition that one might prove not to be another T. S. Eliot, but also some good things, some lessons learned, some "rags of time" salvaged and precious.

Here and there you could find petty greed or huckstering, now and again a drop into opportunism; but to make much of this would be foolish. Common clay, the New York writers had their share of common ambition. What drove them, and sometimes drove them crazy, was not, however, the quest for money, nor even a chance to "mix" with White House residents; it was finally a gnawing ambition to write something, even three pages, that might live.

The intellectuals should have regarded their entry into the outer world as utterly commonplace, at least if they kept faith with the warning of Stendhal and Balzac that one must always hold a portion of the self forever beyond the world's reach. Few of the New York intellectuals made much money on books and articles. Few reached audiences beyond the little magazines. Few approached any centers of power, and precisely the buzz of gossip attending the one or two sometimes invited to a party beyond the well-surveyed limits of the West Side showed how confined their life still was. What seems most remarkable in retrospect is the innocence behind the assumption, sometimes held by the New York writers themselves with a nervous mixture of guilt and glee, that whatever recognition they won was cause for either preening or embarrassment. For all their gloss of sophistication, they had not really moved very far into the world. The immigrant milk was still on their lips.

6

In their published work during these years, the New York intellectuals developed a characteristic style of exposition and polemic. With some admiration and a bit of irony, let us call it the style of brilliance. The kind of essay they wrote was likely to be wide-ranging in reference, melding notions about literature and politics, sometimes announcing itself as a study of a writer or literary group but usually taut with a pressure to "go beyond" its subject, toward some encompassing moral or social observation. It is a kind of writing highly self-conscious in mode, with an unashamed vibration of bravura. Nervous, strewn with knotty or flashy phrases, impatient with transitions and other concessions to dullness, calling attention to itself as a form or at least an outcry, fond of rapid twists, taking pleasure in dispute, dialectic, dazzle—such, at its best or most noticeable, was the essay cultivated by the New York writers. Until recently its strategy of exposition was likely to be impersonal (the writer did not speak much as an "I") but its tone and bearing were likely to be intensely personal (the audience was to be made aware that the aim of the piece was not judiciousness, but, rather, a strong impress of attitude, a blow of novelty, a wrenching of accepted opinion, sometimes a mere indulgence of vanity).

In some of these essays there was a sense of *tournament*, the writer as gymnast with one eye on other rings, or as skilled infighter juggling knives of dialectic. Polemics were harsh, often rude. And audiences nurtured, or spoiled, on this kind of performance, learned not to form settled judgments about a dispute until all sides had registered their blows: surprise was always a possible reward.

This style may have brought new life to the American essay, but among contemporary readers it often evoked a strong distaste, even fear. "Ordinary" readers could be left with the fretful sense that they were not "in," the beauties of polemic racing past their sluggish eye. Old-line academics, quite as if they had just crawled out of The Dunciad, enjoyed dismissing the New York critics as "unsound." And for some younger souls, the cliffs of dialectic seemed too steep. Seymour Krim has left a poignant account of his disablement before "the overcerebral, Europeanish, sterilely citified, pretentiously alienated" New York intellectuals. Resentful at the fate which drove them to compare themselves with "the overcerebral, etc., etc.," Krim writes that he and his friends "were often tortured and unappeasably bitter about being the offspring of this unhappily unique-ingrown-screwed-up breed." Similar complaints could be heard from other writers who felt that New York intellectualism threatened their vital powers.

At its best the style of brilliance reflected a certain view of the intellectual life: free-lance dash, peacock strut, daring hypothesis, knockabout synthesis. For better or worse it was radically different from the accepted modes of scholarly publishing and middlebrow journalism. It celebrated the idea of the intellectual as antispecialist, or as a writer whose speciality was the lack of a speciality: the writer as dilettante-connoisseur, Luftmensch of the mind, roamer among theories. But it was a style which also lent itself with peculiar ease to a stifling mimicry and decadence. Sometimes it seemed—no doubt mistakenly—as if any sophomore, indeed any parrot, could learn to write one of those scintillating Partisan reviews, so thoroughly could manner consume matter. In the fifties the cult of brilliance became a sign that writers were offering not their work or ideas but their persona as content; and this was but a step or two away from the exhibitionism of the sixties. Brilliance could become a sign of intellect unmoored: the less assurance, the more pyrotechnics.

If to the minor genre of the essay the New York writers made a major contribution, to the major genres of fiction and poetry they made only a minor contribution. As a literary group, they will seem less important than, say, the New Critics, who did set in motion a whole school of poetry. A few poets—John Berryman, Robert Lowell, Randall Jarrell, perhaps Stanley Kunitz—have been influenced by the New York intellectuals, though in ways hardly comprising a major pressure on their work: all were finished writers by the time they brushed against the New York milieu. For one or two poets, the influence of New York meant becoming

aware of the cultural pathos resident in the idea of the Jew (not always distinguished from the idea of Delmore Schwartz). But the main literary contribution
of the New York milieu has been to legitimate a subject and tone we must uneasily
call American Jewish writing. The fiction of urban malaise, second-generation
complaint, Talmudic dazzle, woeful alienation, and dialectical irony, all found
its earliest expression in the pages of *Commentary* and *Partisan Review*—fiction in
which the Jewish world is not merely regained in memory as a point of beginnings, an archetypal Lower East Side of spirit and place, but is also treated as a
portentous metaphor of man's homelessness and wandering.

Such distinguished short fictions as Bellow's *Seize the Day*, Schwartz's "In
Dreams Begin Responsibility," Mailer's "The Man Who Studied Yoga," and Malamud's "The Magic Barrel" seem likely to survive the cultural moment in which
they were written. And even if one concludes that these and similar pieces are
not enough to warrant speaking of a major literary group, they certainly form a
notable addition—a new tone, a new sensibility—to American writing. In time,
these writers may be regarded as the last "regional" group in American literature,
parallel to recent Southern writers in both sophistication of craft and a thematic
dissociation from the values of American society. Nor is it important that during the last few decades both of these literary tendencies, the Southern and the
Jewish, have been overvalued. The distance of but a few years has already made
it clear that except for Faulkner Southern writing consists of a scatter of talented
minor poets and novelists; and in a decade or so a similar judgment may be commonly accepted about most of the Jewish writers.

What is clear from both Southern and Jewish writing is that in a society increasingly disturbed about its lack of self-definition, the recall of regional and traditional details can be intensely absorbing in its own right, as well as suggestive
of larger themes transcending the region. (For the Jewish writers New York was
not merely a place, it was a symbol, a burden, a stamp of history.) Yet the writers
of neither school have thus far managed to move from their particular milieu to a
grasp of the entire culture; the very strengths of their localism define their limitations; and especially is this true for the Jewish writers, in whose behalf critics have
recently overreached themselves.

Whatever the hopeful future of individual writers, the "school" of American
Jewish writing is by now in an advanced state of decomposition: how else to explain the attention it has lately enjoyed? Or the appearance of a generation of
younger Jewish writers who, without authentic experience or memory to draw
upon, manufacture fantasies about the lives of their grandfathers? Or the popularity of Isaac Bashevis Singer, who, coming to the American literary scene precisely

at the moment when writers composing in English had begun to exhaust the Jewish subject, could, by dazzling contrast, extend it endlessly backward in time and deeper in historical imagination?

Just as there appear today young Jewish intellectuals who no longer know what it is that as Jews they do not know, so in fiction the fading immigrant world offers a thinner and thinner yield to writers of fiction. It no longer presses on memory; people can now *choose* whether to care about it. We are almost at the end of a historic experience, and it now seems unlikely that there will have arisen in New York a literary school comparable to the best this country has had. Insofar as the New York intellectual atmosphere has affected writers like Schwartz, Rosenfeld, Bellow, Malamud, Mailer, Goodman, and Philip Roth, it seems to have been too brittle, too contentious, too insecure for major creative work. What cannot yet be estimated is the extent to which the styles and values of the New York world may have left a mark on the work of American writers who never came directly under its influence.

Thinking back upon intellectual life in the forties and fifties, and especially the air of malaise that hung over it, I find myself turning to a theme as difficult to clarify as it is impossible to evade. And here, for a few paragraphs, let me drop the porous shield of impersonality and speak openly in the first person.

7

We were living directly after the holocaust of the European Jews. We might scorn our origins; we might crush America with discoveries of ardor; we might change our names. But we knew that but for an accident of geography we might also now be bars of soap. At least some of us could not help feeling that in our earlier claims to have shaken off all ethnic distinctiveness there had been something false, something shaming. Our Jewishness might have no clear religious or national content, it might be helpless before the criticism of believers; but Jews we were, like it or not, and liked or not.

To recognize that we were living after one of the greatest catastrophes of human history, and one for which we could not claim to have adequately prepared ourselves either as intellectuals or as human beings, brought a new rush of feelings, mostly unarticulated and hidden behind the scrim of consciousness. It brought a low-charged but nagging guilt, a quiet remorse. Sartre's brilliant essay on authentic and inauthentic Jews left a strong mark. Hannah Arendt's book on totalitarianism had an equally strong impact, mostly because it offered a coherent theory, or at least a coherent picture of the concentration-camp universe. We could no longer escape the conviction that, blessing or curse, Jewishness was an integral part of our life, even if—and perhaps just because—there was nothing we could do or say about it. Despite a few simulated seders and literary raids on Hasidism, we could not turn back to the synagogue; we could only express our irritation with "the community" which kept nagging us like disappointed mothers; and sometimes we tried, through imagination and recall, to put together a few bits and pieces of the world of our fathers. I cannot prove a connection between the holocaust and the turn to Jewish themes in American fiction, at first urgent and quizzical, later fashionable and manipulative. I cannot prove that my own turn to Yiddish literature during the fifties was due to the shock following the war years. But it would be foolish to scant the possibility.

The violent dispute which broke out among the New York intellectuals when Hannah Arendt published her book on Eichmann had as one of its causes a sense of guilt concerning the Jewish tragedy—a guilt pervasive, unmanageable, yet seldom declared. In the quarrel between those attacking and those defending *Eichmann in Jerusalem* there were polemical excesses on both sides, since both were acting out of unacknowledged passions. Yet even in the debris of this quarrel there was, I think, something good. At least everyone was acknowledging emotions that had long gone unused. Nowhere else in American academic and intellectual life was there such ferocity of concern with the problems raised by Hannah Arendt. If left to the rest of the American intellectual world, her book would have been praised as "stimulating" and "thoughtful," and then everyone would have gone back to sleep. Nowhere else in the country could there have been the kind of public forum sponsored on this subject by *Dissent*: a debate sometimes ugly and outrageous, yet also urgent and afire—evidence that in behalf of ideas we were still ready to risk personal relationships. After all, it had never been dignity that we could claim as our strong point.

Nothing about the New York writers is more remarkable than the sheer fact of their survival. In a country where tastes in culture change more rapidly than lengths of skirts, they have succeeded in maintaining a degree of influence, as well as a distinctive milieu, for more than thirty years. Apart from reasons intrinsic to the intellectual life, let me note a few that are somewhat more worldly in nature.

There is something, perhaps a quasireligious dynamism, about an ideology, even a lapsed ideology that everyone says has reached its end, which yields force and coherence to those who have closely experienced it. A lapsed Catholic has tactical advantages in his apostasy which a lifelong skeptic does not have. And just as Christianity kept many nineteenth-century writers going long after they had discarded religion, so Marxism gave bite and edge to the work of twentieth-century writers long after they had turned from socialism.

The years in which the New York writers gained some prominence were those in which the style at which they had arrived—irony, ambiguity, complexity, the problematic as mode of knowledge—took on a magnified appeal for the American educated classes. In the fifties the cultivation of private sensibility and personal responsibility were values enormously popular among reflective people, to whom the very thought of public life smacked of betrayal and vulgarity.

An intelligentsia flourishes in a capital: Paris, St. Petersburg, Berlin. The influence of the New York writers grew at the time New York itself, for better or worse, became the cultural center of the country. And thereby the New York writers slowly shed the characteristics of an intelligentsia and transformed themselves into—

An Establishment?

Perhaps. But what precisely is an Establishment? Vaguely sinister in its overtones, the term is used these days with gay abandon on the American campus; but except as a spread-eagle put-down it has no discernible meaning, and if accepted as a put-down, the problem then becomes to discover who, if anyone, is not in the Establishment. In England the term has had a certain clarity of usage, referring to an intellectual elite which derives from the same upper and middle classes as the men who wield political power and which shares with these men Oxbridge education and Bloomsbury culture. But except in F. R. Leavis's angrier tirades, "Establishment" does not bear the conspiratorial overtones we are inclined to credit in this country. What it does in England is to locate the social-cultural stratum guiding the tastes of the classes in power and thereby crucially affecting the tastes of the country as a whole.

In this sense, neither the New York writers nor any other group can be said to comprise an American Establishment, simply because no one in this country has ever commanded an equivalent amount of cultural power. The New York writers have few, if any, connections with a stable class of upper-rank civil servants or with a significant segment of the rich. They are without connections in Washington. They do not shape official or dominant tastes. And they cannot exert the kind of control over cultural opinion that the London Establishment is said to have maintained until recently. Critics like Trilling and Kazin are listened to by people in publishing, Rosenberg and Greenberg by people in the art world; but this hardly constitutes anything so formidable as an Establishment. Indeed, at the very time mutterings have been heard about a New York literary Establishment, there has occurred a rapid disintegration of whatever group ties may still have remained among the New York writers. They lack—and it is just as well—the first requirement for an Establishment: that firm sense of internal discipline which enables it to impose its taste on a large public.

During the last few years the talk about a New York Establishment has taken an unpleasant turn. Whoever does a bit of lecturing about the country is likely to encounter, after a few drinks, literary academics who inquire enviously, sometimes spitefully, about "what's new in New York." Such people seem to feel that exile in outlying regions means they are missing something remarkable (and so they are: the Balanchine company). The cause of their cultural envy is, I think, a notion that has become prevalent in our English departments that scholarship is somehow unworthy and the "real" literary life is to be found in the periodical journalism of New York. Intrinsically this is a dubious notion, and for the future of American education a disastrous one; when directed against the New York writers it leads to some painful situations. As polite needling questions are asked about the cultural life of New York, a rise of sweat comes to one's brow, for everyone knows what no one says: New York means Jews.*

Whatever the duration or extent of the influence enjoyed by the New York intellectuals, it is now reaching an end. There are signs of internal disarray: unhealed wounds, a dispersal of interests, the damage of time. More important, however, is the appearance these last few years of a new and powerful challenge to the New York writers. And here I shall have to go off on what may appear to be a long digression, since one cannot understand the present situation of the New York writers without taking into account the cultural-political scene of America in the late sixties.

8

There is a rising younger generation of intellectuals: ambitious, self-assured, at ease with prosperity while conspicuously alienated, unmarred by the traumas of the totalitarian age, bored with memories of defeat, and attracted to the idea of power. This generation matters, thus far, not so much for its leading figures and their meager accomplishments, but for the political-cultural style—what I shall call the "new sensibility"—it thrusts into absolute opposition against both the New York writers and other groups. It claims not to seek penetration into, or accommodation with, our cultural and academic institutions; it fancies the pros-

---

* Not quite no one. In an attack on the New York writers (*Hudson Review*, Autumn 1965) Richard Kostelanetz speaks about "Jewish group-aggrandizement" and "the Jewish American push." One notices the delicacy of his phrasing.

pect of a harsh generational fight; and given the premise with which it begins—
that everything touched by older writers reeks of betrayal—its claims and fancies
have a sort of propriety. It proposes a revolution—I would call it a counterrevolution—in sensibility. Though linked to New Left politics, it goes beyond any
politics, making itself felt, like a spreading blot of anti-intellectualism, in every
area of intellectual life. Not yet fully cohered, this new cultural group cannot yet
be fully defined, nor is it possible fully to describe its projected sensibility, since it
declares itself through a refusal of both coherence and definition.

There is no need to discuss once more the strengths and weaknesses of the
New Left, its moral energies and intellectual muddles. Nor need we be concerned
with the tactical issues separating New Left politics from that of older left-wing
intellectuals. Were nothing else at stake than, say, "coalition politics," the differences would be both temporary and tolerable. But in reality a deeper divergence
of outlook has begun to show itself. The new intellectual style, insofar as it ap-
proximates a politics, mixes sentiments of anarchism with apologies for authoritarianism; bubbling hopes for "participatory democracy" with manipulative elitism; unqualified populist majoritarianism with the reign of the cadres.

A confrontation of intellectual outlooks is unavoidable. And a central issue is
certain to be the problem of liberalism, not liberalism as one or another version
of current politics, nor even as a theory of power, but liberalism as a cast of mind,
a structure of norms by means of which to humanize public life. For those of us
who have lived through the age of totalitarianism and experienced the debacle of
socialism, this conflict over liberal values is extremely painful. We have paid heavily for the lesson that democracy, even "bourgeois democracy," is a precious human achievement, one that, far from being simply a mode of mass manipulation,
has been wrested through decades of struggle by the labor, socialist, and liberal
movements. To protect the values of liberal democracy, often against those who
call themselves liberals, is an elementary task for intellectuals as a social group.

Yet what I have just been saying has in the last few years aroused opposition,
skepticism, open contempt among professors, students, and intellectuals. On
the very crudest, though by no means unpopular level, we find a vulgarization
of an already vulgar Marxism. The notion that we live in a society that can be
described as "liberal fascism" (a theoretic contribution from certain leaders of
the Students for a Democratic Society) isn't one to be taken seriously; but the
fact that it is circulated in the academic community signifies a counterrevolution
of the mind: a refusal of nuance and observation, a willed return to the kind of
political primitivism which used to declare the distinctions of bourgeois rule—
democratic, authoritarian, totalitarian—as slight in importance.

For the talk about "liberal fascism" men like Norman Mailer must bear a heavy responsibility, insofar as they have recklessly employed the term "totalitarian" as a descriptive for present-day American society. Having lived through the ghastliness of the Stalinist theory of "Social Fascism" (the granddaddy of "liberal fascism") I cannot suppose any literate person really accepts this kind of nonsense, yet I know that people can find it politically expedient to pretend that they do.

There are sophisticated equivalents. One of these points to the failings and crises of democracy, concluding that the content of decision has been increasingly separated from the forms of decision-making. Another emphasizes the manipulation of the masses by communication media and declares them brainwashed victims incapable of rational choice and acquiescing in their own subjugation. A third decries the bureaucratic entanglements of the political process and favors some version, usually more sentiment than scheme, for direct plebiscitary rule. With varying intelligence, all point to acknowledged problems of democratic society; and there could be no urgent objection were these criticisms not linked with the premise that the troubles of democracy can be overcome by undercutting or bypassing representative institutions. Thus, it is quite true that the masses are manipulated, but to make that the crux of a political analysis is to lead into the notion that elections are mere "formalities" and majorities mere tokens of the inauthentic; what is needed, instead, is Herbert Marcuse's "educational dictatorship" (in which, I hope, at least some of the New York intellectuals would require the most prolonged reeducation). And in a similar vein, all proposals for obligatory or pressured "participation," apart from violating the democratic right not to participate, have a way of discounting those representative institutions and limitations upon power which can alone provide a degree of safeguard for liberal norms.

Perhaps the most sophisticated and currently popular of anti-democratic notions is that advanced by Marcuse: his contempt for tolerance on the ground that it is a rationale for maintaining the status quo, and his consequent readiness to suppress "regressive" elements of the population lest they impede social "liberation." About these theories, which succeed in salvaging the worst of Leninism, Henry David Aiken has neatly remarked: "Whether garden-variety liberties can survive the ministrations of such 'liberating tolerance' is not a question that greatly interests Marcuse." Indeed not.

Such theories are no mere academic indulgence or sectarian irrelevance; they have been put to significant use on the American campus as rationalizations for breaking up meetings of political opponents and as the justification for imaginary coups d'état by tiny minorities of enraged intellectuals. How depressing that "men of the left," themselves so often victims of repression, should attack the values of tolerance and freedom.*

These differences concerning liberal norms run very deep and are certain to affect American intellectual life in the coming years; yet they do not quite get to the core of the matter. In the Kulturkampf now emerging there are issues more consequential than the political ones, issues that have to do with the nature of human life.

One of these has been with us for a long time, and trying now to put it into simple language, I feel a measure of uneasiness, as if it were bad form to violate the tradition of antinomianism in which we have all been raised.

What, for "emancipated" people, is the surviving role of moral imperatives, or at least moral recommendations? Do these retain for us a shred of sanctity or at least of coercive value? The question to which I am moving is not, of course, whether the moral life is desirable or men should try to live it; no, the question has to do with the provenance and defining conditions of the moral life. Do moral principles continue to signify insofar as and if they come into conflict with spontaneous impulses, and more urgently still, can we conceive of moral principles retaining some validity if they do come into conflict with spontaneous impulses? Are we still to give credit to the idea, one of the few meeting points between traditional Christianity and modern Freudianism, that there occurs and must occur a deep-seated clash between instinct and civilization, or can we now, with a great sigh of collective relief, dismiss this as still another hang-up, perhaps the supreme hang-up, of Western civilization?

For more than one hundred and fifty years there has been a line of Western thought, as also of sentiment in modern literature, which calls into question not

---

* That Marcuse chooses not to apply his theories to the area of society in which he himself functions is a tribute to his personal realism, or perhaps merely a sign of a lack of intellectual seriousness. In a recent public discussion, recorded by the *New York Times Magazine* (May 26, 1968), there occurred the following exchange:

Hentoff: We've been talking about new institutions, new structures, as the only way to get fundamental change. What would that mean to you, Mr. Marcuse, in terms of the university, in terms of Columbia?

Marcuse: I was afraid of that because I now finally reveal myself as a fink. I have never suggested or advocated or supported destroying the established universities and building new anti-institutions instead. I have always said that no matter how radical the demands of the students and no matter how justified, they should be pressed within the existing universities. . . . I believe—and this is where the finkdom comes in—that American universities, at least quite a few of them, today are still enclaves of relatively critical thought and relatively free thought.

one or another moral commandment or regulation, but the very idea of commandment and regulation; which insists that the ethic of control, like the ethic of work, should be regarded as spurious, a token of a centuries-long heritage of repression. Sometimes this view comes to us as a faint residue of Christian heresy, more recently as the blare of Nietzschean prophecy, and in our own day as a psychoanalytic gift.

Now even those of us raised on the premise of revolt against the whole system of bourgeois values did not—I suppose it had better be said outright—imagine ourselves to be exempt from the irksome necessity of regulation, even if we had managed to escape the reach of the commandments. Neither primitive Christians nor romantic naifs, we did not suppose that we could entrust ourselves entirely to the beneficence of nature, or the signals of our bodies, as a sufficient guide to conduct. (My very use of the word "conduct," freighted as it is with normative associations, puts the brand of time on what I am saying.)

By contrast, the emerging new sensibility rests on a vision of innocence: an innocence through lapse or will or recovery, an innocence through a refusal of our and perhaps any other culture, an innocence not even to be preceded by the withering away of the state, since in this view of things the state could wither away only if men learned so to be at ease with their desires that all need for regulation would fade. This is a vision of life beyond good and evil, not because these experiences or possibilities of experience have been confronted and transcended, but because the categories by which we try to designate them have been dismissed. There is no need to taste the apple: the apple brings health to those who know how to bite it: and look more closely: there is no apple at all; it exists only in your sickened imagination.

The new sensibility posits a theory that might be called *the psychology of unobstructed need*: men should satisfy those needs which are theirs, organic to their bodies and psyches, and to do this they must learn to discard or destroy all those obstructions, mostly the result of cultural neurosis, which keep them from satisfying their needs. This does not mean that the moral life is denied; it only means that in the moral economy costs need not be entered as a significant item. In the current vocabulary it becomes a matter of everyone doing "his own thing," and once everyone is allowed to do "his own thing," a prospect of easing harmony unfolds. Sexuality is the ground of being, and vital sexuality the assurance of the moral life.

Whether this outlook is compatible with a high order of culture or a complex civilization I shall not discuss here; Freud thought they were not compatible, though that does not foreclose the matter. More immediately, and on a less exalted plane, one is troubled by the following problem: what if the needs and impulses of human beings clash, as they seem to do, and what if the transfer of energies from sexuality to sociality does not proceed with the anticipated abundance and smoothness? The new sensibility, as displayed in the writings of Norman Brown and Norman Mailer, falls back upon a curious analogue to laissez-faire economics: Adam Smith's invisible hand, by means of which innumerable units in conflict with one another achieve a resultant of cooperation. Is there, however, much reason to suppose that this will prove more satisfactory in the economy of moral conduct than it has in the morality of economic relations?

Suppose that, after reading Mailer's "The White Negro," my "thing" happens to be that, to "dare the unknown" (as Mailer puts it), I want to beat in the brains of an aging candy-store keeper; or after reading LeRoi Jones, I should like to cut up a few Jews, whether or not they keep stores—how is anyone going to argue against the outpouring of my need? Who will declare himself its barrier? Against me, against my ideas it is possible to argue, but how, according to this new dispensation, can anyone argue against my *need*? Acting through violence I will at least have realized myself, for I will have entered (to quote Mailer again) "a new relation with the police" and introduced "a dangerous element" into my life; thereby too I will have escaped the cellblock of regulation which keeps me from the free air of self-determination. And if you now object that this very escape may lead to brutality, you reveal yourself as hopelessly linked to imperfection and original sin. For why should anyone truly heeding his nature wish to kill or wound or do anything but love and make love? That certain spokesmen of the new sensibility seem to be boiling over with fantasies of blood, or at least suppose that a verbal indulgence in such fantasies is a therapy for the boredom in their souls, is a problem for dialecticians. And as for skeptics, what have they to offer but evidence from history, that European contamination?

When it is transposed to a cultural setting, this psychology—in earlier times it would have been called a moral psychology—provokes a series of disputes over "complexity" in literature. Certain older critics find much recent writing distasteful and tiresome because it fails to reach or grasp for that complexity which they regard as intrinsic to the human enterprise. More indulgent critics, not always younger, find the same kind of writing forceful, healthy, untangled. At first this seems a mere problem in taste, a pardonable difference between those who like their poems and novels knotty and those who like them smooth; but soon it becomes clear that this clash arises from a meeting of incompatible world outlooks. For if the psychology of unobstructed need is taken as a sufficient guide to life, it all but eliminates any place for complexity—or, rather, the need for complexity comes to be seen as a mode of false consciousness, an evasion of true feelings, a psychic bureaucratism in which to trap the pure and the strong. If good sex signifies good feeling; good feeling, good being; good being, good action; and good action, a healthy polity, then we have come the long way round, past the Reichian way or the Lawrentian way, to an Emersonian romanticism minus Emerson's complicatedness of vision. The world snaps back into a system of burgeoning potentialities, waiting for free spirits to attach themselves to the richness of natural object and symbol—except that now the orgasmic blackout is to replace the Oversoul as the current through which pure transcendent energies will flow.

9

We are confronting, then, a new phase in our culture, which in motive and spring represents a wish to shake off the bleeding heritage of modernism and reinstate one of those periods of the collective naif which seem endemic to American experience. The new sensibility is impatient with ideas. It is impatient with literary structures of complexity and coherence, only yesterday the catchwords of our criticism. It wants instead works of literature—though literature may be the wrong word—that will be as absolute as the sun, as unarguable as orgasm, and as delicious as a lollipop. It schemes to throw off the weight of nuance and ambiguity, legacies of high consciousness and tired blood. It is weary of the habit of reflection, the making of distinctions, the squareness of dialectic, the tarnished gold of inherited wisdom. It cares nothing for the haunted memories of old Jews. It has no taste for the ethical nail-biting of those writers of the left who suffered defeat and could never again accept the narcotic of certainty. It is sick of those magnifications of irony that Mann gave us, sick of those visions of entrapment to which Kafka led us, sick of those shufflings of daily horror and grace that Joyce left us. It breathes contempt for rationality, impatience with mind, and a hostility to the artifices and decorums of high culture. It despises liberal values, liberal cautions, liberal virtues. It is bored with the past: for the past is a fink.

Where Marx and Freud were diggers of intellect, mining deeper and deeper into society and the psyche, and forever determined to strengthen the dominion of reason, today the favored direction of search is not inward but sideways, an "expansion of consciousness" through the kick of drugs. The new sensibility is drawn to images of sickness, but not, as with the modernist masters, out of dialectical canniness or religious blasphemy; it takes their denials literally and does not even know the complex desperations that led them to deny. It seeks to charge itself into dazzling sentience through chemicals and the rhetoric of violence. It gropes for sensations: the innocence of blue, the ejaculations of red. It *ordains* life's simplicity. It chooses surfaces as against relationships, the skim of texture rather than the weaving of pattern. Haunted by boredom, it transforms art into a sequence of shocks which, steadily magnified, yield fewer and fewer thrills, so that simply to maintain a modest frisson requires mounting exertions. It proposes an art as disposable as a paper dress, to which one need give nothing but a flicker of notice. Especially in the theater it resurrects tattered heresies, trying to collapse aesthetic distance in behalf of touch and frenzy. (But if illusion is now worn out, what remains but staging the realities of rape, fellatio, and murder?) Cutting itself off from a knowledge of what happened before the moment of its birth, it repeats with a delighted innocence much of what did in fact happen: expressionist drama reduced to skit, agitprop tumbled to farce, Melvillean anguish slackened to black humor. It devalues the word, which is soaked up with too much past history, and favors monochromatic cartoons, companionate grunts, and glimpses of the ineffable in popular ditties. It has humor, but not much wit. Of the tragic it knows next to nothing. Where Dostoevsky made nihilism seem sinister by painting it in jolly colors, the new American sensibility does something no other culture could have aspired to: it makes nihilism seem casual, good-natured, even innocent. No longer burdened by the idea of the problematic, it arms itself with the paraphernalia of postindustrial technique and crash-dives into a Typee of neoprimitivism.

Its high priests are Norman Brown, Herbert Marcuse, and Marshall McLuhan,* all writers with a deeply conservative bias: all committed to a stasis of the given: the stasis of unmoving instinct, the stasis of unmovable society, the stasis of endlessly moving technology. Classics of the latest thing, these three figures lend the new sensibility an aura of profundity. Their prestige can be employed to suggest an organic link between cultural modernism and the new sensibility, though in reality their relation to modernism is no more than biographical.

---

* John Simon has some cogent things to say about Brown and McLuhan, the pop poppas of the new: ". . . like McLuhan, Brown fulfills the four requirements for our prophets: (1) to span and reconcile, however grotesquely, various disciplines to the relief of a multitude of specialists; (2) to affirm something, even if it is something negative, retrogressive, mad; (3) to justify something vulgar or sick or indefensible in us, whether it be television-addiction (McLuhan) or schizophrenia (Brown); (4) to abolish the need for discrimination, difficult choices, balancing mind and appetite, and so reduce the complex orchestration of life to the easy strumming of a monochord. Brown and McLuhan have nicely apportioned the world between them: the inward madness for the one, the outward manias for the other."

Perhaps because it is new, some of the new style has its charms—mainly along
the margins of social life, in dress, music, and slang. In that it captures the yearnings of a younger generation, the new style has more than charm: a vibration of
moral desire, a desire for goodness of heart. Still, we had better not deceive ourselves. Some of those shiny-cheeked darlings adorned with flowers and tokens of
love can also be campus *enragés* screaming "Up Against the Wall, Motherfuckers,
This Is a Stickup" (a slogan that does not strike one as a notable improvement
over "Workers of the World, Unite").

That finally there should appear an impulse to shake off the burdens and entanglements of modernism need come as no surprise. After all the virtuosos of
torment and enigma we have known, it would be fine to have a period in Western
culture devoted to relaxed pleasures and surface hedonism. But so far this does
not seem possible. What strikes one about a great deal of the new writing and
theater is its grindingly ideological tone, even if now the claim is for an ideology of pleasure. And what strikes one even more is the air of pulsing *ressentiment*
which pervades this work, an often unearned and seemingly inexplicable hostility. If one went by the cues of a critic like Susan Sontag, one might suppose that
the ethical torments of Kamenetz Podolsk and the moral repressiveness of Salem,
Massachusetts, had finally been put to rest, in favor of creamy delights in texture,
color, and sensation. But nothing of the sort is true, at least not yet; it is only
advertised.

Keen on tactics, the spokesmen for the new sensibility proclaim it to be still
another turn in the endless gyrations of modernism, still another revolt in the permanent revolution of twentieth-century sensibility. This approach is very shrewd,
since it can disarm in advance those older New York (and other) critics who still
respond with enthusiasm to modernism. But several objections or qualifications
need to be registered:

Modernism, by its very nature, is uncompromisingly a minority culture, creating and defining itself through opposition to a dominant culture. Today, however,
nothing of the sort is true. Floodlights glaring and tills overflowing, the new sensibility is a success from the very start. The middle-class public, eager for thrills
and humiliations, welcomes it; so do the mass media, always on the alert for
exploitable sensations; and naturally there appear intellectuals with handy theories. The new sensibility is both embodied and celebrated in the actions of Mailer,
whose condition as a swinger in America is not quite comparable with that of
Joyce in Trieste or Kafka in Prague or Lawrence anywhere; it is reinforced with
critical exegesis by Susan Sontag, a publicist able to make brilliant quilts from

grandmother's patches. And on a far lower level, it has even found its Smerdyakov in LeRoi Jones, that parodist of apocalypse who rallies enlightened Jewish audiences with calls for Jewish blood. Whatever one may think of this situation, it is surely very different from the classical picture of a besieged modernism.

By now the search for the "new," often reduced to a trivializing of form and matter, has become the predictable old. To suppose that we keep moving from cultural breakthrough to breakthrough requires a collective wish to forget what happened yesterday and even the day before: ignorance always being a great spur to claims for originality. Alienation has been transformed from a serious revolutionary concept into a motif of mass culture, and the content of modernism into the decor of kitsch. As Harold Rosenberg has pungently remarked:

> The sentiment of the diminution of personality is an historical hypothesis upon which writers have constructed a set of literary conventions by this time richly equipped with theatrical machinery and symbolic allusions. . . . The individual's emptiness and inability to act have become an irrefrangible cliché, untiringly supported by an immense, voluntary phalanx of latecomers to modernism. In this manifestation, the notion of the void has lost its critical edge and is thoroughly reactionary.

The effort to assimilate new cultural styles to the modernist tradition brushes aside problems of value, quality, judgment. It rests upon a philistine version of the theory of progress in the arts: all must keep changing, and change signifies a realization of progress. Yet even if an illicit filiation can be shown, there is a vast difference in accomplishment between the modernism of some decades ago and what we have now. The great literary modernists put at the center of their work a confrontation and struggle with the demons of nihilism; the literary swingers of the sixties, facing a nihilist violation, cheerfully remove the threat by what Fielding once called "a timely compliance." Just as in the verse of Swinburne echoes of Romanticism sag through the stanzas, so in much current writing there is indeed a continuity with modernism, but a continuity of grotesque and parody, through the doubles of fashion.

Still, it would be foolish to deny that in this Kulturkampf, the New York intellectuals are at a severe disadvantage. Some have simply gone over to the other camp. A critic like Susan Sontag employs the dialectical skills and accumulated knowledge of intellectual life in order to bless the new sensibility as a dispensation of pleasure, beyond the grubby reach of interpretation and thereby, it would seem, beyond the tight voice of judgment. That her theories are skillfully rebuilt

versions of aesthetic notions long familiar and discarded; that in her own critical writing she interprets like mad and casts an image anything but hedonistic,
relaxed, or sensuous—none of this need bother her admirers, for a highly literate
spokesman is very sustaining to those who have discarded or not acquired intellectual literacy. Second only to Sontag in trumpeting the new sensibility is Leslie
Fiedler, a critic with an amiable weakness for thrusting himself at the head of
parades marching into sight.*

But for those New York (or any other) writers not quite enchanted with the current scene there are serious difficulties.

They cannot be quite *sure*. Having fought in the later battles for modernism,
they must acknowledge to themselves the possibility that, now grown older, they
have lost their capacity to appreciate innovation. Why, they ask themselves with
some irony, should "their" cultural revolution have been the last one, or the last
good one? From the publicists of the new sensibility they hear the very slogans,
catchwords, and stirring appeals which a few decades ago they were hurling
against such diehards as Van Wyck Brooks and Bernard de Voto. And given the
notorious difficulties in making judgments about contemporary works of art,
how can they be certain that Kafka is a master of despair and Burroughs a symptom of disintegration, Pollock a pioneer of innovation and Warhol a triviality of
pop? The capacity for self-doubt, the habit of self-irony which is the reward of decades of experience, renders them susceptible to the simplistic cries of the new.

---

* Fiedler's essay "The New Mutants" (*Partisan Review*, Fall 1965) is a sympathetic charting
of the new sensibility, with discussions of "pornoesthetics," the effort among young people to
abandon habits and symbols of masculinity in favor of a feminized receptiveness, "the aspiration to take the final evolutionary leap and cast off adulthood completely," and above all, the
role of drugs as "the crux of the futurist revolt."

With uncharacteristic forbearance, Fiedler denies himself any sustained or explicit judgments of this "futurist revolt," so that the rhetorical thrust of his essay is somewhere between
acclaim and resignation. He cannot completely suppress his mind, perhaps because he has
been using it too long, and so we find this acute passage concerning the responses of older
writers to "the most obscene forays of the young": ". . . after a while, there will be no more Philip
Rahvs and Stanley Edgar Hymans left to shock—antilanguage becoming mere language with
repeated use and in the face of acceptance; so that all sense of exhilaration will be lost along
with the possibility of offense. What to do then except to choose silence, since raising the ante
of violence is ultimately self-defeating; and the way of obscenity in any case leads as naturally to
silence as to further excess?"

About drugs Fiedler betrays no equivalent skepticism, so that it is hard to disagree with Lionel Abel's judgment that, "while I do not want to charge Mr. Fiedler with recommending the
taking of drugs, I think his whole essay is a confession that he cannot call upon one value in
whose name he could oppose it."

Well, the answer is that there can be no certainty: we should neither want nor need it. One must speak out of one's taste and conviction, and let history make whatever judgments it will care to. But this is not an easy stand to take, for it means that after all these years one may have to face intellectual isolation, and there are moments when it must seem as if the best course is to be promiscuously "receptive," swinging along with a grin of resignation.

10

In the face of this challenge, surely the most serious of the last twenty-five years, the New York intellectuals have not been able to mount a coherent response, certainly not a judgment sufficiently inclusive and severe. There have been a few efforts, some intellectual polemics by Lionel Abel and literary pieces by Philip Rahv; but no more. Yet if ever there was a moment when our culture needed an austere and sharp criticism—the one talent the New York writers supposedly find it death to hide—it is today. One could imagine a journal with the standards, if not the parochialism, of *Scrutiny*. One could imagine a journal like *Partisan Review* stripping the pretensions of the current scene with the vigor it showed in opposing the Popular Front and neoconservative cultures. But these are fantasies. In its often accomplished pages *Partisan Review* betrays a hopeless clash between its editors' capacity to apply serious standards and their yearnings to embrace the moment. Predictably, the result leaves everyone dissatisfied.

One example of the failure of the New York writers to engage in criticism is their relation to Mailer. He is not an easy man to come to grips with, for he is "our genius," probably the only one, and in more than a merely personal way he is a man of enormous charm. Yet Mailer has been the central and certainly most dramatic presence in the new sensibility, even if in reflective moments he makes clear his ability to brush aside its incantations.* Mailer as thaumaturgist of orgasm; as metaphysician of the gut; as psychic herb-doctor; as advance man for literary

---

* Two examples: "Tom Hayden began to discuss revolution with Mailer. 'I'm for Kennedy,' said Mailer, 'because I'm not so sure I want a revolution. Some of those kids are awfully dumb.' Hayden the Revolutionary said a vote for George Wallace would further his objective more than a vote for RFK." (*Village Voice*, May 30, 1968—and by the way, some Revolutionary!) "If he still took a toke of marijuana from time to time for Auld Lang Syne, or in recognition of the probability that good sex had to be awfully good before it was better than on pot, yet, still!—Mailer was not in approval of any drug, he was virtually conservative about it, having demanded of his eighteen-year-old daughter . . . that she not take marijuana, and never LSD, until she completed her education, a mean promise to extract in these apocalyptic times." (*The Armies of the Night.*)

violence;* as dialectician of unreason; and above all, as a novelist who has laid waste his own formidable talent—these masks of brilliant, nutty restlessness, these papery dikes against squalls of boredom—all require sharp analysis and criticism. Were Mailer to read these lines he would surely grin and exclaim that, whatever else, his books have suffered plenty of denunciation. My point, however, is not that he has failed to receive adverse reviews, including some from such New York critics as Norman Podhoretz, Elizabeth Hardwick, and Philip Rahv; perhaps he has even had too many adverse reviews, given the scope and brightness of his talent. My point is that the New York writers have failed to confront Mailer seriously as an intellectual spokesman, and instead have found it easier to regard him as a hostage to the temper of our times. What has not been forthcoming is a recognition, surely a painful one, that in his major public roles he has come to represent values in deep opposition to liberal humaneness and rational discourse. That the New York critics have refused him this confrontation is both a disservice to Mailer and a sign that, whatever it may once have been, the New York intellectual community no longer exists as a significant force.

An equally telling sign is the recent growth in popularity and influence of the *New York Review of Books*. Emerging at least in part from the New York intellectual milieu, this journal has steadily moved away from the styles and premises with which it began. Its early dependence on those New York writers who lent their names to it and helped establish it seems all but over. The Jewish imprint has been blotted out; the *New York Review*, for all its sharp attacks on current political policies, is thoroughly at home in the worlds of American culture, publishing, and society. It features a strong Anglophile slant in its literary pieces, perhaps in accord with the *New Statesman* formula of blending leftish (and at one time, fellow-traveling) politics with Bloomsbury culture. More precisely, what the *New York Review* has managed to achieve—I find it quite fascinating as a portent of things to come—is a link between campus "leftism" and East Side stylishness, the worlds of Tom Hayden and George Plimpton. Opposition to Communist politics and ideology is frequently presented in the pages of the *New York Review* as if it were an obsolete, indeed a pathetic, hangover from a discredited past or, worse yet, a dark sign of the CIA. A snappish and crude anti-Americanism has swept

---

* In this regard the editor of *Dissent* bears a heavy responsibility. When he first received the manuscript of "The White Negro," he should have expressed in print, if he chose to publish the essay, his objections to the passage in which Mailer discusses the morality of beating up a fifty-year-old storekeeper. That he could not bring himself to risk losing a scoop is no excuse whatever.

over much of its political writing—and to avoid misunderstanding, let me say that by this I do not mean anything so necessary as attacks on the ghastly Vietnam War or on our failures in the cities. And in the hands of writers like Andrew Kopkind (author of the immortal phrase "morality . . . starts at the barrel of a gun"), liberal values and norms are treated with something very close to contempt.

Though itself too sophisticated to indulge in the more preposterous New Left notions, such as "liberal fascism" and "confrontationism," the *New York Review* has done the New Left the considerable service of providing it with a link of intellectual respectability to the academic world. In the materials it has published by Kopkind, Hayden, Rahv, Edgar Z. Friedenberg, Jason Epstein, and others, one finds not an acceptance of the fashionable talk about "revolution" which has become a sport on the American campus, but a kind of rhetorical violence, a verbal "radicalism," which gives moral and intellectual encouragement to precisely such fashionable (self-defeating) talk.

This is by no means the only kind of political material to have appeared in the *New York Review*; at least in my own experience I have found its editors prepared to print articles of a sharply different kind; and in recent years it has published serious political criticism by George Lichtheim, Theodore Draper, and Walter Laqueur. And because it is concerned with maintaining a certain level of sophistication and accomplishment, the *New York Review* has not simply taken over the new sensibility. No, at stake here is the dominant tone of this skillfully edited paper, an editorial keenness in responding to the current academic and intellectual temper—as for instance in that memorable issue with a cover featuring, no doubt for the benefit of its university readers, a diagram explaining how to make a Molotov cocktail. The genius of the *New York Review*, and it has been a genius of sorts, is not, in either politics or culture, for swimming against the stream.

Perhaps it is too late. Perhaps there is no longer available among the New York writers enough energy and coherence to make possible a sustained confrontation with the new sensibility. Still, one would imagine that their undimmed sense of the zeitgeist would prod them to sharp responses, precise statements, polemical assaults.

Having been formed by, and through opposition to, the New York intellectual experience, I cannot look with joy at the prospect of its ending. But not with dismay either. Such breakups are inevitable, and out of them come new voices and energies. Yet precisely at this moment of dispersion, might not some of the New York writers achieve renewed strength if they were to struggle once again for whatever has been salvaged from these last few decades? For the values of liberalism, for the politics of a democratic radicalism, for the norms of rationality and intelligence, for the standards of literary seriousness, for the life of the mind as a humane dedication—for all this it should again be worth finding themselves in a minority, even a beleaguered minority, and not with fantasies of martyrdom but with a quiet recognition that for the intellectual this is likely to be his usual condition.

Irving (on right) at a farm or Fresh Air Camp (?) in the Catskills at age about 10 or 11. This is the earliest known picture of Irving.

Irving with violin at about age 11 or 12.

Irving's graduation picture from CUNY, 1939.

Irving with daughter, Nina, and son, Nicholas, about 1954.

Irving at Stanford University, 1962. Photo credit: Jose Mercado/Stanford News Service.
© Stanford University.

Irving Howe photographed by Jill Krementz on December 18, 1973,
in his apartment on Riverside Drive, New York City.

The 1970s

A Grave and Solitary Voice: An Appreciation of Edwin Arlington Robinson

{1970}

THE CENTENNIAL OF Edwin Arlington Robinson passed several years ago—he was born on December 22, 1869—with barely a murmur of public notice. There were a few academic volumes of varying merit, but no recognition in our larger journals and reviews, for Robinson seems the kind of poet who is likely to remain permanently out of fashion. At first, thinking about this neglect, I felt a surge of anger, since Robinson seems to me one of the best poets we have ever had in this country. But then, cooled by reflection and time, I came to see that perhaps it doesn't matter whether the writers we most care about receive their "due." Only the living need praise. Writers like Robinson survive in their work, appreciated by readers who aren't afraid to be left alone with an old book.

Robinson himself would hardly have expected any other fate, for he was not the sort of man to make demands on either this world or the next. Shy of all literary mobs, just managing to keep afloat through a workable mixture of stoicism and alcohol, he lived entirely for his poetry. Most of the time he was very poor, and all of the time alone, a withdrawn and silent bachelor. He seems to have composed verse with that single-mindedness the rest of us keep for occasions of vanity and profit. As a result he wrote "too much," and his *Collected Poems*, coming almost to

1,500 crowded pages, has a great deal of failed work. But a small portion is very fine, and a group of fifteen or twenty poems unquestionably great.

This, to be sure, is not the received critical judgment—though a few critics, notably Conrad Aiken in some fine reviews of the 1920s and Yvor Winters in a splendid little book published in 1946, have recognized his worth. The public acclaim of a Robert Frost, however, Robinson could never hope to match; the approval of the *avant-garde*, when it came at all, came in lukewarm portions, since T. S. Eliot had declared his work to be "negligible" and that, for a time, was that. Robinson stood apart from the cultural movements of his day, so much so that he didn't even bother to *oppose* literary modernism: he simply followed his own convictions. He was one of those New England solitaries—great-grandsons of the Puritans, nephews of the Emersonians—whose lives seem barren and pinched but who leave, in their stolid devotion to a task, something precious to the world.

The trouble in Robinson's life was mostly interior. Some force of repression, not exactly unknown to New England character, had locked up his powers for living by, or articulating openly, the feelings his poems show him to have had. Even in the poems themselves a direct release of passion or desire is infrequent; they "contain," or emerge out of, enormous depths of feeling, but it is a feeling pressed into oblique irony or disciplined into austere reflection. He was not the man to yield himself to what Henry James once called "promiscuous revelation."

Robinson lived mainly within himself, and sometimes near a group of admiring hangers-on who, as he seems to have known, were unworthy of him. Among his obsessive subjects are solitude and failure, both drawn from his immediate experience and treated with a richness of complication that is unequaled in American poetry. For the insights Robinson offered on these grim topics, in poems such as "The Wandering Jew" and "Eros Turannos," he no doubt paid a heavy price in his own experience. But we should remember that, finally, such preoccupations are neither a regional morbidity nor a personal neurosis: they are among the permanent and inescapable themes of literature. In his own dry and insular way, Robinson shared in the tragic vision that has dominated the imagination of the West since the Greek playwrights. By the time he began to write, it had perhaps become impossible for a serious poet to compose a tragedy on the classical scale, and as a result his sense of the tragic, unable to reach embodiment in a large action, had to emerge—one almost says, leak through—as a tone of voice, a restrained and melancholy contemplativeness.

At the age of twenty-two, Robinson could already write, half in wisdom and half in self-defense, sentences forming an epigraph to his whole career:

Solitude . . . tends to magnify one's ideas of individuality; it sharpens his sympathy for failure where fate has been abused and self demoralized; it renders a man suspicious of the whole natural plan, and leads him to wonder whether the invisible powers are a fortuitous issue of unguided cosmos.

Like Hawthorne and Melville before him, Robinson came from a family that had suffered both a fall in circumstances and a collapse of psychic confidence. To read the one reliable biography, by Herman Hagedorn, is gradually to be drawn into a graying orbit of family nightmare, an atmosphere painfully similar to that of a late O'Neill play. Tight-lipped quarrels, heavy drinking, failing investments, ventures into quack spiritualism and drugs—these were the matter of his youth. Hagedorn describes the few months before the death of the poet's father:

[The elder Robinson's] interest in spiritualism had deepened and, in the slow disintegration of his organism, detached and eerie energies seemed to be released. There were table rappings and once the table came off the floor, "cutting my universe . . . clean in half." . . . Of these last months with his father, he told a friend, "They were a living hell."

Not much better were Robinson's early years in New York, where he slept in a hall bedroom and worked for a time as a subway clerk. He kept writing and won some recognition, including help from President Theodore Roosevelt, who was impressed by one of Robinson's (inferior) poems but had the honesty to admit he didn't understand it. Toward the end of his career Robinson scored his one commercial success with *Tristram*, the least interesting of his three lengthy Arthurian poems. This success did not much affect his life or, for that matter, his view of life. He died in 1935, a victim of cancer. It is said that as Robinson lay dying one of his hangers-on approached him for a small loan: life, as usual, trying to imitate art.

II

The imprint of New England on Robinson's sensibility is strong, but it is not precise. By the time he was growing up in the river-town of Gardner, Maine (the Tilbury Town of his poems), Puritanism was no longer a coherent religious force. It had become at best a collective memory of moral rigor, an ingrained and hardened way of life surviving beyond its original moment of strength. Yet to writers like Hawthorne and Robinson, the New England tradition left a rich inheritance:

the assumption that human existence, caught in a constant inner struggle between good and evil, is inherently dramatic; and the habit of intensive scrutiny,
at once proud and dust-humble, into human motives, such as the old Puritans
had used for discovering whether they were among the elect. Writers like Hawthorne and Robinson were no longer believers but since they still responded to
what they had rejected, they found themselves in a fruitful dilemma. They did
not wish entirely to shake off the inflexible moralism of the New England past;
yet they were fascinated by the psychological study of behavior that would come
to dominate twentieth-century literature and, meanwhile, was both a borrowing
from nineteenth-century European romanticism and a distillation of Puritan habits of mind. The best of the New England writers tried to yoke these two ways of
regarding the human enterprise, and if their attempt is dubious in principle, it
yielded in practice a remarkable subtlety in the investigation of motives. As for
Emersonianism, by the time Robinson was beginning to think for himself it was
far gone in decay, barely discernible as specific doctrine and little more than a
mist of genteel idealism.

Robinson borrowed from both traditions. His weaker poems reveal an Emersonian yearning toward godhead and transcendence, which is an experience
somewhat different from believing in God. His stronger poems share with the
Puritans a cast of mind that is intensely serious, convinced of the irreducibility
of moral problems, and devoted to nuance of motive with the scrupulosity his
grandfathers had applied to nuance of theology. Even in an early, unimpressive
sonnet like "Credo," which begins in a dispirited tone characteristic of much late-
nineteenth-century writing,

> I cannot find my way: there is no star
> In all the shrouded heavens anywhere

Robinson still felt obliged to end with an Emersonian piety:

> I know the far-sent message of the years,
> I feel the coming glory of the Light.

Whenever that "Light" begins to flicker, so tenuous a symbol for the idea of
transcendence, it is a sure sign of trouble in Robinson's poems. A straining toward an optimism in which he has no real conviction, it would soon be overshad-
owed, however, by Robinson's darkening fear, as he later wrote in a long poem
called *King Jasper*, that

No God,
No Law, no Purpose, could have hatched for sport
Out of warm water and slime, a war for life
That was unnecessary, and far better
Never had been—if man, as we behold him,
Is all it means.

Such lines suggest that Robinson's gift was not for strict philosophizing in verse: he was eminently capable of thinking as a poet, but mainly through his arrangement of dramatic particulars and the casual reflections he wove in among them. What makes Robinson's concern with God and the cosmos important is not its doctrinal content, quite as vague in statement and dispirited in tone as that of other sensitive people of his time, but the way in which he would employ it as the groundwork for his miniature dramas. Fairly conventional doctrine thereby becomes the living tissue of suffering and doubt.

It is an advantage for a writer to have come into relation with a great tradition of thought, even if only in its stages of decay, and it can be a still greater advantage to struggle with the problem of salvaging elements of wisdom from that decayed tradition. For while a culture in decomposition may limit the scope of its writers and keep them from the highest achievement, it offers special opportunities for moral drama to those who can maintain their bearing. The traps of such a moment are obvious; nostalgia, on the one extreme, and sensationalism, on the other. Most of the time Robinson was strong enough to resist these temptations, a portion of the old New England steel persisting in his soul; or perhaps he could resist them simply because he was so entirely absorbed in his own sense of the human situation and therefore didn't even trouble about the cultural innovations and discoveries of his time. He made doubt into a discipline, and failure into an opening toward compassion. The old principles of his culture may have crumbled, but he found his subject in the problems experienced by those to whom the allure of those principles had never quite dulled.

III

Many of Robinson's shorter poems—lyrics, ballads, sonnets, dramatic narratives—are set in Tilbury Town, his Down East locale where idlers dream away their lives in harmless fantasy, mild rebels suffer the resistance of a community gone stiff, and the tragedy of personal isolation seems to acquire a universal character, as if speaking for Robinson's vision of America, perhaps all of life. Other

nineteenth-century writers had of course employed a recurrent setting in their
work, and later Faulkner would do the same with Yoknapatawpha County. Yet
Robinson's use of Tilbury Town is rather different from what these writers do: he
makes no attempt to fill out its social world, he cares little about details of place
and moment, he seems hardly to strive for historical depth. Tilbury Town is more
an atmosphere than a setting, it is barely drawn or provisioned, and it serves to
suggest less a vigorous community than a felt lack of historical continuity. The
foreground figures in these poems are drawn with two or three harsh, synoptic
strokes, but Tilbury Town itself is shadowy, fading into the past and no longer able
to bind its people. Robinson eyes it obliquely, half in and half out of its boundaries, a secret sharer taking snapshots of decline. To illuminate a world through
a glimpsed moment of crisis isn't, for him, a mere strategy of composition; it
signifies his deepest moral stance, a nervous signature of reticence and respect.
He seems always to be signaling a persuasion that nothing can be known with
certainty and the very thought of direct assertion is a falsehood in the making.

Some of these Tilbury pieces, as Robinson once remarked, have been "pickled
in anthological brine." Almost "everybody" knows "Miniver Cheevy" and "Richard Corey," sardonic vignettes of small-town character, Yankee drop-outs whose
pitiable condition is contrasted—in quirky lines and comic rhymes—with their
weak fantasies. These are far from Robinson's best poems, but neither are they
contemptible. In the sketch of poor Miniver, who "loved the days of old," there
are flashes of cleverness:

> Miniver mourned the ripe renown
>   That made so many a name so fragrant;
> He mourned Romance, now on the town,
>   And Art, a vagrant.

Such pieces lead to better ones of their kind, such as the tautly written sonnets
about Reuben Bright, the butcher who tears down his slaughterhouse when told
his wife must die, and Aaron Stark, a miser with "eyes like little dollars in the
dark." My experience in teaching these poems is that students trained to floun-
der in The Waste Land will at first condescend, but when asked to read the poems
again, will be unsettled by the depths of moral understanding Robinson has hidden away within them.

The finest of Robinson's sonnets of character is "The Clerks." Describing a return to Tilbury Town, the poet meets old friends, figures of "a shopworn brotherhood," who now work as clerks in stores. The opening octet quietly evokes this

scene, and then in the closing sestet Robinson widens the range of his observation with a powerful statement about the weariness of slow defeat:

> And you that ache so much to be sublime,
> And you that feed yourselves with your descent,
> What comes of all your visions and your fears?
> Poets and kings are but the clerks of Time,
> Tiering the same dull webs of discontent,
> Clipping the same sad alnage of the years.

Without pretending to close analysis, I would like to glance at a few of the perceptual and verbal refinements in these six lines. The opening "ache . . . to be sublime" has its workaday irony that prepares for the remarkable line which follows: to "feed" with "your descent" is a characteristic Robinsonian turn, which in addition to the idea of consuming oneself through age suggests more obliquely that indulgence in vanity which claims distinction for one's decline. Poets and kings who are "clerks of Time" are helplessly aligned with the Tilbury clerks, yet Robinson sees that even in the democracy of our common decay we cling to our trifle of status. For in the "dull webs of discontent" which form the fragile substance of our lives, we still insist on "tiering" ourselves. Coming in the penultimate line, the word "tiering" has enormous ironic thrust: how long can a tier survive as a web? And then in the concluding line Robinson ventures one of his few deviations from standard English, in the use of "alnage," a rare term meaning a measure of cloth, that is both appropriate to the atmosphere of waste built up at the end and overwhelming as it turns us back to the "shop-worn" clerks who are Robinson's original *donnée*.

Now, for readers brought up in the modernist tradition of Eliot and Stevens, these short poems of Robinson will not yield much excitement. They see in such poems neither tangle nor agony, brilliance nor innovation. But they are wrong, for the Tilbury sonnets and lyrics do, in their own way, represent a significant innovation: Robinson was the first American poet of stature to bring commonplace people and commonplace experience into our poetry. Whitman had invoked such people and even rhapsodized over them, but as individual creatures with warm blood they are not really to be found in his pages. Robinson understood that

> Even the happy mortals we term ordinary or commonplace act their own
> mental tragedies and live a far deeper and wider life than we are inclined to
> believe possible. . . .

The point bears stressing because most critics hail poets like Eliot and Stevens for their innovations in metrics and language while condescending toward Robinson as merely traditional. Even if that were true, it would not, of course, be a sufficient reason for judgments either favorable or hostile; but it is not true. Robinson never thought of himself as a poetic revolutionary, but like all major poets he helped enlarge for those who came after him the possibilities of composition. The work of gifted writers like Robert Lowell, James Dickey, and James Wright was enabled by Robinson's muted innovations.

His dramatic miniatures in verse—spiritual dossiers of American experience, as someone has nicely called them—remind one a little of Hawthorne, in their ironic undercurrents and cool explorations of vanity, and a little of James, in their peeling away of psychic pretense and their bias that human relationships are inherently a trap. Yet it would be unjust to say that Robinson was a short-story writer who happened to write verse, for it is precisely through the traditional forms he employed—precisely through his disciplined stanzas, regular meters, and obbligatos of rhyme—that he released his vision. Robinson's language seldom achieves the high radiance of Frost, and few of his short poems are as beautifully complexioned as Frost's "Spring Pools" or "The Most of It." But in Robinson there are sudden plunges into depths of experiences, and then stretches of earned contemplativeness, that Frost can rarely equal. Here, for example, is the octet of a Robinson sonnet, "The Pity of the Leaves," that deals with an experience—an old man alone at night with his foreboding of death—which in "An Old Man's Winter Night" Frost also treated memorably but not, I think, as well:

> Vengeful across the cold November moors,
> Loud with ancestral shame there came the bleak
> Sad wind that shrieked and answered with a shriek,
> Reverberant through lonely corridors.
> The old man heard it; and he heard, perforce,
> Words out of lips that were no more to speak—
> Words of the past that shook the old man's cheek
> Like dead remembered footsteps on old floors.

It is always to "the slow tragedy of haunted men" that Robinson keeps returning. One of his greatest lyrics on this theme, the kind of hypnotic incantation that *happens* to a poet once or twice if he is lucky, is "Luke Havergal": a grieving man hears the voice of his dead love and it draws him like an appetite for death, a beauty of death quiet and enclosing.

The greatest of these Tilbury poems, and one of the greatest poems about the tragedy of love in our language, is "Eros Turannos." Yvor Winters aptly calls it "a universal tragedy in a Maine setting." It deals with a genteel and sensitive woman, advancing in years and never, apparently, a startling beauty, who has married or otherwise engaged herself to a charming wastrel with a taste for the finer things of life:

> She fears him, and will always ask
> What fated her to choose him;
> She meets in his engaging mask
> All reasons to refuse him. . . .

With a fierce concentration of phrase, the poem proceeds to specify the entanglements in which these people trap themselves, the moral confusions and psychic fears, all shown with a rare balance of exactness and compassion. The concluding stanza reaches a wisdom about the human lot such as marks Robinson's poetry at its best. Those, he writes, who with the god of love have striven,

> Not hearing much of what we say,
> Take what the god has given;
> Though like waves breaking it may be,
> Or like a changed familiar tree,
> Or like a stairway to the sea
> Where down the blind are driven.

Thinking of such poems and trying to understand how it is that in their plainness they can yet seem so magnificent, one finds oneself falling back on terms like "sincerity" and "honesty." They are terms notoriously inadequate and tricky, yet inescapable in discussing poets like Robinson and Thomas Hardy. It is not, after all, as if one wants to say about more brilliant poets like Eliot and Yeats that they are insincere or lacking in honesty; of course not. What one does want to suggest is that in poems like Robinson's "Eros Turannos" and "Hillcrest," as in Hardy's "The Going" and "At Castle Boterel," there is an abandonment of all pretense and pose, all protectiveness and persona. At such moments the poet seems beyond decoration and defense; he leaves himself vulnerable, open to the pain of his self; he cares nothing for consolation; he looks at defeat and does not blink. It is literature beyond the literary.

IV

Robinson was also a master of a certain genre poem, Wordsworthian in tone and perhaps source, which Frost also wrote but not, in my judgment, as well. These are poems about lost and aging country people, mostly in New England: "Isaac and Archibald," "Aunt Imogen," and "The Poor Relation." The very titles are likely to displease readers whose hearts tremble before titles like "Leda and the Swan," "The Idea of Order at Key West," and "The Bridge." A pity!

"Isaac and Archibald" is the masterpiece of this group, a summer idyll tinged with shadows of death, told by a mature man remembering himself as a boy who spent an afternoon with two old farmers, lifelong friends, each of whom now frets that the other is showing signs of decay. The verse is exquisite:

> So I lay dreaming of what things I would,
> Calm and incorrigibly satisfied
> With apples and romance and ignorance,
> And the still smoke from Archibald's clay pipe.
> There was a stillness over everything,
> As if the spirit of heat had laid its hand
> Upon the world and hushed it; and I felt
> Within the mightiness of the white sun
> That smote the land around us and wrought out
> A fragrance from the trees, a vital warmth
> And fulness for the time that was to come,
> And a glory for the world beyond the forest.
> The present and the future and the past,
> Isaac and Archibald, the burning bush,
> The Trojans and the walls of Jericho,
> Were beautifully fused; and all went well
> Till Archibald began to fret for Isaac
> And said it was a master day for sunstroke.

Another kind of poem at which Robinson showed his mastery, one that has rarely been written in this country, is the dramatic monologue of medium length. "Rembrandt to Rembrandt," "The Three Taverns" (St. Paul approaching Rome), and "John Brown" are the best examples. The pitfalls of this genre are notorious: an effort to capture the historic inflections of the speaker's voice, so that both conciseness of speech and poetic force are sacrificed to some idea of verisimilitude; a tendency toward linguistic exhibitionism, blank verse as a mode of preening; and a lack of clear focusing of intent, so that the immediate experience of the speaker fails to take on larger resonance. Robinson mostly transcends these difficulties. He chooses figures at moments of high crisis, Rembrandt as he plunges into his dark painting, St. Paul as he ruminates upon his forthcoming capture, and John Brown as he readies himself for hanging. The result is serious in moral perception, leading always to the idea of abandonment of the self, and dignified in tone, for Robinson had little gift for colloquial speech and was shrewd enough to maintain a level of formal diction.

It is Frost who is mainly honored for this kind of dramatic poem, but a sustained comparison would show, I think, the superiority of Robinson's work. Though not nearly so brilliant a virtuoso as Frost, Robinson writes from a fullness of experience and a tragic awareness that Frost cannot equal. Frost has a strong grasp on the melodramatic extremes of behavior, but he lacks almost entirely Robinson's command of its middle ranges. Frost achieves a cleaner verbal surface, but Robinson is more abundant in moral detail and insight.

There remains finally a word to be said about Robinson's Arthurian poems, *Merlin*, *Lancelot*, and *Tristram*, the first two of which are very considerable productions. I am aware of straining my readers' credulity in saying that *Merlin* and *Lancelot*, set in the court of King Arthur and dealing with the loves and intrigues of his knights, are profound explorations of human suffering.

Tennyson's *Idylls of the King*, dealing with the same materials, is mainly a pictorial representation of waxen figures, beautiful in the way a tapestry might be but not very gripping as drama. Robinson's Guinevere and Lancelot, however, are errant human beings separated from us only by costume and time; his Merlin is an aging man of worldly power and some wisdom who finds himself drawn to the temptations of private life. Long poems are bound to have flaws, in this case excessive talk and a spun-thin moral theorizing that can become tedious. There is the further problem that any effort at sustained blank verse will, by now, lead to padding and looseness of language. Still, these are poems for mature men and women who know that in the end we are all as we are, vulnerable and mortal. Here Merlin speaks at the end of his career, remembering his love:

> Let her love
> What man she may, no other love than mine
> Shall be an index of her memories.
> I fear no man who may come after me,
> And I see none. I see her, still in green,

> Beside the fountain. I shall not go back . . .
> 　　　If I come not,
> The lady Vivian will remember me,
> And say: "I knew him when his heart was young.
> Though I have lost him now. Time called him home,
> And that was as it was; for much is lost
> Between Broceliande and Camelot."

In my own experience Robinson is a poet who grows through rereading, or perhaps it would be better to say, one grows into being able to reread him. He will never please the crowds, neither the large ones panting for platitude nor the small ones supposing paradox an escape from platitude. All that need finally be said about Robinson he said himself in a sonnet about George Crabbe, the eighteenth-century English poet who also wrote about commonplace people in obscure corners of the earth:

> Whether or not we read him, we can feel
> From time to time the vigor of his name
> Against us like a finger for the shame
> And emptiness of what our souls reveal
> In books that are as altars where we kneel
> To consecrate the flicker, not the flame.

What's the Trouble? Social Crisis, Crisis of Civilization, or Both
{1971}

*We must get it out of our heads that this is a doomed time, that we are waiting
for the end, and the rest of it, mere junk from fashionable magazines.*
—SAUL BELLOW, *Herzog*

The rhetoric of apocalypse haunts the air and naturally fools rush in to use it.
Some of it is indeed "mere junk from fashionable magazines," and even those of
us who know that we have lived through a terrible century can become impatient
with the newest modes in *fin du mondisme*. Yet people who are anything but fools
seem also to yield themselves to visions of gloom, as if through a surrender of
rationality and will they might find a kind of peace. And there is a feeling abroad,
which I partly share, that even if our cities were to be rebuilt and our racial conflicts to be eased, we would still be left with a heavy burden of trouble, a trouble
not merely personal or social but having to do with some deep if ill-located regions of experience. To be sure, if we could solve social problems of the magnitude I have just mentioned, our sense of the remaining troubles would come to
seem less ominous. But they would still be there. They would be symptoms of a
crisis of civilization through which Western society has been moving for at least
a century and a half.

A social crisis signifies a breakdown in the functioning of a society: it fails to feed the poor, it cannot settle disputes among constituent groups, it drags the country into an endless war. If local, a social crisis calls for reform; if extensive, for deep changes in the relationships of power. Yet both those defending and those attacking the society may well be speaking with complete sincerity in behalf of a common heritage of values. Even a major social change doesn't necessarily lead to a radical disruption of the civilization in which it occurs. The American Revolution did not. By contrast, the Russian Revolution not only overturned social arrangements, it also signified a deep rent within the fabric of civilization—or so it seemed only a few decades ago, though today, with the increasing "bourgeoisification" of Russia, we can no longer be certain. Romantic writers like Pilnyak and Pasternak looked upon the Revolution less as a step to proletarian power than as an upheaval within the depths of their country that would force it toward a destiny sharply different from that of the West. Trotsky attacked these writers for this heresy, but in retrospect it does not seem that they were quite as foolish as he made out. They were talking about a crisis of civilization.

Though it may coincide with a social crisis and thereby exacerbate its effects, a crisis of civilization has to do not so much with the workings of the economy or the rightness of social arrangements as it does with the transmission of values, those tacit but deeply lodged assumptions by means of which men try to regulate their conduct. At least in principle, a social crisis is open to solutions by legislation and reform, that is, public policy. But a crisis of civilization, though it can be muted or its effects postponed by the relief of social problems, cannot as a rule be dissolved through acts of public policy. It has more to do with the experience of communities and generations than with the resolution of social conflict. It works itself out in ways we don't readily understand and sometimes, far from working itself out, it continues to fester. A social crisis raises difficulties, a crisis of civilization dilemmas. A social crisis is expressed mainly through public struggle, a crisis of civilization mainly through incoherence of behavior.

To speak of a crisis of civilization is not, of course, to suggest that our civilization is coming to an end: it may be but we have no way of knowing. Nor is it to suggest that every change taking place at the deeper and more obscure levels of our experience should immediately be submitted to moral judgment. There are many things about which we simply cannot know. We can only say that developments occur which occupy a longer time span and are more deeply lodged in the intangibles of conduct than is true for the issues of a given moment.

II

Let us now turn abruptly away from our present concerns and move backward to a point some 75 or 80 years ago, in order to see how an English left-laborite or German Social Democrat might have felt about the experience of his time.*

The main historical fact about the nineteenth century—and for socialists, one of the greatest facts in all history—is that the masses, dumb through the centuries, began to enter public life. A Berlin worker had heard August Bebel speak; he was struck by the thought that, for all his limitations of status, he might help shape public policy; and indeed, he might even form or join his "own" party. He would, in the jargon of our day, become a subject of history rather than its object. What the worker came dimly to realize was not merely that history could be made, the lesson of the French Revolution, but that he himself might make it, the message of socialism.

The whole tragic experience of our century demonstrates this to be one of the few unalterable commandments of socialism: the participation of the workers, the masses of human beings, as self-conscious men preparing to enter the arena of history. Without that, or some qualified version of it, socialism is nothing but a mockery, a swindle of bureaucrats and intellectuals reaching out for power. With it, socialism could still be the greatest of human visions. This belief in the autonomous potential of the masses lay at the heart of early Marxism, in what we may now be inclined to regard as its most attractive period: the years in which European social democracy gradually emerged as a popular movement.

Meanwhile there had flowered in England the theory and practice of classical liberalism. By classical liberalism I have in mind not a particular economic doctrine, as the term has come to be understood in Europe, but rather a commitment to political openness, the values of tolerance, liberties such as were embodied in the American Bill of Rights, and that most revolutionary of innovations, the multi-party system. Among Marxists the significance of this liberal outlook was far from appreciated, and in the Marxist tradition there has undoubtedly been a · line of opinion systematically hostile to liberal values. In time that would be one source of the Marxist disaster. So, unless he were the kind of laborite or social democrat who had become a bit skeptical of his received orthodoxies, our observer of 1895 wasn't likely to grasp the revolutionary implications of the liberal premise, or to see it as part of a large encompassing democratic transformation that ideally would link the bourgeois and socialist revolutions.

* The central idea for this section was suggested to me by Max Shachtman, though I cannot say whether he would have approved of the way in which I develop it.

Our socialist observer might also have noted, in the somewhat reductive terms prevalent on the Left, that science was triumphant and religion in decay. He would surely not have suspected that the weakening of religious belief, a development to which he had contributed, might bring unexpected difficulties to the lives of skeptics. Nor would he have paid attention to the views of, say, Dostoevsky on this matter, for as a rule he felt comfortable in the self-contained world that, together with an ideology proclaiming competence in almost all branches of knowledge, socialism had created for itself.

Finally, he might have become aware of certain trends in Western culture, such as the fierce hostility to bourgeois life shown by almost all writers and artists, including the reactionary ones, and the rapidity of change, indeed the absolute triumph of the principle of change, within European culture. A new sense of time, as Daniel Bell has remarked, came to dominate the arts, and the result would be that thrust toward restlessness and hunger for novelty, that obsession with progress as an end in itself, which has since characterized much of modern culture.

Let us now propose a brutal exaggeration, yet one that has its analytic uses: *by the time the nineteenth century comes to an end, at a point usually agreed to be 1914, the basic direction of world politics starts to be reversed.* The First World War—as it reveals not only the hypocrisies of the European states, including the liberal bourgeois states, but the inability of the social democrats to prevent a global bloodbath—proves to be a terrible blow to the inherited attitudes of the earlier age of progress. If the nineteenth century promised, roughly speaking, an ever-increasing movement toward democracy and liberality, then the twentieth, even while exploiting the catchwords and passions of the nineteenth, would be marked by an overwhelming drift toward various kinds of authoritarianism. This would not of course be the only direction of political change in the twentieth century; vast popular movements, some burned out in defeat and others twisted into betrayals, would also appear in Europe and Asia. But if we remember that ours has been the century of Hitler and Stalin, then my "brutal exaggeration" about the main political drift may not seem . . . well, quite so brutal. The self-activity of the working class, that essential fulcrum of socialist power, would now be replaced in all too many instances by an authoritarian manipulation of plebeian energies (Communism in all its forms) or by an accommodation to the limited goals of the existing society (social democracy in most of its forms). Liberalism as both idea and value came under fierce attack. The expected benefits of Reason were scorned, as being either deceptive or unneeded. Modern culture was recruited as an authority in the assault upon liberal styles of feeling. What I propose to assert is that we have been living not—certainly not merely—in the Age of Revolution about which Trotsky spoke but in an Age of Counterrevolution that has assailed mankind from Right and Left. This, I know, is a view distasteful to what passes today for orthodox Marxism, and so I mean it to be.

The central expectation of Marxism—that by its own efforts the working class could transform history—was called into question. Every political tendency on the Left had to face the question: if the working class turns out not to be the revolutionary force that Marxists had supposed, what then? The spectrum of nominated substitutes, from union bureaucracies to insurgent kindergartens, from technocratic experts to soulful drop-outs, has not been reassuring.

It is still too soon to speak with certainty. Has the vision of the self-activization of the masses, a vision democratic in its essence, proved to be false? Premature? Or merely delayed by historical interruptions and accidents?* I shall not try to answer this question, in part because I am not certain how to answer it, except to note the cogency of a remark attributed to Cournot: "The fact that we repeatedly fail in some venture merely because of chance is perhaps the best proof that chance is not the cause of our failure." In any case, for us this failure is the central problem of modern political experience, and it helps explain—even while being far from the sole explanation for—the fact that every mode of politics in our century succumbs in varying degrees to authoritarianism.

People employing another set of categories will no doubt see the politics of this century in other terms; but other terms can often veil similar perceptions. What seems likely is that all who share the view that democratic norms are essential to

* In 1948, writing on the occasion of the hundredth anniversary of *The Communist Manifesto*, Jean Vannier, one of Trotsky's close associates, remarked about the working class that

It has shown itself capable of outbursts of heroism, during which it sacrifices itself without a thought, and develops a power so strong as to shake society to its very foundations. It can rid itself in an instant of the most inveterate prejudices, while there seems to be no limit to its audacity. But by and by, whatever the consequences of its action, whether victory or defeat, it is finally caught up in the sluggish, quotidian flow of things.

The fetid backwaters of the past seep back; the proletariat sinks into indolence and cynicism. And even in its triumphant moments, it exhibits a want of consciousness in its choice of leaders. The "instinctive sense of reality" attributed to it by Auguste Comte, which it so readily reflects in many a circumstance, abandons it at such moments. Its courage and self-sacrifice are not enough to give it what, precisely, is needed in order to act out the role assigned to it by Marx: political capacity.

The question Vannier is raising here is not merely whether the working class can take power—that is an old and well-rehearsed question. He is asking something more troublesome: can a triumphant working class, once in power, display the political "capacity" to rule over a modern society or will it, in effect, cede power to an alliance of bureaucrats, intellectuals, and technocrats?

a tolerable life would be ready to grant some credit to the sketch that has been drawn here.

III

How are we now to relate the two lines of speculation I have thus far advanced — first, that we are experiencing the repercussions of a crisis of civilization (a few signs of which will shortly be noted) and second, that we are living through the consequences of the failure of socialism? Perhaps by a third line of speculation: that it is precisely the recurrent political-social difficulties of Western capitalism, significantly eased but not removed by the welfare state, which create a fertile ground for the emerging symptoms of a long-festering crisis of civilization. The social-political problems of the moment and the deeper crisis of civilization have, so to say, a habit of collaboration; they even maliciously assume the guise of one another. There follows a terrible confusion in which problems open to public solution become encumbered with metaphysical and quasi-religious issues while efforts are vainly made to bring into the political arena metaphysical and quasi-religious issues beyond the capacity of politics to cope with.

Why we should be experiencing this confusion of realms is a question to which the answers are either too easy or too hard. Let us not rehearse them at length. The atom bomb has made us aware that the very future of the race hangs on political decision. The Nazi and Stalinist concentration camps have raised questions as to the nature of our nature: is there an inherent bestiality in mankind beyond the correction of collective activity? The Vietnam war, in a more recent moment, has been felt by segments of the young as an international trauma, serving to break ties of loyalty with both society and earlier generations. In the West a generation has arisen accustomed to affluence and therefore able to devote itself to problems of life, sometimes merely life-style, as against the problems of making a living. Higher education on a mass scale is becoming a reality in Western society, yet no one quite knows what its purpose, content, or outcome is or should be. A counter society, half-real and half-myth, has appeared as the Third World, imbued by its admirers with a mixture of utopianism and authoritarianism, revolution and primitive nobility: all arising from a revulsion against advanced society. Such are the reasons that might be given for a situation in which the crisis of modern civilization, recurrent for at least a century and a half, is again felt as immediate and pressing; but what we do not really know is the relative weights to assign to these reasons, and that means we do not know very much.

The difficulty — let us say, one difficulty — of living at this moment in history is that we experience, both as *simultaneity and contradiction*, the problems of three stages of modern society. Or to be more modest we experience problems that in our thought we have assigned to three stages of society: precapitalist (race, illiteracy, backwardness); capitalist (class conflict, economic crisis, distribution of wealth); and postcapitalist (quandaries concerning work, leisure, morality, and style, such as are sometimes described as "existential," a term meant to indicate significant imprecision). But it is crucial to note that we experience these three orders of difficulty within the context of an advanced or "late" capitalism. Problems therefore suddenly appear in this late capitalist society that we had supposed would emerge only under socialism—problems not to be described merely or mainly in terms of social class but rather as pertaining to all human beings. (It ought to be said that the more intelligent socialists had foreseen the possibility that by liberating men from material want socialism might impose upon them a severe crisis of civilization, though impose it under circumstances more favorable to the human imagination than had been possible in the past.)

In the industrialized countries capitalism has entered a phase of unprecedented affluence, not justly distributed yet still reaching almost every class in society. Many people, especially those drawn from the upper and middle classes, have thereby come to experience a certain freedom to see their lives in generalized or abstract "human" terms. In the long run this is surely what one hopes for all humanity—that men should free themselves, to the extent that they can, from the tyranny of circumstances and confront their essential being. In the short run, however, this occurs, to the extent that it does occur, within a social context that distorts and frustrates the newly acquired sense of the human. For it occurs within a context of class domination and social snobbism, as well as at a historical moment forcing upon the young ghastly dilemmas. At one and the same time, a young person of middle-class origin can feel free to experiment with his life, yet must also live under the shadow of a war perceived to be unjust and even criminal. He can feel himself free to abandon the norms of bourgeois society, yet in doing so he will often unwittingly reinstate them as self-alienating masks and phantasms.

I am aware here of a possible criticism: that in speaking of these three stages of recent history as they had been thought of by socialists, I am referring not to objective realities but to conceptions nurtured, perhaps mistakenly, by people on the Left, and that there is nothing inherent in modern history which requires that certain problems be correlated with early capitalism or others with socialism. I accept this criticism in advance, but would only add that all of us see, as we must see, historical developments through the lens of our assumptions, and that those who reject socialist categories may come to similar conclusions through their own terms about the mixture of problems I have been discussing. We might, for example, choose to say that during the past decade we have become aware that the religious disputes of the nineteenth and the social anxieties of the twentieth century are related—with the issues that obsessed the nineteenth century, issues that had to do with the desanctification of the cosmos, surviving into our own moment in surprisingly powerful ways. For what should interest us here is not the "rightness" of a particular intellectual vocabulary or tradition, but a cluster of insights that might be reached through different vocabularies and traditions.

In any case, the jumble of interests and needs I have been associating with various stages of modern history could also be regarded as distinctive elements— elements of conflict and tension—within the welfare state. It is in the very nature of the welfare state that through its formal, ideological claims it should arouse steadily increasing expectations which as an economic system still geared mainly to a maximization of profit it does not always or sufficiently satisfy. The welfare state systematically creates appetites beyond its capacity to appease—that, so to say, is the principle of dynamism which keeps it both in motion and off-balance. The welfare state cannot count upon those fierce sentiments of national loyalty which, precisely insofar as it has come to dominate the industrialized portion of the world, it replaces with an array of group and sectional interests—that much-vaunted pluralism of interests often concealing an imbalance of opportunity. The welfare state has small attraction as an end or ideal in its own right, and little gift for inspiring the loyalties of the young. It is a social arrangement sufficiently stable, thus far, to all but eliminate the prospect of revolution in the advanced countries; but it is also a social arrangement unstable enough to encourage the militant arousal of previously silent groups, the intensification of political discontents, and the reappearance, if in new and strange forms, of those tormenting "ultimate questions" with which modern man has beset himself for a century and a half. These "ultimate questions" as to man's place in the universe, the meaning of his existence, the nature of his destiny—that they now come to us in rather modish or foolish ways is cause for impatience and polemic. But we would be dooming ourselves to a philistine narrowness if we denied that such questions do beset human beings, that they are significant questions, and that in our moment there are peculiarly urgent reasons for coming back to them.

IV

How does one know that we, like our fathers, grandfathers, and great-grandfathers, are living through a crisis of civilization? What could possibly constitute evidence for such a claim? Even to ask such questions may strike one as both comic and impudent: comic because it seems a little late to be returning to a theme that has been pursued to the point of exhaustion, impudent because it can hardly be approached in a few pages. One is tempted simply to say what Louis Armstrong is supposed to have said when he was asked to define jazz, "If you don't know, I can't tell you." For if felt at all, a crisis of civilization must be felt as pervasive: as atmospheric and behavioral, encompassing and insidious.

How shall we live?—this question has obsessed thoughtful people throughout the modern era, which is to say, since at least the French Revolution, and it has obsessed them with increasing anxiety and intensity. I don't suppose there has ever been a time when the question hasn't been asked, but in those centuries when religious systems were commonly accepted as revealed truth, the problems of existence necessarily took on a different shape and eventuated in a different emotional discipline from anything we know in our time. Some of the more spectacular symptoms of disaffection we are now witnessing ought to be taken not as historical novelties revealing the special virtue or wickedness of a new generation, but as tokens of that continuity of restlessness and trouble which comprises the history of Western consciousness since the late eighteenth century.

One major sign is the decay or at least partial breakdown of the transmission agencies—received patterns of culture, family structure, and education—through which values, norms, and ideals are handed down from generation to generation. It would be self-deceiving, if for some comforting, to suppose that we are going through just another "normal" struggle between generations which "in time" will work itself out through familiar mechanisms of social adjustment. The present conflict between generations or, if you prefer, between segments of the generations, is "normal" only insofar as it seizes upon, intensifies, and distorts those philosophical, moral, and religious themes which we have inherited from the nineteenth century.

The decay or partial breakdown in the transmission of values occurs most dramatically among middle-class and upper-middle-class youth secure enough in the comforts of affluence to feel that in the future our primary concern will be existence rather than survival. Some declare an acceptance of received values but cry out against their betrayal by the system or the men who run it; others reject the received values (sustained work, restraint as a social discipline, postponement of gratifications in behalf of ultimate ends, goals of success, etc.). In practice, it is hard to keep the two kinds of response completely separate. Young protesters often believe they are motivated by a fundamental denial of Western civilization when in reality they are unhappy with their private lot. But more important by far is the fact, as I take it to be, that those who believe they are motivated merely by a revulsion against the betrayal of accepted values are in reality being moved, at least in part and at least with partial consciousness, by the more extreme visions of life-style that we associate with postindustrial society. One result is that in the name of rejecting their elders' betrayal of liberal values they slide into contempt for those values.

The immediate social form through which such young people try to organize their responses is a cluster of distinctively generational groups lying somewhere between family and occupation. Torn between the problems of too much freedom and the problems of too little, between the fear of an endless chaos and the claustrophobia of rigid social definition, they create, in the words of Richard Flacks, "institutions which can combine some of the features of family life with those of the occupational structure. Youth groups, cultures, movements serve this function, combining relations of diffuse solidarity with universalistic values." One immediate cause for establishing these institutions is frustration with the external society: there is less and less socially useful or meaningful labor for young people to do and the consequence is that while the process of socialization is sped up the prospect of maturation is delayed. These fragile institutions of the youth culture also reveal themselves as testing grounds for experiment with, or acting-out for, the crisis of values which long antedates their appearance. Miniature settings serve as laboratories, sometimes mere sickrooms, for dealing with the largest problems of modern life.

Now, it has been argued by writers who are skeptical of the above description that signs of disaffection, whether trivial or profound, are mostly confined to segments of affluent youth and that the blue-collar young, still facing a struggle for economic survival, cannot indulge themselves in such existential luxuries. Perhaps so. But even if true, this hardly minimizes the importance of what has happened within large and significant segments of middle-class youth—especially in the United States where the middle class sprawls across the social map and strongly influences the ways in which adjacent classes live.

If your main concern is to plot out lines of voting behavior, then it is indeed crucial to notice the class limitations of the new youth styles; but if you are concerned with long-range social trends, then you must recognize that by their very nature these are likely first to appear among minorities. (It does not follow that everything to be found among minorities will become a long-range social trend.) What needs, then, to be estimated, or simply guessed, is the extent to which such minorites—in our case, a rather substantial one—may shape the conduct of tomorrow. Clearly, it is too soon to say whether we are witnessing a transient outbreak of malaise reflecting the privileges and disadvantages of middle-class youth or a fundamental revision in the patterns of our life reflecting the emergence of postindustrial society, the loss of faith in traditional values, and the persistence of moral and metaphysical problems thrown up by the crisis of civilization. To insist merely upon the former might be parochial; merely upon the latter, grandiose. But even if we lean toward skepticism, we ought to recognize the possibility that a series of intermittent generational traumas, and the current one is hardly the first, might constitute a long-range historical trend of major importance.*

About the gravity of a second major symptom that points to a crisis of civilization there is likely to be less dispute. The whole enterprise of education is in grave trouble. It is marked by anxieties bordering on demoralization and often a retreat from serious purpose that becomes sheer panic. In part this seems due to immediate causes that might let up in a few years; in part it signifies a thread of confusion that has kept recurring throughout the history of modern education. There seems barely any consensus among professors as to what they are supposed to profess, barely any agreement among educators as to what they believe education to be or do. There is little concurrence in our universities, and not much more in our high schools, as to the skills, disciplines, kinds of knowledge, and attitudes

* A few points about the significance of the new youth styles:

1. It is hard to suppose that the feelings of disaffection or dismay one encounters among young people are confined to those who come from a single class, though it may well be that such feelings are most strongly articulated by them. Even among plebeian segments of our population there are visible strong feelings of rage and resentment, sometimes turned against "the students," but in origin and character often sharing with "the students" sentiments of powerlessness and dismay.

2. Today's middle-class style can become tomorrow's working-class style. In this country, the lines of social and cultural demarcation between the classes are not nearly so firm as in other capitalist societies. Youth mobility is high; working-class children go to college in increasing, if not sufficient, numbers; they are likely to share at least some of the responses of other students; and they do not bring with them a strong sense of class allegiance or definition to which they feel obliged to cling and which might create psychic barriers between them and their middle-class peers.

3. Mass culture quickly provides lower-class equivalents to middle-class styles, and often succeeds in spilling across class barriers. There are overwhelming cultural or pseudo-cultural experiences shared by the young of all classes, certainly more so than in any previous society. Movies, rock music, drugs—these may not figure with equal force in the lives of both working- and middle-class youth, but they do create a generational consciousness that, to an undetermined extent, disintegrates class lines.

There have recently appeared reports of widespread and serious drug usage among young workers, both white and black, in major American industries. Whatever this may signify, and I don't pretend to know, it ought to be sufficient evidence to dismiss the claim that somehow the less attractive features of the "counter culture" are unique to disoriented or spoiled middle-class youth. For good or bad, illumination or contamination, young workers in a mass society increasingly share the surrounding general culture.

of mind we wish to develop. The more education is exalted in our social mythology, the less do we seem to know what it means.

Curricula discussions at faculty meetings are notoriously tiresome, yet they finally do reflect disputes and mirror disorientation concerning the very idea of education and thereby, perhaps, the very nature of our civilization. What, beyond the rudiments of literacy, do people need to know? What, beyond such needs, should they wish to learn? What do we hope to pass on from one generation to the next in regard to moral and cultural values? What is our image of an educated man? Around such questions disputes rage, and rage so harshly that connections can barely be made between the antagonists. For these are disputes that come down to the question of how or whether we shall maintain a vital continuity with traditional Western culture.

When a society does not know what it wishes its young to know, it is suffering from moral and spiritual incoherence. It has no clear sense of the connections it would maintain—or whether it even wishes to maintain them—with the civilization of which presumably it is a part. And when to this incoherence is added the persuasion that young people should be kept in schools for increasing lengths of time (often with the parallel notion that schools should be made to resemble the external society, which is to say, to be as unlike schools as possible), then immediate and long-range troubles are thrust into a dangerous friction.

The United States, and to a lesser extent other advanced countries of the West, have embarked on a project which, we socialists would like to think, might better have coincided with the growth of a democratic socialist order. It is a project that declares every citizen to be entitled to a higher education and soon may enable every citizen to obtain one. Who can fault this premise? But who would deny that there are extremely troubling results from undertaking so revolutionary a task under social circumstances often inhospitable to it? Those of us who spoke for a universalization of culture and education were not, I think, wrong; but we were naive in our sense of how it might be brought about, or what the cost of bringing it about might be. We failed to see that some problems are not open to quick public solution, and we refused to see that the solution of other problems might lead to new and unforeseen ones. In the short run—and who knows, perhaps even the long run—a conflict develops between the values of high culture and the values of universal education, to both of which we are committed but between which we would hardly know how to choose, if choose we had to. Millions of young people are thrust into universities and no one quite knows why or toward what end. The immediate result is social bitterness and clash. One of the few things these millions of young people may discover in the universities is, however, that learning and culture, since they are but faintly credited by many of their teachers, need hardly be credited by them. That expresses and intensifies a crisis of civilization.

Ultimately, one suspects, this crisis has to do with residual sentiments of religion and vague but powerful yearnings toward transcendence. For to the extent that the transmission of values is blocked and a lack of faith in the power of education spreads among the educated classes, there must follow a more pervasive uncertainty as to the meanings and ends of existence. Let me turn to a vocabulary not spontaneously my own and suggest that we are beginning to witness a new religious experience—or, perhaps, an experience of religious feelings. Partly because of the sterility of traditional religious institutions, this experience cannot easily be embodied in religious terms and it must therefore assume the (often misshapen) masks of politics, culture, and life-style. Our socialist of 75 or 80 years ago, smug in his rationalism and convinced that all would be well once "we" took power, could hardly understand such a development; his first inclination would have been to regard it as a sign of reaction. For that matter, it is by no means clear that a socialist of the present moment can understand it, either. Yet, no matter how alien we remain to the religious outlook, we must ask ourselves whether the malaise of this time isn't partly a consequence of that despairing emptiness which followed the breakup in the nineteenth century of traditional religious systems; whether the nihilism every sensitive person feels encompassing his life like a spiritual smog isn't itself a kind of inverted religious aspiration (so Dostoevsky kept saying); and whether the sense of disorientation that afflicts us isn't due to the difficulties of keeping alive a high civilization without a sustaining belief. All questions of the nineteenth century; all returning to plague us at the end of the twentieth.

Richard Lowenthal has remarked on this score:

> We have not yet had a civilization that was not based on a transcendent belief. And what we are trying to do is to maintain our values and move upon the momentum of these values originally created by religion—but after the transcendent belief is gone. The question is: will we succeed?

To such questions a simple answer is neither possible nor desirable. Even if we conclude that the breakdown of religious systems, enormously liberating as in part it was, also yielded unforeseen difficulties for those who might never have stepped into a church or a synagogue, this is not to be taken, of course, as a token of support for those who wish to recreate through will the dogmas that once were supported by faith. Perhaps we have no choice but to live with the uncomfortable aftereffects of the disintegration, aftereffects that range from moving efforts at private spiritual communion to flashy chemical improvisations for pseudoreligious sects. I am convinced, in any case, that the coming era will witness a proliferation of such sects, some betraying the corrupting effects of the very technology they will repudiate, others mixing antinomian ecstasies with utopian visions, and still others seeking to discover through simplicities of custom the lost paradise of love.

Again experience proves far more recalcitrant and complicated than any of our theories has enabled us to suppose. It may indeed be that the religious impulse is deeply grounded in human existence and that men need objects of veneration beyond their egos. "The Golden Age," wrote Dostoevsky, "is the most unlikely of all the dreams that have been, but for it men have given up their life. . . . For the sake of it prophets have died and been slain, without it the peoples will not live and cannot die." If the impulse Dostoevsky invokes here cannot be expressed through religious channels, then it must turn to secular equivalents. It turns to the fanaticism of ideology (which may explain the continued hold Marxism has on the imaginations of the young). It turns to heretical sects seeking an unsullied pantheism. It turns to communities of the faithful who repudiate technology and civilization itself, a repudiation as old as religion itself.

Who can say? Remembering the certainties of our socialist of 75 or 80 years ago, good, decent, and even heroic fellow that he was, we might be a little cautious in dismissing the needs and aspirations of our fellowmen, especially those we find difficult to understand. All we can say with assurance or good will is that the themes of religious desire appear and reappear in the experience of our epoch, tokens of "the missing All," whether as harmony or dissonance. And they will surely be heard again.

An anxiety,
  A caution,
    And a caution against the caution.

The anxiety: whenever there occurs that meeting of social crisis and crisis of civilization I have sketched here, democratic norms and institutions are likely to be in danger. If we look at the collapse of democratic societies in our century, we must conclude that the usually cited causes—economic depression, unemployment, etc.—are necessary but not sufficient elements; there must also occur some loss of conviction in the animating ethos of the nation or culture, some coming-apart of that moral binder which holds men in the discipline of custom. Anyone observing the intellectual life of the West during the past decade may be struck by the thought that some such loss of conviction, or some such coming-apart of moral binder, seems to be happening, if not among the masses, then certainly among growing segments of the educated classes. The bourgeois mythos has been losing its hold on the bourgeois mind, though nothing has come along to replace it. Nothing, that is, except that vulgarized quasi-Marxism which has been improvised by a small though significant minority of the intellectual young. Nor should this, by the way, come as a surprise, for no other twentieth-century ideology has been so powerfully able to stir or corrupt the nascent religious impulses of sensitive and uprooted people.

By an irony too painful to underscore, it is only in Eastern Europe that intellectuals have come to appreciate the value of liberal institutions. In the West, a mere three decades after the ravages of totalitarianism, there is again visible a strident contempt for the ethic of liberal discourse and the style of rationality. In part this arises from the mixed failings and successes of the welfare state, but in part from an upswell of unacknowledged and ill-understood religious sentiments that, unable to find a proper religious outlet, become twisted into moral and political absolutism, a hunger for total solutions and apocalyptic visions. Impatience with the sluggish masses, burning convictions of righteousness, the suffocation of technological society, the boredom of overcrowded cities, the yearning for transcendent ends beyond the petty limits of group interest, romantic-sinister illusions about the charismatic virtues of dictatorship in underdeveloped countries—all these tempt young people into apolitical politics, at best communes and at worst bombs, but both sharing an amorphous revulsion from civilization itself.

Why then should one suppose that such sentiments can pose a threat to democratic institutions? Because, if carried through to the end, they release yearnings and desires that by their very nature cannot be satisfied through the limited mechanisms of democratic politics. Because, if carried through to the end, they summon moods of desperation and fanaticism which lead to a dismissal of democratic politics.

The caution: nothing could be more disastrous for our political life in the immediate future than to have the modest, perhaps manageable and (as some intellectuals like to suppose) "boring" problems of the welfare state swept aside in behalf of a grandiose, surely unmanageable and (as some intellectuals would feel) "exciting" *Kulturkampf* between the up-tight and the loose, the repressive and the permissive. If, say, in the next decade figures like Spiro Agnew and Jerry Rubin, or to choose less disreputable substitutes, William Buckley and Charles Reich, were allowed to dominate public debate, people would vote according to their prejudices concerning drugs, sex, morality, pornography, and "permissiveness."

A bleak prospect; for while such a situation might arise out of spontaneous passions on all sides, it might just as well have been arranged as a political maneuver
for the far Right, the only political group that could profit from it. And even if I
am wrong in supposing that only the far Right could profit politically from a *Kulturkampf*, how much comfort is that? For the one thing that is entirely clear is that
a politics or a social outlook devoted to democratic social change and the style of
rationality would lose.

What is required here is a measure of social and intellectual discipline, the
capacity for keeping one's various interests distinct and in a hierarchy of importance. Furthermore, we must recognize that at least in a democratic society politics has built-in—and in the long run, desirable—limitations. It may be possible
through legislation to remove some of the socioeconomic causes of alienation
but it is not possible through politics to cope directly with that seething cluster of
emotions we call alienation; it may be possible through legislation to improve the
conditions under which men work but it is not possible through politics to cope
with the growing uncertainties men have as to work and leisure.

That in a society so beset as ours with ideological noise and cultural clatter
we should expect the necessary discipline—give unto the ballot box its due, and
leave for your life-style what your taste requires—seems all but utopian. But if we
lack that discipline, we will pay heavily.

The caution against this caution: There are limits to common sense and pragmatism, which those who favor these qualities ought to be the first to recognize.
The Fabian course to which democratic socialists in the United States are, by and
large, committed, seems to me the closest we can come to political realism; but
precisely for that reason we ought to recognize the points at which it fails to stir
the imagination or speak to the troubles and passions of many people. Such a
politics offers a possible way of improving and extending the welfare state, which
is about as much as one can hope for in the immediate future, but it has little
to say about problems that the welfare state is barely equipped to cope with. A
politics of limitation, of coalition, of step-by-step change is desirable; the alternatives are neither real nor attractive; yet we must not allow strategy to blot out
vision.

So let us be ready to acknowledge to others and ourselves that between the
politics we see as necessary and the imaginative-expressive needs we have as men
living in this time, there are likely to be notable gaps. The chaotic but profoundly
significant urges and passions that sweep through modern society—at once innocent and nihilistic, aspiring and gloom-ridden, chiliastic and despairing—

must touch us as well as those with whom we have political quarrels. How could it be otherwise? Who, looking upon the experience of our century, does not feel repeated surges of nausea, a deep persuasion that the very course of civilization has gone wrong? Who, elbowing his way past the wastes of our cities, does not feel revulsion against the very stones and glass, the brick and towers, all the debris of inhumaneness? Who, thinking of our bombs and our pollution, does not wish, at least on occasion, to join in the jeremiads against all that we are and have?

What we must do is recognize the distance, perhaps the necessary distance, between political strategy and existential response. We are saying that many things requiring remedy are open to social-political solution (provided intelligence and will are present). We are also saying that we live at a moment when problems beyond the reach of politics—problems that *should* be beyond the reach of politics—have come to seem especially urgent and disturbing. We have learned that the effort to force men into utopia leads to barbarism, but we also know that to live without the image of utopia is to risk the death of imagination. Is there a path for us, a crooked path for men of disciplined hope?

A Postscript

To say "No" as one's answer to the question at the end of the above paper would be neither hard nor even foolish. By reasoning alone, or the appearance of it, one can readily conclude that the future humanity can expect, say, fifty or sixty years from now is, mostly, to live in a low-charged authoritarian state, very advanced in technology and somewhat decadent in culture, in which there will be little terror and not much freedom, in which most men will eat fairly well and only a few suffer despair over their condition, and in which order, control, efficiency will coexist with tolerated areas of their opposites.

The famous theory of convergence—which sees the major forms of modern society gradually coming closer to one another, in a kind of eclectic elitism that satisfies none of the traditional social outlooks—has far more defenders than is commonly recognized. It is a theory that easily allows, though it does not necessarily require, a certain bland disdain for political freedom. To believe in such a theory—according to which the trend toward economic collectivism inherent in modern technological conditions comes together with the trend toward authoritarianism inherent either in the sheer complexity of things or the sheer recalcitrance of human nature—it is simply necessary to float with "the given," to accept the effectiveness but not the claims of ideology, and to rid oneself of old-fashioned liberal "illusions."

It hardly seems necessary to elaborate the many ways in which the conditions of modern society militate against the survival or growth of freedom. That technology becomes increasingly complicated, the province of a highly trained elite, and thereby less and less open to democratic controls or social arrangements premised on a high degree of popular participation; that modern urban life tends to create large masses of semi-educated men, vulnerable to the newest modes of manipulation and essentially passive in their responses to political decision; that the steadily exacerbated division between industrialized and backward nations encourages charismatic desperadoes and deracinated intellectuals toward "revolutionary" coups which, whatever else they fail to do, do not fail to destroy all liberties; that the heritage of totalitarian ideology weighs heavily upon us, a poison long settled in the minds of men; that fierce new apocalyptic moods, recklessly blending politics and religion, arise throughout the world, though perhaps most notably in the industrialized nations—all this is by now familiar, commonplace, requiring no detail.

We know that a society which tolerates extreme inequalities of wealth and income runs the risk of revolt that can endanger liberties. But we also know that a society which insists upon enforcing an absolute egalitarianism can do so only by destroying liberties.

We know that a society in which the masses of men, drugged by affluence and the mass media, become passive and inert is one in which liberties may slowly erode. But we also know that a society shaken by the tremors of pseudomessianism, in which willful idealistic minorities seek to impose their vision upon sluggish majorities, is one in which liberties may be quickly undone.

We know that a society trapped in economic primitivism and clannishness, traditionalist or premodern casts of thought, is not likely to be one in which liberties can flourish. But we also know that it is entirely possible for political tyranny to coexist with an advanced economy.

If, then, we can specify certain conditions—a measure of affluence, the absence of extreme inequalities, a coherent political structure, a high level of education, and perhaps most crucial, a tradition of belief in freedom—which make possible or encourage the survival of liberties, these are at best necessary and not sufficient conditions. In truth, we can only guess at the optimum conditions for the survival and growth of liberties. I think it would be a social democratic society, in which a certain proportion of the central means of production would be socialized, that is, democratically owned and controlled; extremes of inequality in wealth, and thereby, ultimately in power, would be evened out; and liberties, extending from the political to the socioeconomic areas of life, would flourish.

Whether such a society can in fact ever be achieved is an open question: I cannot have the simple faith of my socialist forbears of a century ago. For, as I now see it, such a society would require not merely certain structures of economic relationships and political power—that, by comparison, is *almost* easy to envisage—but also certain structures of shared values, bringing together restraint and cooperativeness, discipline and social initiative. Nor can one believe any longer, as radicals once did, that the mere establishment of the envisaged economic and political structures will necessarily create the required values. I still think it reasonable to suppose that they would *enable* men to create those values, but there is no certainty whatever. For we have learned in recent years that a society can be threatened not merely by external assault or economic breakdown but by something harder to specify yet at least as insidious in effect: namely, the disintegration of those tacit and binding beliefs which enable men to live together. This disintegration, which affects the sons of the bourgeoisie in the West and the sons of the party leadership in the East, can have curiously mixed implications: it can be against gross injustice *and* contemptuous of liberal values, it can be outraged by unjust wars *and* prone to a mystique of violence. At least at this point, Schumpeter seems to have been a better prophet than Marx.

The question that must then follow, and which it would be foolish to try to answer, is this: can a reasonably decent society, liberal in its political style and egalitarian in its socioeconomic outlook, survive in the conditions likely to exist during the next fifty or sixty years? Apart from the factors I have listed a page or two earlier that militate against such a survival, and apart from others that could be added, there is a problem here of the gravest difficulty though one that has come to seem acute only recently. Such a liberal or social democratic society may well provide the best conditions for human beings to live in; but insofar as it comes closer to realization, it may not provide spiritual or psychic goals that will satisfy the people who live in it, at least those most inclined to sentience and restlessness.

To raise this speculation at a moment when most human beings on this globe live in societies that do not satisfy their minimal physical needs and, furthermore, hold them in authoritarian subjection may seem idle. But it is not. For while intelligent socialists have always said that "the good society" would for the first time make it possible for men to confront freely and with adequate consciousness their metaphysical problems, they hardly could have foreseen the ferocity with which at least some people would try to attack these problems even before reaching, and indeed in the name of reaching, "the good society." If there is in reality a deep, though not always manifest, religious hunger in human beings, or at least the intellectually and spiritually aware minority; if this hunger fails in the twentieth century to find outlets through adequate religious institutions, ceremonies, and doctrines; and if it then turns, with a kind of self-alienated violence, into a secular expression, at once apocalyptic, messianic, and fanatic—then we may suppose that the closer we approach "the good society," or the more single-mindedly we become preoccupied with approaching it, the more severe the problem will become. The values of a liberal society may indeed be in conflict, immediate or potential, with the religious or quasi-religious impulses among human beings that seem to break out recurrently with varying degrees of passion and force. And insofar as such a society clears away the gross troubles of survival that have afflicted most human beings throughout history, it leaves the way open to what we might call the risks and terrors of the metaphysical.

At this point in our speculations, the intellectuals as a group come straight to center stage. One might hope that they, in the turmoil of a civilization beset by inner doubts and a confusion between political and religious goals, would be the most unyielding, even "unreasonable," in their defense of liberties. Intellectuals, after all, are the single group in society that would seem to have the highest stake in freedom; it is their minimal requirement for professional existence; it is the very element that makes it possible to be an intellectual. But of course, the history of intellectuals in the twentieth century is, not least of all, a history of betrayal and self-betrayal, a history of repeated surrenders to authoritarian and totalitarian ideology and power. The value of freedom stirs only some intellectuals, or it stirs them only at moments when it least needs defense. For this, there are a great many reasons, and I do not pretend to know them all; but let me cite a few. By their very outlook and vocation, intellectuals are peculiarly susceptible to ideological melodrama: it is their form of faith. The grandiosity of the abstract, the willfulness of schemes of perfection imposed through iron and blood, the feeling that anything short of a total measure is "boring," the refusal to examine the possibility that intertwined with utopian visions can be coarse yearnings for power, the infatuation with charismatic figures who represent decisiveness, rapidity, daring, intuitive authority—these are some of the elements in the experience of intellectuals that make them susceptible to authoritarian movements.

There are also mundane considerations. Modern bureaucratic societies, formally structured as one-party dictatorships, have great need for intellectuals—at least for their skills, if not their vocation. If we take enormous pride in those intellectuals who rebel in the name of freedom, men like Djilas, Solzhenitsyn, and Kolakowski, we must also recognize that at least some of those who persecute them are also intellectuals of a sort. And for intellectuals in the underdeveloped countries, dispossessed and estranged, deracinated and unemployed, the prospect of an authoritarian regime resting on ideology signifies a future of prestige, power, and privilege. At a certain cost, to be sure. It is therefore silly to expect that in the coming decades the intellectuals as a class will be unconditional defenders of freedom—indeed, it is a notion so silly that only intellectuals could entertain it.

Yet freedom remains our signature. We may know and have to say that many other things are needed if freedom is to exist—a society that satisfies the material and social needs of human beings, a society that gives people a sense of participation and opportunity, a society that does not kill off its young in ghastly wars, etc. But it is freedom that remains the fundament of the intellectual's vocation: he honors or betrays, but he cannot avoid it.

Yet we may ask, what is the historical sanction for this commitment to freedom? what forces in history, what laws of development, what dynamic of the society or the economy?

No doubt, at various points in the future there will be some historical forces enabling or smoothing the way for those persons or groups who will speak in defense of basic liberties. No doubt, it is of the greatest importance to try to estimate the nature and range of those forces, whether they be "impersonal" elements of the social structure or collective movements of classes and groups. But that is not what I propose to do here, partly because I do not feel competent to do it.

I want, instead, to assume that we cannot be "certain," as many of us were in the past, that there is an ineluctable motion within history toward a progressive culmination. I want to discard any faith in the necessary movement of History—even in its much-advertised cunning. Not that I would create instead a gnostic melodrama in which man stands forever pitted against his own history, a promethean loneliness against the runaway of civilization. I simply want to put the question aside, and then to say: the obligation to defend and extend freedom in its simplest and most fundamental aspects is the sacred task of the intellectual, the one task he must not compromise even when his posture seems intractable, or unreasonable, or hopeless, or even when it means standing alone against fashionable shibboleths like Revolution and The Third World.

I am aware that to offer this liberal/social democratic truism as a central idea for the future will not excite many sensibilities or set many hearts beating. Precisely that fact reinforces my conviction that, just as in the perspective of the past two centuries it is the liberal idea that now seems the most permanently revolutionary, so in the world as we know it and are likely to know it the idea of freedom, always perilous, remains the most urgent and therefore the most problematic.

I take as my model Alexander Solzhenitsyn. It seems clear that since publishing his great novels, The First Circle and The Cancer Ward, Solzhenitsyn has moved
to a kind of elemental Christianity, for which there is of course a great tradition
in Russia going back to and beyond Tolstoy. This tradition is not mine, though
I understand how revolutionary it can be in relation to a total state. But in the
Solzhenitsyn novels there is a steady commitment to the idea of freedom, not
because it is seen as the logical consequence of history, nor as an unquenchable
desire arising from our natures; there is too much evidence against both these
views. Solzhenitsyn brings to bear no determinist argument in behalf of freedom.
He simply suggests that freedom is the only condition under which people like
ourselves can breathe; that freedom is required, as well, by all human beings insofar as they would pursue their particular interests, as groups or classes; that
freedom is, for modern man, a supreme good. Let us say—and surely at least a
few will still be saying it seventy-five years from now—that it is the name of our
desire.

The City in Literature
{1971}

S IMPLICITY, *AT LEAST IN LITERATURE,* is a complex idea. Pastoral poetry, which has been written for more than two thousand years and may therefore be supposed to have some permanent appeal, takes as its aim to make simplicity complex. With this aim goes a convention: universal truths can be uttered by plebeian figures located in a stylized countryside often suggestive of the Golden Age. In traditional or sophisticated pastoral these plebeian figures are shepherds. In naive pastoral they can be dropouts huddling in a commune. Traditional pastoral is composed by self-conscious artists in a high culture, and its premise, as also its charm, lies in the very "artificiality" untrained readers dislike, forgetting or not knowing that in literature the natural is a category of artifice. As urban men who can no more retreat to the country than could shepherds read the poems celebrating their virtues, we are invited by pastoral to a game of the imagination in which every move is serious.

With time there occurs a decline from sophisticated to romantic pastoral, in which the conventions of the genre are begun to be taken literally, and then to naive pastoral, in which they *are* taken literally. Yet in all these versions of pastoral there resides some structure of feeling that seems to satisfy deep psychic needs. Through its artifice of convention, the pastoral toys with, yet speaks to, a nagging doubt concerning the artifice called society. It asks a question men need not hurry to answer: Could we not have knowledge without expulsion, civilization without conditions?

Now, between such questions and pastoral as a genre, there is often a considerable distance. We can have the genre without the questions, the questions without the genre. We can also assume that pastoral at its best represents a special, indeed a highly sophisticated version of a tradition of feeling in Western society that goes very far back and very deep down. The suspicion of artifice and cultivation, the belief in the superior moral and therapeutic uses of the "natural," the fear that corruption must follow upon a high civilization—such motifs appear to be strongly ingrained in Western Christianity and the civilization carrying it. There are Sodom and Gomorrah. There is the whore of Babylon. There is the story of Joseph and his brothers, charmingly anticipating a central motif within modern fiction: Joseph, who must leave the pastoral setting of his family because he is too smart to spend his life with sheep, prepares for a series of tests, ventures into the court of Egypt, and then, beyond temptation, returns to his fathers. And there is the story of Jesus, shepherd of his flock.

Western culture bears, then, a deeply grounded tradition that sees the city as a place both inimical and threatening. It bears, also, another tradition, both linked and opposed, sacred and secular: we need only remember St. Augustine's City of God or Aristotle's view that "Men come together in the city in order to live, they remain there in order to live the good life." For my present purpose, however, the stress must fall on the tradition, all but coextensive with culture itself, which looks upon the city as inherently suspect.

It is a way of looking at the city for which, God and men surely know, there is plenty of warrant. No one can fail to be haunted by terrible stories about the collapse of ancient cities; no one does not at some point recognize the strength of refreshment to be gained from rural life; no one can look at our civilization without at moments wishing it could be wiped out with the sweep of a phrase.

II

Our modern disgust with the city is foreshadowed in the 18th-century novelists. Smollett, connoisseur of sewage, has his Matthew Bramble cry out upon the suppurations of Bath—"Imagine to yourself a high exalted essence of mingled odors, arising from putrid gums, imposthumated lungs, sour flatulencies, rank arm-pits, sweating feet, running sores." In London Bramble feels himself lost in "an immense wilderness . . . the grand source of luxury and corruption." Fore-shadowing the late Dickens, Smollett is also a literary grand-uncle of Louis Ferdinand Céline, impresario of Parisian *pissoirs* and New York subway toilets.

Smollett helps create the tradition of disgust, but Fielding, a greater writer, helps set in motion the dominant literary pattern of discovery and withdrawal in regard to the city. It is the pattern of *Tom Jones* and later, in more complicated ways, of those 19th-century novels recording the travels of the Young Man from the Provinces: the youth leaving the wholesomeness of the country and then, on the road and in the city, experiencing pleasures, adventures, and lessons to last a lifetime. Fielding has little interest in blunt oppositions between mountain air and pestilent streets such as Smollett indulges. Smollett's city is more vivid than Fielding's, but Smollett rarely moves from obsessed image to controlled idea: the city, for him, is an item in that accumulation of annoyance which is about as close as he comes to a vision of evil. And thereby, oddly, Smollett is closer to many 20th-century writers than is Fielding. A man of coherence, Fielding knows that the city cannot be merely excoriated, it must be imaginatively transformed. Just as Tom Jones's journey is a shaping into circular or spiral pattern of the picaro's linear journey, so the city of the picaresque novel—that setting of prat-falls, horrors, and what the Elizabethan writer Robert Greene had called "pleasant tales of foist"—becomes in Fielding an emblem of moral vision. The picaro learns the rules of the city, Fielding's hero the rules of civilized existence. In Fielding the city is a necessary stopping-point for the education of the emotions, to be encountered, overcome, and left behind.

It is customary to say that the third foreshadower of the 18th century, Daniel Defoe, was a writer sharing the later, 19th-century vision of the city, but only in limited ways is this true. For Defoe's London is bodiless and featureless. Populated with usable foils, it provides less the substance than the schema of a city; finally, it is a place where you can safely get lost. The rationality of calculation Max Weber assigns to capitalism becomes in *Moll Flanders* an expert acquaintance with geographic maze. Moll acts out her escapade in a city functional and abstract, mapped out for venture and escape—somewhat like a ballet where scenery has been replaced by chalk-marks of choreography. Defoe anticipates the design of the city, insofar as it is cause and token of his heroine's spiritual destitution, just as Kafka will later dismiss from his fiction all but the design of the city, an equivalent to his dismissal of character psychology in behalf of metaphysical estrangement.

III

The modern city first appears full-face—as physical concreteness, emblem of excitement, social specter, and locus of myth—in Dickens and Gogol. Nostalgic archaism clashes with the shock of urban horror, and from this clash follows the myth of the modern city. Contributing to, though not quite the main component of this myth, is the distaste of Romanticism for the machine, the calculation, the city.

"The images of the Just City," writes W. H. Auden in his brilliant study of Romantic iconography, "which look at us from so many Italian paintings . . . are lacking in Romantic literature because the Romantic writers no longer believe in their existence. What exists is the Trivial Unhappy Unjust City, the desert of the average from which the only escape is to the wild, lonely, but still vital sea."

Not all Romantics go to sea, almost all bemoan the desert. Wordsworth complains about London in *The Prelude*:

> The slaves unrespited of low pursuits,
> Living amid the same perpetual flow
> Of trivial objects, melted and reduced
> To one identity, by differences
> That have no law, no meaning, and no end.

This Romantic assault upon the city continues far into our century. Melville's Pierre says, "Never yet have I entered the city by night, but, somehow, it made me feel both bitter and sad." "I always feel doomed when the train is running into London," adds Rupert Birkin in *Women in Love*. Such sentences recur endlessly in modern writing, after a time becoming its very stock in trade. And the assault they direct against the modern city consists of more than sentimentalism, or archaism, or *Gemeinschaft*-nostalgia. The Romantic attack upon the city derives from a fear that the very growth of civilization must lead to a violation of traditional balances between man and his cosmos, a Faustian presumption by a sorcerer who has forgotten that on all but his own scales he remains an apprentice. Nothing that has happened during this past century allows us easily to dismiss this indictment.

Darkened and fragmented, it is an indictment that comes to the fore in Dickens's later novels. In the earlier ones there is still a marvelous responsiveness to the youthfulness of the world, an eager pleasure in the discoveries of streets.

Almost every *idea* about the city tempts us to forget what the young Dickens never forgot: the city is a place of virtuosity, where men can perform with freedom and abandonment. And it is Dickens's greatness, even in those of his books which are anything but great, that he displays London as theater, circus, vaudeville: the glass enlarging upon Micawber, Sarry Gamp, Sam Weller. If the city is indeed pesthole and madhouse, it is also the greatest show on earth, continuous performances and endlessly changing cast. George Gissing notes that Dickens seemed "to make more allusions throughout his work to the *Arabian Nights* than to any other book," a "circumstance illustrative of that habit of mind which led him to discover infinite romance in the obscurer life of London." Continues Gissing: "London as a place of squalid mystery and terror, of the grimly grotesque, of labyrinthine obscurity and lurid fascination, is Dickens's own; he taught people a certain way of regarding the huge city."

In Dickens's early novels there are already ominous chords and frightening overtones. The London of *Oliver Twist* is a place of terror from which its young hero must be rescued through a country convalescence, and the London of *The Old Curiosity Shop*, as Donald Fanger* remarks, "impels its victims . . . to flee to the quasi-divine purity of the country . . . repeatedly identified with the remote springs of childhood, innocence and peace." Yet throughout Dickens's novels London remains a place of fascination: he is simply too great a writer to allow theory to block perception.

In his earlier novels sentimental pastoral jostles simple pleasure in color and sound; and the pattern toward and away from the city, as classically set forth by Fielding, is used in a somewhat casual way until it receives a definitive rendering in *Great Expectations*. But it is in his three great novels—*Bleak House, Little Dorrit,* and *Our Mutual Friend,* with their commanding images of fog, prison, dust-heap— that Dickens works out that vision of our existence which has so brilliantly and oppressively influenced later writing. Here the by-now worn notions of our culture—alienation, depersonalization, forlornness—are dramatized with an innocence of genius. That in cities men become functions of their function; go crazy with the dullness of their work; transform eccentricities into psychic paralysis; soon come to look as if they themselves *were* bureaucracies; and die without a ripple of sound —all this Dickens represents with a zest he had not yet learned to regard as ill-becoming. He enlarges his earlier comic gifts into the ferocious

---

* Let me here record my debt to the brilliant writings on the theme of the city and literature by Donald Fanger and John Raleigh.

splendor of the Smallweeds, the Guppys, the Snagsbys, so that even as the city remains a theater, the play is now of a hardening into death.

Not only, as Edmund Wilson remarks, does Dickens develop the novel of the social group; he becomes the first to write the novel of the city as some enormous, spreading creature that has gotten out of control, an Other apart from the men living within it. By the time he writes his last complete novel, the savage and underrated *Our Mutual Friend*, Dickens sees London as "a hopeless city, with no rent in the leaden canopy of its sky . . . a heap of vapour charged with muffled sound of wheels, and enfolding a gigantic catarrh."

We have learned to speak lightly of "society" as something pressing and enclosing us, but imagine the terror men must have felt upon first encountering this sensation! Reading these late novels of Dickens we seem to be watching a process like that of the earth being buried beneath layers of ice: a process we now can name as the triumph of the Collective. And to this process Dickens's most intimate response is a bewilderment he projects onto an alienated space, in that multiplying chaos where Mr. Krook, double of the Lord High Chancellor, reigns and the dust-heap becomes a symbol of the derangements of exchange value. The indeterminacy of urban life, for Dostoevsky a frightening idea, is for Dickens a frightening experience.

As if in echo, one of Gogol's clerks cries out, "There is no place for me." Not in Petersburg there isn't nor in the grotesque emblem of Petersburg Gogol created. Meek spiritual cripples, his clerks lure us for a moment into sympathy with the smallness of their desires. But perhaps out of that awe at the endlessness of suffering which leads Faulkner and Leskov into harshness, Gogol treats pathos not as pathetic but as the material for comedies of irreducible disorder. The grander the city, the more wormlike its creatures. Socially fixed, the clerks are personally erased. Reduced to clerkness, one of them takes home documents to copy for pleasure—this zero reveling in his zero-ness recalls another zero, Peretz's Bontche Shveig, who when asked in heaven to name his ultimate desire, requests a hot roll with butter each morning.

How can one bear such a world, this Gogol-city of innumerable petty humiliations? By a gesture signifying the retribution of arbitrariness. In "The Overcoat" Akaky Akakievich (in Russian a name with cloacal associations) affirms himself only after death, when Petersburg is haunted by an Akakyish specter: an excremental cloud hanging over this excremental city. In "The Nose" a character finds that his nose has simply quit his face, with a sauciness he would not himself dare. But how can a nose quit a face? (As like ask Kafka how a man can turn into a cockroach.) When the weight of the determined becomes intolerable, the arbitrary gesture that changes nothing yet says everything may come to seem a token of freedom. The nose leaves the face because Gogol *tells* it to.

The figures and atmospheres of Dickens and Gogol are appropriated by Dostoevsky, but in his novels men appear as conscious beings, their alienated grotesqueness elevated to psychological plenitude. The life of man in the city becomes a metaphysical question, so that in those airless boarding houses into which Dostoevsky crams his characters there is enacted the fate of civilization. Raskolnikov's ordeal relates to Petersburg and Christianity: Can man live in this world, is there a reason why he should? *Crime and Punishment* offers a wide repertoire of city sensations, not as a catalogue of display but as a vibrant correlative to Raskolnikov's spiritual dilemmas. God and the Devil still live in this city, the former as idiot or buffoon, the latter as sleazy good-natured petit-bourgeois. That is why in Dostoevsky the city of filth retains a potential for becoming the city of purity. The city brings out Raskolnikov's delusions: it is the locale of the modern fever for mounting sensations, for the modern enchantment with the sordid as a back-alley to beatitude. The city is also the emblem of Raskolnikov's possible redemption: it is the locale of men who share a community of suffering and may yet gain the ear of Christ. Never does Dostoevsky allow the attractions of nihilism to deprive him of the vision of transcendence. In "Notes from Underground" the city bears a similar relation, what might be called a dialectical intimacy, with the narrator: each of his intellectual disasters is publicly reenacted as a burlesque in the streets. More than social microcosm or animated backdrop, the city provides Dostoevsky with the contours and substance of his metaphysical theme.

IV

Let us abruptly turn from what literature may tell about the city to what the city does in and to literature.

The city as presence brings major changes in narrative patterns. Abandoning the inclusive tourism of the picaresque, the 19th-century novel often employs a spiral-like pattern; first a pull toward the city, then a disheartened retreat to some point of origin (the blacksmith shop in *Great Expectations*, the chestnut tree in *The Charterhouse of Parma*). Elements of pastoral seem still attached to this narrative configuration, for one of its tacit ends is to retain in the novel clusters of feeling that flourished best in earlier genres. Lionel Trilling describes this kind of narrative:

. . . equipped with poverty, pride and intelligence, the Young Man from the Provinces stands outside life and seeks to enter. . . . It is his fate to move from an obscure position into one of considerable eminence in Paris or London or St. Petersburg, to touch the life of the rulers of the earth. He understands everything to be "a test."

And then? Always the same denouement: the Young Man's defeat or disillusion, and his retreat to the countryside where he can bind his wounds, cauterize his pride, struggle for moral renewal. Even more striking than its presence in novels as explicitly hostile to the city as *Great Expectations* and *Sentimental Education* is the way this pattern dominates novels in which the author seems consciously to intend a celebration of the city. For Balzac Paris is a place of "gold and pleasure," and the central portion of *Lost Illusions* evokes a stormy metropolis of excitement and sheer animatedness. Yet even this most cosmopolitan of novels follows the pattern of attraction and withdrawal, bringing its hero Lucien back to the countryside in bewilderment and thereby offering a distant nod to pastoral. At the end, to be sure, Balzac's cynicism triumphs (one almost adds, thank God) and Lucien is seen in the tow of the devil, who will take him to the city where life, naturally, is more *interesting*: the city, as Balzac said, that "is corrupt *because* it is eminently civilized."

If the pattern of 19th-century fiction forms a spiral to and away from the city, it is in the sharpest contrast to later novels in which the city becomes a maze beyond escape. In *Ulysses* and *The Trial* the traditional journeys of the hero are replaced by a compulsive backtracking: there is no place else to go, and the protagonist's motions within the city stand for his need, also through backtracking, to find a center within the self.

The city allows for a more complex system of social relationships than any other locale. Sociologists keep repeating that the city impels men into relationships lacking in warmth, often purely functional and abstract; and from this once-revolutionary perception they slide into nostalgia for an "organic community" located at notoriously imprecise points in the past. For the novelist, however, the city's proliferation of casual and secondary relationships offers new possibilities: the drama of the group and the comedy of the impersonal. The experiences of Ulysses for which Homer had to arrange complicated journeys, Joyce can pack into a day's wandering through a single city. There follows the possibility of fictions constructed along the lines that the Soviet critic M. M. Bakhtin calls a "polyphonic" structure, in which social loss may yield literary advance. Dostoevsky's novels, writes Bakhtin, "caught intact a variety of social worlds and groups which had not [yet] . . . begun to lose their distinctive apartness" and thereby "the objective preconditions were created for the essential multilevel and multivoice structure of the polyphonic novel."

To which I would add two observations: 1) The rise of the city is a blessing for minor characters who might otherwise never see the light of day; and 2) The inclination of some novelists to employ a multiplicity of narrative points of view has much to do with the rise of the city.

As the city becomes a major locale in literature, there occur major changes in regard to permissible subjects, settings, and characters. The idea of literary decorum is radically transformed, perhaps destroyed. Literature gains a new freedom; everything, which may be too much, is now possible. Out of the dogmas of anticonvention, new conventions arise. The city enables the birth of new genres: who could imagine surrealism without Paris?

In the novel of the city, a visit to a slum can serve as a shorthand equivalent to a descent into hell, as in *Bleak House* or *Redburn*. An address, a neighborhood, an accent—these identify the condition of a man, or the nature of an act, quite as much as social rank or notations of manners once did. So powerful, at first liberating and then constricting, do these new conventions become that in *The Waste Land* their rapid evocation permits a summary vision of an entire culture. The typist's life as a familiar barrenness, the dialogue in the bar as a characteristic plebeian mindlessness, the conversation between upper-class husband and wife as a recognizable sterility—these serve as the terms of an overarching spiritual assessment.

As the city breaks down traditional rankings, there emerges the plebeian writer or the writer of fallen circumstances. The city erases family boundaries, in one direction toward those rootless wanderers of the streets first imagined by Edgar Allan Poe, and in the other direction toward the extended families pictured by Dostoevsky. The city yields stunning and rapid juxtapositions: "In Paris," gloats Balzac, "vice is perpetually joining the rich man to the poor, and the great to the humble."

The city thereby offers endless possibilities of symbolic extension. In Gissing's *New Grub Street* it becomes a place of paralyzing fatigue, a grayness of spirit that finds its extension in the grayness of a London winter. To Flaubert in *Sentimental Education*, as if to anticipate Max Weber's fear that we are entering "a long polar night of icy darkness and hardness," Paris comes to represent a collective yielding to *acedia* and nihilism, and as we read we have the sensation of watching men turn slowly into stone, a whole civilization in the process of quiet petrifaction.

The city affects literature in still another way: it provides a new range of vocabularies, from the street argot of a Céline to the ironic urbanities of the early

Auden, from the coarse eloquence of Balzac's Parisians to the mixture of racy street-Jewishness and intellectual extravaganza of Bellow. The city also encourages that flavorless language, the language of sawdust, we associate with naturalism, as if the denial of will must be reflected in the death of words; yet the city also yields writers like Dickens and Gogol new resources for grotesquerie and mockery. Language can be reduced to bureaucratic posture, as in Guppy's proposal to Esther Summerson in Bleak House, employing the terms of a brief for a small-claims court. Or it can be used by Gogol in a style the Russians call skaz, described by Yevgeny Zamyatin as "The free, spontaneous language of speech, digressions . . . coinages of the street variety, which cannot be found in any dictionary . . . [and in which] the author's comments are given in a language close to that of the milieu depicted."

One of the great temptations for the writer dealing with city life is to think of it as a "creature" or "being" independent from and looming over the people who live in it. Apostrophes to London and Paris are frequent in Dickens and Balzac, but these are only feeble rhetorical intimations of what they are struggling to apprehend. The sense that somehow a city has "a life of its own" is so common, it must have some basis in reality; but precisely what we mean by such statements is very hard to say. For Dickens and Gogol, as for Melville, such metaphors become ways of expressing the sense of littleness among people forming the anonymous masses. For other writers, such as Zola, Andrey Biely, and Dos Passos, these metaphors prepare the way for an effort to embody the life of the group in its own right, to see the collective as an autonomous and imperious organization.

The city as presence in modern literature gives rise to a whole series of new character types, and these come to be formidable conventions in subsequent writing. A few of them:

The clerk, soon taken to represent the passivity, smallness, and pathos of life in the city: Gogol, Melville, Dickens, Kafka.

The Jew, bearer of the sour fruits of self-definition: Joyce, Proust, Mann.

The cultivated woman, one of the triumphs of modern writing, inconceivable anywhere but in the city, a woman of femininity and intelligence, seductiveness and awareness, traditional refinement and modern possibilities: Tolstoy's Anna, James's Madame Vionnet, Colette's Julie.

The underground man, a creature of the city, without fixed rank or place, burrowing beneath the visible structure of society, hater of all that flourishes aboveground, meek and arrogant, buried in a chaos of subterranean passions yet gratified by the stigmata of his plight: Dostoevsky and Céline.

"The psychological basis of the metropolitan type of individual," writes Georg Simmel in his essay, "The Metropolis and Mental Life," "consists in the intensification of nervous stimulation which results from the swift and uninterrupted change of outer and inner stimuli. . . . Lasting impressions . . . use up, so to speak, less consciousness than does the rapid crowding of changing images, the sharp discontinuity in the grasp of a single phrase, and the unexpectedness of onrushing impressions." Dostoevsky and Joyce best capture this experience in the novel, Baudelaire and Hart Crane in verse.

In *Crime and Punishment* Raskolnikov is assaulted by repeated impressions during his dazed wanderings through Petersburg. He walks along the street and sees a coachman beating his horse with gratuitous brutality. He watches a street entertainer grinding out a tune on a barrel organ, tries to strike up a nervous conversation with a stranger and frightens the man away. Another man approaches him and without warning mutters. "You are a murderer." At still another moment he notices a woman in front of him, "at first reluctantly and, as it were, with annoyance, and then more and more intently"; he supposes her a victim of a seduction; the terribleness of the city seems flaringly vivid to him. Each of these apparently stray incidents becomes a tonal equivalent to Raskolnikov's condition, and the seemingly chaotic business of the city is transformed into a map of the protagonist's turmoil.

V

Together with what I have called the myth of the modern city—enemy of man: pesthole, madhouse, prison—there appear in modern literature at least two other significant visions of urban life. The first is benign, fairly frequent among American writers who have grown up in a culture devoted to the virtues of the countryside. For Henry James the city serves as a token of the possibilities of a high civilization. The Paris of *The Ambassadors* is a mixture of Balzac's Paris (without Balzac's greasepaint, vulgarity, and financial delirium) and an American dream of a European City of Beauty. Paris becomes the shining gloss of man's history, the greatness of the past realized in monuments and manners. Paris stands for the Jamesian vision of a culture far gone in sophistication yet strangely pure, as if no dollar were exchanged there or loyalty betrayed. James was not a naif, he knew he was summoning a city of his desire; and in an earlier novel, *The American*, he had shown himself capable of presenting a Paris sinister and shabby. But now Paris has become the home of civilization, with the splendor of its history yielding the materials for his myth of idealization.

Quite as benign is Whitman's vision of New York. His poems do not capture
the terrible newness of the industrial city, for that he does not really know. Whitman's city flourishes in harmony with surrounding forests and green; it figures
modestly in the drama of democracy; there is still psychic and social roominess,
so that this bohemian singing of the masses can easily knock about in the streets,
a New World *flâneur*, without feeling crowded or oppressed. Between the noisy
groping city and Whitman's *persona* as the Fraternal Stranger there are still large
spaces, and this very spaciousness allows him to celebrate the good nature and
easy style of his "camerados" in New York. Not many 19th-century writers can
share that comfort.

The second and by far more influential vision of the city proceeds in a cultural
line from Baudelaire through Eliot and then through Eliot's many followers. In
the smudge of our time, this vision of the city has come to seem indistinguishable
from the one I have attributed to the 19th-century masters; but it is distinguishable. There is in Baudelaire little of that recoil from the city about which I have
spoken and little, if any, pastoral indulgence. He accepts the city as the proper
stage for his being; he apprehends, better than anyone, the nervous currents that
make cosmopolitan life exciting and destructive; he writes in the *Tableaux Parisiens*
not only of ugliness and debauchery but also, in Proust's words, of "suffering,
death, and humble fraternity." A famous passage celebrates the public concerts,
"rich in brass," that "pour some heroism into the hearts of town dwellers."

Walter Benjamin notes that "Baudelaire placed the shock experience at the
very center of his artistic work," and he remarks also on the relation between that
"shock experience" and Baudelaire's "contact with the metropolitan masses . . .
the amorphous crowd of passers-by" with whom he "becomes an accomplice
even as he dissociates himself from them." In Baudelaire's poems shock serves
more than a social end; it has to do with his struggle for a scheme of moral order,
a struggle conducted, *in extremis*, through images of disorder. Baudelaire's fear is
not, as others had already said before him, that the city is hell: his fear is that it
is *not* hell, not even hell. His strategy of shock comes to seem a modernist terror-
raid in behalf of classical resolution—not always so, of course, since poets can
become secret sharers of the devils they grapple with. It hardly matters whether
Baudelaire is seen as a figure of urban satanism or inverted Christianity; he moves
in the orbits of both, emanating, in Mallarmé's wonderful line, "a protective poison that we must go on breathing even if we die of it." For Baudelaire, Paris embodies the fear of a life reduced from evil to the merely sordid, a life sinking into
the triviality of nihilism.

This is the side of Baudelaire that Eliot appropriates in *The Waste Land*: "Unreal City . . . I had not thought death had undone so many." Eliot lacks Baudelaire's capacity for surrendering himself to the quotidian pleasures of a great city, but he narrows the Baudelairean vision into something of enormous power, perhaps the single most powerful idea of our culture. Eliot's idea of the city has become assimilated to that of the great 19th-century writers, though it is imperative to insist on the difference between madhouse and wasteland, even prison and wasteland. Eliot's vision is then taken up, more and more slackly, by the writers of the last half-century, charting, mourning, and then—it is unavoidable—delectating in the wasteland. Life in the city is shackled to images of sickness and sterility, with a repugnance authentic or adorned; and what seems finally at the base of this tradition is a world view we might designate as *remorse over civilization*. "When one has a sense of guilt after having committed a misdeed," says Freud gloomily, "the feeling should . . . be called remorse." Our guilt, almost casual in its collective sedimentation, proceeds from the feeling that the whole work of civilization— and where is that to be found but in cities?—is a gigantic mistake. This remorse appears first as a powerful release of sensibility, in imaginative works of supreme value, and then as the clichés of *kitsch*, Madison Avenue modernism. The strength of the masters remains overwhelming, from Baudelaire to Eliot to Auden, as they fill their poems with forebodings of the collapse of cities, the crumbling of all man's works. Auden writes in "The Fall of Rome":

> Private rites of magic send
> The temple prostitutes to sleep;
> All the literati keep
> An imaginary friend.
> [. . . . .]
> Caesar's double-bed is warm
> As an unimportant clerk
> Writes I DO NOT LIKE MY WORK
> On a pink official form.

And the Greek poet Cavafy writes about a city waiting, with impatient weariness, for the barbarians to take over:

> What does this sudden uneasiness mean,
> And this confusion? (How grave the faces have become!)

Why are the streets and squares rapidly emptying,
and why is everyone going back
home lost in thought?

Because it is night and the barbarians have not come,
and some men have arrived from the frontiers
and they say there are no barbarians any more
and now, what will become of us without barbarians?
These people were a kind of solution.

VI

The suspicion of the city and all it represents seems to run so deep in our culture that it would be impossible to eradicate it, even if anyone were naive enough
to wish to. In its sophisticated variants it is a suspicion necessary for sanity. And
perhaps, for all we know, it is a suspicion emblematic of some ineradicable tragedy in the human condition: the knowledge that makes us cherish innocence
makes innocence unattainable.

In traditional pastoral, suspicion of the city is frequently contained through
a discipline of irony proceeding through a sequence something like this: game
of the shepherds, seriousness of the game, recognition of how limited are the
uses of that seriousness. In modern literature, which can have but little interest
in shepherds, there is a violence of response to the city which breaks past the
discipline of irony—our experience demands that. But then, just as traditional
pastoral suffers the corruptions of literalism, so must the modernist assault upon
the city. How, we ask ourselves, can we bring together, in some complex balance
of attitude, our commitment to the imaginative truth in what the modern writers
show us about the city and our awareness that it may no longer be quite sufficient
for us?

We are the children, or step-children, of modernism. We learned our abc's lisp-
ing "alienation, bourgeoisie, catastrophe." As against those who brushed aside
the 20th century, we were right in believing our age to be especially terrible, especially cursed, on the rim of apocalypse. But today loyalty to the tradition of modernism may require a rejection of its academic and marketplace heirs, and far
more important, a questioning of its premises and values.

To deride the epigones of modernism who have reduced it from a vision to a
fashion is no great intellectual risk. We should go farther and ask whether the
masters must, in some sense, be held responsible for their corrupted followers, if

only insofar as the corruption may point back to some little-noticed or half-hidden flaw in the world-view of the masters. Our problem then becomes to ask whether the visions of the great modernist writers can retain for us the moral urgency and emotional command they so powerfully exerted only a few decades ago.

Clearly this is not a question to be answered in a few paragraphs, though I have tried on an earlier occasion to indicate some opinions.* What matters, in behalf of a serious confrontation with our dominant literary heritage, is to move past (which is not to say abandon) both the authentic pieties we retain from an earlier moment and the false ones that have followed them.

I propose a hypothesis: We have reached the point in our cultural history where it seems both possible and useful to remove ourselves from the partisanship that cultural modernism evoked throughout the past century. Modernism is no longer threatened, nor in question. Its achievements are solid and lasting, its influence is incalculable. It is beginning to take a place in the development of Western culture somewhat like that which Romanticism can be said to have taken by the last two or three decades of the 19th century. *Modernism is beginning to become part of history*, and thereby, for those of us responsive to history, a complex of styles and values we can accept through the mediation of its classical works. Modernism can now enter our moral experience complicated by that awareness of historical distance which is a mark of a cultivated sensibility, and thereby it remains a crucial part of our experience, as Romanticism does too. But if we ask ourselves questions as to the truth of the vision of a Lawrence or an Eliot or a Yeats—and I have some awareness of how tricky such questions can be—then we are no longer likely, and younger people are certainly no longer likely, to answer them with an unbroken passion, that total assent or denial elicited by a cultural movement both contemporary and embattled.

If we lose much by no longer seeing modernism as a contemporary cultural presence, we may gain something too. We may gain a certain detached perspective upon its nature and its achievements, as in recent decades, through discovery, polemic, and reassessment, we have been gaining such a perspective upon the nature and achievements of Romanticism. And if we do approach modernism in this way—as a major component of our culture which the motions of history are transporting into that segment of our experience we call the past—then we may discover that a good many of our earlier enthusiasms will have to be qualified. Not repudiated; qualified. The famous "revolutionary" aspect of modernism may come to have for us an ambiguous value: in part an authentic response to the

* In my essay "The Culture of Modernism," *Decline of the New.*

terribleness of the age and in part a nostalgia for a historically unlocatable and morally dubious "organic past"; in part a profound engagement with the inner nerves of city life and in part a snobbism of the fastidious embraced by those who look down upon the commonplace desires of commonplace mankind; in part an assault upon the calculation that lies at the heart of the bourgeois ethic and in part a cruel dismissal of those fragmented solutions and moderate comforts which it has become easy to dismiss as bourgeois. And we may then have to conclude that the now established hostility to the idea of the city, which is one portion of the modernist legacy, will no longer serve as well as in the past. The vision of the city we inherit from Eliot and Baudelaire, Céline and Brecht—with its ready nausea, packaged revulsion, fixed estrangement—will have to be modulated and itself seen as a historical datum. If we ask ourselves whether we accept the ideas of Shelley or the vision of Blake, their very distance allows us to answer with a sense of ironic qualification that would be difficult to summon for an embattled contemporary. Something of the sort should soon be true in regard to the great figures of modernism.

To remain faithful to its tradition means to call it sharply into question. Can we not, for example, say, yes, the city remains the pesthole and madhouse, the prison and setting of spiritual void that you have shown it to be; nevertheless we can no longer be satisfied with this perception and this perception alone.

Nor is it as if we lack an inspiring model from within literary modernism itself. No writer has portrayed the city with such severity as James Joyce. Every assault that the modernist literary tradition can make upon the city appears in *Ulysses*, magnified in scope and feverish with intensity. Yet that assault is also, in *Ulysses*, transcended through a skeptical humaneness, a tolerance beyond tolerance, a recognition that man was not put on this earth to scratch his eyes out. Of all the writers who render the modern city, it is Joyce who engages in the most profound struggle with nihilism, for he sees it everywhere, in the newspaper office and the church, on the street and in the bed, through the exalted and the routine. Joyce, says Richard Ellmann, shows that "the world of cigars is devoid of heroism only to those who don't understand that Ulysses' spear was merely a sharpened stick . . . and that Bloom can demonstrate the qualities of man by word of mouth as effectively as Ulysses by thrust of spear." The theme of *Ulysses*, says Ellmann, is simply that "casual kindness overcomes unconscionable power." Does it? In reality? In Joyce's book? I hardly know but cherish Ellmann's sentence, as I believe Joyce would have too.

We may destroy our civilization, but we cannot escape it. We may savor a soured remorse at the growth of civilization, but that will yield us no large or lasting reward. There is no turning back: our only way is a radical struggle for the City of the Just.

The City of the Just . . . the phrase rings a little hollow right now, so far do we seem to be from it. Still, we shall create genuine cities, which means vital civilizations, or we shall perish. We shall create a high culture, serious and gay, or we shall sink into a rocklike, mainline stupor. Assault upon the city is now to be valued only when understood as the complex play of men who live in cities and would live nowhere else. It is too late for tents and sheep and lutes, or whatever surrogates we may invent. "Perhaps the best definition of the city in its higher aspects," says Lewis Mumford, "is that it is a place designed to offer the widest facilities for significant conversation."

So we must turn again, to build the Just City where men can be decent and humane and at ease, that ease Wallace Stevens speaks of:

> One's grand flights, one's Sunday baths,
> One's tootings at the wedding of the soul
> Occur as they occur . . .

And what will we do in the city? Take our Sunday baths, toot at "the wedding of the soul," read Colette, marvel at Balanchine, and with proper modulations of irony, realize the claims of pastoral, that indestructible artifice of the urban imagination. More than 400 years ago Barnaby Googe understood it all: "God sends me Vittayles for my nede, and I synge Care awaye."

Tribune of Socialism: Norman Thomas

{1976}

W A. SWANBERG HAS WRITTEN an old-fashioned biography of Norman Thomas, and mostly the book is the better for it. No strands of political theorizing, no dips into Freudianism, no lumps of sociology. All is narrative—the story of a splendid man told simply and with a controlled affection.

Swanberg has understood that a lifelong devotion to the poor and the exploited is not something that needs—in the style of current sophistications—to be "explained." The kind of life Norman Thomas led is always a possibility for us, and the biographer need only show it forth as an exemplary instance. If this book has some pedestrian pages, if it rarely breaks into eloquence or profundity, the story it tells is nevertheless a deeply moving one.

The pedestrian pages come at the start, in sketches of Thomas's early years in a high-minded Presbyterian family. The earnestness of young Norman preparing for the ministry, his search for a social vision that might give substance to his ethical-religious sentiments, his turn to pacifism in World War I and then to a larger social rebelliousness—these are described with a shade too much detail and stolidity of tone. But once Thomas shifts in the early 1920s from Social Gospel to Socialist Party, trying to pull together a movement ripped apart by Government persecution and Communist defection, the story comes entirely to life.

Ferociously energetic, endowed with a loud crackling voice, quick in debate and wonderfully free of the public man's self-importance, Thomas now became both the leader of his floundering party and an all-American circuit rider. He ran for office again and again, speaking at street corners, union halls, and universities, and touring the country in a beat-up car with his wife Violet, a patrician lady who gave her heart to her husband and his cause. (In one campaign they barnstormed through New England for 10 days—at a grand cost of $55.45!) Old-party spokesmen learned to avoid Thomas in debate: he knew more, he talked faster, and—miracle of American miracles!—he came out with comely sentences and coherent paragraphs.

Wherever there was injustice, Thomas spoke up. Boss Hague in Jersey City tried to institute a vest-pocket fascism? Thomas was there to challenge him, suffering rough treatment and jail. Gov. Paul McNutt of Indiana proposed informally to repeal the Bill of Rights? Thomas was there to say it couldn't be done. Some of Mr. Swanberg's best pages concern Thomas's one-man crusade to help the Southern Tenant Farmers' Union, formed in 1934 by desperately poor sharecroppers in Arkansas. Thomas kept going down there, risking his neck, defying vigilante terrorists, winning the affection of farm workers who had never before dared speak for their rights. And up North, Thomas kept needling Secretary of Agriculture Henry Wallace (later the fellow-travelers' darling) to do something for the Arkansas sharecroppers, but Wallace steadily refused to meet with him and, instead, made a shameful speech saying the trouble in Arkansas was due to "Communistic and Socialistic gentlemen" who "have gone in to stir up trouble."

In the late 1930s, Thomas tangled with President Roosevelt (who nevertheless seems to have liked him). He tried to persuade the president that his embargo on arms to Loyalist Spain was enabling a major fascist victory in Europe, but as Thomas caustically reported, Roosevelt "in his own inimitable way changed the subject."

As a man who tried to bring together the imperatives of morality and the devices of politics, and as leader of a small socialist party who felt keenly the intellectual crisis that socialism was undergoing throughout the world, Thomas made a lot of mistakes. He let himself be excessively influenced by the sectarian-academic Marxists of the 1930s. He came too close to the isolationists during the years before World War II.

Thomas was a superb tribune for socialism, but an indifferent party leader. Partly this was due to his temperament, which drew him more strongly to the rostrum than the desk. But mostly it was a result of overwhelming, perhaps insoluble, problems that the socialist movement was facing in the mid-30's and later.

The failure of the German Left to fight against Hitler's seizure of power seemed to the young radicals gathered near Thomas evidence that social democratic reformist policies were futile and that more militant methods were needed. Thomas half agreed, though he also sensed that in the United States revolutionary policies could only lead to the hermeticism of the sect. The right-wing Socialists, the Old Guard that was dug into the Jewish garment unions, welcomed F.D.R.'s New Deal as a partial fulfillment of the demands they had long been making. Thomas half agreed, though he also argued that the New Deal provided no more than minor palliatives to a sick society.

Meanwhile, the Communists had turned rightward and were barraging the Socialists with appeals for a "united front." The Old Guard distrusted the Communists on principle, and often with good reason, while the left-wing Socialists felt that the threat of fascism warranted at times the risk of limited blocs with the Communists. Thomas saw justice in both views, so much so that some of his friends, on both left and right, made the mistake of seeing his intelligence as indecision.

Retrospective wisdom (in which we're all rich) suggests that the Socialists might have supported New Deal reforms as far as they went while not abandoning their basic critique of our society. Or it might have been possible to recognize the need for militant struggle against European fascism while also grasping that American circumstances did not lend themselves to the revolutionary outlook.

But Thomas suffered from the defects of his virtues. He wasn't single-minded or devious enough to be a strong party leader; he couldn't content himself with easy formulas, left or right. The result was that his party, which had grown encouragingly in the early 1930s, was destroyed by splits and defections. The Old Guard settled into a passive friendship with the New Deal; the left-wing got cut up in a romance with the Trotskyists; ordinary members quit in disgust. Thomas remained, loyal to the end, but increasingly a leader without followers.

Yet it was in these last years that he reached his peak as a public man. Aging, sick, lonely, he was always on call, always ready to speak, write, debate, picket, organize. He rethought some of his ideas, writing a friend that "various grim experiences, including the record of the Russian Revolution, make me far more doubtful of easy collectivist . . . alternatives," and his socialism now consisted of a rather loose democratic egalitarianism. His mind grew more subtle, he cut away the barnacles of dogmatism.

And he kept his sense of humor. A lady told him he'd been running for President since she was a little girl. "Madam," he replied, "I've been running for President since I was a little boy." Once, as Mr. Swanberg tells it, "Thomas made histrionic use of his aches . . . he seated himself at the far end of the platform so that when he was introduced he limped very slowly to the podium, cane in one hand . . . then turned to the audience and rasped, 'Creeping Socialism!'"

Among those who had abandoned him politically, it became the custom to honor him with sentimental tributes, sometimes even speaking of him as a saint. He was nothing of the sort. The few of us who remained his political friends in the 1950s and 60s knew him as something more than saint—we knew him as a passionate, troubled, eager, sometimes irascible man. He could be impatient with fools, especially the sort who bored him with elaborate introductions when he gave a speech. He could twist your arm if he wanted you to do something for a cause. He could be sharp and sour: after debating William F. Buckley Jr., he did a very funny imitation of Buckley's self-adoring superciliousness. His sight failed, but his voice kept booming out. ("I'm a tottering wreck, and it's annoying.")

Here he is, close to the end, as Dwight Macdonald describes him speaking at a SANE rally against the Vietnam War:

"So now he is 82 and he has to be helped to the speaker's stand, but once there, in the old, familiar stance, facing the crowd—they are on their feet applauding, calling out to him—he takes a firm grip on the rostrum, throws his head back, and begins to talk in a voice that is quavering. . . . For ten minutes he baits the President, modulating from irony to polemic to indignation to humor to fact to reasoning, speaking in a rapid businesslike way without rhetorical effects. . . .

"He winds up briskly, professional brio, as how many times, how many times? We get to our feet again to clap, to cheer timidly, to smile at one another as members of the same family do when one of them acquits himself well in public. The old man endures the applause politely for a reasonable time, then begins to make his way back to his seat. . . ."

Norman Thomas was the only great man I have ever met, and if I never meet another I will not feel deprived.

Postscript

I'm not sure this piece fits into the scheme of this book [*Celebrations and Attacks*]. But it gives me pleasure to say these words of tribute to a wonderful man, and so I say them.

Strangers

{1977}

B EING AN AMERICAN, we have been told repeatedly, is a complex fate, and being an American writer still more so: traditions ruptured, loyalties disheveled. Yet consider how much more complex, indeed, how utterly aggravating, it could have been to grow up in an American subculture, one of those immigrant enclaves driving itself wild with the clashing hopes that it would receive the New World's blessing and yet maintain a moment of identity neither quite European nor quite American. The rise and fall of such subcultures is said to be intrinsic to the American experience, and no doubt it is. But when one looks into conventional accounts of our literature, it is hard to find much evidence that our writers ever felt themselves to be strangers in the land—though about their estrangement from the cosmos everyone speaks. It is hard to find evidence of that deep, rending struggle which marked those writers who had to make, rather than merely assume, America as their native ground.

The whole of our literary history for the past century might be reworked so as to encourage a richer sense of what cultural influence really signifies—a sense, for example, that it is not enough simply to trace lines of continuity, since these lines are blocked, distorted, and even obliterated by recurrent outcroppings of transported Europe. Toward such a history I would here offer a few words, based not on hard evidence, of which we have little, but on recollections of the experiences shared by a generation of American Jewish writers. I will use the first person plural, though with much uneasiness, since I am aware that those for whom I claim to speak are likely to repudiate that claim and wish to provide their own fables of factuality. Here, in any case, is mine.

Lines of connection from writer to writer are never as neat or as "literary" as historians like to make out. Between master and disciple there intervene history, popular culture, vulgarization, organized forgetting, decades of muck and complication. Still, if only to ease my argument, we may agree that for writers like Robinson and Frost, Ralph Waldo Emerson towered as an ancestor imposing and authoritative, sometimes crippling, and that he figured for them not merely through the books they picked up at home or had to read in school, but through the very air, the encompassing atmosphere, of their culture. How much of "transcendentalism" remains in their writing everyone can estimate on his own, since no one has yet found a scale for weighing weightlessness; but that the pressures of this weightlessness are at work upon their writing seems beyond dispute. Despite inner clashes and discontinuities, American culture moves from the generation of Emerson to that of Robinson and Frost, as a bit later, that of Crane and Stevens, with a more or less "natural" or spontaneous rhythm. There is a passing on of the word.

But for young would-be writers growing up in a Jewish slum in New York or Chicago during the twenties and thirties, the main figures of American literature, as well as the main legends and myths carried through their fictions and stories, were not immediately available. What could Emerson mean to a boy or girl on Rivington Street in 1929, hungry for books, reading voraciously, hearing Yiddish at home, yet learning to read, write, and think in English? What could the tradition of American romanticism, surely our main tradition, mean to them?

Together with the poems of Browning and Tennyson, such young people took in the quasi- or pseudo-Emersonian homilies their Irish teachers fed them at school. They took in the American legends of an unspoiled land, heroic beginnings, pioneer aloneness, and individualist success. All of these had a strong, if sometimes delayed, impact. In the course of this migration of myth from lady teachers to immigrant children there had, however, to occur twistings, misapprehensions. Besides, we immigrant children did not come as empty vessels. We had *other stories*. We had stories about legendary endurance in the Old World; stories about the outwitting of cruel priests; stories about biblical figures still felt to be contemporaries though by now largely ripped out of their religious setting; stories about endless martyrs through the ages (while America seemed to have only one martyr and he, in beard and shawl, had a decidedly Jewish look).

These stories of ours were the very material out of which cultures are made, and even as we learned to abandon them with hurried shame and to feign respect for some frigid general who foolishly had never told a lie, or to some philosopher of freedom who kept slaves, we felt a strong residue of attachment to our own stories. We might be preparing to abandon them, but they would not abandon us. And what, after all, could rival in beauty and cleverness the stories of Isaac and Ishmael, Jacob and the angel, Joseph and his brothers?

Raised to a high inclusiveness, a story becomes a myth. It charts the possibilities and limits for the experience of a people, dramatizing its relations with the universe. We are speaking here of *possession*: that which we know, or remember, or remember that we have been forgetting. We are speaking about those tacit gestures, unseen shrugs, filaments of persuasion which form part of subverbal knowledge.

For a time, then, we tried to reconcile our stories with the American stories. The two of them would coexist in our minds, awkwardly but fruitfully, and we would give to the one our deep if fading credence and to the other our willed if unsure allegiance.

With American literature itself, we were uneasy. It spoke in tones that seemed strange and discordant. Its romanticism was of a kind we could not really find the key to, for while there were figures of the Jewish past who had striking points of kinship with the voices of Concord, we had partly been deprived of the Jewish past. (When the comparison was first made between Whitman's poetry and the teachings of Hasidism, it came from a Danish critic, Frederick Schyberg; but most of us, who ought to have noticed this immediately, knew little or nothing about Hasidism, except perhaps that it was a remnant of "superstition" from which our fathers had struggled to free themselves.)

Romanticism came to us not so much through the "American Renaissance" as through the eager appropriations that East European Jewish culture had made in the late nineteenth century from Turgenev and Chernyshevsky, Tolstoy and Chekhov. The dominant outlook of the immigrant Jewish culture was probably a shy, idealistic, ethicized, "Russian" romanticism, a romanticism directed more toward social justice than personal fulfillment. The sons and daughters of this immigrant milieu were insulated from American romanticism by their own inherited romanticism, with the differences magnified and the similarities, for a time, all but suppressed.

American romanticism was more likely to reach us through the streets than the schools, through the enticements of popular songs than the austere demands of sacred texts. We absorbed, to be sure, fragments of Emerson, but an Emerson denatured and turned into a spiritual godfather of Herbert Hoover. This American sage seemed frigid and bland, distant in his New England village—and how could we, of all generations, give our hearts to a writer who had lived all his life "in the country"? Getting in touch with the real Emerson, whoever that might be—say, with the Emerson radiant with a sense of universal human possibility yet aware enough, in his notebooks, of everything that might thwart and deny— this was not for us a natural process of discovering an ancestor or even removing the crusts of misconstruction which had been piled up by the generations. It was a task of rediscovering what we had never really discovered and then of getting past the barriers of sensibility that separated Concord, Massachusetts, from the immigrant streets of New York.

These were real barriers. What could we make of all the talk, both from and about Emerson, which elevated individualism to a credo of life? Nothing in our tradition, little in our experience, prepared us for this, and if we were growing up in the thirties, when it seemed appropriate to feel estranged from whatever was "officially" American, we could hardly take that credo with much seriousness. The whole complex of Emersonian individualism seemed either a device of the Christians to lure us into a gentility that could only leave us helpless in the worldly struggles ahead, or a bit later, when we entered the phase of Marxism, it seemed a mere reflex of bourgeois ideology, especially that distinctive American form which posited an "exceptionalist" destiny for the New World.

Perhaps a more fundamental way of getting at these matters is to say that we found it hard to decipher American culture because the East European Jews had almost never encountered the kind of Christianity that flourished in America. The Christianity our fathers had known was Catholic, in Poland, or Orthodox, in Russia, and there was no reason to expect that they would grasp the ways or the extent to which Protestantism differed. We knew little, for instance, about the strand of Hebraism running through Puritan culture—I recall as a college student feeling distinct skepticism upon hearing that the Puritan divines had Hebrew. (If they had Hebrew, how could they be Gentiles?) It was only after reading Perry Miller in later years that this aspect of American Protestant culture came alive for me. All that was distinctive in Protestant culture, making it, for better or worse, a radically different force in confrontation from Catholicism or Eastern Orthodoxy, we really could not grasp for a long time. We read the words but were largely deaf to the melody.

2

For most of us, individualism seemed a luxury or deception of the Gentile world. Immigrant Jewish culture had been rich in eccentrics, cranks, and individualist display; even the synagogue accepted prayer at personal tempos. But the idea of an individual covenant with God, each man responsible for his own salvation; the claim that each man is captain of his soul (picture those immigrant kids, in white middy blouses, bawling out, "O Captain, My Captain"); the notion that you not only have one but more than one chance in life, which constitutes the American version of grace; and the belief that you rise or fall in accord with your own merits rather than the will of alien despots—these residues of Emersonianism seemed not only strange but sometimes even a version of that brutality which our parents had warned was intrinsic to Gentile life. Perhaps our exposure to this warmed-over Emersonianism prompted us to become socialists, as if thereby to make clear our distaste for these American delusions and to affirm, instead, a heritage of communal affections and responsibilities.

Then, too, Jewish would-be writers found the classical Americans, especially Emerson and Thoreau, a little wan and frail, deficient in those historical entanglements we felt to be essential to literature because inescapable in life. If we did not yet know we surely would have agreed with Henry James's judgment that Emerson leaves "a singular impression of paleness" and lacks "personal avidity." Born, as we liked to flatter ourselves, with the bruises of history livid on our souls, and soon to be in the clutch of New World "avidities" that would make us seem distasteful or at least comic to other, more secure, Americans, we wanted a literature in which experience overflowed. So we abandoned Emerson even before encountering him, and in later years some of us would never draw closer than to establish amiable diplomatic relations.

Hardest of all to take at face value was the Emersonian celebration of nature. Nature was something about which poets wrote and therefore it merited esteem, but we could not really suppose it was as estimable as reality—the reality we knew to be social. Americans were said to love Nature, though there wasn't much evidence of this that our eyes could take in. Our own tradition, long rutted in shtetl mud and urban smoke, made little allowance for nature as presence or refreshment. Yiddish literature has a few pieces, such as Mendele's "The Calf," that wistfully suggest it might be good for Jewish children to get out of the heder (school) and into the sun; but this seems more a hygienic recommendation than a metaphysical commitment. If the talk about nature seemed a little unreal, it became still more so when capitalized as Nature; and once we reached college age and heard that Nature was an opening to God, perhaps even his phenomenal mask, it seemed quite as farfetched as the Christian mystification about three gods collapsed into one. Nothing in our upbringing could prepare us to take seriously the view that God made his home in the woods. By now we rather doubted that He was to be found anywhere, but we felt pretty certain that wherever He might keep himself, it was not in a tree, or even leaves of grass.

What linked man and God in our tradition was not nature but the commandment. Once some of us no longer cared to make such a linkage, because we doubted either the presence of God or the capacity of man, we still clung to the commandment, or at least to the shadow of its severities, for even in our defilements it lay heavily upon us.

I think it ought to be said that most of us were decidedly this-worldly, in that sardonic Yiddish style which, through the genius of a Sholom Aleichem or occasionally a Peretz, can create its own darkly soothing glow. Our appetites for transcendence had been secularized, and our messianic hungers brought into the noisy streets, so that often we found it hard to respond to, even to hear, the vocabulary of philosophical idealism which dominates American literature. Sometimes this earth-boundedness of ours was a source of strength, the strength of a Delmore Schwartz or a Daniel Fuchs handling the grit of their experience. Sometimes it could sour into mere candy-store realism or sadden into park-bench resignation. If the imagination soared in the immigrant slums, it was rarely to a Protestant heaven.

I am, of course, making all this seem too explicit, a matter of words. It went deeper than words. We had grown up, for instance, with the sovereign persuasion, which soon came to seem our most stringent imprisonment, that the family was an institution unbreakable and inviolable. Here, though we might not yet have known it, we were closer to the Southern than to the New England writers. For where, if you come to think of it, is the family in Emerson, or Thoreau, or Whitman? Even in Melville the family is a shadowy presence from which his heroes have fled before their stories begin. And where is the family in Hemingway or Fitzgerald? With Faulkner, despite all his rhetoric about honor, we might feel at home because the clamp of family which chafed his characters was like the clamp that chafed us. When we read Tolstoy we were witness to the supremacy of family life; when we read Turgenev we saw in Bazarov's parents a not-too-distant version of our own. But in American literature there were all these strange and homeless solitaries, motherless and fatherless creatures like Natty and Huck and Ishmael. Didn't they know where life came from and returned to?

Glance at any significant piece of fiction by an American Jewish writer—Schwartz's "America, America," Malamud's "The Magic Barrel," Bellow's "The Old System"—and you will see that the family serves as its organizing principle, just as in Jewish life it had become the last bulwark of defenselessness. Even in the stories of Philip Roth, which herald and perhaps celebrate the breakup of immigrant culture, there is finally a crabbed sort of admiration for the family. The Jewish imagination could not so much as conceive a fiction without paying tribute, in both senses of the word, to the family.

We had, to be sure, other and more positive reasons for keeping an uneasy distance from American literature. We felt that together with the old bedclothes, pots, and pans that our folks had brought across the ocean, they had also kept a special claim on Russian culture. Tolstoy, Turgenev, Chekhov—though not the sensationalist and anti-Semite Dostoevsky—were very close to us. They had been liberally translated into Yiddish and read by the more advanced Jewish youth of Eastern Europe. Breathing moral idealism, they spoke for humanity at large; they told us to make life better and, as it seemed to us then, what better word could literature tell? The works of these masters revealed a generosity of spirit at the very moment that the spirit of the East European Jews was straining for secular generosity. In the devotion of the Yiddish-speaking intelligentsia to Tolstoy, Turgenev, and Chekhov it almost came to seem as if these were *Jewish* writers! Tolstoy presented some problems—perhaps we regarded him as a Jew for Jesus. But the other two, they were ours! I remember Isaac Rosenfeld, the most winning of all American Jewish writers, once explaining to me with comic solemnity that Chekhov had really written in Yiddish but Constance Garnett, trying to render him respectable, had falsified the record. Anyone with half an ear, said Rosenfeld, could catch the tunes of Yiddish sadness, absurdity, and humanism in Chekhov's prose—and for a happy moment it almost seemed true.

Coming as strangers who possessed, so to say, the Russian masters, we could afford to be a little cool toward the American ones. What was Dreiser to Tolstoy, Anderson to Turgenev, and the sum of all American short stories to one by Chekhov? These Russians formed a moral dike guarding the immigrant Jewish intelligentsia and then their children from the waves of American sensibility and myth. Like the Yiddish culture from which we had emerged, we were internationalist in our sentiment before we were part of *any* nation, living in the exalted atmospheres of European letters even as we might be afraid, at home, to wander a few streets away.

The situation was further complicated by the fact that the young would-be Jewish writers were themselves only tenuously connected with the Jewish culture from which they had emerged. They were stamped and pounded by the immigrant experience, but that was something rather different from the Jewish tradition. Brilliant and vital as the immigrant experience may seem to us now, it was nevertheless a thinned-out residue of the complex religious culture that had been built up over the centuries by the East European Jews. A process of loss was being enacted here—first, the immigrant culture was estranged from its Old World sources, and second, we were estranged from the immigrant culture. Especially were we estranged from—in fact, often ignorant of—those elements of religious mysticism and enthusiasm, ranging from the Cabalists to Hasidism, which had wound their way, as a prickly dissidence, through East European Jewish life. It was, for many of us, not until our late teens that we so much as heard of Sabbatai Zevi or Jacob Frank, the false messiahs who had torn apart the life of the East European Jews in the seventeenth and eighteenth centuries. Even as the fierce self-will of the immigrant culture kept us at a certain distance from American literature, so did it also screen out "reactionary" elements of the Jewish past.

I sometimes think that respectful Gentile readers have been badly gulled by the American Jewish writers into believing that they, the writers, possess a richer Jewish culture than in fact they do. The truth is that most of the American Jewish writers are painfully ignorant of the Jewish tradition. When they venture to use a Yiddish phrase they are liable to absurd mistakes. There is a delicious bit revealing this condition in a story by Irvin Faust about a Brooklyn boy who has gone for a season to Vermont and is asked by the farmer's daughter, "Myron, talk Jew to me." He has to scramble in his memories to find a phrase: "Ish leeba Dick."

> "Oh," Rita Ann moaned softly, "say that again."
> "Ish . . . leeba . . . Dick."
> "Oooh. What's it mean?"
> This I remembered, at least to a point. "I love you . . . Dick."

The work of the American Jewish writers represented an end, not a beginning—or perhaps more accurately, its end was in its beginning. It was a sign of the breakup of Jewish community and the crumbling of Jewish identity; it spoke with the voice of return, nostalgia, retrospection, loss. And even if we chose to confine our sense of Jewish experience to the immigrant milieu, something that would already constitute a major contraction, many of these writers didn't even command that milieu in a deep, authentic way. Abraham Cahan, Henry Roth, and Daniel Fuchs did command it, with their very bones; Delmore Schwartz and Michael Seide made wry poetry out of their boyhood recollections; Saul Bellow re-created the immigrant world through ironic scaffoldings and improvisations; Bernard Malamud, by some miracle of transmutation, summoned in English an occasional true replica of the Yiddish story. But the work of many American Jewish writers is filled not only with cultural and linguistic errors; more important, it also suffers from a gross sentimentalism, a self-comforting softness, with regard to the world they suppose themselves to be representing or reconstructing. Especially is this true of those younger writers who are, so to say, exhausting the credit of their grandfathers' imaginations, making of the East Side a sort of black-humored cartoon, half-Chagall, half-Disney. By now it is clear that the world of our fathers, in its brief flare of secular passion, gave the American Jewish writers just enough material to see them through a handful of novels and stories. The advantages of remembered place soon gave way to the trouble of having lost their place. Which is why so many of the American Jewish writers seem to enter the second half of their careers as displaced persons: the old streets, the old songs, have slipped away, but the mainstream of American life, whatever that may be, continues to elude their reach. America, it turns out, is very large, very slippery, very recalcitrant.

For the American Jewish poets, whom I have largely ignored here, things may yet turn out more favorably. Once milieu and memory are exhausted, Jewishness can take on the strangeness of a fresh myth, or at least myth rediscovered; that myth need have no precise location, no street name or number; and the Bible may lose its tyranny of closeness and become a site to be ransacked. Something of the sort has happened in the last few decades among Yiddish writers, the novelists and storytellers among them finding it more and more difficult to locate their fictions in a recognizable place, while precisely an awareness of this dilemma has yielded the poets a rich subject.

3

But now I must retrace my steps and make things a little more complicated. For if I've been talking about the pressures that kept us at a certain distance from American literature, it must surely be remembered that there were other pressures driving us, sometimes feverishly, toward it.

With time we discovered something strange about the writing of Americans: that even as we came to it feeling ourselves to be strangers, a number of the most notable writers, especially Whitman and Melville, had also regarded themselves as strangers, though not quite in the blunt and deprived way that we did. Whitman saw himself as a poet-prophet who necessarily had to keep a certain distance from his culture—a stranger in the sense proposed by Georg Simmel, that is, a potential wanderer who "has not quite lost the freedom of coming and going," so that even when "fixed within a particular spatial group . . . his position in this group is determined, essentially, by the fact that he has not belonged to it from the beginning, that he imports qualities into it. . . ." The Whitman who has often been seen as "furtive," the wanderer of the streets who comes into touch with everyone but remains close to no one, is a stranger, making of that condition the metaphysical coloring of his persona.

In the early years of the immigrant culture, Whitman was the most popular American writer (except perhaps Poe) among Yiddish readers and writers; there are odes addressed to him in Yiddish and some rough translations of his shorter poems. One reason for this affection was that to the Yiddish-speaking immigrant intelligentsia Whitman seemed really to *mean* it when he invited everyone to make himself at home in the New World. They detected in Whitman an innocence of soul which touched their own innocence; they heard in his voice strains of loneliness which linked with their own loneliness; they saw him as the American who was what Americans ought to be, rather than what they usually turned out to be. They may have been misreading him, but, for their purposes, very usefully.

By the time our turn came—I mean, those of us who would be writing in English—Whitman had lost some of his charm and come to seem portentous, airy, without roots in the griefs of the city, not really a "modern" sensibility. In 1936 "Crossing Brooklyn Ferry" might not speak very strongly to a boy in the slums, even one who had often crossed on the Staten Island ferry on Saturday nights; it would take several decades before the poem could reveal itself in its grandeur, this time to the aging man that boy had become. But probably not until the late thirties or early forties did there come into our awareness another American writer who seemed to speak to us as comrade to comrade, stranger to stranger. Herman Melville was a "thicker" writer than Whitman, "thicker" with the pain of existence and the outrage of society, a cousin across the boundaries of nationality and religion who seemed the archetypal young man confronting a world entirely prepared to do him in. Had we known *Redburn* in time, we might have seen Melville as the tenderfoot only a step or two away from the greenhorn, and we would have been enchanted by the great rhetorical outpouring in that book where Melville welcomes immigrants, all peoples, to the American fraternity. We would have seen the young Melville as a fellow who had to work in a ship—I was about to say, in a shop—where he was hooted at because he wanted to keep some of the signs of his delicate youth. And we would have seen him as a writer who bore the hopes, or illusions, that we were bearing about the redemptive possibilities of "the people."

But the Melville book that we knew was, of course, *Moby-Dick*, quite enough to convince us of a true kinship. Melville was a man who had worked—perhaps the only authentic proletarian writer this country has ever known—and who had identified himself consciously with the downtrodden plebs. Melville was a writer who took Whitman's democratic affirmations and made them into a wonderfully concrete and fraternal poetry. If he had been willing to welcome Indians, South Sea cannibals, Africans, and Parsees (we were not quite sure who Parsees were!), he might have been prepared to admit a Jew or two onto the *Pequod* if he had happened to think of it.

The closeness one felt toward Melville I can only suggest by saying that when he begins with those utterly thrilling words, "Call me Ishmael," we knew immediately that this meant he was not Ishmael, he was really Isaac. He was the son who had taken the blessing and then, in order to set out for the forbidden world, had also taken his brother's unblessed name. We knew that this Isaac-cum-Ishmael was a mama's boy trying to slide or swagger into the world of power; that he took the job because he had to earn a living, because he wanted to fraternize with workers, and because he needed to prove himself in the chill of the world. When he had told mother Sarah that he was leaving, oh, what a tearful scene that was! "Isaac," she had said, "Isaac, be careful," and so careful did he turn out to be that in order to pass in the Gentile world he said, "Call me Ishmael." And we too would ask the world to call us Ishmael, both the political world and the literary world, in whose chill we also wanted to prove ourselves while expecting that finally we would still be recognized as Isaacs.

The stranger who wore Redburn's hunting jacket and subjected himself to trials of initiation on Ahab's ship, this stranger seemed "one of us," as we could never quite suppose the heroes of Cooper or Twain or Hawthorne were "one of us." These remained alien writers, wonderful but distant, while Melville was our brother, a loose-fish as we were loose-fish.

To be a loose-fish seemed admirable. Alienation was a badge we carried with pride, and our partial deracination—roots loosened in Jewish soil but still not torn out, roots lowered into American soil but still not fixed—gave us a range of possibilities. Some we seized. The American Jewish writers began developing styles that were new to American literature. That we should regard ourselves as partisans of modernism, defenders of the European experimentalists against middlebrow sluggards and know-nothing nativists—this followed a pattern already established in America. Decades earlier the first struggling painters to escape from the immigrant Jewish milieu, figures like Abraham Walkowitz and Max Weber, had leapt across their worthy American contemporaries in order to become pupils at the School of Paris. That, simultaneously, we should respond with pleasure and draw upon the styles of the popular Jewish entertainers, from Fanny Brice to the Marx Brothers, from Willie and Eugene Howard to S. J. Perelman— this too was made possible by the freedom of our partial deracination.

Not fixed into a coherent style, we could imitate many. Not bound by an enclosing tradition, we could draw upon many. It was a remarkable feat for Alfred Kazin, still under thirty and living in Brooklyn, to write a book called *On Native Grounds*, in which he commandeered the whole of American prose fiction. It was a canny self-insight for Paul Goodman to declare his cousinship with Emerson and his American patriotism as a sign of anarchist desire, even though most of his friends, including me, were not quite sure what he was up to. And it was a display of sheer virtuosity, the virtuosity of a savored freedom, for Saul Bellow to write in *Henderson the Rain King* a pure Emersonian fiction, quite as if he had finally wrenched loose from Napoleon Street and the Hotel Ansonia.

Imitation could not always be distinguished from improvisation. If I ask myself, where did the style of the *Partisan Review* essay come from, I think I know a few of the sources. The early Van Wyck Brooks may be one, Edmund Wilson another, and some Continental writers too. But I want also to add that *we made it up*, or, rather, the writers of a decade earlier, those who started out in the middle thirties, dreamed it out of their visions or fantasies of what a cosmopolitan style should be. They drew upon Eliot and Trotsky, perhaps also Baudelaire and Valéry, but finally they made it up: a pastiche, brilliant, aggressive, unstable.

It remains, then, an interesting question why it was that while the first literary passions of the American Jewish intellectuals were directed toward modernism, there was rather little modernist experimentation among the American Jewish writers of fiction. I have a few simple answers. In their imaginations these writers were drawn to Eliot and Joyce, Kafka and Brecht, but the stories most of them composed had little to do with the styles or methods of modernism. Modernism had come to America a decade earlier, in the twenties, with Hemingway and Faulkner, Eliot and Stevens, Crane and Williams. By the thirties, when the generation of Schwartz and Bellow began to write, experimentalism no longer seemed so very experimental; it was something one rushed to defend but also, perhaps, with some inner uneasiness. To the revolution of modernism we were latecomers.

But more. Reaching American literature with heads full of European writing yet also still held by the narrowness of experience in the cities, the American Jewish writers turned inevitably and compulsively to their own past, or to that feverish turf of the imagination they declared to be their past. It was the one area of American life they knew closely and could handle authoritatively, no more able to abandon it in memory than bear it in actuality. The sense of place is as overpowering in their work as, say, in the stories of Eudora Welty and Flannery O'Connor; it soon becomes a sense of fate: hovering, lowering, confining, lingering, utterly imperious.

In the end, as we like to say, it was upon language that the American Jewish writers left their mark. Just as the blacks left theirs upon the vocabulary of American music, so the Jews brought to the language of fiction turnings of voice, feats of irony, and tempos of delivery that helped create a new American style— probably a short-lived style and brought to fulfillment in the work of a mere handful of writers, but a new style nonetheless. Style speaks of sensibility, slant, vision; speaks here of a certain high excitability, a rich pumping of blood, which the Jews brought with their baggage, a grating mixture of the sardonic and sentimental, a mishmash of gutter wisdom and graduate-school learning. I think it no exaggeration to say that since Faulkner and Hemingway the one major innovation in American prose style has been the yoking of street raciness and high-culture mandarin which we associate with American Jewish writers.

Not, to be sure, all of them. There really is no single style that is shared by these writers, and some—Delmore Schwartz in the artifice of his antirhetoric, Michael Seide in the mild purity of his diction, Tillie Olsen in her own passionate idiom—clearly challenge the generalizations I shall nevertheless make. For what I want to assert is that the dominant American Jewish style is the one brought to a pitch by Saul Bellow and imitated and modified by a good many others.

In the growth of this style one can see reenacted a pattern through which our nineteenth-century writers created the major American styles. Cooper and Hawthorne, though fresh in their matter, still employed versions of formal Augustan prose; even as they were doing so, however, a language of native storytellers and folkloristic colloquialism was being forged by the humorists of the Old Southwest and the Western frontier; and then, to complete a much-too-neat triad, Twain and Melville blended formal prose with native speech, the heritage from England with the improvisations of American regions, into a style that in Twain might be called "purified demotic" and in Melville "democratic extravagance."

A similar development, on a much smaller scale, has been at work in the fiction of the American Jewish writers. The first collection of stories by Abraham Cahan, *Yekl*, is written in a baneful dialect so naturalistically faithful, or intent upon being faithful, to the immigrant moment that it now seems about as exotic and inaccessible as the argot of Sut Lovingood. Cahan's major novel, *The Rise of David Levinsky*, employs, by contrast, a flavorless standard English, the prose of an earnest but somewhat tone-deaf student worried about proper usage. More interesting for its mythic narrative line than for verbal detail, this novel shows Cahan to be not quite in possession of *any* language, either English or Yiddish, a condition that was common enough among the immigrants, and in the case of their occasionally talented sons would become the shifting ground upon which to build a shifty new style. The problem foreshadowed in Cahan's work is: How can the Yiddishisms of East Side street talk and an ill-absorbed "correct" prose painfully acquired in night school be fused into some higher stylistic enterprise?

One answer, still the most brilliant, came in Henry Roth's *Call It Sleep*, a major novel blending a Joyce roughened to the tonalities of New York and deprived of his Irish lilt with a Yiddish oddly transposed into a pure and lyrical English but with its rhythms slightly askew, as if to reveal immigrant origins. In Roth's novel the children speak a ghastly mutilated sort of English, whereas the main adult characters talk in Yiddish, which Roth renders as a high poetic, somewhat offbeat, English. Thus, the mother tells her little boy: "Aren't you just a pair of eyes and ears! You see, you hear, you remember, but when will you know? . . . And no kisses? . . . There! Savory, thrifty lips!" The last phrase may seem a bit too "poetic" in English speech, but if you translate it into Yiddish—*Na! geshmake, karge lipelakh!*—it rings exactly right, beautifully idiomatic. Roth is here continuing the tradition of Jewish bilingualism, in the past a coexistence of Hebrew as sacred and Yiddish or Ladino as demotic language; but he does this in an oddly surreptitious way, by making of English, in effect, two languages, or by writing portions of this book in one language and expecting that some readers will be able to hear it in another.

Yet, so far as I can tell, Roth has not been a major stylistic influence upon later American Jewish writers, perhaps because his work seems so self-contained there is nothing much to do with it except admire. Perhaps a more useful precursor is Daniel Fuchs, a lovely and neglected writer, especially in his second novel, *Homage to Blenholt*, where one begins to hear a new music, a new tempo, as if to echo the beat of the slums.

This American Jewish style, which comes to fulfillment and perhaps terminus with Bellow, I would describe in a few desperate phrases:

A forced yoking of opposites: gutter vividness and university refinement, street energy and high-culture rhetoric.

A strong infusion of Yiddish, not so much through the occasional use of a phrase or word as through an importation of ironic twistings that transform the whole of language, so to say, into a corkscrew of questions.

A rapid, nervous, breathless tempo, like the hurry of a garment salesman trying to con a buyer or a highbrow lecturer trying to dazzle an audience.

A deliberate loosening of syntax, as if to mock those niceties of Correct English which Gore Vidal and other untainted Americans hold dear, so that in consequence there is much greater weight upon transitory patches of color than upon sentences in repose or paragraphs in composure.

A deliberate play with the phrasings of plebeian speech, but often the kind that vibrates with cultural ambition, seeking to zoom into the regions of higher thought.

In short, the linguistic tokens of writers who must hurry into articulateness if they are to be heard at all, indeed, who must scrape together a language. This style reflects a demotic upsurge, the effort to give literary scale to the speech of immigrant streets, or put another way, to create a "third language," richer and less stuffy, out of the fusion of English and Yiddish that had already occurred spontaneously in those streets. Our writers did not, of course, create a new language, and in the encounter between English and Yiddish, the first has survived far better than the second; but still, *we* have left our scar, tiny though it be, on *their* map.

The other day a gentile friend of mine remarked that in getting from City College in uptown Manhattan to the City University's Graduate Center at Forty-Second Street she had had a long *shlep*. She used this word without a trace of self-consciousness, and she was right, for what she had experienced was not quite an inconvenience nor even a drag; it was a *shlep*. The word in Yiddish bears a multitude of burdens, as if to take a New York subway comes, as indeed it does, to taking on the weight of the world. *Shlep* is becoming part of the American language and in the hard days ahead it can only help.

But there is more. There is the *shlepper*, in whom the qualities of *shlepping* have become a condition of character. There is a *shleppenish*, an experience that exhausts the spirit and wearies the body. And as virtual apotheosis there is *shlepperei*, which raises the burdens of *shlepping* into a statement about the nature of the world. Starbuck unable to resist Ahab was a bit of a *shlepper*; Prufrock afraid to eat his peach made his life into a *shleppenish*; Herzog ground down by his impossible women transformed all of existence into sheer *shlepperei*.

Of such uncouth elements is the American language made and remade. Upon such renewals does the American experience thrive. And if indeed our dream of a New World paradise is ever to be realized, this time beyond mere innocence, how can we ever expect to get there except through the clubfoot certainties of *shlepping?*

Introduction: Twenty-five Years of Dissent
{1979}

TO BE A SOCIALIST IN EUROPE means to belong to a movement commonly accepted as part of democratic political life, a contender in the battle of interest and idea. To be a socialist in America means to exist precariously on the margin of our politics, as critic, gadfly, and reformer, struggling constantly for a bit of space. Lonely and beleaguered as it may be, this position of the American socialist has, nevertheless, an advantage: it forces one to the discomforts of self-critical reflection. And that, sometimes fruitfully and sometimes not, has been a central concern of Dissent, the democratic socialist quarterly which, as I write early in 1979, has reached its twenty-fifth anniversary (notable for any "little magazine," all the more so for one holding unpopular views). You will find in this book a representative sample of the best work that has appeared in Dissent this past quarter of a century, though not, of course, a systematic exposition of the democratic socialist point of view. But rather than discuss the merits or failings of one or another article—the reader can do that perfectly well, unaided—I would like in this introduction to say a few words about the historical context in which our work has occurred.

The story of the left in America is one of high initial hopes, followed by considerable if not major achievements, and ending with painful, even disastrous collapse. Why this recurrent rhythm, enacted now three times in the last seventy-five years?

The first and strongest upsurge of the American left occurred as Debsian socialism, starting before the First World War. Of all the radical movements we've had, this was the most "American." It was the least ideologically "pure," the most inclined to speak in a vocabulary—evangelistic, folksy, shrewd, idealistic—that ordinary Americans might respond to. By 1912 this loosely strung Socialist Party had over 100,000 members; had elected some 1,200 public officials; and was sponsoring 300 periodicals, one of which, the erratic *Appeal to Reason*, had a circulation of three quarters of a million. While not yet a force capable of seriously challenging the major parties, the Socialist Party of that era was genuinely rooted in native experience, blessed in Eugene Victor Debs with a leader of high sincerity and eloquence, able to command a respectable minority of delegates at AFL conventions, and increasingly winning support among intellectuals. This was a real movement, not a petrified sect. Internally, it was extremely heterogeneous, as all American parties tend to be. There were municipal reformers and social democrats on its right; anti-political syndicalists and Marxist theoreticians on its left. There were Midwestern populists, called socialists mainly by courtesy. There were Christian Socialists, for whom socialism meant a latter-day version of Jesus's word. What prompted thousands of ordinary Americans to become socialists was an impulse to moral generosity, a readiness to stake their hopes on some goal other than personal success. It was an impulse that drew its strength from an uncomplicated belief in freedom and fraternity; or to use an almost obsolete word, goodness.

Today, of course, it is hard not to feel that this socialism contained too large a quota of innocence, too great a readiness to let spirit do the work of mind. For the vision of the future which most early American socialists held was remarkably unproblematic—in an odd way, it took over the optimism of the early Emersonian, indeed, the whole American individualist tradition, and transported it to new communal ends. Part of the success experienced by Debsian socialism was probably due to precisely this link to native modes of feeling; its collapse toward the end of the First World War may also, however, have been due to the fact that this native tradition did not prepare it for the toughness that an oppositional party has to cultivate, especially one that, like the Socialists, opposed American participation in the war. The party disintegrated under the blows of government attack and war hysteria; also, because its growing left wing was lured to the nascent Communist movement after the Russian Revolution.

More than a decade would go by before a new resurgence could begin in the early 1930s, smaller in scope than Debsian socialism but with somewhat greater intellectual sophistication. A successor to Debs appeared: Norman Thomas, self-less, energetic, intelligent, a superb speaker. Thousands of young people flocked into the movement, shaken by the Depression, convinced there was no choice for America but fundamental social transformation. The party had a footing in the trade unions, among such gifted figures as the Reuther brothers, Walter and Victor, and it won the allegiance of an influential circle of intellectuals. It was marked by a spirit of liveliness and openness. But again the pressures of histori-cal circumstance undid this burgeoning movement—especially as they presented themselves in the form of difficult new problems American socialists were not yet prepared to solve. These problems have, in fact, been major concerns of all contemporary political thought: first, how to respond to the "welfare state" intro-duced through Roosevelt's New Deal and, second, what to make of the terrifying new phenomenon of Stalinist totalitarianism.

At the right pole of the Socialist Party in the thirties was clustered a group of old-timers, mostly veterans of the Jewish garment unions, who saw the New Deal as a partial embodiment of their hopes. What mattered for them was im-mediate social reform, not a shadowy dream of "complete" transformation. But for the party's younger and more militant people, who soon won over Norman Thomas, the New Deal, though some of its particular measures were desirable, represented a patchwork meant to salvage a sick and unjust system. Roosevelt's reforms, they pointed out, had not really ended unemployment or changed the basic situation of the worker in capitalist society. It was a dispute that seemed be-yond compromise. The older trade unionists knew that the New Deal had brought crucial improvements: there was now the opportunity to strengthen unions and improve the conditions of millions of people. The left-wing socialists, harden-ing into a semi-Leninist ideology, were responding not just to American condi-tions—indeed, to American conditions least of all. They were trying to maintain an international perspective at a time when it seemed that social breakdown cut across national lines. They felt they were living through the apocalypse of inter-national capitalism—had not the Depression, the rise of fascism, the collapse of bourgeois democracy in Europe provided sufficient evidence? Capitalism, they said, could not be reformed nor peaceably changed; social revolution (ill-defined, vaguely invoked) was the way out. Whatever pertinence this outlook may have had in a Europe overcome by fascism, it had precious little in America even dur-ing the Depression years, a country in which the democratic tradition remained very strong.

In retrospect (the easiest source of wisdom) one feels there might have been a more flexible socialist stand, acknowledging that the New Deal was indeed a significant step toward desirable reform yet by no means removing the need for a basic socialist critique. But such a nuanced policy was impossible to either side: the problem was still too fresh and stark for compromise, and besides, the classical socialist division between incremental reformers and strict ideologues had already set in.

About the problem of Stalinism, the socialists of the thirties were clearer. A few did begin to flirt with "the Soviet experiment," but most were repelled by its ghastly terrorism, its destruction of working class, indeed, all human rights. Gradually the Socialists began to develop an analysis of Stalinism as a new order of social oppression—but to that we will return a bit later.

Vexed by these problems, the Socialists now destroyed themselves in a round of bitter factional disputes. Meanwhile, the Communist movement, with its mindless loyalty to every turn of Moscow policy and its own deeply authoritarian structure and rigid ideology, was gaining support among a growing number of young American radicals. The tragic outcome of this story is by now well known—a coarse violation of the human spirit, a terrible waste of energy and hope, which left a generation of American radicals broken and demoralized. After the Hitler-Stalin pact, and then the infamous governmental persecutions during the Cold War years, the Communist movement dwindled into an elderly sect; but the damage it had done to American radicalism is beyond calculation.

There was to be one more leftist upsurge in America, that of the New Left in the sixties, passionate, ill-defined, and in the end crashing, like its predecessors, to disaster. In its first phase, the New Left seemed hopeful to us. This was a phase of populist fraternity, stressing a desire to make real the egalitarian claims of the American tradition, a non- and even anti-ideological approach to politics, and a strategy of going into local communities in order to help oppressed minorities. A major stimulant was the rising protest of American blacks in the early sixties as they began to struggle for their rights as citizens and human beings. The main New Left slogan of this moment, appealing if vague, was "participatory democracy," a hope that democracy could be extended from the forms of representation to the substance of experience.

Things went bad. Perhaps it was due to the desperation engendered among many young people by the Vietnam war, which they rightly saw as a political and moral outrage; perhaps to a romanticism of "revolution" arising from a naïve identification with "charismatic" leaders like Castro and Mao. But by the mid-sixties there had begun a shift from fraternal sentiment to ill-absorbed dogma, from the good-spirited shapelessness of "participatory democracy" to the bitter rigidity of "vanguard" sects, from the spirit of nonviolence to a quasi-Leninist fascination with violence. In this second phase the New Left grew in numbers, yet through the sterile authoritarianism of its now-dominant Maoist and Weathermen wings, made certain that it, too, would end up as no more than a reincarnation of the radical sects of the past.

We had the heart-sickening sense of reliving the disasters of the past (e.g., the way some leaders of Students for a Democratic Society contrived a theory of "liberal fascism"—that the liberalism of American society is "really" fascist—which bore a fatal resemblance to the idiotic Stalinist theory of the thirties called "social fascism"—that social democrats were "really" fascists). What had begun with a bang ended with a whimper: the pathological terrorism of the Weathermen, the brutal factionalism within SDS between the Maoists and other sects, the waste (once more, once more!) of all that splendid hope and energy. Unheeded, we could do little but warn and criticize.

The conclusions, the "lessons," to be drawn from these experiences are obviously far more substantial than can here be put forward. But with a ruthless sort of condensation, let me list—as I see them, some of my friends contributing to this book [*Twenty-five Years of Dissent: An American Tradition*] may not agree—a few points:

- The ideological baggage of Marxism, especially Marxism-Leninism, must largely be dropped if we are to have in America a socialist movement open, alive, and responsive to native feelings. "Vanguard" parties, ideological systems, sneering at "bourgeois democracy"—all this can lead only to the petrifaction of sects. Which is not, of course, to deny the possible uses of a flexible Marxism in political and historical analysis.

- The postures of righteousness that have often marked American radicalism, sometimes deriving more from Emersonian testimony than Marxist theory, can at times stand in the way of a realistic left politics. All three of the radical upsurges of the century suffered from such postures—as, for instance, the notion that working within the Democratic Party is a form of "betrayal." Political conditions in America make increasingly unlikely that we shall have here a mass socialist or labor party on the European model. But that does not mean that socialists cannot exert significant political influence.

- By this point in history, socialism can no longer be seen as a vision of perfection; it cannot be a surrogate for religious yearnings, though all too often, in the left-wing experiences of America, it has become that. We want to build a better world, but even a better world is not heaven on earth.

Those with religious needs must try to satisfy them through religious experience.

- Socialism must be committed, without qualification, to democracy—yes, the flawed and inadequate democracy we have today—in order to be able to bring a heightened democratic content to every department of life: political, economic, social, cultural. There can be no socialism without democracy, nor any compromise with apologists for dictatorship or authoritarianism in any shape or form.

II

Dissent, which started as a quarterly in winter 1954, arose out of the decomposition of the socialist movement of the thirties. Some of us rebelled against the sterility of the sects that still remained from the thirties, even as we wanted to give new life to the values that had been petrified in those sects. Others came from different places, some being independent writers and intellectuals drawn to the idea of socialism or the need for social criticism.

When intellectuals can do nothing else, they start a magazine. But starting a magazine is also doing something: at the very least it is thinking in common. And thinking in common can have unforeseen results.

The kind of magazine we had in mind was perhaps without precedent in the history of the American left. Though it would be devoted to democratic socialism, there would be no "party line" on political topics. Authors would not be published merely because they were counted among the faithful. The idea of socialism was itself to be treated as problematic rather than as a fixed piety. The socialist movement having reached its nadir in American life, we felt that our main task was to deal with socialism in the realm of ideas. This, to be sure, can never be enough. Yet there are moments when patience is all, and stubbornness too. And then I recall a few lines from our friend Harold Rosenberg: "The weapon of criticism is doubtless inadequate. Who on that account would choose to surrender it?"

Even this modest goal was not easy to achieve. The early fifties were not merely afflicted with McCarthyism and repressions attendant upon the Cold War; they were also the years during which the "American Celebration," involving a systematic reconciliation between American intellectuals and commercial society, reached its climax. A good many intellectuals were deluded by the feverish prosperity of a war-production economy into believing that all, or almost all, of our socioeconomic problems had been solved and that poverty had been effectively removed from American life. Susceptible to the genteel chauvinism of the Cold

War years, they often lapsed into a mood of political complacency—sometimes apathy—in which the traditional symbols and phrases of liberalism did service for new impulses of conservatism.

Whatever else, we of *Dissent* did not succumb to this mood. We kept insisting that American society, even in its flush of postwar prosperity, remained open to the most severe and fundamental criticism: some of which we tried to provide.

For certain of our writers and readers it was this aspect of our magazine, symbolized by its title, that counted most. The idea of socialism, though it might still elicit their approval, seemed to them distant, abstract, and academic; what interested them most was analysis, reportage, polemic about American society today, eventuating in a sustained radical criticism of its claims and pretensions.

For others among us, the idea of socialism as both problem and goal remained central. We suspected that for an indefinite time there would be no major socialist movement in America, but as intellectuals we tried to retain a long-range perspective, to live for more than the immediate moment. And we felt that for a radical criticism of American society to acquire depth and coherence it needed as an ideal norm some vision of the good—or at least of a better—society. This vision was what we meant by socialism.

But as soon as we tried to grapple with the problems of socialist thought; to discover what in the ideology of Marxism remained significant and what had gone dead; to comprehend the failures of socialism as a world movement and to analyze the bewildering complex of moral and political problems that had come with the rise of Communist totalitarianism, the new forms of economy in the West, and the bureaucratization of the labor and socialist movements—as soon as we approached these matters it became clear that any expectation of constructing a new socialist ideology was premature, perhaps a fantasy. We had to learn to work piecemeal, to treat socialist thought as inherently problematic, and to move pragmatically from question to question—with general theories or notions, to be sure, but without a total, world-encompassing ideology.

Socialists, we felt, could make a contribution to intellectual and political life, precisely by projecting an image of a fraternal society in which men planned and controlled their political and economic affairs through democratic participation and in which no small group of owners, managers, or party bosses could dominate the lives of millions. But to do this, socialists had first to question their own assumptions. Necessarily, this led us to place a heavy stress upon the moral component of socialism. We opposed the status quo not merely because it had led, and might again lead, to depressions and human misery, but also because it rested upon a fundamentally unjust arrangement of social relations. It was a society that not only created material hardships for millions of people but gave rise to an ethic of inhumane competitiveness and to a psychic insecurity which in America had reached frightening proportions. And it was for similar reasons that we remained intransigent opponents of Communism.

A second major stress in the *Dissent* re-examination of socialism has been upon the indispensability of democracy. Modern society, no matter what form it takes, shows an underlying tendency toward an idolatry of the state, a worship of the bureaucratic machine. All modern societies share in this drive toward transforming man into a passive object manipulable in behalf of abstract slogans, production plans, and other mystifying apparitions. The Western democracies are still far less guilty in this respect than the Communist nations; but the drift toward industrial bureaucratism seems universal. For us, therefore, the idea of socialism could retain value only if a new stress were placed on democratic participation and control. Statified or nationalized economy was not an end in itself; it could be put to desirable or despicable uses. These are the main emphases dominating the essays on socialism that open this anthology.

We had—and have—still other intentions. One of them is to propose intellectual relations with the more independent sections of American liberalism, in order to extend welfare legislation and human rights, further the black and women's movements, and defend civil liberties. It is this perspective which largely motivates Part II of this book and has also been dominant in the pages of *Dissent*. For we have been concerned not only with political theory but also with the immediate realities of American society. We have tried, in our modest way, to contribute to the reconstruction of a democratic left in the United States.

III

Two problems of social analysis concerned us with a special intensity during these years, and I think we have made some contribution toward clarifying them—though, of course, other problems pile up, with their predicaments and puzzles. Let me say a few words about these two:

The Problem of Stalinism. A crucial, perhaps *the* crucial, experience of our century has been the appearance of totalitarian systems yoking terror and ideology and claiming to shape the entirety of existence: the relentless assault by the party-state upon a defenseless population in the name of a total utopia.

Stalinism seemed a cruel parody, perhaps a self-parody, of the socialist dream, and it forced thoughtful socialists to reconsider the terms of their conviction. In

Russia a Marxist party had seized power; it had destroyed private property in the means of production; it had elicited overwhelming sacrifice and idealism; yet the result was a brutal and oppressive society, ruled by terror, erasing free expression, allowing the working class none of the rights it possessed even under capitalism, and in its essential quality alien to the socialist vision.

Within this society there sprang up a new social stratum: the party-state bureaucracy which found its roots in the bureaucratic intelligentsia, the factory managers, the military officials, and above all the Communist functionaries. This new social stratum looked upon the workers as material to be shaped, upon intellectuals as propagandists to be employed, upon the international Communist movement as an auxiliary to be exploited, and upon Marxist thought as a crude process for rationalizing its power and ambitions.

What was the nature of the new society that had arisen in Russia during the twenties and thirties?

A growing number of socialists concluded that the loss of political power by the Russian working class meant that it no longer ruled in any social sense, for, as a propertyless class, it could exercise power only through direct political means and not in those indirect ways that the bourgeoisie had sometimes employed in its youthful phase. Stalinism showed no signs of either producing from within itself a bourgeois restoration or of gliding into democracy. The bureaucracy had become a new ruling class, with interests of its own fundamentally opposed to both capitalism and socialism.

This view of communist society—which Djilas popularized through the phrase The New Class—held that what is decisive is not the forms of property ownership (i.e., nationalized economy) but the realities of property relations (i.e., who controls the state that owns the property). Can the workers, in whose name power is held, organize themselves into trade unions to strike against "their" state? Can they form parties to openly challenge the domination of "their" party? As Djilas has remarked: "An unfree people can have no scope in the economic organism."

From such theoretic analyses and speculations enormous consequences followed for socialist thought:

- There is no necessary or inevitable sequence from capitalism to socialism, as many Marxists had believed, nor is there any inherently "progressive" movement within history. New, unforeseen, and retrogressive societies can intervene in the sequence of change.
- The mere abolition of capitalism is not, in and of itself, necessarily a step toward either freedom in general or socialism in particular; it can lead—

indeed, in some instances it has led—to societies more repressive than capitalism at its worst.

- Neither working-class rule nor socialism can be defined merely as a society in which private property has been abolished or the means of production nationalized; what is decisive is the nature of the political regime exercised over postcapitalist or nationalized property.

- In the long run the Communist movement may come to seem, not the vanguard of "proletarian revolution," but a movement that could achieve success only in underdeveloped countries, where there was neither a self-confident bourgeoisie nor an advanced working class. The "historic function" of this movement came to be the provision of ideological rationales for a draconian socioeconomic modernization of backward societies.

- The idea of a total transformation of humanity under the guidance of the "vanguard party" is a corrupt fantasy which soon leads to an alternation of terror and apathy.

- Socialism must then be redefined as a society in which the means of production, to an extent that need not be determined rigidly in advance, are collectively owned and in which they are democratically controlled; a society requiring as its absolute prerequisite the preservation and extension of democracy. Without socialism, democracy tends to be limited in social scope, to apply its benefits unequally, and to suffer from coexistence with unjust arrangements of social power; but without democracy, socialism is impossible.

The Problem of the Welfare State. The welfare state preserves the essential character of capitalist economy, in that the interplay of private or corporate owners in the free market remains dominant; but it modifies the workings of that economy, in that the powers of free disposal by property owners are regulated and controlled by political organs. Within limits that need not be rigidly fixed in advance, the welfare state can be regarded as an algebraic container that can be filled with the arithmetic of varying sociopolitical contents. More important, the welfare state is the outcome, not necessarily a "final" one, of prolonged social struggle to modulate and humanize capitalist society. It would be hard to say to what extent the welfare state is the result of a deliberate intent to stabilize capitalist society from above, so that it will avoid breakdown and revolutionary crises; to what extent it is the outcome of relatively autonomous economic processes; and to what extent it is the partially realized triumph in the struggle of masses of people to satisfy their needs. At the moment—by contrast to those who feel the major need for the immediate future to be a kind of benevolent social engineering and those who see the welfare state as a manipulative device for maintaining traditional forms of economic coercion—it seems necessary to stress that the welfare state represents a conquest that has been *wrested* by the labor, socialist, and liberal movements.

For those of us who wish to preserve a stance of criticism without the sterility of total estrangement, the welfare state has been a somewhat unsettling experience. Here are some of the characteristic responses of leftist intellectuals in the last few decades:

1. *A feeling that the high drama (actually, the vicarious excitement) of earlier Marxist or "revolutionary" politics has been lost and that in the relatively trivial struggles for a division of social wealth and power within a stable order there is neither much room nor need for political-intellectual activity.* Much of this response strikes us as, by now, unearned and tiresome. The snobbism of "revolutionary" nostalgia can easily decline into a snobbism of political abstention.

2. *A belief that the welfare state will, in effect, remain stable and basically unchanged into the indefinite future; that conflict will be contained within the prescribed limits and that problems of technique will supersede the free-wheeling or "irresponsible" tradition of fundamental criticism.* This view accepts the "givenness" not merely of the welfare state but also of its present forms and boundaries. It thereby underestimates the need for and significance of basic moral-political criticism. If I am right in saying this, the traditional responses of the radical intellectual—dismissed though they may be in some quarters as utopian, impractical, etc.—remain quite as necessary as before. Even for making new practical proposals to alleviate social troubles within the present society, a degree of utopian perspective and intellectual distance is required. For essential to such alleviation is a continued redefinition of what, indeed, is practical.

3. *A belief that the welfare state is characteristic of all forms of advanced industrial society; that it offers bread and television, palliatives and opiates, to disarm potential opposition; and that it thereby perpetuates, more subtly but insidiously than in the past, class domination.* Despite its seeming intransigence, this view strikes me as essentially conservative, for it leads to passivity, not action—and inhumane,—for it minimizes the improvements in the life conditions of millions of human beings. Minimizes, above all, the fact that the welfare state has meant that large numbers of working-class people are no longer ill fed, ill clothed, and insecure, certainly not to the extent they were thirty years ago. That automobile workers in Detroit can today earn a modest if still insufficient income; that through union intervention they have some, if not enough, control over their work conditions; that they can expect pensions upon getting old which may be inadequate but are far better than

anything they could have expected thirty years ago—all this is *good*: politically, socially, and in the simplest human terms. To dismiss or minimize this enormous achievement on the lordly grounds that such workers remain "alienated" is to allow ideology to destroy human solidarity.

In contrast to these three attitudes, we would propose the following general stance toward the welfare state: The struggles and issues raised within the welfare state are "real," not mere diversionary shadow plays or trivial squabbles. They matter; they affect the lives of millions. No matter how mundane the level at which they are conducted, the struggles for social betterment within the arena of the welfare state merit our concern and active involvement. That is why we write and act in relation to poverty, civil rights, education, urban renewal, Medicare, a host of immediate problems. At the same time, radical intellectuals seek to connect these problems with the idea of a qualitative transformation of society. Socialism not being an immediate option, it is necessary for radicals, while continuing to speak for their views in full, also to try to energize those forces that are prepared to stretch the limits of the welfare state and improve the immediate quality of our life. Such a dynamic once set in motion, there may be possibilities for going still further.

IV

Let your mind go back in time. At a meeting of workers in Berlin in the 1870s, a social democrat named August Bebel speaks. He advances a new vision of human possibility. He tells his audience that men who work with their hands need not be subordinate and mute, need not assume that the destinies of nations are always to be decided by superiors in power. He tells his listeners that they, too, count. They count in their numbers, they count in their capacities to come together, they count in their crucial role in the productive process, they count in their readiness to sacrifice. The mute will speak; the objects of history will become subjects prepared to transform it. This was the socialist message as it began to be heard a little more than a century ago. It was heard in England in the night schools, in the labor colleges, sometimes on the edges of the dissident chapels. It was heard in France through the more revolutionary traditions of that country, in the Paris Commune where organs of plebeian autonomy were being improvised. And even here in America, it was heard among immigrants packed into slums or sweating over railroad beds. It was heard among freewheeling sailors and lumbermen who preferred a syndicalist version of revolt. It was heard among Jewish immigrants on the East Side. It was heard among intellectuals and Christian pastors in New

York who found that the promptings of thought and sympathy drove them to the socialist vision.

After more than a century, many hopes have been burned out into ashes, whole generations have perished in despair, movements have been drowned in blood, and many people in those movements have lapsed into silence. The socialist idea is no longer young, no longer innocent, and now must compete in a world of sophistication. It cannot hope to grow through mere simple reiteration of simple slogans. Yet anyone looking at the world today must be struck by the power which this idea still holds: the devotion that millions of people, mostly in Europe but elsewhere too, still give to it.

We know the mistakes and the failures of this past century. The notion that as soon as *we* take power, all would be well: this, serious people can no longer believe. Who is that *we*—which self-appointed "vanguard"? The notion that democracy, even in its most corrupted forms, is anything but a precious human conquest, that it's just a façade for the rule of the oppressors: this serious people can surely no longer believe. The notion that social change will come about through the automatic workings of the economy, without human will or intention, just like the opposite notion that history can be forced or raped through the will of a tiny band of chosen intellectuals: this, too, serious people can no longer believe. Intellectuals today, despots tomorrow.

We know that the socialist movement declined at many points into a mere appendage of laborite institutions, and that these institutions could not bring about the changes that we want in society. We know that in some countries the socialist movement degenerated through the Communist heresy into totalitarianism, bringing a kind of "salvation"—the "salvation" of terror and fear. Yet these failures notwithstanding, there remains a living core of socialist belief, commitment, value.

At one point that living core is very close to liberalism: a belief in the widest possible political freedoms, a belief that democracy remains the foundation of all that we want. Without that democracy, nothing is possible, life becomes unbearable. But socialism introduces something new, historically and analytically. It introduces the idea that the plebes, the masses, the ordinary people can rise to articulation, rise to rulership, to power.

We have faith in the capacities of ordinary people, not to become experts in finance, not to understand the mysteries of inflation—though they can hardly do worse than the experts—but to come to sensible, humane conclusions about the major direction of social decisions. If you deny this, you deny not only socialism, you deny the moral basis of democracy as well.

Socialism also introduces a stress on communal life, on the sharing of values, the sharing of responsibility, the sharing of power. We believe the democracy that prevails, more or less, in our political process should also prevail in our economic life, in the ownership and the running of our corporations. The major economic direction of modern society, at least in the advanced nations, is toward an increasing state domination of the economy; the vision of laissez-faire has no reality, except in certain magazines. We believe the fundamental issue is this: what will be the relationship between the democratic political process and the increasingly complex economy of modern society? And the control that we want to exert upon the modern economy is not through a vast state bureaucracy, not through some fantasy of total nationalization, but rather through democratic and autonomous agencies which will represent the people who work in a given industry as well as the population at large, so that there can be a balance between particular interests of those in a given industry and the larger interests of the entire society. This commitment to the democratization of economic life is at the heart of the socialist idea today. Democracy here, democracy there, democracy everywhere. The idea is simple, the techniques necessarily complex and difficult.

With this, there goes an emphasis on egalitarianism. That word is not very fashionable these days in American intellectual life, but we will survive that too. Egalitarianism doesn't mean that everyone has to make exactly the same each week. It does mean that the vast disproportions of opportunity and power, which bring with them vast disproportions of the capacity for human fulfillment, should be shaved down a lot.

In the last few years, we've been living through some disappointments with America's quasi-welfare state. People see that partial reforms bring only partial relief, that partial reforms inadequately financed can bring unexpected trouble, that partial reforms occurring in the context of the market and distorted by the priorities of corporate interests and mismanaged by government bureaucracy can lead to anti-social consequences. But the conclusion to be drawn from this is not some churlish desire—impossible in the modern economy, in any case—to return to a laissez-faire or private economy. If, for instance, Medicare as we have it now leads to ripoffs by doctors, the answer isn't to abolish it or to turn down national health insurance; the answer is to deepen the social content and democratic control of health insurance, making certain that such ripoffs don't persist.

A lot of the traditional socialist criticisms of capitalist society—the simplest, most fundamental criticisms—still apply. We read that citrus growers in Florida are delighted by bad weather because it cuts down their crops and will keep up their prices. As long as these people have to function in this economy, I cannot blame them. It makes economic sense. But in terms of any larger social value, it's pure insanity. We should be unhappy at cutbacks in citrus production. There are lots of kids in the United States who could use those oranges. We could all use them at cheaper prices, or we could even—there go those "socialist do-gooders"—ship them at low prices to other places. But that would mean a socially planned economy, a society that, as we used to say and could well say again, is organized for use and not profit.

Just at the time when there are so many troubles, so many social ills, when clearly the system is not working well, we can detect a new wave of neo-conservatism or really reactionary thought. Conservative sages demonstrate that the poor remain poor because they are improvident: you need a Ph.D. for that. Others teach us that there are limits to social policy, more urgently felt as it happens with regard to providing employment for black youth than rescue or bounty for Lockheed and Penn Central. Still other curators of wisdom invoke the fallen nature of mankind—as if once Eve bit into that disastrous apple, it was forever decreed that humanity might rise as high as the peaks of laissez-faire capitalism but not an inch beyond. The assault on the welfare state during the late 1970s is an assault on the deprived, the poor, the blacks. But we believe that this retreat from liberalism, this retreat from the welfare state and social generosity, is not going to take care of the problems that we find all about us. A bit sooner or a bit later, we shall again, as a society, have to confront the inequities of our economic arrangements, the maldistribution of our income and wealth, the undemocratic nature of our corporate structures.

When that happens, the overall perspective suggested in this book ought to have a growing relevance. It is a two-sided view of political and social action within a democratic society. On one side, a constant battle for all those "little" things—better health care, new housing programs, more equitable taxation, the rights of women and blacks—that occupy the attention of liberals. On the other side, a fundamental critique of the society in the name of democratic socialist values. To say both kinds of things, to say them at the same time, to keep a humane balance between the near and the far: that is the view we have tried to advance in the twenty-five years of Dissent . . .

Introduction: The Best of Sholom Aleichem with Ruth Wisse

{1979}

ＨOW DO TWO EDITORS WRITE an essay together when one lives in New York City and the other in Montreal? They follow the epistolary tradition of Yiddish literature and send one another letters. That is what we did, sent real letters that we soon began to look forward to receiving. It could have gone on almost forever, but we stopped because Sholom Aleichem said, "Enough, children, enough."

IH TO RW

Reading through the Sholom Aleichem stories we have brought together, I have an uneasy feeling that this is a Sholom Aleichem seldom before encountered. Or at least, seldom before recognized. Yet the stories, apart from the few translated here for the first time, are familiar enough, part of the Sholom Aleichem canon.

The writer universally adored as a humorist, the writer who could make both Jews and Gentiles laugh, and most remarkable of all, the writer who could please *every kind of Jew*, something probably never done before or since—this writer turns out to be imagining, beneath the scrim of his playfulness and at the center of his humor, a world of uncertainty, shifting perception, anxiety, even terror.

Let no innocent reader be alarmed: the stories are just as funny as everyone has said. But they now seem to me funny in a way that almost no one has said. Certainly if you look at the essay on Sholom Aleichem by the preeminent Yiddish critic S. Niger, which Eliezer Greenberg and I anthologized in our *Voices from the Yiddish*, you will find described there a writer of tenderness and cleverness, with a profound grasp of Jewish life (all true, of course)—but not the Sholom Aleichem I now see.

Is my view a distortion, the kind induced by modernist bias and training? I'm aware of that danger and try to check myself, but still. . . . As I read story after story, I find that as the Yiddish proverb has it, "a Jew's joy is not without fright," even that great Jew who has in his stories brought us more joy than anyone else. True, there are moments of playfulness, of innocent humor, as in the portions of the adventures of Mottel the orphan that we've excerpted here—he, so to say, is Sholom Aleichem's Tom Sawyer. But the rest: a clock strikes thirteen, a hapless young man drags a corpse from place to place, a tailor is driven mad by the treachery of his perceptions, the order of *shtetl* life is undone even on Yom Kippur, Jewish children torment their teacher unto sickness. And on and on.

Perhaps the ferocious undercurrent in Sholom Aleichem's humor has never been fully seen, or perhaps Jewish readers have been intent on domesticating him in order to distract attention from the fact that, like all great writers, he can be very disturbing.

No, he isn't Kafka, and I don't at all want him to be. (The world doesn't need more than one Kafka.) Still, aren't there some strands of connecting sensibility? When Kafka read his stories aloud, he roared with laughter. And now, in reading Sholom Aleichem, I find myself growing nervous, anxious, even as I keep laughing. Like all great humorists, he attaches himself to the disorder which lies beneath the apparent order of the universe, to the madness beneath the apparent sanity. In many of the stories one hears the timbre of the problematic.

Of course, I'm exaggerating a little—but not much. And what I'm not trying to say is merely that we now see Sholom Aleichem as a self-conscious, disciplined artist rather than merely a folk-voice (or worse yet, the "folksy" tickler of Jewish vanities). For while it is true that Sholom Aleichem is tremendously close to the oral tradition of Yiddish folklore (you once remarked that a number of his stories are elaborations, or complications, of folk anecdotes), still, that folk material is itself not nearly so comforting or soft as later generations of Jews have liked to suppose.

Given the nature of Jewish life in Europe these past several centuries, how could the folk tradition have been as comforting or soft as it has come down to us through both the popularizers and the sentimentality of people who have broken from the Jewish tradition even as they have felt drawn to it? The Chelm stories, the Hershel Ostropolier stories, the Hasidic tales, even sometimes the folk songs: all have their undercurrents of darkness. Life may have been with people, but the people often lived in fright. Sholom Aleichem, then, seems to me a great writer who, like all the Yiddish writers of his moment, was close to folk sources yet employed them for a complicated and individual vision of human existence. That means terror and joy, dark and bright, fear and play. Or terror in joy, dark in bright, fear in play.

Am I wrong?

RW TO IH

Your concluding words remind me of the description by Ba'al Makhshoves (the Yiddish critic and one of Sholom Aleichem's earliest admirers) of the feeling we have when we think we've committed a terrible sin, or experienced catastrophe, and wish it were all just a dream. This, according to him, is Sholom Aleichem's incomparable achievement: he conjures up the collective anxiety and then dispels it magically, laughing the danger away.

I guess Sholom Aleichem's contemporaries took the nightmarish uncertainties for granted and enjoyed the relief he alone provided. But you're right. Nowadays his name has become such a byword for folksy good humor, innocent "laughter through tears," that we're surprised to rediscover the undertone of threat in his work. It may be, as you say, our "modernist bias" that attracts us to the darker side, but there it is, menacing and grotesque. There is fear, not just confusion, and guilt, a nastier emotion than sorrow. That recurring image of the sick father, once powerful but now coughing fitfully between sentences, or the humiliated teacher, never able to recover his authority, suggests the fatal weakness in the culture and—more to the point—the narrator's sense of his own shared culpability in having brought it low.

And actually, how could it be otherwise? For the author of these works is a sophisticated literary man, living at some remove from the insular and cohesive society he delights in depicting. Remember I told you how startled I was to find that all the correspondence between the author and his family, his wife and children, was in Russian, obviously the language of the home. Unlike Tevye, Sholom Aleichem encouraged his children's Russification, realizing that the centrifugal force of change would leave little of the old way of life intact. Oh, to be sure, he was still the product of "tradition," and confined to a Jewish fate. Raised in a Ukrainian *shtetl*, he later suffered the indignities of living in Kiev without a residence permit, scrambled like a thousand other Menachem-Mendels to provide for his family, fled the pogroms, joined the great migration to America. In some ways it's the very typical Jewish story. But he was also the consummate artist, working the full range of modern literary genres; the shrewd journalist, attuned to every nuance of socialist, Zionist, or assimilationist politics and polemics; the exacting editor, forging a new cultural idiom and enjoying a cosmopolitan milieu. Small wonder that there is so much masking and unmasking in his stories, so many instances of dislocation and social ambiguity. Everyone was remaking himself, with varying degrees of success. And among them was Sholom Rabinowitz, experiencing all the personal and social upheavals that as "Sholom Aleichem" he would reorder with amusing grace.

Far from distorting, your comments begin to set the record straight. And if you're particularly struck by the generally overlooked "ferocity" of the work, I'm amazed by the ingenious and *self-conscious* artist behind the widely accepted notion of the folk-voice. Take "Station Baranovich," one of the train stories we decided to include. Early Yiddish readers were likely to know that their author, the man you once called "the only modern writer who may truly be said to be a culture-hero," had suffered a complete collapse at that fateful stop during a grueling speaking tour, an attack of "acute pulmonary tuberculosis" that was followed by years of convalescence. At Baranovich the great entertainer, the spellbinding story teller, had almost left the train for good.

So much for fact. What about the fiction? The story is narrated by a traveling salesman. The passengers' conversation runs appropriately grim—to pogroms, murders, anti-Jewish decrees. The interior story of a certain Kivke, alternately a victim of the czarist regime and a blackmailer of his own community, might have been used by many another Jewish writer (God save us!) to demonstrate the demoralizing effects of persecution. But Sholom Aleichem, who at Baranovich was warned of his own mortality, makes this a writer's story: the fate of Kivke and of the Jewish community are ultimately in the hands of the gifted *story teller* whose untimely departure at Baranovich constitutes the story's only really fatal event. The artist can transform reality at will—a potent charm in desperate times— but his magic is subject to temporal claims. Hilarious the story is. But doesn't it also comment bitingly on the relation of the artist to his audience and to his material, of the audience to its artists and environment, of reality to art? It even manages a stroke of revenge in its parting shot: "May Station Baranovich burn to the ground!" Our colleagues analyzing "self-reflexiveness in art" should have a field day here!

It must be some fifty years since Van Wyck Brooks drew attention to Samuel Clemens lurking behind the sprightlier Mark Twain. If anything, we're a little late in exposing the negative, the harsher "World of Sholom Aleichem" and the canny Mr. Sholom Rabinowitz behind the man with the avuncular smile. Or should we stick to the compulsively naive and cheerful? As in his, "What's new with the cholera epidemic in Odessa?"

IH to RW

We've been stressing, so far, the "modern" Sholom Aleichem, a comic writer whose view of Jewish, and perhaps any other, life tends to be problematic, rather nervous, and streaked with those elements of guilt and anxiety that we usually associate with writers of the twentieth century. To see Sholom Aleichem in this way seems a necessary corrective to the view, now prevalent in Jewish life, that softens him into a toothless entertainer, a jolly gleeman of the shtetl, a fiddler cozy on his roof. And insofar as we reject or at least complicate this prevailing view, it's especially important to remark that Sholom Aleichem is not a "folk writer," whatever that might mean. No, he is a self-conscious artist, canny in his use of literary techniques, especially clever in his use of the monologue, which in his stories may seem to be meandering as pointlessly as an unemployed Jew on market day in the shtetl but which actually keeps moving toward a stringent and disciplined conclusion.

Still we should not go too far in trying to revise the common view of Sholom Aleichem. He came out of a culture in which the ferment of folk creation was still very lively, and in which the relationship between writer and audience was bracingly intimate, certainly different from what we have come to accept in Western cultures. A good many of Sholom Aleichem's stories are drawn from familiar or once-familiar folktales and anecdotes. One of his best stories, "The Haunted Tailor," is based on such materials, though as Sholom Aleichem retells it, the story emerges intellectually sharpened and complicated. It moves in its tone toward both the grotesque and the satiric, and in characterization it progresses from folk figure to individual. Tevye the dairyman, probably Sholom Aleichem's greatest character, emerges from the depths of Jewish folk experience in Eastern Europe, yet he is far more than a representative type. Tevye is a particularized Jew with his own nuances and idiosyncrasies, even as we also recognize in him a shtetl Everyman.

In Sholom Aleichem, then, the balance between collectivity and individual, between Jewish tradition and personal sensibility, is very fine. Coming at the point in the history of the Eastern European Jews where the coherence of traditional life has been shattered, only to let loose an enormous, fresh cultural energy, Sholom Aleichem stands as both firm guardian of the Jewish past and a quizzical, skeptical Jew prepared (as the unfolding of the Tevye stories makes clear) to encounter and maybe accept the novelty and surprise of modern Jewish life. It's just this balance, so delicate and precarious, that I find enchanting in his work. And this may be one reason that I think of him as a "culture hero," in the sense that Dickens and Mark Twain were culture heroes in their time and place. For Sholom Aleichem embodies the culture of the Eastern European Jews at a high point of consciousness, at the tremor of awareness that comes a minute before dissolution starts.

He embodies the essential values of Eastern European Jewish culture in the very accents and rhythms of his language, in the pauses and suggestions, the inside jokes and sly references. This relationship between the writer as culture hero and the culture itself is something so intimate and elusive we hardly have a way to describe it—except to say that every Jew who could read Yiddish, whether he was orthodox or secular, conservative or radical, loved Sholom Aleichem, for he heard in his stories the charm and melody of a common *shprakh*, the language that bound all together. The deepest assumptions of a people, those tacit gestures of bias which undercut opinion and rest on such intangibles as the inflection of a phrase, the movement of shoulders, the keening of despair, the melody of a laugh—all these form the inner substance of Sholom Aleichem's work.

Take as an example the brilliant little story, "A Yom Kippur Scandal." Wit and cleverness turn upon one another; the bare anecdote on which the story is based becomes an occasion for revealing the deepest feelings of a culture. Yet Sholom Aleichem's own quizzical voice is also heard at the end. There are at least two scandals: one that a stranger, a guest of the synagogue on the holiest of days, Yom Kippur, is robbed of a substantial sum of money (or pretends that he has been robbed); the other that a youth is a violator of the fast, discovered at the service with chicken bones hidden away. Both scandals are serious, but in the eyes of the rabbi, one of Sholom Aleichem's innocents, the first seems a sin against man, the second a sin against God, and thereby the second is the greater. Sholom Aleichem doesn't stop there, for he leaves the story up in the air—it is a characteristic narrative strategy of his—so that we don't know whether the stranger really was robbed, who did it, or how the problem was solved. As if that matters in the light of the greater scandal of the chicken bones, wildly funny as it struck many of the congregants! The story follows the Jewish habit of answering a question with another question: all life is a question, and if you ask me why, I can only answer, how should I know?

The dominant quality of Sholom Aleichem's work, then, seems to me not his wit or verbal brilliance or playfulness, remarkable as all these are; it is his sense of moral poise, his assurance as both Jew and human being, his ease in a world of excess. The image of the human, drawing upon traditional Jewish past and touching upon the problematic Jewish future, has seldom received so profound a realization as in these stories. His controlling voice tells us of madness, to be sure; but so long as we can hear *that* voice, we know the world is not yet entirely mad.

So I'd like to keep in balance the two Sholom Aleichems, the traditional and the modern, who, as we read him, are of course really one.

RW TO IH

I've been thinking about your emphasis on the cultural balance and "moral poise" of Sholom Aleichem, wondering how much of what you describe derives from the historical moment, and just what is specific to him. The end of the nineteenth century, that very critical period for East European Jews, when they were still thickly rooted in their traditions but freshly vulnerable to social and political changes, provided great artists with a unique literary opportunity. Yiddish, the common language, was ripe for the kind of harvest yielded during the Renaissance, when Western European writers in an analogous period of secularization and rising national awareness, plowed their vernaculars with heady expectations of gain. There are periods when the culture and its language seem to be at just the right point of tension between maturity and untried possibilities. No accident that all three of the Yiddish classical masters—Mendele Mocher Sforim (Abramovitch), I. L. Peretz, and Sholom Aleichem (Rabinowitz)—flourished almost together.

But of the three, Sholom Aleichem alone really struck the note of balance. Mendele and Peretz were both embattled writers, fiercely critical of their society, and only gradually softened by pity, doubt, and age. As underpaid employees of the Jewish community—Mendele was a school principal and Peretz a bureaucratic official—they spent most of their adult years torn between the daily routine of duty and the personal drive for literary self-expression. The strain of this divided existence, and the resentment, shows in their work. Their writing has a strong dialectic tendency, pitting the old and new, the impulses and ideas against one another in sharp confrontations. Peretz's favorite literary arena is the law court. As for Abramovitch-Mendele, his fictional autobiography literally splits his personality in two and has the critical, crotchety intellectual facing the kindly philosophic book peddler with no middle ground between them.

Sholom Aleichem is different. Though he too felt the impending break in the "golden chain" of Jewish tradition, and felt the cracks in his own life, he makes it his artistic business to close the gap. In fact, wherever the danger of dissolution is greatest, the stories work their magic in simulating or creating a terra firma. Maybe this, in part, is what the Yiddish critic, Borukh Rivkin, had in mind when he wrote that Sholom Aleichem provided the East European Jews with a fictional territory to compensate for their lack of a national soil.

The Tevye stories, of which we include a few, provide the most striking instance of stability where one would least expect it. If you follow the line of the plot, it traces nothing less than the breakup of an entire culture. At the beginning Tevye "makes a fortune," becomes a dairyman, and begins to provide for his large family. By the end he is a widower, supporting a destitute widowed daughter. A second daughter is in Siberia, a third is a convert, a fourth has committed suicide, the fifth—who married for money—has fled with her bankrupt husband to America. Tevye is attacked (albeit mildly) by his peasant neighbors and forced to flee from the land to which he feels he has as good a claim as anyone. He says, "What portion of the Bible are they reading this week? Vayikro? The first portion of Leviticus? Well, I'm on quite another chapter. Leykh lekho: get thee out. Get going, Tevye, they said to me, get out of thy country and from thy father's house, leave the village where you were born and spent all the years of your life and go—unto the land that I will show thee—wherever your two eyes lead you!" Pretty bitter stuff! God's mighty prophecy to Abraham of a promised land is applied by Tevye to himself with the caustic inversion of all the terms. This is Lear on the heath, but as his own jester. Tevye, who is actually defenseless against the barrage of challenges and attacks that lay him low, should have been a tragic victim. Instead, balancing his losses on the sharp edge of his tongue, he maintains the precarious posture of a comic hero.

All Tevye's misquotations, puns, and freewheeling interpretations that cause such hardship to even our best translators have been offered as proof of his simplicity and ignorance. Ridiculous! Tevye may not be the Vilna Gaon, but he is the original stand-up comic, playing to an appreciative audience of one: his impresario, Sholom Aleichem, who then passes on this discovered talent to us readers. Tevye has been endowed with such substantiality, so much adaptive vigor of speech and vision, that the dire events he recounts almost cease to matter. He gives proof of his creative survival even as he describes the destruction of its source. (I thought it was very fine when the Broadway production of Fiddler on the

Roof placed Tevye, in the finale, on a revolving stage, as though he were taking his world along with him wherever he went.)

This character worked so well for Sholom Aleichem it's not surprising that he created other versions of Tevye, including the narrator of "A Thousand and One Nights" whom we're introducing here. Yankel Yonever of Krushnik is another sturdy father, telling Sholom Aleichem the sorry tales of his children—only here the events are uglier and deadlier. The Jews are trapped between the anti-Semitic Cossacks and the invading Germans in the murderous chaos of World War I. The survivors, Yankel the narrator and Sholom Aleichem his listener, are in flight from Russia, suspended aboard ship in midocean with no ground at all underfoot. Yet even here the effect is one of moral and psychological balance, though the author has gone as far as he can go in achieving it. Yankel describes how the venerable rabbi was murdered by the Cossacks and left hanging for three days in the public square. This is the kind of brutal reality Sholom Aleichem had always avoided, and, in fact, Yankel says that at first he refused to pass the square, unwilling to witness the shame with his own eyes. When he finally goes, though, what does he see? Not the terrifying symbol of Cossack might, but the rabbi *"hanging shimenesre,"* the eighteen benedictions. Whereas ordinary Jews stand in their daily recitation of these blessings, the rabbi sways back and forth in an ultimate act of devotion. The image is so comfortingly homey; it domesticates the violence and shows us the rabbi as we can bear to look at him. Without inflated rhetoric, it also transforms a vile humiliation into triumphant martyrdom. It's just the turn of the phrase that does it, the simple substitution of "hanging" for "standing" *shimenesre* in one of the commonest Yiddish terms for praying. The English, because of the need for explanation, has to work almost too hard for the required effect, pressing on consciousness as a deliberate interpretive act. In Yiddish the redemption seems effortless.

Reading the last chapters of Tevye and this ironic version of Sheherezade, the tales of "A Thousand and One Nights," all written during Sholom Aleichem's final years, I wonder whether he could have kept the "comedy" going much longer. It is almost impossible to avoid sentimentalizing on the one hand or falling into cynicism on the other when attempting a balanced humanism in the face of this kind of barbarity.

IH TO RW

I know we have to be moving along to the literary aspects of Sholom Aleichem's work: his inventiveness with language, his fondness for the monologue as a narrative form, his curious habit of seeming to end a story before it comes to climax. But I can't resist a few more words on the matter of "moral poise"—by which, of course, we mean not some abstract doctrine but a vibrant quality of the stories themselves, communicated through details of language. It's when you come to Sholom Aleichem's stories about children that you see how balanced, at once stringent and tender, severe and loving, is his sense of life.

Some of the children's stories, like "Robbers" and "The Guest," are not at all carefree. Their dominant tone is nervousness and fright, their dominant theme, the enforced discovery, at too early an age, of the bitterness of the world. Sholom Aleichem does not hesitate to register the psychic costs of traditional Jewish life, costs in denial, repression, narrowness. But there are other stories, happier in voice, where the life-force, the child's sheer pleasure in breathing and running, breaks through. In the group translated as "Mottel the Cantor's Son," from which we've taken a few self-contained portions, the tone is lighthearted and playful. If Tom Sawyer could speak Yiddish, he'd be at home here. It's as if Sholom Aleichem were intent upon reminding his Jewish readers that we too deserve a little of the world's innocence.

Mottel represents the sadly abbreviated childhood of the traditional *shtetl*, where life does not flow evenly from one phase of experience to another, but all of them, childhood, adolescence, and manhood, are compressed into one. But Mottel does not yet know this, or pretends not to know it—who can be sure which? He is a wonderful little boy, celebrating his friendship with a neighbor's calf and stealing apples from the gardens of the rich. He is full of that spontaneous nature which Jewish upbringing has not yet suppressed ("Upon one leg I hop outside and—naturally straight to our neighbor's calf"). But he has an eye for the life about him; he is beginning to seep up that quiet Jewish sorrow which is part of his life's heritage ("That's an old story: a mother's got to cry. What I'd like to know is whether all mothers cry all the time, like mine"). Perhaps in a kind of tacit rebellion against the heaviness, the weighted ethicism, of Jewish life, Sholom Aleichem makes Mottel into something of a scamp, especially in the breezy chapters we've excerpted here, where Mottel, after the death of his father the cantor, becomes a little businessman, selling the cider and ink that his overimaginative brother manufactures ("Jews, here's a drink: Cider from heaven / If you order just one / You'll ask for eleven").

The Mottel stories are notable because the note they strike is heard infrequently in Yiddish literature. The hijinks of an adventurous boy, so favored in American and English writing, is something (I would guess) that Sholom Aleichem chose to write about only after conscious deliberation, as if to show his fellow Jews in

Eastern Europe and in the American slums what life might be, or in their long-lost youth might once have been. In his autobiography Sholom Aleichem writes about childhood pleasures: ". . . this is not meant for you, Jewish children! Yellow sunflowers, sweet-smelling grass, fresh air, fragrant earth, the clear sun—forgive me, these are not meant for you. . . ." Mottel shows us what has been lost.

Still, even in the saddest and most burdened Yiddish writing, there is something else shown about the life of Jewish children, and now, in retrospect, this seems to form an overwhelming positive contrast to the literatures of our century. In Yiddish literature the family is still a cohesive unit; fathers may be strict, mothers tearful, brothers annoying, but love breaks through and under the barriers of ritual. If there are few carefree children in Yiddish literature, there are few unloved or brutalized children.

Perhaps all that I'm saying is that in the world of Sholom Aleichem there are still some remnants of community. And this gives him strength and security as a writer; simply because he is so much at home with his materials, he can move from one tone to another. The Mottel stories can be casual, offhand, charming, even mischievous, but then suddenly Sholom Aleichem will drop to a fierce irony, a harrowing sadness. At the end Mottel and his family are aboard ship for America. All is fun, pranks, jokes, and then comes a brief lyrical description of a Yom Kippur service in the hold of the ship, "a Yom Kippur," says this Jewish little boy, "that neither God nor man would ever forget." And it is a token of Sholom Aleichem's genius, his "moral poise," that we are entirely prepared to accept the claim that these words come from the same boy who sells cider and ink and hops on one leg toward the neighbor's calf.

RW TO IH

The other day I came across a 1941 essay by Max Weinreich that runs oddly parallel to some of our main concerns. I say "oddly" because as a linguist Weinreich was dealing strictly with Sholom Aleichem's language and linguistic influence: yet he too concludes that the folksiness of Sholom Aleichem received undue attention and had a deleterious effect on its imitators, while the hard precision and richness of his language have gone almost unnoticed. Weinreich argues that the compulsive association of Yiddish with joking—an unfortunate tendency among modern Jews—has prevented a deeper appreciation of the master's verbal craftsmanship and artistic range.

It does seem that in its literary imitations of the voices and mannerisms of ordinary Jews, Sholom Aleichem's oral styles were almost *too* effective. Even sophisticated readers were so amused and dazzled by the natural flow of the language that they considered the writer to be a ventriloquist, his art a superior form of realism. As if Sholom Aleichem had anticipated the tape recorder!

This may be a compliment in its way, but in fact, the "artless garrulousness" of the characters is under surprisingly tight control, and in ways that translation may sometimes have to sacrifice. What, for example, can we do with the opening sentence of "Dos tepl" ("The Pot")—that famous Sholom Aleichem monologue: "Rebbe! Ikh vil aykh fregn a shayle vil ikh aykh!" Natural English can't attempt much more than "Rabbi, I've come to ask you a question." But the original circles back on itself, rather like this: "Rabbi, I want to ask you a question is what I want to do." The woman's circular style is the most accurate literary expression of the closed circle of her thoughts and her life. She labors within the same rounds of work and obligation set out for her by her mother; her son is dying of the very illness that claimed her husband; her poverty traps her in such narrow constraints of time and space that she cannot grasp those very possibilities that might mitigate her poverty. Above all, her mind is imprisoned in its own obsessive circularity, unable to come to the point even long enough to pose her question. Though her speech may be generally "true to life," it is actually used to give truth to her particular embattled consciousness, self-protecting and self-defeating in equal measure, and preoccupied with impending death.

At some point we would also have to admit that Sholom Aleichem's success as a stylist has frustrated our editorial choices, at least in part. The sly mockery of American Jewish assimilation, rendered through the crude, overeager borrowings of Yiddish immigrants fresh off the boat, falls flat in English, the host language. It's also difficult to distinguish in translation, as Sholom Aleichem does in the original, the many degrees of social climbers who oil their Yiddish with Russian phrases to ease the way up, and then slip comically on their malapropisms and mistakes. Sholom Aleichem's speakers are characterized as much by the quality of their language as by its apprehended meaning. I doubt that any translation can get this across.

In addition to being a marvelous tool, Yiddish is also Sholom Aleichem's metaphor for the culture. While many of his contemporaries and even some of his successors were hampered by the novelty of Yiddish as a modern literary language, Sholom Aleichem turned the fluidity and newness of Yiddish prose style to penetrating advantage. What better medium for conveying the critical changes of East European Jewish life than a "language of fusion"—to use Max Weinreich's term—in which the sources of fusion are still identifiable and in active flux? Sholom Aleichem uses the nuances of Yiddish to communicate the degree to which a speaker is integrated into the traditional culture or deviates from it in any direction—toward the "German" enlightenment, the Slavic identification with the folk, or the higher pretensions of St. Petersburg society. From the speaker's tendency to use certain aspects of the German or Slavic components of the language, one can determine his origins and aspirations, his relation to the values of his home, and the lure of the environment.

Yet too extreme an emphasis on the Hebraic element, the most indigenous component of Yiddish, is not a good sign either. Characters who affect too traditional a language are either sanctimonious hypocrites, like the members of the Burial Society in the story "Eternal Life," or con-artists of whom Sholom Aleichem provides a peerless variety. The positive characters are those who tend neither inward nor outward but speak a perfectly balanced tongue.

For Tevye, the most trustworthy of Sholom Aleichem's speakers, the fused elements of Yiddish are an eternal delight. Like a true musician, he enjoys showing the speed and grace with which he can skip from one note or one tone to another. His best jokes and quotations are polyglot, drawing attention to their mixture of high and low, old and new, indigenous and imported. He can use these combinations to achieve both comic and sentimental effects.

Even this technique of linguistic crosscutting, however, does not automatically guarantee a reliable character. Shimon-Eli, the haunted tailor, is like Tevye, a man who loves to speak in quotations which he translates, or mistranslates, or occasionally invents. His level of speech, like Tevye's, reveals his limited *cheder* education, his easy familiarity with the tradition, and an intellectual reach that exceeds its grasp. But Shimon-Eli uses quotations and linguistic jokes as clichés, the same stock phrases reappearing whoever the listener and whatever the situation. He moves instinctively back and forth through his repertoire, just as he passes through the same phases of his journey over and over again without reflection or insight. At the end, his failure to adapt, his application of tried explanations instead of fresh, deductive questions, dooms him to madness. Tevye's movement through levels of speech is the manifestation of his adaptive intelligence. Shimon-Eli's automatic movement through a similar set of paces is the surest sign of his stultification.

By the end of the nineteenth century, I. L. Peretz, who was quickly becoming the dominant influence in Yiddish literature, tried to stabilize a literary language for the purposes of normal narration. He drew attention away from the specificities of Yiddish, away from its folk expressions, the interplay of its source languages, the different dialects and levels of its various speakers. In Peretz's stories a Lithuanian rabbi and a Polish Hasid speak the same Yiddish.

But for Sholom Aleichem the unfixed nature of Yiddish was its greatest attraction, and its infinite range of dialects and oral styles the best literary means of
capturing the dynamic changes—or the resistance to change—in the culture.
There are times, reading Sholom Aleichem in the pulsating original, when I think
we ought to have put out a Yiddish reader for the fortunate few who can use it,
leaving translation to the gods.*

IH TO RW

In talking about Sholom Aleichem's stories, we both remarked on the seeming
oddity that many of them do not really end. Especially in those told by an internal
narrator (a character who is seen and heard telling a story either to other characters or to "Mr. Sholom Aleichem"), there is roughly the following sequence:
the stories move toward climax, they arouse suspense, they bring together the
elements of conflict, and then, just when you expect the writer to drive toward
resolution, they seem deliberately to remain hanging in the air. They stop rather
than end. And this happens often enough to make us suspect that it cannot be a
mere accident or idiosyncrasy. Sholom Aleichem is a self-conscious artist and he
must have had something in mind. Thus, in "A Yom Kippur Scandal" we never
really find out who stole the money; in "The Haunted Tailor" we are spared following the central figure to his fate; and in "Station Baranovich" the story teller
provocatively refuses to complete his story. What is this all about? I have a few
speculations:

* The difficulties of translating Sholom Aleichem are almost beyond recounting. They go far
deeper than the problem of rendering Yiddish idiom into English, a problem sometimes solved
by finding enough English equivalents, and more often acknowledged as beyond solution because the Yiddish idiom is so deeply planted in Jewish tradition it is virtually untranslatable. A
more serious problem is that of rendering the Hebraic component, which in some stories like
"The Haunted Tailor" and "Tevye Strikes It Rich," is crucial to the development of both narrative
and meaning.
    Previous translators have simply evaded this problem by omitting the Hebrew, either in
translation or transliteration, and the result has been a serious impoverishment of the work. In
the present volume such gifted translators as Leonard Wolf and Hillel Halkin struggle heroically
with this difficulty, each employing a different approach. What compounds the difficulty here is
that the relationship between the two languages, Hebrew and Yiddish, is so complex: at some
points they are two separate languages, though historically linked, but at other points they form
a linguistic continuum. Yet we may also be certain that for some of Sholom Aleichem's Yiddish
readers these Hebrew passages, many of them taken from the Bible and some cleverly distorted
for comic effect, were almost as inaccessible as they are for most English readers. The jokes,
then, are not only on one or another character, but also on us, readers who have lost or abandoned the tradition.

1. Sholom Aleichem is persisting in the old tradition of oral story telling (though, in fact, he is a literary artist and not an oral story teller) which takes pleasure in leading the listener on, teasing him further and further. Then, as if to demonstrate the emotional power of the narrator or the moral perplexities of existence, there is a sudden, abrupt blockage—as if to say, figure out the rest for yourself, make up whatever denouement you can, it's all equally puzzling. . . .

2. Sholom Aleichem is suggesting rather slyly that, really, there are far more important things in the world than the resolution of an external action, suspenseful and exciting though it may be; indeed, what one learns along a narrative journey matters more than the final destination. Thus in "A Yom Kippur Scandal" the question of the visitor's money—was it ever really there? did someone steal it? is he a confidence man?—counts for very little in comparison with the scandal, the shocked laughter, when it is discovered that one of the shtetl's pious young favorites has been secretly nibbling on chicken bones during the fast day of Yom Kippur. And the reasoning is obvious once you ponder it: the money is merely a worldly matter, while the behavior of the youth raises an issue of faith.

3. Sholom Aleichem often uses in these stories a narrating figure that might be called "the clever Jew," one who is rather worldly though still tied to some of the old ways of piety. This narrator has "been around," as merchant or traveler. In his ambiguous person he seems to straddle old world and new. Almost always there is a duel between the narrator and his audience of gullible and / or skeptical listeners within the story; or between the narrator and the readers of the story, who are in effect challenged to figure out what to make of him; or sometimes, one ventures to say, between the narrator and Sholom Aleichem himself, who stands somewhat bemused by his own creation. The puzzlement this narrator spins out in a story like "A Yom Kippur Scandal" becomes a trail toward evident laughter and possible wisdom. In "Eternal Life" the narrator is now an experienced man, one of those solid but still reasonably pious merchants that Yiddish writers liked to use as the center of their fictions. He recalls the foolishness but also the charming innocence of his youth; and if he now flees from the prospect of seeking "eternal life," is that, within the bounds of the world view by which he purports to live, so entirely a gain in maturity and rightness? In "Dreyfus in Kasrilevke" the narrator is placed within the action; he tells his "stories" (the reports he reads in the paper about the Dreyfus case) to other Jews in the little shtetl of Kasrilevke. At the end they refuse to believe him; they cannot credit so gross an injustice. In their "rejection" of this narrator figure, Sholom Aleichem has created an overpowering moment, a deeply poignant image of the Jewish refusal to believe in the full evil of

the world. The "clever Jew" is thus shown in many aspects—complicated, quiz-zical, problematic.

4. Sholom Aleichem uses, as I've said, traditional devices of oral story tell-ing, but he is also a sophisticated writer very much aware of his departures from that tradition. He can no longer regard a story as something that is always fixed, secure, knowable (e.g., the rebellious clock in "The Clock That Struck Thirteen," a wonderfully appropriate and homey image for the sense of collapsing order). Sholom Aleichem lived at a time when stories could be begun but not always brought to an end. Before him stories could be brought to an end; after him they could hardly be begun. What, then, one wonders, would he have made of Coc-teau's remark that "Literature is a force of memory that we have not yet under-stood"? Perhaps he would have amended the last clause to "that we can no longer understand."

5. Sholom Aleichem knew intuitively that the boundary between comedy and tragedy is always a thin and wavering line—and for Jews, often nonexistent. Al-most all of his best comic stories hover on the edge of disaster. All exemplify the truth of Saul Bellow's remark that in Jewish writing "laughter and trembling are so curiously intermingled that it is not easy to determine the relations of the two." Reading Sholom Aleichem is like wandering through a lovely meadow of laughter and suddenly coming to a precipice of doom. At the end of "The Haunted Tailor" we have a vista of madness, at the end of "A Yom Kippur Expropriation" a pros-pect of social violence, at the end of "A Yom Kippur Scandal" the shame of Jewish disintegration. Sholom Aleichem takes us by the hand, we are both shaking with laughter, and he leads us. . . . "And would you like to hear the rest of the story?" asks one of his narrators. "The rest isn't so nice." Assuredly not.

RW TO IH

I appreciated your speculations on Sholom Aleichem's endings and narrative art. As a mundane footnote, one could also note the influence in this—as in ev-ery conceivable linguistic, stylistic, and narrative aspect of Sholom Aleichem's work—of Mendele Mocher Sforim, the man he dubbed the grandfather of mod-ern Yiddish literature, the man who was really his own artistic progenitor. Indeed some of Mendele's finest work, also in the oral tradition, does not seem to end; but Sholom Aleichem draws attention to the inconclusiveness of his conclusions in a way his forerunner did not. It's as you say: he actively challenges our notion of the denouement or solution and avoids the verdict, the finality, of what would usually be an unhappy fate.

In general, Sholom Aleichem did not do very well with a direct approach to the great, climactic, and decisive moments of plot. When he did attempt a big love scene, or a tough social confrontation, he could be surprisingly inept. You have only to look at one of his earliest efforts, the thinly disguised autobiographical novella where the wealthy young heroine, who has been playing fantasias by moonlight, rushes through the garden and into the arms of her indigent tutor to the following momentous dialogue:

HE: Polinka!
SHE: Rabovsky!

Impossible to read the scene without laughing—at the author's expense.

Lest this seem just the failure of a novice, one could turn to a ripe novel, like The Storm (1905), where Sholom Aleichem depicts the ideological clashes among the Jews in pre-Revolutionary Russia. At the moment of intended climax, when the Zionist hero is to win over the uncommitted heroine to both his politics and himself, he can do no better than to stop in the middle of the street, whip from his pocket a famous poem by Chaim Nachman Bialik, and *read* her its text for the better part of the chapter! It is not that Sholom Aleichem avoided the romantic subject, the heroic possibility, the grand style of the novel: he was simply unconvincing and demonstrably *uncomfortable* in this mode, especially at the high points of resolution, and of course, conclusion.

No, his mastery is of quite the opposite order. Beginning with no more than an anecdote, sometimes an item that his adoring readers sent him, sometimes a joke that already had whiskers on it, he would invent a speaker, give him a story to tell and the merest pretext for a tale—the amusement of a fellow passenger, the enlightenment of a stranger to town, etc. The story would be either about himself, or more often, about a third party, someone from his *shtetl* perhaps, more of a character type than a differentiated personality. And if that were not layered and indirect enough, the speaker would tell the story not to the readers, but to an intermediary who was often the author's invented self, this all-embracing soul called "Sholom Aleichem." Veiled, then, like Salome, the anecdote begins its tantalizing, captivating play, a dance of words that is meant to leave you, as the author boasts, laughing your head off!

The kernel "story" of "On Account of a Hat," one of your favorites, I know, was once told to me as a regional Jewish joke, in about ten seconds. Out of this insubstantial matter, Sholom Aleichem has woven a masterpiece with a dozen interpretations: it is the plight of the Diaspora Jew, an exposure of rootlessness,

a mockery of tyranny, the comic quest for identity, a Marxist critique of capitalism, and, of course, an ironic self-referential study of literary sleight of hand. . . .
It's easy to mock the highfalutin readings this story has received, but those who
catch its serious import are not wrong either. Magically witty and unpretentious
as it is, the story leaves you with an eerie, troubling sense of reality that begs
attention. (Isaac Bashevis Singer, whose anecdotal style owes much to Sholom
Aleichem, occasionally forces the serious mien of his stories with sermonettes on
good, evil, and the meaning of existence. In Sholom Aleichem, you get no such
prompting.)

What we have is an author who works best by indirection, in the smaller modes
of fiction, from the worm's angle of vision, and with apparently flimsy materials.
Even the main, archetypal figures of Sholom Aleichem are not full-blown heroes of novels, but characters or speakers in short story sequences, written over
a period of years and later assembled in book form. The stature and personali-
ties of Tevye, Menachem-Mendel, Mottel the Cantor's Son, as well as the town
of Kasrilevke (Sholom Aleichem's fourth, collective "hero"), emerge from a run
of episodes, each only slightly different from the one before it, that cumulatively
establish their dimensions. As distinct from the normal novel, which develops
a single architectonic structure, growing from introduction to a central point of
resolution, Sholom Aleichem's major works beat like waves against a shore, one
chapter resembling and reinforcing the last in variations of a theme. The normal
novel lays human destiny out as a one-way trip, with important encounters, in-
tersections, and moments of decision that determine one's rise or fall, success or
failure, happiness or misery. The major works of Sholom Aleichem have no such
suspenseful vision. A man is what he is to begin with—even Mottel, the child.
He confronts all the things that happen to him and forces himself upon life again
and again, and the sum of these trials shape the rhythm, constitute the meaning,
of his existence.

It's the old literary knot of form and content. Sholom Aleichem's admiration
for the stubborn ruggedness of Jewish faith and the surprising vitality of the people comes to expression not just thematically, in story after story, but in the resil-
ient, recuperative *shape* of all his major works.

Before ending, I should tell you that this serious correspondence of ours about
Sholom Aleichem appeared to me the other day in a comical light. I was lecturing
about Sholom Aleichem to a nice synagogue audience, and every time I illustrated
a point with a quotation or the plot of a story, the audience broke into happy, appreciative laughter. After a while I must admit I found myself adding quotations

and dramatizing more stories to elicit that laughter, and when the lecture was over, people came over to tell me what a good story teller I was!

You see the point. Expostulate on Kafka or Dostoevsky and people are fairly begging for your explanations and interpretations. Lecture on any other Yiddish writer—Mendele, Peretz, Asch, Grade, the brothers Singer—and your words will illumine, clarify, edify. But set out to discuss the "narrative structure" or "comic techniques" of Sholom Aleichem, and he undercuts your very best attempt. I have the uncomfortable feeling that readers may look through these letters not for any insights, but for their illustrative examples. And Sholom Aleichem would be right behind, egging them on. Consider the deliberate irreverence of his literary memoir, *Once There Were Four*, and contrast this mountaineering saga of Jewish writers with all the high, serious climbs of other European literati. He gives us no disquisitions on literature, no pen portraits of his contemporaries, no contemplative philosophy from the heights. Just four "anecdotes" on the subject of forgetting, in which three of the greatest Jewish writers of the age, and one choleric literary companion, are revealed as ordinary, anxious Jews, faltering and trembling in ordinary, if not humiliating circumstances. He deflates intellectual and artistic pretentiousness, and even undercuts the grandeur of the Alps!

We set out—I think justifiably—to take a serious new look at a well-known but not well-appreciated author. What confronts us, finally, is the quizzical smile of the author, compulsively skeptical about everything but the story.

The 1980s

Mission from Japan:
Review of The Samurai
{1982}

A S THE MEREST BEGINNER and very much a latecomer, I started recently to look into Japanese fiction. What I can report is fragmentary, a record of uncertainties, confusions, and probable mistakes such as many Western readers are likely to share upon encountering Japanese fiction.

My first response was a shock of pleasure. Even through the dim channel of translation one can quickly see that contemporary Japanese fiction contains a large body of distinguished work. Much of it is marked by psychological finesse, and still more by a formalism of manner occasionally broken by thrusts into the sensual and perverse. My second response was a sense of anxiety, since nothing seemed to fall into place or settle into clarity. The forms, subjects, and even voices of gifted writers like Tanizaki, Dazai, Mishima, and Endo seemed reasonably familiar, so much so that I would ask myself: is it possible that Tanizaki, before writing the "Firefly Hunt" chapter in The Makioka Sisters, had read Virginia Woolf? Did Dazai know Dostoevsky? Or Endo, Silone? But soon such questions came to seem pointless, as I found myself sinking into a chasm of strangeness or, to put it differently, suffered a break in the premises of understanding that bind reader to writer.

Part of the strangeness may be due to no more than differences in literary method. There is, to start with a small matter, a greater tolerance for repetition of incident and remark in Japanese fiction than in Western. Japanese novelists appear to be less concerned than those in the West with devices that make for tension and foreshortening; they favor a more even pace of narrative; they do not seem to try nearly so hard for radical variations of stress from one part of a novel to another. The verbal surfaces of the Japanese novels I have read struck me as more pacific, perhaps more laconic than our fiction has trained us to expect. And in Japanese fiction there are often stretches of material, apparently flat detail and routine transcription of events, that a Western reader is likely to find puzzling. Even as sophisticated a novelist as Tanizaki includes such "nonfunctional" segments, causing one to wonder what thematic or dramatic purpose they may have.

These difficulties are still fairly simple and can be negotiated with a little impatience (skip a page or two). A greater obstacle in reading Japanese fiction, even as one may be steadily engrossed by it, is that the norms of expectation regarding conduct and judgment are often subtly and therefore radically at variance with our own. Least available are those cues to systems of manners through which Western fiction helps us release quick intuitions.

In Japanese novels the characters are often finely portrayed, in part because the autobiographical narrative has been popular and in part because the entrance of a culture into modernity creates the grounds for psychological nuance. But the *concept* of individuality seems elusive, as if it only gradually entered Japanese fiction and continues to meet resistance from traditionalist codes. Even among consciously "modern" Japanese writers there is, it seems to me, rather less tolerance than among us for strong assertions of will or virtuosities of self; and still more alien is our notion that achieving an absolute selfhood is a primary human goal.

Equally hard to grasp are various rituals depicted or recalled by Japanese writers, especially in novels written by more traditionalist figures like Kawabata. Some of these rituals are public, so that one can try to bone up on them, but others form a half-hidden skein of suggestion which, in their refinements, come to seem almost impenetrable.

Reading Kawabata's admirable novel *Thousand Cranes*, one can hardly fail to recognize that the tea ceremony plays an important part, but only an expert Western reader is likely to know that the novel, as Kawabata said in his Nobel Prize speech, "is an expression of doubt and warning against the vulgarity into which the tea ceremony has fallen." A Japanese reader learning about the importance of the death watch in certain of Emily Dickinson's poems might feel similar puzzlements.

But what troubles one most in reading Japanese fiction is a nagging sense that one is missing something; it may seem close at hand yet quite elusive; and no Japanese, you may be sure, will ever explain. Reading Kawabata or Tanizaki, I could detect faint signals—a smile? a mild irony? a clarifying allusion?—but could not shape them into coherence. It's as if there is always some undervoice, the true voice, overheard but not grasped.

In a fine little book called *In Praise of Shadows* Tanizaki confirms some of these impressions: "In conversations we [Japanese] prefer the soft voice, the understatement. Most important of all are the pauses. . . . Westerners are amazed at the simplicity of Japanese rooms, perceiving in them no more than ashen walls bereft of ornament. Their reaction is understandable, but it betrays a failure to comprehend the mystery of shadows." And a "mystery," at least in part, it remains.

No doubt, with greater knowledge and prolonged reading, some of these difficulties fade away. They are, after all, not very different from the obstacles to understanding that an American may encounter in reading Latin American fiction. But I suspect that there must always be a residue of intractable difficulties, signaling the really great distance between Japanese culture and our own. The only solution for the beginning reader, I have found, is to abandon any irritable quest for certainty and take pleasure in one's experience of strangeness and uncertainty. Accept that one must fumble, guess, wonder.

The novels of Shusaku Endo seem at first to be free of many of these problems. Surely one of the most accomplished writers now living in Japan or anywhere else, Endo is a Catholic who after the war studied in France and there came under the spell of Mauriac and Bernanos. The exact nature of this influence is hard to know: I suspect it has less to do with literary matters than with an attachment to Catholicism gaining its intensity from a persuasion that in our time any serious religious commitment must also be a questioning one.

The Catholic imagination straining against the limits of the Catholic institutional presence—this is something we certainly know about from many Western writers. On first encountering Endo one may therefore experience a certain relief of familiarity, but mostly it's an illusion.

In an early novel, *Volcano* (1959), Endo's Catholic preoccupations tend, through sheer earnestness, to overwhelm the often vivid materials of the book. In another early novel, *Wonderful Fool* (1959), the theme is more successfully, perhaps because less explicitly, realized. Endo pits ambiguous Christian sentiments against an indifferent modern Japan, often with pleasing comic effects. He places in the chaos of postwar Tokyo a sweet-tempered Frenchman named Gaston, something of a holy fool "who, no matter how often he is deceived or betrayed, continues to keep his flame of love and trust from going out." Charming and touching as Gaston is, he cannot really carry enough fictional weight to sustain that emulation of Christ which Endo evidently desires for him; nor can he serve to embody Endo's obsession with the entanglements and ultimate irreconcilability between Christianity and Japanese tradition.

It is in two later books that Endo fulfills himself as a novelist—*Silence*, first published in Japan in 1966, and *The Samurai*, first published there in 1980 and now available in a fluent and persuasive English translation. Both novels are set in or near early seventeenth-century Japan, when the Christian missionaries gained successes only to suffer brutal persecution, and both are partly based on historical fact. *Silence* I regard as a masterpiece, a lucid and elegant drama about a Portuguese missionary tormented by Japanese inquisitors. The missionary agrees finally to apostatize, not merely or even mainly because he cannot bear his ordeal but because he hears a voice of Christ telling him that to relieve the torments of his Japanese flock it is right that he place his foot on the *fumie*—a wooden box bearing the image of Christ which the inquisitors use to enact their victims' apostasy. "Trample! Trample! I more than anyone know of the pain in your foot. Trample! It was to be trampled on by men that I was born into this world."

Less well formed than *Silence*, *The Samurai* is a more ambitious and complex work, richer in contemplative matter though also more uneven in its effects. *The Samurai* contains episodes set in Japan, Mexico, and Spain; there is a striking variety of Japanese and European figures; but parts of the novel suffer from a "documentary" inertness and the narrative as a whole lacks the single-track rapidity of *Silence*.

The story of *The Samurai* is simple enough. In 1613 there sets sail from Japan a ship laden with emissaries and merchants, their declared aim to open trade relations with Nueva España (Mexico). As interpreter and guide (also, misleader), a Franciscan missionary, Father Velasco, accompanies them. He has, naturally, purposes of his own: to gain for the Franciscans, in opposition to the more fanatical Jesuits, a monopoly of the Japanese mission and for himself the title of Bishop of Japan. But there is a trick all along: the emissaries are of low rank, a group of samurai chosen by the Japanese rulers as decoys in a scheme to appropriate Western technology (*plus ça change . . .*). The central figure among the samurai, and in the book, is a stolid, honest retainer named Hasekura, whose whole life has been devoted to work and obedience.

This journey, which takes them round the world, lasts four years: they have experiences at once comic and painful in Mexico and Spain. Hoping that a formal conversion to Christianity will help them fulfill their political mission, the emissaries are baptized—though with only the slightest interest in Christian mystery or faith. Finally back in Japan, they encounter a new regime that is bitterly hostile to opening any relations with the West and determined to uproot Christianity by force.

Through the journey it charts and the lengthy stops along the way, *The Samurai* offers numerous set-pieces: the impoverished and long-suffering Japanese peasants, with whom Hasekura shares an obscure marshland; the Japanese nobility caring for nothing but the consolidation of its power and regarding Christian converts quite as if they were alien "cosmopolitans"; the minor Japanese officials surrounding Hasekura, all neatly distinguished within their hierarchical order; the Catholic bureaucracy of Spain, sodden with worldliness yet still open to memories of faith.

Hasekura and Father Valasco dominate the book: their contrasting steadiness and stealthiness, Japanese rootedness and European impatience, come together, more or less, in a culminating martyrdom. At this point Endo presses too hard, the theologian in him overcoming the novelist. Hasekura, in his humiliation on returning to a Japan that has become anti-Christian, finds some glimmers of sympathy for Jesus, a faith or at least an acceptance of martyrdom which conventional Christian preaching could not give him. But the novel hardly provides enough preparatory cues to enable us to give this ending full credence.

The strand of Catholic sensibility that Endo has made his own dominates both *Silence* and *The Samurai*, though mainly through negations—doubt and muted despair. Perhaps sensing that his austere version of the faith is more appropriate for the training of martyrs than the worship of common mortals, Endo gives way to an inner Christian grieving over the helplessness of a Christianity that demands more of men than they can give. The historical clash between the Christian mission and Japan thus becomes for Endo an instance, though the crucial one, of a universal predicament.

Europeans are often central figures in these novels, and Endo is remarkably gifted at a sort of Western impersonation, and edging into alien consciousness. He writes with considerable humor about the mixture of submissiveness and worldliness animating the missionaries, so that unexpectedly one comes rather to like these stranded Fathers.

Yet if one supposes that Endo is writing here "as a European," that is a misconception quickly to be put to rest. It helps a Western reader to situate himself through the references to Mauriac; it may even help to notice that Endo's conception of Jesus as the deformed and weak victim has something in common with Silone's. But one soon recognizes that, while marked by the West, Endo is not of it. He is a very strange figure, profoundly alienated, and moving in ways I can't entirely explain.

What puzzles and obsesses him is the apparently unshakable Japanese "essence," a national character that has been formed by centuries of historical and geographical isolation. He keeps calling Japan "the mudswamp," a place, that is, where everything sinks and loses its identifying shape. He speaks about the "threefold insensitivity" of Japan, "the insensitivity to God, the insensitivity to sin, the insensitivity to death." He believes Christianity must fail in Japan because it cannot bring itself to see the Japanese as they really are, in their radical otherness. It must fail because its institutions, theologies, and practices keep even its Japanese converts apart from the one thing that might (and in *The Samurai* finally does) break past the stolidity of the Japanese character—and that would be an act of piercing empathy with Jesus. Most Japanese, according to Endo, tend to be contemptuous of so passive and weak a figure as Jesus: what sort of a God can this "emaciated man" be? Yet precisely this contempt may, through the traumas of history, turn at least a few of them to an imitation of Christ.

Like all serious novelists, Endo prompts one not only to live with his fictions but to engage with his thought. One wonders, then: Is it really true that the Japanese character is so hopelessly locked into the triple insensitivity that Endo attributes to it? One is repeatedly struck by the fact that in both *Silence* and *The Samurai* Buddhism rarely, if ever, makes a strong appearance, speaking in its own right and from the depth of its own traditions. For Endo, apparently, Buddhism possesses little moral or metaphysical authority: it offers, in these novels, no crucial reply to the claims of Christianity. But it seems hard to believe that this is really so. Might not a writer like Kawabata, in the gentlest of replies to Endo, have identified authentic values within the Buddhist traditions—values that might be set against Endo's rigid polarities of "the emaciated man" and "the mudswamp"?

And another point: if institutional Christianity must fail and all that remains is the example of the forlorn Jesus, where does that leave all those who lack the vocation of sainthood or the talent for martyrdom? Can Jesus survive without Christianity, without the very institutions, rituals, and doctrines that must often twist his word? To such questions Endo offers no answers, at least in these two of his novels, and from a strictly literary point of view it hardly matters. But the power of a first-rate work of fiction lies partly in its capacity to make us think beyond fictions, and there Endo leaves one uneasy.

Distinguished as *The Samurai* is, it seems too much the product of a mind lost to itself. I have before me the image of a remarkable figure, standing neckdeep in his native mudswamp, but head still aflame with stories of the crucified god. It is hard to believe that more than a few can live by so lacerating a vision.

Absalom in Israel:
Review of Past Continuous
{1985}

S O MANY SECRET DISAPPOINTMENTS and betrayed visions accumulate over the years and bear down upon the consciousness of people who may not even know the source of their dismay. In the culture of Israel, this burden is perhaps the very idea of Israel itself, as if people—at least, some people—were haunted by a vision of what Israel was supposed to be but, in the nature of things, never could become.

This weight of feeling clouds, yet ultimately defines, *Past Continuous*, an Israeli novel of great distinction which was first published in 1977 and has now been put into fluent English. (But with one "concession" to American readers: the occasional paragraphing of what in the Hebrew text is an unbroken flow of language.) I cannot recall, these past several years, having encountered a new work of fiction that has engaged me as strongly as *Past Continuous*, both for its brilliant formal inventiveness and for its relentless truth-seeking scrutiny of the moral life. While a difficult book requiring sharp attentiveness on the part of the reader, it still satisfies traditional expectations that a novel should lure one into an imaginary "world."

Until this book Yaakov Shabtai had been an Israeli literary figure of middle stature. A tremendous breakthrough, which can be compared to that of Faulkner when he moved from his early novels to *The Sound and the Fury*, occurred in Shabtai's middle age, the kind of breakthrough that becomes possible when a writer gains possession of his own culture, uncovering its deepest sentiments and secrets. Shabtai died of heart disease in 1981 at the age of forty-seven, leaving behind another unfinished novel.

The opening pages of *Past Continuous* plunge us into a bewildering mixture of fact, memory, reflection. A voice speaks, and it is of an omniscient narrator who seems in complete control. Nothing can be heard or seen except through its mediation. Neither colloquial nor very eloquent, it is self-assured, exhaustive. It records; it quietly corrects both itself and the book's characters; and, although rarely, it keens over their fate. Above all, this voice tries to get things exactly right, as if some higher power had assigned it the obligation of making final judgment.

The opening sentence—"Goldman's father died on the first of April, whereas Goldman himself committed suicide on the first of January"—sets the bounds of time and the tone for all to follow. The present in *Past Continuous* consists of the months between the deaths of father and son, with the speaker, whose identity we don't yet know but whose authority we accept, leading us back, through his own associations of events and impressions, to events in the past. As the relatives and friends of Goldman's father, Ephraim, gather after the funeral, there begins an unraveling of shared memories. The local detail is very dense, matted into synoptic vignettes of the characters' lives. There are dozens of characters, though strictly speaking they are glimpsed rather than developed. Shabtai offers only sparse physical descriptions of these people, yet one soon comes to feel that one "knows" a good many of them, for his is an art of the representative, an art of the group. A community is releasing its experience, a generation is sliding toward extinction: the community, the generation of "labor Israel," socialist Zionism, which was central in the creation of the young country but has by now—say, the late 1970s—succumbed to old age and debility. If there can be such a thing as a collective novel, then *Past Continuous* is one.

The book takes off from one of the conventions of Western literature: a myth of historical and moral decline. By no means (and this is worth stressing) should it be taken as a straight account of Israel's recent condition. It offers something more complex and ambiguous: a voice of the culture quarreling with itself, an evocation of buried yearnings and regrets, a social elegy whose tone is somber and unsentimental. Like Faulkner, Shabtai subjects to merciless scrutiny the very myth upon which his book rests and to which he seems residually attached. The griefs weighing upon his characters may thereby, perhaps, be unpacked and allowed to settle in the calm of memory.

In the forefront, though not quite at the center, of *Past Continuous* stand three men in early middle age: Goldman, a reflective and melancholy man, Chekhovian in the way he registers losses, and the book's uncertain center of intelligence; Caesar, whose lechery is almost comic and who registers nothing, but serves, in the novel, as a kind of foil to Goldman; and Israel, a pianist of sensitivity but feeble will, who forms a connecting link with the other characters. These three can be seen as "representing" a generation that has inherited the life of Tel Aviv but not the strength of its founders, a generation, indeed, that in moments of self-pity feels crushed by that strength. As in all myths of decline, the sons have been weakened. Behind this myth there is history, but history bent and misshaped.

Through these younger characters Shabtai reaches toward the older generation, which engages him more keenly. Men and women in their sixties and beyond—one can see them sitting at the beachfront cafés of Tel Aviv, soaking up the sun and reading *Davar*, the labor newspaper—this older generation consists of an elite in an advanced stage of decomposition. Nothing about the manners or appearance of these people would suggest this, and they would hotly deny they ever did form an elite, except perhaps an elite formed to eliminate all elites. Israeli readers would have no more trouble in recognizing these figures—the people of the Histadrut, the cadres of labor Zionism—than southern readers a few decades ago would have had in recognizing the aristocracy of the Sartorises and the Compsons.

Mostly, Shabtai's older characters come from Eastern Europe and have settled, not quite at ease, in Eretz Yisroel with a budget of expectations as wildly improbable as they are (for some of us) affecting: to establish a Jewish nation, to live by an egalitarian ethic, and to create a new kind of Jew, standing erect, doing his own work with his own hands. To put it this way is to yield to abstraction, for what was really involved was a tremendous yearning for social and moral transfiguration, a leap through history, a remaking of souls.

This "design," to lift a phrase from Faulkner's Thomas Sutpen, was partly realized, but for the plebeian veterans of Tel Aviv, stirred in their youth by a whiff of the absolute, the very process of realization brought disappointment. History gave a little but not enough, and now it has left these people—Shabtai's people—with a grief they cannot comprehend or shake off. They seldom talk about it any longer, and some of them have begun to doubt the genuineness of their own feelings, but this hardly matters since those feelings continue to oppress them.

What—as Sutpen asks in *Absalom, Absalom!* about a very different sort of "design"—what went wrong? External circumstances? Strategic blunders?

Impossible expectations? Or some deep flaw in the original "design"? Shabtai's older figures have put these questions largely behind them, for it's as if he had deposited them at a point where neither asking nor answering can do much good. Political people stranded in a post-political moment, either they cling to their received values, tightening themselves into righteousness as their world slips away from them, or they slump into an irritable mixture of rectitude and cynicism, a condition Shabtai is very shrewd in depicting, as if it were the atmosphere of his own years.

After Ephraim's funeral the mourners sit in the Goldman apartment, nibbling cakes and chatting emptily. There is little for these people to look forward to, but there is little pleasure in looking back, so they become entangled in foolish quarrels, as blocked in their love as in their enmity. Individually, Shabtai's characters are mostly pitiable, but collectively they bear the stamp of history—history the destroyer—and this lends a certain magnitude to their plight. By its technique, the book creates an enlarged reflection of its theme, with the intricacies of memory cast as emblems of human entanglement. Voice gives way to voice, through the narrator's "overvoice." Goldman's father, Ephraim, a tyrant of idealism who feels "his anger had to be everyone's anger" and believes "in a world order with good and bad and no neutral ground between them," towers over the book, and it's around him that a good many of the other figures turn. The pianist Israel recalls that as a child he had seen Ephraim kill a neighbor's dog because the neighbor, a "dissolute" woman, violated the standards of the "new society." Later, this trivial, chilling incident comes to seem a preparation for a terrible moment illustrating the costs of fanatic purity: Ephraim refuses to meet his brother Lazar, who years earlier, against Ephraim's Zionist advice, had gone off to fight in the Spanish Civil War, ended somehow in Stalin's arctic wastes, and has finally been freed. Ephraim is a man of strong feelings, but they have been corked and soured by the monolith of a redemptive faith.

It is, or was, a faith calling for self-transformation, and the desire for this goal, at once noble and destructive, has many versions, twisted and parodied. Manfred, the old lover of Ephraim's wife, Regina, had begun as a Communist, only to become a student of Christianity "mapping hell as it was described in lay and ecclesiastic literature," and now, stripped of belief, he returns to a love that is nothing but the love of loving "the memory of their love." Shortly after Ephraim's death, Regina acts out a fantasy in reply to the mania for self-transformation: she regresses into the Polish past, calling herself Stefana, "painting her lips in a subtle shade of violet-red," wearing "old silks and velvets," as if to undo all the grim years of Tel Aviv.

Others find different strategies. Erwin, Caesar's father, who had emigrated to Palestine as a pioneer, concludes that there is "always a gap between the world of values and that of action, and that actually everything [is therefore] permitted"—a lesson Caesar takes to heart as he races from woman to woman. Moishe Tzellermaer remakes himself through a religion "which contained neither a belief in God nor reflections on the nature of God," but consists of mere dry rituals dryly observed. Goldman, who has never known the idealistic raptures of the older generation, also turns to religion, dabbling briefly in cabala, "but his religion had nothing to sustain it and died." After this he turns to Taoism and Jungian psychology, which also "die."

The handful of Shabtai's characters who find their way do so by remaining still, accepting the thin margin onto which history has thrust them and trying nonetheless to survive decently. Uncle Lazar, though still acknowledging a "redemptive instinct" in man, concludes "that there [is] no single act in public or private life, however right or revolutionary, which [is] redemptive in the sense that from a certain point onward a new era would commence in which everything would be perfectly good." The thought itself is familiar enough, but the dignity it allows Uncle Lazar is impressive. He forms an alliance with Yehudit Tanfuss, a modest, unassuming woman, and "in the early hours of the evening, they would sit on the balcony talking or reading . . . or [go] for walks arm in arm, which [is] the way they always liked to walk together." And Aunt Zipporah (who made me think of Dilsey) keeps washing clothes and ironing and cooking and helping her sisters and friends through sickness and old age, for she believes in "the dignity of labor" and that "it was forbidden to lose the will to live," and that the difficulties of life "were not accidental but the very stuff of life."

Only the Goldmans, father and son, cannot make their peace with limitation. Pure, sterile, Ephraim resists the trickeries of history until "all of a sudden he turned into an old man . . . and all that was left of him was obduracy and bitter but helpless rage." The aggressions of the father become the self-torments of the son, who before ending his futile life gains a moment of illumination that may be no more—but it is enough—than ordinary sympathy: "Love and hate, together with the force of habit and family ties [reflects Goldman], chained people to each other in a way over which logic and will had no control, and . . . even death could not sever these bonds, except through the stubborn strength of time, which wore everything away, and even then something of the other person remained behind as part of your being forever. . . ." All—rectitude and opportunism, hedonistic frenzy and calm acquiescence—melt into a life that was once to be transfigured but now, simply continuing, must be endured.

About the older generation Shabtai writes with great assurance. About the younger generation, Shabtai's own—Goldman, Israel, Caesar, and the women they pursue and abandon—he is neither judgmental nor very sympathetic, but wary and bemused, as if a writer can understand the chaos of those who came before him but not of his contemporaries. Shabtai describes Caesar's "deepest feeling about life . . . that it was fluid and formless and aimless, and everything was possible in it to an infinite degree, and it could be played backward and forward like a roll of film, just as he wished"—a feeling that's the very opposite of the one held by Goldman's father or Uncle Lazar and Aunt Zipporah.

In certain respects *Past Continuous* seems closer to a chronicle, in which the past is granted a stamp of certainty and contrivances of plot are not allowed to interfere with the passage of events, than to a traditional or even modernist novel, in which events, whether or not ordered by plot, may still be represented as being in flux. But the book's density of texture is closer to the novel than to the chronicle.

Here is a close look at one of the book's most attractive figures, Uncle Lazar, who was caught up in the political struggles of Europe but is now quietly aging in Tel Aviv:

> Although the truth is that Uncle Lazar was not a taciturn man by nature, and if he hardly ever spoke it was only because he knew the limitations of human knowledge, the invalidity of human reason, and the restrictions of human possibilities, and everything was so contradictory and ambiguous that doubt seemed the only thing which possessed any reality, and the ability to believe was possessed by only a few, and there was no use hoping for much, and he also knew just how far a person had to deceive himself in order to live through a single day, and how fate could play tricks on people, as it had on him, and that all the words in the world were incapable of moving the world a single centimeter from its course, or bringing back one single day that had passed, or filling in the gaps, or consoling a man whose eyes had been opened, and Uncle Lazar's eyes had been opened, and they remained open, although he was not at all despairing or embittered, but simply very realistic and sober, with all the calm detachment of a man who had experienced much and who saw clearly and for whom life, to which he continued to relate seriously and positively, held no more surprises, because he had already died and risen again.

The Hebrew title, far more evocative than the English one, is *Zikhron Devarim*, signifying a protocol or memorandum, and indeed, the pace and tone of the book are rather like that of a protocol or memorandum: precise, measured, detached. Shabtai's technique is in radical opposition to the prescriptions for the modern novel of Joseph Conrad and Ford Madox Ford: dramatize, dramatize, show rather than tell. There are few large scenes in the book; it consists mostly of compressed biographies, life histories in miniature. The voice of *Past Continuous* tells more than it shows, on the valid premise that, with enough pressure of thought and feeling, the act of telling can become a way of showing.

Chronicling the rise and fall of a generation, almost never stopping for psychological detail or nuance, steadily widening its reach so as to gain the illusion of totality, the voice of *Past Continuous* achieves an authority quite beyond that of the omniscient narrator in the traditional novel. And while its use of associations bears a similarity to "stream of consciousness," especially as practiced by Faulkner, Shabtai's method is finally quite different, since in his book we do not enter the inner life of the characters. Brooking no pretense of relativism, the narrative voice does not hesitate to say with assurance about Ephraim or Lazar or Caesar, "The truth is. . . ." If only as a premise of reading, we come to suppose we are listening to a communal recorder, a choral observer who may just possibly be the consciousness of a city.

The narrator speaks:

From one day to the next, over the space of a few years, the city was rapidly and relentlessly changing its face, and right in front of [Goldman's] eyes it was engulfing the sand lots and the virgin fields, the vineyards and citrus groves and little woods and Arab villages, and afterward the changes began invading the streets of the older parts of the town, which were dotted here and there with simple one-storied houses surrounded by gardens with a few shrubs and flower beds, and sometimes vegetables and strawberries, and also cypress trees and lemon and orange and mandarin trees, or buildings which attempted to imitate the architectural beauties and splendors of Europe, in the style of Paris or Vienna or Berlin, or even of castles and palaces, but all these buildings no longer had any future because they were old and ill adapted to modern tastes and lifestyles, and especially because the skyrocketing prices of land and apartments had turned their existence into a terrible waste and enabled their owners to come into fortunes by selling them, and Goldman, who was attached to these streets and houses because they, together with the sand dunes and virgin fields, were the landscape in which he had been born and grown up, knew that this process of destruction was inevitable, and perhaps even necessary, as inevitable as the change in the population of the town, which in the course of a few years had been filled with tens of thousands of new people, who in Goldman's eyes were invading outsiders who had turned him into a stranger in his own city.

The culminating effect, for this reader at least, is overwhelming. Dispassionate in grief, this narrative voice seldom drops to judgment, though once or twice there is a sentence that can be taken as a judgment of sorts. At the funeral of Goldman's father, a mourner says, "In spite of everything he deserved to be loved." ("Why do you hate the South? . . . *I dont. I dont. I dont hate it. I dont hate it.*")

Kafka once said, "We must have those books that come upon us like ill-fortune, and distress us deeply, like the death of one we love better than ourselves, like suicide. A book must be an ice-ax to break the sea frozen within us." Before he died Yaakov Shabtai wrote such a book.

Why Has Socialism
Failed in America?
{1985}

AMERICA NEVER STOOD STILL for Marx and Engels. They did not attempt a systematic analysis of the possibilities for socialism in the New World, but if you look into their *Letters to Americans* you will find many interesting aperçus, especially from Engels. Almost all the numerous theories later developed about the fate of American socialism are anticipated in these letters.

As early as 1851, when the socialist Joseph Weydemeyer migrated to the United States, Engels wrote him:

> Your greatest handicap will be that the useful Germans who are worth anything are easily Americanized and abandon all hope of returning home; and then there are the special American conditions: the ease with which the surplus population is drained off to the farms, the necessarily rapid and rapidly growing prosperity of the country, which makes bourgeois conditions look like a beau ideal to them. . . .*

It isn't farfetched to see here a germ of what would later be called American exceptionalism, the idea that historical conditions in the United States differ

---

* August 7, 1851, *Letters to Americans, 1848–1895* (1953), pp. 25–26.

crucially from those set down in the Marxist model for the development of capitalism, or differ crucially from the way capitalism actually developed in Europe. Consider those remarks of Engels: a recognition of, perhaps irritation with, the sheer attractiveness of America; a casual anticipation of the Turner thesis in the claim that "surplus population is drained off to the farms"; a wry observation about American eagerness to accept the bourgeois style, though this might better have been phrased in the language of American individualism.

At about the same time, Marx was taking a somewhat different approach. "Bourgeois society in the United States," he was writing, "has not yet developed far enough to make the class struggle obvious"*; but he also expected that American industry would grow at so enormous a rate that the United States would be transformed into a major force in the world market, delivering heavy blows against English imperial domination.

Now, if one cares to, it is possible to reconcile Engels's approach with that of Marx. Engels was thinking tactically, about the problems of building a movement, while Marx was thinking historically, about events anticipated but not yet encountered. Marx was asking why the social consequences of the rise of capitalism, such as an intensified class struggle, had not yet appeared in the United States — even though, according to his theory, these consequences were inevitable. He was "testing" a particular historical sequence against his theoretical scheme, and this led him to believe that capitalism would emerge in the United States in its purest and strongest form—purest, because unencumbered by the debris of the pre-capitalist past, and strongest, because able, both technologically and financially, to leap past the older capitalism of England. Thereby, he concluded, the United States would—or was it, should?—become "the world of the worker, par excellence,"† so that socialist victory might even occur first in the New World. Here Marx was verging on a materialist or "economist" reductionism, and he would repeat this line of reasoning some thirty years later, in 1881, when he wrote that, capitalism in the United States having developed "more rapidly and more shamelessly than in any other country,"‡ the upsurge of its working class could be expected to be all the more spectacular.

Engels's observations, because more "local," tend to be more useful. He writes in his 1891 preface to Marx's *The Civil War in France*: "There is no country in which 'politicians' form a more powerful and distinct section of the nation

---

* March 5, 1852, *Letters to Americans*, pp. 44–45.
† Quoted in R. Laurence Moore, *European Socialists and the American Promised Land* (1970), p. 9.
‡ June 20, 1881, *Letters to Americans*, p. 129.

than in North America. There each of the two great parties which alternately suc-ceed each other in power is itself controlled by people who make a business of politics. . . ."*

Had the later American Marxists picked up Engels's tip here, they might have avoided some of their cruder interpretations of the role of the state in this coun-try. More interesting still is Engels's introduction to the 1887 reprint of his book *The Condition of the Working Class in England*, where he acknowledges "the peculiar difficulties for a steady development of a workers party"† in the United States. Engels first makes a bow toward the overarching Marxist model: ". . . there can-not be any doubt that the *ultimate* platform of the American working class must and will be *essentially* the same as that now adopted by the whole militant working class of Europe. . . . [Emphasis added.]" Engels would elsewhere stress the "ex-ceptionalist" aspect, largely tactical, of the American problem. In order to play a role in politics, he says, the American socialists "will have to doff every remnant of foreign garb. They will have to become out and out American. They cannot expect the Americans to come to them; they, the minority and the [German] im-migrants [in the Socialist Labor Party] must go to the Americans. . . . And to do that, they must above all else learn English."‡

What may we conclude from all this? That, like other thinkers, Marx and En-gels cherished their basic models; that the more closely they examined a particu-lar situation, the more they had to acknowledge "deviations" from their models; that they anticipated, quite intelligently, a good many of the major themes in the discussions about socialist failure in the United States; and that in their efforts to suggest adaptations of the nascent socialist movement, mostly immigrant in composition, to the American setting, they were not very successful. You might suppose, however, that Engels's proposal that the Germans learn English would be regarded, in leftist terminology, as "a minimum demand."

If I have overstressed the differences in approach between Marx and Engels, it is for a reason: to show that both the orthodox view of later socialists, clinging to the authority of the Marxist model, and the heterodox emphasis upon American distinctiveness can legitimately be attributed to the founding fathers of Marxism. An interesting comment on this comes from Theodore Draper in a personal com-munication: "Whenever the two old boys considered real conditions in real coun-tries, they gave way to the temptation of 'exceptionalism' (I seem to remember

---

* *The Civil War in France*, 1891 edition (1934), p. 24.
† *The Condition of the Working Class in England*, 1887 edition.
‡ December 2, 1893, *Letters to Americans*, p. 258.

that it crops up in their writings on India, Italy, Ireland as well). Reality always
breaks in as 'exceptions' to the rule."*

2

Werner Sombart's *Why Is There No Socialism in the United States?* first appeared in
1906, and though its thesis has been rendered more sophisticated in numerous
later writings, it remains a basic text. I propose here somewhat to minimize—
though not to dismiss—Sombart's reasons, which tend mainly to stress objective historical factors standing in the way of socialism in America. But since he
saw that some of these factors, like the supply of free land in nineteenth-century
America, would not be operative much longer, he concluded—like the Marxists,
though not one himself—that in a few decades socialism would thrive in America. In this prediction he was mistaken, and it is important to know why. Here, in

---

* One notable exception, at the opposite extreme from the American, is worth glancing at.
Among the Russian radicals of the second half of the nineteenth century there was an intense
and significant debate as to the possibility that socialist development in Russia might bypass
capitalist and urban industrialization. Must Russia follow the familiar lines of Western development, or can it proceed along its own, "exceptional" path? The concrete issue was the *mir*, or
traditional peasant commune. When the Russian Marxist Vera Zasulich wrote Marx in 1881 for
his opinion, he devoted himself to this problem with much greater energy than to American
problems—it may have seemed more important, or at least closer. After preparing four drafts
of a reply, Marx sent the last one to his correspondent, writing that the account in *Capital* of the
development of capitalism was "*expressly* limited to the *countries of western Europe*" and therefore
provided "no reasons for or against the vitality of the rural community." He added, however,
that he had become convinced that "this community is the mainspring of Russia's social re-
generation." (Quoted in Russell Jacoby, "Politics of the Crisis Theory," *Telos*, Spring 1975, p. 7.)
Later he and Engels wrote that the *mir* could pass on to a higher form of "communal ownership"
and avoid the "dissolution which makes up the historical development of the west . . . if the Russian Revolution is the signal of proletarian revolution in the West, so that both complete each
other. . . ." (Ibid., p. 8.)

Whether this judgment was correct need hardly concern us here. What matters is Marx's
evident readiness to grant that Russia might be an "exception" to the developmental scheme of
Capital. There is no similar readiness in his writings with regard to the United States, not even
to the limited extent one finds it in Engels's letters; and one wonders why. An obvious reason is
that Engels lived longer and, as the gray eminence of the movement, had to cope with the hopeless sectarianism of the German exiles who formed the Socialist Labor Party in America during
the 1880s. More speculatively, I would say that it was easier for Marx to grant an "exception" to a
precapitalist economy mired in absolutism than to an economy becoming quintessentially capitalist, and easier, as well, to acknowledge the political consequences of a "basic" socioeconomic
institution like the *mir* in Russia than the political significance of a "superstructural" element
like the national culture of America.

schematic form, are some of the Sombartian "objective" factors that account for the failure, or at least difficulties, of American socialism:

1. Since this country had no feudal past, Americans could feel that as free citizens of a "new nation" they were able to express their needs and complaints within the democratic system; in consequence, the sense of class distinctions was much less acute here than in Europe.

2. Material prosperity in the United States, the result of a tremendous economic expansion, undercut the possibilities of socialist growth, since it enabled segments of the working class to gain a measure of satisfaction and imbued others with the hope that America would be their "golden land."

3. The greater opportunities America offered for upward social mobility led most Americans to think in terms of individual improvement rather than collective action—they hoped to rise out of, rather than with, their class.

4. The open frontier, with its possibility of free or cheap land, served as a safety valve for discontent.

5. The American two-party system made it hard for a third party to establish itself and enabled the major parties to appropriate, at their convenience, parts of the programs advanced by reform-oriented third parties.

6. [This comes not from Sombart but from labor historian Selig Perlman:] The massive waves of immigration led to deep ethnic cleavages within the working class, so that earlier, "native" workers rose on the social scale while newer groups of immigrants took the least desirable jobs. It therefore became extremely hard to achieve a unified class consciousness within the American working class.

Neatly bundled together, such "factors" can seem more than sufficient for explaining the distinctive political course of America. But when examined somewhat closely, these factors tend—not, of course, to disappear—but to seem less conclusive: they *are* present, some of them all the time and all of them some of the time, but their bearing upon American socialism remains, I would say, problematic.

A methodological criticism of the Sombartian approach has been made by Aileen Kraditor: that Sombart, like the Marxists, takes for granted a necessary historical course against which American experience is to be found, if not wanting, then deviant, and therefore requiring "special explanation." But it's quite likely, argues Kraditor, that no such over-all historical direction can be located and that what really needs explaining is not why socialism failed in America, but why anyone thought it might succeed. Well, I am prepared to grant the dubiousness of the European model/American deviation approach, but would argue that there is some value in pursuing it tentatively, if only to see *where else* it might lead.

The Sombartian "factors" are too encompassing and thereby virtually ahistorical: they explain too much and thereby too little. They can hardly tell us why the American working class in the 1880s and 1890s engaged in very militant and even violent strikes yet did not "move ahead" to any large-scale socialist beliefs, nor can they tell us why the American socialist movement thrived, more or less, at one moment and collapsed at another. Such large historical "factors" as Sombart invokes may be overdetermining. Insofar as they apply, they leave little room for human agency, diversity, and surprise; they fall too readily into a "vulgar Marxist" assumption that human beings act exclusively or even mainly out of direct economic interest. And as a result, the problem for historians becomes to explain how *any* significant socialist movement ever did appear in this country. Between the Sombartian "factors" and the fate of a particular political movement there is, so to say, too much space; what is missing is the whole range of national culture—how people think, the myths by which they live, the impulsions that move them to action, and, not least of all, the circumstances and approaches of particular socialist movements.*

In any case, let us now glance at some of the Sombartian causes for the failure of American socialism.

Absence of a Feudal Past

This argument has been most skillfully restated by the political theorist Louis Hartz. He isolates

> three factors stemming from the European feudal inheritance, the absence of which in the United States precluded the possibility of a major socialist experience. One is a sense of class which an aristocratic culture communicates to the bourgeoisie and which both communicate to the proletariat. Another is the experience of social revolution implemented by the middle

---

* "Most of the attempted [Sombartian] answers," writes Daniel Bell, "have discussed not *causes* but *conditions*. . . . An inquiry into the fate of a social movement has to be pinned to the specific questions of time, place, and opportunity. . . ." (*Marxian Socialism in the United States* [1967], p. 5.) Bell's distinction between "condition" and "cause" is suggestive, but hard to maintain. He means, I suppose, that a condition is a relatively stable or latent circumstance that enables or disables a certain course of action—as when we say that the condition of prosperity in the 1920s made the growth of socialism unlikely. A cause is a closely operative, precipitating event—as when we say the Socialist Party's decline during and after World War I was partly caused by governmental repression. Yet I can see the Sombartians replying that if a condition is sufficiently strong and enduring, it may, in its workings, be all but indistinguishable from a cause.

class which the proletariat also inherits. . . . Finally . . . the memory of the medieval corporate spirit which, after liberal assault, the socialist movement seeks to recreate in the form of modern collectivism.*

Behind Hartz's analysis there is a historical truth: that European socialist movements gained part of their following through alliances with bourgeois democratic movements in a common struggle against traditional or "feudal" institutions; and that the socialist movements kept their following by making demands that the plebs be granted political rights, promised but not fully delivered. Hartz makes much of the absence of this enabling condition in America, and, before him, Lenin had noted that America has one of "the most firmly established democratic systems, which confronts the proletariat with purely socialist tasks."[†]

In part at least, both Hartz and Lenin are wrong. For just as French socialists in the nineteenth century worked, as the Marxist phrase goes, to "fulfill the bourgeois revolution" by creating social space for the working class, and just as Chartism strove to gain for the English workers political rights within the bourgeois system, so there were in America major "democratic [as distinct from so-called purely socialist] tasks" to be undertaken by socialists and liberals. These concerned large segments of the population: for instance, the struggle for woman suffrage, in which the socialists played an important part, and the struggle for black rights, in which the socialists could have played an important part had it not been for the sectarian Debsian claim that black freedom could be achieved "only" through socialism and consequently required no separate movement or demands. The struggle in Europe to do away with "feudal" or aristocratic hangovers has an equivalent, *mutatis mutandis*, in America as a struggle to live up to the promise of the early republic.

It's interesting that Marx and Engels could not decide whether the distinctiveness of American society was a boon or a burden for American socialism. At one point Engels, quite as if he had just read Hartz, wrote that Americans are "born conservatives—just *because* America is so purely bourgeois, so entirely without a feudal past and therefore proud of its purely bourgeois organization."[‡] At another point, quite as if he had just read Hartz's critics, Engels cited "the more favorable soil of America, where no medieval ruins bar the way. . . ."[§]

---

* "Reply," in John H. M. Laslett and Seymour Martin Lipset, eds., *Failure of a Dream? Essays in the History of American Socialism* (1974), p. 421.

[†] *Letters to Americans*, Appendix, p. 275.

[‡] February 8, 1890, in *Karl Marx and Friedrich Engels: Selected Correspondence, 1846–1895* (1942), p. 467.

[§] *Letters to Americans*, Appendix, p. 287.

The argument, then, can cut both ways. Absence of a feudal past has made for greater "civic integration," a feeling among all (except the blacks) that they "belonged." The American working class seems never quite to have regarded itself as the kind of "outsider" or pariah that the working classes of Europe once did. Whatever discontents might develop—numerous and grave in nineteenth-century America, from abolitionism to major strikes—were likely to be acted out within the flexible consensus of American myth, or as a complaint that our values had been betrayed by the plutocrats. Only the Marxists were feckless enough to attempt a head-on collision with the national myth, and what it mostly brought them was a bad headache.

But if America, in S. M. Lipset's phrase, was "a new nation" that gave its citizens a strong sense of independence and worth, then precisely this enabled them to fight staunchly for their rights. American labor strikes in the late nineteenth and early twentieth centuries were often more bloody than those in Europe. And it was, I think, two utterly divergent variants of the American myth, two simplified crystallizations at the right and left extremes, that made the class struggle so fierce in America. The capitalists, persuaded that Americans should be able to do as they wished with their property and pay whatever wages they proposed to pay, and the workers, persuaded that Americans (or Americans-in-the-making) should stand up as free men and resist exploitation, appealed to the same deeply embedded myth of the native citizen blessed with freedom by God.

There was a sharp class struggle in America during the decades after the Civil War, even without the questionable benefits of feudal hangovers, and in stressing its presence, as against those who kept talking about "classlessness," the Marxists were right. There was even a kind of class consciousness in the American working class, though this was hard to specify and the Marxists rarely succeeded in doing so, if only because it was a class consciousness that took the form, mostly, of an invocation of early republican values and a moralistic evangelicism. Werner Sombart put the matter well: "There is expressed in the worker, as in all Americans, a boundless optimism, which comes out of a belief in the mission and greatness of his country, a belief that often has a religious tinge."* This belief, with its "religious tinge," could be turned toward Social Darwinism or toward unionism, populism, and early socialism.

As for Hartz's third factor—the lack of a remembered "medieval corporate spirit" which might help re-create "modern collectivism"—one may suppose that such a memory did have some influence on European workers in the mid-

---

* *Why Is There No Socialism in the United States?*, C. T. Husbands, ed. (1976), p. 18.

nineteenth century. (I suspect it has more influence on historians of romanticist inclination.) But it's hard to believe that by the 1920s or 1930s this "memory" played much of a role in the collective expression of, say, the French workers. And if Americans had no such tradition to draw upon, it would be a crude exaggeration to conclude that the only other tradition remaining to us has been an unmodulated "possessive individualism." Herbert Gutman, a historian of the American working class, has nicely distinguished between individualist and independent traditions. There are traditions of independent Americans cooperating for common ends, in everything from frontier communities to utopian colonies, from abolitionist movements to the early unions; and Gutman has further noted that the agitational literature of American unionism in the late nineteenth century echoed these very themes of the unionism of the 1830s.

It would be wrong simply to dismiss Hartz's analysis, for it speaks to commonly perceived realities and, even with all reasonable qualifications, it has an evident power. But it has to be put forward in more nuanced terms than Hartz has proposed, and this means that his now famous "factors," even if they rendered the rise of socialism in America difficult, do not suffice to explain its unhappy fate.

On the Reefs of Roast Beef

America, wrote Sombart, was "the promised land of capitalism," where "on the reefs of roast beef and apple pie socialistic Utopias . . . are sent to their doom."[*] This pithy sentence appears to carry a self-evident validity, but recent historical and sociological investigations create enough doubts so that, at the very least, we must qualify Sombart's conclusion.

It is an exaggeration to suggest that the American workers, or members of the lower classes, have enjoyed a steady material abundance. Large segments of the population, gasping for breath, have never reached those famous "reefs of roast beef." There is a profound truth in Nathaniel Hawthorne's remark that "in this republican country, amid the fluctuating waves of our social life, somebody is always at the drowning-point."

From the 1870s until the present we have had sharply varying times of wellbeing and distress, largely in accord with the cyclical character of capitalist boom and crisis; times when the standard of living rose visibly for many workers, as during World War I and the decades between 1940 and 1970; and times when, as in the last third of the nineteenth and first two decades of the twentieth centuries, certain American workers, like the building mechanics, did improve their

---

[*] *Why Is There No Socialism in the United States?*, p. 18.

lot while those working in mills, packing plants, and clothing factories did not. Differentiations of income and material condition among American workers have often been sharper than those in class-ridden Europe. They continue to our present moment, between skilled and/or unionized workers and that segment of the "secondary" work force consisting of ill-paid and largely unorganized blacks, Hispanics, and illegal immigrants in fugitive light industries.

Still other shadows fall across Sombart's bright picture—for example, the extent to which American workers have been subject to industrial accidents because this country, until recently, refused to pass the kind of social legislation that had long been enacted in Europe. For a good many historians it has nevertheless been the supposed objective advantages of American society when compared with European societies of the late nineteenth and early twentieth centuries—a higher standard of living, a greater degree of social mobility—that largely explain the failures of American socialism. But, as far as I have been able to gather from various historical studies, the evidence regarding standards of living and social mobility remains inconclusive. For one thing, the technical problems in making comparisons on such matters are very severe. It is hard to know exactly how to "measure" standards of living and social mobility, since so many elements of experience, some by no means readily quantifiable, enter into them.

Seymour Martin Lipset, a close observer in this area, writes that "a number of students of social mobility in comparative perspective (Sorokin, Glass, Lipset and Bendix, Miller, Blau and Duncan, and Bourdon) have concluded from an examination of mobility data collected in various countries that the American rate of mass social mobility is not uniquely high, that a number of European countries have had comparable rates. . . ."[*]

By contrast, Stephan Thernstrom, who has assembled valuable data about working-class mobility in Boston and Newburyport during the nineteenth and first two decades of the twentieth centuries, concludes that mobility was significantly higher in a big city like Boston than in a town like Newburyport, and, indeed, that in Boston "the dream of individual mobility was [not] illusory [during the nineteenth century] and that collective advance was [not] the only realistic hope for the American worker."[†]

A more recent and notably meticulous study by Peter R. Shergold comparing real wage rates and real family income in Pittsburgh, Pennsylvania, and two En-

---

[*] "Comment," in Laslett and Lipset, eds., *Failure of a Dream?*, p. 528.
[†] "Socialism and Social Mobility," in Laslett and Lipset, eds., *Failure of a Dream?*, p. 519.

glish cities, Birmingham and Sheffield, for the years 1899–1913, demonstrates, however, the enormous difficulties of such comparisons. Shergold concludes

> that assertions of relative American affluence must be severely qualified. Unskilled workers experienced similar levels of material welfare in Britain and the United States in the 1900s, and it is quite possible that English laborers actually enjoyed a higher standard of living during the last quarter of the nineteenth century. The dominant characteristic of the American labor force was not comparative income superiority, but the much greater inequality of wage distribution. The most highly-paid manual employees, primarily skilled workers, earned substantially larger incomes than those in equivalent English occupations, whereas low-paid workers received incomes similar to those in England. In short, the fruits of economic growth, the benefits of emergent corporate capitalism, were far more unevenly distributed among wage earners in the United States than in England.

And again:

> It is the comparative inequality of wage rewards in the United States, an income gulf widened by ethnic heterogeneity and racial prejudice, that must provide the socioeconomic context within which to analyze the American labor movement. American workers found it profoundly difficult to perceive their very diverse lifestyles as the product of a common exploitation. It was not a high average standard of living that dictated how they behaved. Rather, in a supreme historical paradox, it was the combination of a uniquely egalitarian ideology—"Americanism"—with extravagant inequality of material circumstances.*

Helpful as Shergold's material is in undermining older assertions about the "objective" reasons for the difficulties of American socialism (and, for that matter, of the American labor movement), the exact pertinence of his work remains debatable. Had he chosen to compare an American industrial city with cities in Eastern or Southern Europe, areas from which so many industrial workers in America emigrated, the economic disparities would probably have been more dramatic—and the statistical difficulties still greater—than in the work he did. In any case, his evidence that skilled workers in an American industrial city were better off than those in a similar English one may help explain the varying fates

---

* *Working-Class Life* (1982), pp. 225, 229.

of socialism in America and England, since skilled workers played an important part in the early socialist movements.

Though the scholarly material on standards of living and social mobility is valuable—indeed, one wishes there were a good deal more—it doesn't by itself sustain Sombartian generalizations about American material conditions as the central cause of the difficulties and failures of American socialism. Even if one believes that Stephan Thernstrom's conclusions about the possibilities of individual improvement in late-nineteenth-century America probably hold for the country as a whole, the evidence is not sufficiently stark or unambiguous to form, or contribute heavily to, a *sufficient* explanation for the sharply different fates of socialism in the United States and Europe.

3

Nor is there any reason to believe, either from experience or research, that affluence necessarily makes for docility among workers. To argue that it does is to succumb to a crude sort of reductive economism, according to which the outlook of the worker is determined by nothing more than his personal circumstances. There has, to the contrary, been a strand of social thought that has seen extreme poverty as a demoralizing condition, likely to inhibit rather than stimulate political activism. S. M. Lipset cites the fact that "strong socialist movements exist in countries with high rates of social mobility," such as Australia and New Zealand, and Michael Harrington that German social democracy's greatest growth occurred at a time of relative prosperity, between the 1870s and World War I. A paper by Philip Dawson and Gilbert Shapiro, following Tocqueville's lead, shows that just before the French Revolution of 1789 those segments of the French bourgeoisie which had significantly improved their position were more vigorous in expressing opposition to the ancien régime than those which had not.

Studies comparing in close detail the conditions of American and European workers tend to be cautious regarding the Sombartian conclusion about "roast beef." A brilliant essay by James Holt comparing trade unions in the British and U.S. steel industries from 1880 to 1914 finds that the main factors thwarting class solidarity among the Americans were the rapidity of technological advance, which reduced the need for skilled workers, who were often the most militant unionists; and the ferocity of American employers, who often used brutal methods to break the unions. "The most striking difference between the two situations [American and British steel industries] concerns the behavior of employers rather than employees. In both countries, the impulse to organize was present among steelworkers but in one [Britain] most employers offered little resistance to union growth while in the other [the United States] they generally fought back vigorously." Holt concludes suggestively:

> The weakness and political conservatism of the American labor movement in the late 19th and early 20th centuries have often been seen primarily as the product of a lack of class consciousness among American workingmen. In the United States, it is suggested, class lines were more fluid and opportunities for advancement more rapid than in European countries. . . . Perhaps so, yet . . . in some ways the American workingman was more rather than less oppressed than his British counterpart. The retreat of so many American union leaders from a youthful socialism to a cautious and conservative "business unionism" may have reflected less a growing enthusiasm for the . . . status quo than a resigned acknowledgment that in a land where the propertied middle classes dominated politically and the big corporations ruled supreme in industry, accommodation was more appropriate than confrontation.*

Insofar as the roast-beef argument finds most American workers refusing socialism because they were relatively satisfied with their lot, it would seem to follow that, *for the same reason*, they would also reject militant class action. But many did turn to militant class or labor action. The history of American workers suggests not at all that a surfeit of good things led to passivity and acquiescence; it suggests only—and this is something very different—that the intermittent outbursts of labor militancy did not often end in socialist politics.

The Sombartian argument in its blunt form is not defensible. But to say this isn't to deny that the varying degrees of material comfort among segments of the American working class have probably constituted (to borrow a phrase from Daniel Bell) a limiting condition on the growth of American socialism. This relative or partial material comfort may help explain why American socialism was never likely to become a mass movement encompassing major segments of the working class; but it doesn't suffice for explaining something more interesting: why American socialism has had so uneven a history, with modest peaks and virtual collapse at several points.

What seems crucial is that social mobility in this country has been *perceived* differently from the way it has been perceived in Europe. The myth of opportunity

* "Trade Unionism in the British and U.S. Steel Industries, 1880–1914: A Comparative Study," *Labor History*, 1977, p. 35.

for energetic individuals rests on a measure of historical actuality but also has taken on a power independent of, *even when in conflict with*, the social actuality. This myth has held the imagination of Americans across the decades, including immigrants dreadfully exploited when they came here but who apparently felt that almost anything in the New World, being new, was better than what they had known in the old. Here we enter the realm of national psychology and cultural values, which is indeed what we will increasingly have to do as we approach another of the "objective factors" commonly cited among the reasons for the failure of American socialism.

The Lure of Free Land

As it turns out, escape from onerous work conditions in the East to free land in the West was largely a myth. "In the 1860s, it took $1,000 [then a lot of money] to make a go of a farm, and the cost increased later in the century. So for every industrial worker who became a farmer, twenty farmers became city dwellers. And for every free farm acquired by a farmer [under the Homestead Act of 1862], nine were purchased by railroads, speculators, or by the government itself." There follows, however, a crucial proviso: if free land did not actually fulfill its mythic function, many people did not give up the dream that it would.[*] And perhaps, I'd add, not so much the dream of actually moving to a farm in the West as a shared feeling that the frontier and the wilderness remained powerful symbolic forces enabling Americans to find solace in the thought of escape even when they were not able to act upon it.

But is there not a contradiction between the last two of the Sombartian "objective factors"? If the American worker felt so contented with his life as the roast-beef-and-apple-pie argument suggests, why should he have wanted to escape from it to the rigors of pioneering on the American prairie? This question—the force of which is hardly diminished by the fact that not many workers actually did set out for the West—was asked by the German Social Democratic paper *Vorwärts* when it came to review Sombart's book: ". . . Why under such circumstances [does] the American worker 'escape into freedom' . . . that is, withdraw from the hubbub of capitalism, by settling on hitherto uncultivated land [?] If capitalism is so good to him, he could not help but feel extraordinarily well-off under its sceptre. . . . There is clearly a glaring contradiction here."[†]

The lure of the frontier, the myth of the West surely held a strong grip on the imaginations of many Americans during the late nineteenth century—and later

---

[*] Michael Harrington, *Socialism* (1972), p. 116.
[†] Quoted in Introduction, Sombart, *Why Is There No Socialism in the United States?*, p. xxiii.

too. But it soon became an independent power quite apart from any role the West may actually have played as a "safety valve" for urban discontent.

You have surely noticed the direction my argument is taking: away from a stress upon material conditions (even while acknowledging that in the last analysis they may well have constituted a large barrier to socialist growth) and toward a focusing on the immediate problems of American socialists that were or are in part open to solution through an exertion of human intelligence and will. Let me mention two: large-scale immigration, which created ethnic divisions within the working class, and the distinctive political structure of the United States.

The Immigrant Problem

The rise of American socialism in the late nineteenth and early twentieth centuries coincides with the greatest wave of immigration this country has ever experienced, an immigration drawn largely from Eastern and Southern Europe, with large numbers of Italians, Slavs, Jews, and Poles. When a nonspecialist looks into the historical literature, the main conclusion to be drawn is that it would be foolhardy to draw any large conclusions. Or, if pressed, I would say that the waves of the "new immigrants"—the more poorly educated, largely peasant stock from premodern countries—presented more of a problem to the American *unions* than to the socialists.

Many immigrants in this "second wave" came with a strong desire to work hard, save money, and go back home; they thought of themselves as what we'd call "guest workers," and that is one reason many came without their wives. The rate of return among East Europeans and Italians was very high. Between 1908 and 1910, for South and East Europeans, forty-four out of a hundred who came went back; between 1907 and 1911, for Italians, seventy-three out of a hundred who came went back. Such people were not likely to be attracted to political movements, especially those that might get them in trouble with the authorities or might interfere with their projects for self-exploitation as workers; nor, for the same reasons, were these immigrants often good material for unionization, though a study by Victor Greene has shown that the Slavs in western Pennsylvania, if conditions grew desperate enough, could be recruited as strong supporters of strike actions. As Jerome Karabel has shrewdly remarked: "If . . . a 'safety valve' did indeed exist for the discontented American worker, it was apparently to be found less on the frontier than in tired old Europe."*

* "The Failure of American Socialism Reconsidered," in Ralph Miliband and John Saville, eds., *The Socialist Register, 1979* (1979), p. 216.

Upon arrival, South and East European immigrants often took the worst jobs. Usually without industrial skills, these people were shunted to brute labor, on the railroads and in the steel mills. Their presence enabled the "first wave" of immigrants, from Northern Europe, to rise on the social scale and, above these, the native-born to enter new supervisory posts created by a rapid industrial expansion. The American working class was thereby split into competing ethnic segments—and the contempt native-born and earlier immigrants often showed the newer immigrants did nothing to heal this split. No matter what the Marxist schema might propose, these ethnic divisions were often felt more strongly than any hypothetical class consciousness, except perhaps during strikes, in which a momentary solidarity could be achieved.

Partly in reaction to the ethnic and racial antagonisms they met from other workers, but partly from a natural desire to live with those who spoke the same language, ate the same foods, and shared the same customs, many immigrant workers huddled into ethnic neighborhoods, miniature strongholds in which to beat off the contempt of their "betters." These neighborhoods could often be controlled by shrewd politicians offering practical advice and social help; among the Italians, for instance, by *padroni* doubling as labor contractors in the construction industry. This heavy concentration in ethnic neighborhoods usually made for political conservatism and obviously served to thwart class or political consciousness. Later students would see such neighborhoods as enclaves of parochial narrowness or as communities enabling their members to accumulate strength for a move into the larger American world—obviously they could be both. Recently a more sophisticated analysis, by Ira Katznelson and others, has made much of the split between the immigrant as worker in the plant and as resident in the ethnic community, sometimes able to achieve an intense militancy in bitter economic struggles against employers, yet docile in relation to the conservative leadership of the ethnic neighborhood.

Harsh as the exploitation of immigrant workers often was, many of them retained a stubborn conviction that if they accepted deprivation in the short run, their lot would ultimately be bettered—or at least that of their children would be. Certain immigrant groups, especially the Jews, staked almost everything on the educational opportunities offered by America. Often accompanied by desperate homesickness for the old country and harsh curses for the crudity of life in America, the promise of the New World nevertheless gripped the imagination of the immigrants. American radicals might point to real injustices, but to newcomers who had left behind autocratic and caste-ridden nations, our easy manners and common acceptance of democratic norms could seem wonderfully attractive. And there is a psychological point to be added: it was hard enough to be a Slav in Pittsburgh or a Pole in Chicago without the additional burden of that "anti-Americanism" with which the socialists were often charged.

Much of the "new immigration" consisted of Catholics, people still close to the faith, in whom a suspicion of socialism had been implanted by a strongly conservative clergy. The labor historian Selig Perlman believed that the immigrant character of American labor was a major reason for the difficulties of the socialists: "American labor remains one of the most heterogeneous laboring classes in existence. . . . With a working class of such composition, to make socialism . . . the official 'ism' of the movement, would mean . . . deliberately driving the Catholics . . . out of the labor movement. . . ."[*]

Now Perlman's point seems beyond dispute if taken simply as an explanation of why socialism could not, or should not, have become the dominant outlook of the American labor movement. But it does not explain very much about socialist fortunes in general—unless, of course, you assume that domination of the American Federation of Labor was the crucial requirement for socialist success in America. That such domination would have helped the socialists is obvious; but it's not at all obvious that, lacking it, they were doomed to extinction or mere sect existence. In truth, the socialists had plenty of possibilities for recruitment within the country at large before they could so much as reach the new immigrants.

Nor should it be supposed that the immigrants formed a solid conservative mass. In the Debsian era, socialist strength was centered in a number of immigrant communities: the Germans, the Jews, and the Finns, all of whom clustered in ethnic neighborhoods that some recent analysts have seen as bulwarks of conservatism. As if to illustrate how the same data can be used for sharply opposing claims, one historian, John H. M. Laslett, has argued that it was the "process of ethnic assimilation" rather than ethnic isolation that hindered the socialists:

> This is perhaps clearest in the case of the Brewery Workers Union, whose socialism may in large part be ascribed to the influences of socialists who came to this country after the abortive German revolution of 1848, and in greater numbers after Bismarck's antisocialist legislation of 1878. The radicalism of the union noticeably declined as these older groups either died off, moved upward into the entrepreneurial or professional middle class, or were replaced by ethnic groups whose commitment to socialism was less intense.[†]

The immigrants, to be sure, presented practical and moral-political problems for the socialists. Many immigrants, even if friendly to the movement, could not

---

[*] Quoted in Harrington, *Socialism*, p. 131.

[†] "Socialism and American Trade Unionism," in Laslett and Lipset, eds., *Failure of a Dream?*, p. 214.

vote, nor did they rush to acquire citizenship. There were segments of the party that harbored disgraceful antiforeign sentiments, and this led to internecine disputes. The plethora of immigrant communities made for difficulties: Morris Hillquit once noted ruefully that the party had to put out propaganda in twenty different languages. For a union trying to organize, say, a steel plant in Pittsburgh, where the work force was split ethnically and linguistically, this could be a devastating problem. For the socialists, however, it would have been crucial only if they had had much of a chance of reaching many of these "new immigrants," or if they had already scored such successes among the indigenous American population that all that remained in their way was the recalcitrance of immigrant workers. Such, obviously, was not the case. No; the argument from the divisive consequences of immigration does not take us very far in explaining the difficulties of American socialism.

It is when we reach the last of our "objective factors," that we come closer to the actual difficulties socialists encountered in America. It was . . .

The American Political System

If the authors of the Constitution had in mind to establish a political system favoring a moderately conservative two-party structure—a kind of "centrism" allowing some flexibility within a stable consensus politics but also putting strong barriers in the way of its principled critics—then they succeeded brilliantly. Our shrewdly designed system combines a great deal of rigidity in its governing structure with a great deal of flexibility in its major parties. Our method of electing presidents requires that the parties be inclusive enough to cement political coalitions before Election Day, and that means bargaining and compromise, which blur political and ideological lines. Our method of governing, however, makes for a continuity of elites, tends to give the political center an overwhelming preponderance, and makes it tremendously difficult for insurgent constituencies to achieve political strength unless they submit to the limits of one of the major parties. In recent years, this peculiar mixture of rigidity and flexibility has, if anything, become more prevalent. The tremendous costliness of running for political office, now that television has largely replaced the public meeting and advertising slogans the political oration, makes it all but impossible for minority parties to compete. It also enables rich men—noble, eccentric, or wicked—to take on an excessive role in political life. Yet the growth of the primary system and the fact that most voters pay even less attention to primaries than to elections means that coherent minorities can often achieve their ends through cleverness and concentration.

There are theorists by the dozen who regard all this as a master stroke in behalf of maintaining democracy. Perhaps they are right. At least, they may be right if the society does not have to confront major crises, as during the immediate pre–Civil War years and the Depression era, when the political system comes under severe strain. But if the system helps maintain democracy, it also seriously disables democratic critics of capitalism.

For the most part, all of this constitutes the common coin of American political science. Let me therefore try to sharpen the focus by discussing the problem from the point of view of the socialist movement as it kept trying to establish itself in the country's political life.

One of my most wearying memories, when I think back to years in various socialist groups, is that of efforts we would make to get on the ballot. Most states had rigid requirements, sometimes mere rigged handicaps, for minor parties. In New York State we had to obtain a certain number of qualified signatures from all the counties, and this would mean sending volunteers to upstate rural communities where signatories ready to help socialists were pretty rare. In Ohio during the 1930s the number of required signatures, as I recall, was outrageously high. Well, we would throw ourselves into the effort of collecting signatures, and then have to face a court challenge from a major party, usually the more liberal one, since it had more to lose from our presence on the ballot than the conservatives. (It's amusing how often Republicans turned out to be staunch "defenders" of minority rights.) If, finally, we did get on the ballot, we were often so exhausted that there was little or no energy, to say nothing of money, left for the actual campaign.

Over and over again the socialists would face this problem: friendly people would come up to our candidates—especially Norman Thomas—and say they agreed with our views but would nevertheless vote for "the lesser evil" because they didn't "want to throw away their vote." We tried to scorn such sentiments, but, given the American political system, especially the zero-sum game for presidential elections, there really was a core of sense in what these people said.

One of the few occasions when the socialist vote was relatively large—in 1912, when the party drew six percent of the vote—is partly explained by the fact that, as Thomas put it, "voters that year were pretty sure that the winner would be either Woodrow Wilson or Theodore Roosevelt, not William H. Taft, and they didn't believe that the difference between these two fairly progressive men was important enough to prevent their voting for their real preference," the socialist Eugene Debs. I'd guess Thomas was right when he added that if America had had "a parliamentary rather than a presidential government, we should have had, under some name or other, a moderately strong socialist party."

The idea of a long-range *political* movement slowly accumulating strength for some ultimate purpose has simply not appealed to the American imagination. Movements outside the political process, yes—from abolitionism to feminism, from municipal reform to civil rights. But let the supporters of these movements enter electoral politics, and the expectation becomes one of quick victory. S. M. Lipset has described this phenomenon:

> . . . Extra-party "movements" arise for moralistic causes, which are initially not electorally palatable. Such movements are not doomed to isolation and inefficacy. If mainstream political leaders recognize that a significant seg-ment of the electorate feels alienated . . . they will readapt one of the major party coalitions. But in so doing, they temper much of the extremist mor-alistic fervor. . . . The protestors are absorbed into a major party coalition, but, like the abolitionists who joined the Republicans, the Populists who merged with the Democrats, or the radicals who backed the New Deal, they contribute to the policy orientation of the newly formed coalition.*

To which I need only add a clever observation Sombart made in 1906, which is still, I suspect, largely true: "It is an unbearable feeling for an American to belong to a party that always and forever comes out of the election with small figures. . . . A member of a minority party finds himself on election day . . . compelled to stand at one side with martyr-like resignation—something which in no way ac-cords with the American temperament."†

At least a significant number of Americans have never hesitated to "stand at one side with martyr-like resignation" or even with rage in behalf of moral causes. But, curiously, this has not seemed to extend to the electoral system: *there*, they have to strike it rich. That may be one reason they sometimes strike it so poor.

4

The search for answers often leads to nothing more than a redefining of ques-tions. To discount but not dismiss the customary "objective factors" cited as ex-planations for the failure of American socialism is by no means to reject the idea of "American exceptionalism," namely, that conditions in the United States have differed crucially from the Marxist model for the development of capitalism and/ or the way capitalism actually developed in Europe. It is, rather, to transfer our

---

* "Why No Socialism in the United States?," in Seweryn Bialer, ed., *Sources of Contemporary Radicalism* (1977), p. 128.

† Quoted in Bialer, ed., *Sources of Contemporary Radicalism*, p. 62.

explanatory stress from material conditions to the character of American culture. Exceptionalism among us took primarily an ideological or a mythic form, a devotion to the idea that this country could be exempt from the historical burdens that had overwhelmed Europe. It seems obvious that so distinctive a culture, defining itself through an opposition to, even a rejection of, Europe, cannot finally be understood apart from the shaping context of special historical circumstances: it did not arise merely as an idea in someone's head, or an Idea in a Collective Head. Yet I want to stress the independent power, the all-but-autonomous life, of the American myth and its remarkable persistence, despite enormous changes in social conditions. The ideology or myth—call it what you will, as long as you keep your eye fixed on Gatsby's "green light"—seems *almost* impervious to the modifying pressures of circumstance. It isn't, of course; but what strikes one is the extent to which it continues, in good circumstances and bad, to shape our imagination.

What is this myth? It consists in a shared persuasion, often penetrating deeper into our consciousness than mere language can express, that America is the home of a people shaped by or at least sharing in Providence. America is the land of the settler's paradisial wilderness, the setting of the Puritan's New Israel. America is humanity's second chance. Such sentiments rest on a belief that we have already had our revolution and it was led by George Washington, so that appeals for another one are superfluous and malicious, or that, for the millions who came here from Europe in the last one hundred fifty years, the very act of coming constituted a kind of revolution.

That many Americans have found it entirely possible to yield to this myth while simultaneously attacking our socioeconomic institutions, or complaining bitterly that the slaveocracy disgraced us, the plutocrats stole our inheritance, Wall Street fleeced us, the capitalists exploited us, and the military-industrial complex sent our sons to death—all this seems clear. To a simple rationalist or vulgar Marxist, the ability to hold at once to the animating myth behind the founding of America and the most bitter criticism of its violation or abandonment or betrayal may seem a contradiction; but if so, it is precisely from such contradictions that our collective existence has been formed.

The distinctive American ideology takes on a decidedly nonideological mask. I call it, very roughly, Emersonianism, though I know it had its sources in American and indeed European thought long before Emerson. By now, of course, "Emersonianism" has become as elusive and protean a category as Marxism or Freudianism. What I mean to suggest is that Emerson, in a restatement of an old Christian heresy, raised the I to semidivine status, thereby providing a religious sanction for the American cult of individualism. Traditional Christianity had seen man as a being like God, but now he was to be seen as one sharing, through osmosis with the oversoul, directly in the substance of divinity. This provided a new vision of man for a culture proposing to define itself as his new home—provided that vision by insisting that man be regarded as a self-creating and self-sufficient being fulfilled through his unmediated relation to nature and God. The traditional European view that human beings are in good measure defined or described through social characteristics and conditions was, at least theoretically, discounted; the new American, singing songs of himself, would create himself through spontaneous assertions, which might at best graze sublimity and at worst drop to egoism. The American, generically considered, could make his fate through will and intuition, a self-induced grace.

Now this vision can be employed in behalf of a wide range of purposes—myth is always promiscuous. It can show forth the Emerson who, in behalf of "a perfect unfolding of individual nature," brilliantly analyzed human alienation in a commercial society, attacking the invasion of "Nature by Trade . . . [as it threatened] to upset the balance of man, and establish a new, universal Monarchy more tyrannical than Babylon or Rome." And it can emerge in the Emerson who told his countrymen that "money . . . is in its effects and laws as beautiful as roses. Property keeps the accounts of the world, and is always moral."

This American vision can be turned toward the authoritarian monomania of Captain Ahab or to the easy fraternity of Ishmael and Queequeg. It can coexist with Daniel Webster and inspire Wendell Phillips. It can be exploited by Social Darwinism and sustain the abolitionists. It can harden into a nasty individualism and yield to the mass conformity Tocqueville dreaded. Arising from the deepest recesses of the American imagination, it resembles Freud's description of dreams as showing "a special tendency to reduce two opposites to a unity or to represent them as one thing." No one has to like this vision, but anyone trying to cope with American experience had better acknowledge its power.

This complex of myth and ideology, sentiment and prejudice, for which I use "Emersonianism" as a convenient label, forms the ground of "American exceptionalism." Politically it has often taken the guise of a querulous antistatism, at times regarded as a native absolute—though that seldom kept many people from aligning it with the demands of big business for government subsidies. It can veer toward an American version of anarchism, suspicious of all laws, forms, and regulations, asserting a fraternity of two, sometimes even one, against all communal structures. Tilt toward the right and you have the worship of "the free market"; tilt toward the left and you have the moralism of American reformers, even the syndicalism of the Industrial Workers of the World. Snakelike, this "Emersonianism" can also subside into or next to the Lockean moderation of the American Constitution and political arrangement. ("The American Whig leaders" of the postrevolutionary period, Sacvan Bercovitch shrewdly remarks, "brought the violence of revolution under control by making revolution a controlling metaphor of national identity.")

It is notable that most nineteenth-century critics of American society appealed to the standards—violated, they said—of the early republic. They did this not as a tactical device but out of sincere conviction. "We will take up the ball of the Revolution where our fathers dropped it," declared the agrarian radicals of the New York anti-rent movement, "and roll it to the final consummation of freedom and independence of the Masses." The social historian Herbert Gutman finds the same rhetoric in the propaganda of the late-nineteenth-century trade unions. And Sacvan Bercovitch finds it in the declarations of a large number of American radicals throughout that century:

> William Lloyd Garrison organized the American Anti-Slavery Society as "a renewal of the nation's founding principles" and of "the national ideal." Frederick Douglass based his demands for black liberation on America's "destiny" . . . and "the genius of American institutions. . . ." As a leading historian of the period has remarked: ". . . the typical reformer, for all his uncompromising spirit, was no more alienated—no more truly rebellious—than the typical democrat. . . . He might sound radical while nevertheless associating himself with the fundamental principles and underlying tendencies of America."[*]

It's a pity that our indigenous nineteenth-century radicalism had largely exhausted itself by the time small socialist groups, mostly immigrant in composition, began to be organized in the 1880s—or at least could not find a point of significant relation with them. The abolitionist Wendell Phillips began with a pure Emersonian invocation: ". . . We are bullied by institutions. . . . Stand on the pedestal of your own individual independence, summon these institutions about you, and judge them." Once the fight against slavery was won, Phillips moved ahead to other causes, warning against "the incoming flood of the power of incorporated wealth" and calling—in a political style Richard Hofstadter has described as "Yankee homespun" socialism—for an "equalization of property."[†]

---

[*] "The Rights of Assent: Rhetoric, Ritual and the Ideology of American Consciousness," in Sam B. Girgus, ed., *The American Self: Myth, Ideology and Popular Culture* (1981), p. 21.

[†] Quoted in Hofstadter, *The American Political Tradition* (1948), pp. 139, 159.

He became—almost—a bridge between nineteenth-century radicalism and the new American socialism. And like other American dissenters, he held fast to the tradition of invoking the principles of the republic—principles, he said, that had been violated and betrayed.

Recognizing the power of this traditional response is by no means to acquiesce in the delusions that have often been justified in its name. It isn't, for example, to acquiesce in the delusion that America has been or is a "classless" society. Or that there has been any lack among us of bloody battles between capital and labor. Or that there are not today, as in the past, glaring injustices that call for remedy. To recognize the power of the American myth of a covenant blessing the new land is simply to recognize a crucial fact in our history—and one that seems to me at least as decisive for the fate of socialism in this country as the material conditions that are usually cited.

If you go through the writings of American socialists you can find glimmerings and half-recognitions that they have had to function in a culture ill-attuned to their fundamental outlook. The keenest statements on this matter come from an odd pair; an Italian Marxist, Antonio Gramsci, who had no direct contact with America, and an American radical of the 1930s, Leon Samson, remembered only by historians who make the left their specialty. In his *Notebooks* Gramsci writes: "The Anglo-Saxon immigrants are themselves an intellectual, but more especially a moral, elite. . . . They import into America . . . apart from moral energy and energy of will, a certain level of civilization, a certain stage of European historical evolution, which, when transplanted by such men into the virgin soil of America, continues to develop the forces implicit in its nature. . . ."*

In isolation, this passage could almost be taken for a rhapsody celebrating American culture; but Gramsci was a Marxist, and he proceeded to argue that the elements of uniqueness he found in the American past had reached their fulfillment in an apogee of pure capitalism, what he calls "Fordism," an unprecedented rationalization of production setting America apart from the kinds of capitalism known in Europe.

Leon Samson, a maverick socialist of the 1930s, developed a linked notion, that "Americanism" can be seen as a "substitute socialism":

> Like socialism, Americanism is looked upon . . . as a . . . platonic, impersonal attraction toward a system of ideas, a solemn assent to a handful of final notions—democracy, liberty, opportunity, to all of which the American adheres rationalistically much as a socialist adheres to his socialism— because it does him good, because it gives him work, because, so he thinks,

* *Selections from the Prison Notebooks* (1971), pp. 21–22.

it guarantees his happiness. . . . Every concept in socialism has its substitu-
tive counter-concept in Americanism, and that is why the socialist argument falls so fruitlessly on the American ear. . . .*

Both Gramsci and Samson were shrewd enough to locate their "exceptionalism" in the mythic depths of our collective imagination, among the inner vibra-
tions of our culture. What one may conclude from their perceptions, as perhaps
from my own discussion, is that if socialism is ever to become a major force in
America it must either enter deadly combat with and destroy the covenant myth
or must look for some way of making its vision of the good society seem a fulfillment of that myth. Both are difficult propositions, but I need hardly say which is
the less so.

Many socialists have grasped for intuitions along these lines, but have feared
perhaps to articulate them, since they seemed to suggest that so impalpable a
thing as a culture can have a greater power of influence than industrial structures,
levels of production, and standards of living. And that may explain why many
American socialists, including the intelligent ones, found it safer to retreat into
the comforts of the Marxist system, with its claims to universal applicability and
certain fulfillment.

Would a developed recognition of the problem as I have sketched it here have
brought any large or immediate success to American socialism over the past five
or six decades? Probably not. All that such a recognition might have done—
all!—is to endow the American socialists with a certain independence of mind
and a freedom from ideological rigidity.

So, again, we restate our central question. Not "Why is there no socialism in
America?" There never was a chance for major socialist victory in this society,
this culture. The really interesting question is "Why could we not build a significant socialist movement that would have a sustained influence?" One answer, of
course, is that the kind of culture I've sketched here makes it almost impossible
for a significant minority party to survive for very long. In America, politics, like
everything else, tends to be all or nothing. But whether it might yet be possible
for a significant minority movement to survive—one that would be political in a
broad, educative sense without entangling itself in hopeless electoral efforts—is
another question.

Some Inconclusive Conclusions

The analyses and speculations in this article apply mainly to the earlier decades of the century, into the years just before World War II. But the troubles of

* *Toward a United Front* (1935), pp. 16–17.

American—and not only American—socialism in the decades since the thirties must be located in a more terrible—indeed, an apocalyptic—setting. The triumph of Hitlerism called into question a good many traditional assumptions of progress and schemes for human self-determination—called into question the very enterprise of mankind. The rise of Stalinism, a kind of grotesque "double" of the socialist hope, led to the destruction of entire generations, the disillusionment of hundreds of thousands of committed people, the besmirching of the socialist idea itself. As a consequence of the problems thrown up by Hitlerism and Stalinism, there has occurred an inner crisis of belief, a coming-apart of socialist thought. If we consider the crisis of socialism on an international scale within the last fifty years, then clearly these developments count at least as much as, and probably more than, the indigenous American factors discussed here.

There is a school of opinion that holds that American socialism did not fail, but succeeded insofar as it prepared the way, advanced ideas, and trained leaders for mainstream movements of labor, liberalism, and others. This view has an obvious element of truth, perhaps even consolation. Still, no one could be expected to endure the grueling effort to build a socialist movement simply so that it might serve as a "prep school" for other movements. Our final judgment must be more stringent, harder on ourselves: insofar as American socialism proposed ends distinctively its own, it did not succeed.

There is a more sophisticated argument about the fate of American socialism: that finally it did not matter. Europe, with its strong socialist and social-democratic movements, did not achieve democratic socialism; it could reach only the welfare state. The United States, without a major socialist movement, has also reached a welfare state, if at the moment one that is somewhat broken-down. Hence, this argument goes, what does it matter whether or not we have a socialist movement here? I would respond that, largely because of the strength of European socialism, the welfare state in Western Europe has advanced significantly beyond that of the United States, and that there are groups within European socialism, especially in Sweden and France, that now see a need to move "beyond" the welfare state. The presence of these groups has been made possible by the continuing strength of the socialist movement in those countries.

The usual "objective" socioeconomic factors cited as explanations for the difficulties of American socialism are genuine constraints. But I believe that the distinctiveness of American culture has played the more decisive part in thwarting socialist fortunes. And even after both kinds of reasons—the socioeconomic and the cultural—are taken into account, there remains an important margin with regard to intelligence or obtuseness, correct or mistaken strategies, which helped to determine whether American socialism was to be a measurable force or an isolated sect. That the American socialist movement must take upon itself a considerable portion of the responsibility for its failures, I have tried to show elsewhere.

In the United States, socialist movements have usually thrived during times of liberal upswing. They have hastened their own destruction whenever they have pitted themselves head-on against liberalism. If there is any future for socialism in America, it is through declaring itself to be the partial ally of a liberalism with which it shares fundamental democratic values and agrees upon certain immediate objectives; after that, it can be said that socialists propose to extend and thereby fulfill traditional liberal goals by moving toward a democratization of economic and social life. If some liberals express agreement with that perspective, then all the better.

American socialism has suffered from a deep-grained sectarianism, in part a result of the natural inclination of small groups to huddle self-protectively in their loneliness, and in part, especially during the two or three decades after 1917, a result of the baneful influence of Bolshevism. At least as important have been the fundamentalist, evangelical, and deeply antipolitical impulses rooted in our religious and cultural past, impulses that helped to shape the socialist movements in the times of Debs and Thomas far more than their participants recognized. A damaging aspect of this sectarianism was a tendency to settle into postures of righteous moral witness, to the disadvantage of mundane politics.

During its peak moments American socialism tried to combine two roles—that of moral protest and that of political reform—which in America had traditionally been largely separate, and which our political arrangements make it very difficult to unite. In principle, a socialist movement ought to fulfill both of these roles: moral protest largely beyond the political process, and social reform largely within it. A strong argument could be made that the two roles are, or should be, mutually reinforcing, with the one providing moral luster and the other practical effectiveness. But it would take an extraordinary set of circumstances (say, the moment when abolitionism flourished or the moment when the protest against the Vietnam War reached its peak) for a movement in this country to combine the two roles successfully. And what's more, it would take a movement with a degree of sophistication and flexibility that has rarely been available on the left, or anywhere else along the political spectrum.

Still, no socialist movement, if it is to maintain the integrity of its persuasions, can forgo some effort to be both the voice of protest and the agency of reform. It's not a matter of choosing between the roles of moral witness and political actor.

It's a matter of finding ways through which to link properly the utopian moralism of the protester with the political realism of the activist; to ensure that the voice of high rectitude will reinforce and give breadth to the daily murmur of the reformer; to adapt to the realities of the American political system without succumbing to a small-souled pragmatism or a hermetic moralism. In some large parties, loosely and democratically structured, this has sometimes been possible, as in the British Labour Party during its best years. In a small party, such as the American Socialist Party even during its best years, this has been almost impossible.

Whether some such alliance of forces or union of impulses might still be created in America is very much a question. I do not know, but think it a project worthy of serious people.

Henry James once said that being an American is a complex fate. We American socialists could add: He didn't know the half of it.

Writing and the Holocaust
{1986}

OUR SUBJECT RESISTS the usual capacities of mind. We may read the Holocaust as the central event of this century; we may register the pain of its unhealed wounds; but finally we must acknowledge that it leaves us intellectually disarmed, staring helplessly at the reality, or, if you prefer, the mystery, of mass extermination. There is little likelihood of finding a rational structure of explanation for the Holocaust: it forms a sequence of events without historical or moral precedent. To think about ways in which the literary imagination might "use" the Holocaust is to entangle ourselves with a multitude of problems for which no aesthetic can prepare us.

The Holocaust is continuous with, indeed forms a sequence of events within, Western history, and at the same time it is a unique historical enterprise. To study its genesis within Western history may help us discover its roots in traditional anti-Semitism, fed in turn by Christian myth, German romanticism, and the breakdown of capitalism in twentieth-century Europe between the wars. But it is a grave error to "elevate" the Holocaust into an occurrence outside of history, a sort of diabolic visitation, for then we tacitly absolve its human agents of responsibility. To do this is a grave error even if, so far and perhaps forever, we lack adequate categories for comprehending how such a sequence of events could occur. The Holocaust was long prepared for in the history of Western civilization, though not all those who engaged in the preparation knew what they were doing or would have welcomed the outcome.

In the concentration camps set up by the Nazis, such as those at Dachau and Buchenwald, there was an endless quantity of sadism, some of it the spontaneous doings of psychopaths and thugs given total command by the Nazi government, and some of it the result of a calculated policy taking into cynical account the consequences of allowing psychopaths and thugs total command. Piles of corpses accumulated in these camps. Yet a thin continuity can be detected between earlier locales of brutality and the "concentrationary universe." In some pitiable sense, the prisoners in these camps still lived—they were starved, broken, tormented, but they still lived. A faint margin of space could sometimes be carved out for the human need to maintain community and personality, even while both were being destroyed. Horrible these camps surely were; but even as they pointed toward, they did not yet constitute the "Final Solution."

The Nazis had an idea. To dehumanize systematically both guards and prisoners, torturers and tortured, meant to create a realm of subjugation no longer responsive to the common norms of human society; and from this process of dehumanization they had themselves set in motion, the Nazis could then "conclude" that, indeed, Jews were not human. This Nazi idea would lead to and draw upon sadism, but at least among the leaders and theoreticians, it was to be distinguished from mere sadism: it was an abstract rage, the most terrible of all rages. This Nazi idea formed a low parody of the messianism that declared that once mankind offered a warrant of faith and conduct, deliverance would come to earth in the shape of a savior bringing the good days—a notion corrupted by false messiahs into a "forcing of days" and by totalitarian movements into the physical elimination of "contaminating" races and classes. There was also in Nazi ideology a low parody of that mania for "completely" remaking societies and cultures that has marked modern political life.

When the Nazis established their realm of subjection in the concentration camps, they brought the impulse to nihilism, so strong in modern culture, to a point of completion no earlier advocate had supposed possible. The Italian-Jewish writer Primo Levi, soon after arriving at Auschwitz, was told by a Nazi guard: Hier ist kein warum, here there is no why, here nothing need be explained. This passing observation by a shrewd thug provides as good an insight into the world of the camps as anything found in the entire scholarly literature. What we may still find difficult to grasp is the peculiar blend of ideology and nihilism—the way these two elements of thought, seemingly in friction, were able to join harmoniously, thereby releasing the satanic energies of Nazism.

By now we have an enormous body of memoirs and studies describing the experience of the concentration camps. Inevitably, there are clashes of remembrance and opinion. For the psychoanalyst Bruno Bettelheim, held captive in Dachau and Buchenwald in 1939, it was apparently still possible to cope with life in the camps, if only through inner moral resistance, a struggle to "understand" that might "safeguard [one's ego] in such a way that, if by any good luck he should regain liberty, [the prisoner] would be approximately the same person he was" before being deprived of liberty. Precisely this seemed impossible to Jean Améry, a gifted Austrian-Jewish writer who had been imprisoned in Auschwitz. No survivor, no one who had ever been tortured by the SS, he later wrote, could be "approximately the same person" as before.

Even to hope for survival meant, in Améry's view, to "capitulate unconditionally in the face of reality," and that reality was neither more nor less than the unlimited readiness of the SS to kill. The victim lived under "an absolute sovereign" whose mission—a mission of pleasure—was torture, "in an orgy of unchecked self-expansion." Thereby "the transformation of the person into flesh became complete." As for "the word"—which for Améry signified something akin to what "safeguarding the ego" meant for Bettelheim—it "always dies when the claim of some reality is total." For then no space remains between thought and everything external to thought.

It would be impudent to choose between the testimonies of Bettelheim and Améry. A partial explanation for their differences of memory and understanding may be that Bettelheim was a prisoner in 1939 and Améry in 1943–45. Bettelheim's ordeal predated slightly the "Final Solution," while Améry was held captive in the Auschwitz that Hannah Arendt quite soberly called a "corpse factory." It is also possible that these writers, in reflecting upon more or less similar experiences, were revealing "natural" differences in human response. We cannot be certain.

By the time the Nazis launched their "Final Solution" such differences of testimony had become relatively insignificant. The Holocaust reached its point of culmination as the systematic and impersonal extermination of millions of human beings, denied life, and even death as mankind had traditionally conceived it, simply because they fell under the abstract category of "Jew." It became clear that the sadism before and during the "Final Solution" on the trains that brought the Jews to the camps and in the camps themselves was not just incidental or gratuitous; it was a carefully worked-out preparation for the gas chambers. But for the Nazi leaders, originating theoreticians of death, what mattered most was the *program* of extermination. No personal qualities or accomplishments of the victims, no features of character or appearance, mattered. The abstract perversity of categorization declaring Jews to be *Untermenschen* as determined by allegedly biological traits was unconditional.

No absolute division of kind existed between concentration and death camps, and some, like the grouping of camps at Auschwitz, contained quarters for both slave laborers and gas chambers, with recurrent "selections" from the former feeding the latter. Still, the distinction between the two varieties of camps has some descriptive and analytic value: it enables us to distinguish between what was and was not historically unique about the Holocaust.

Whatever was unique took place in the death camps, forming a sequence of events radically different from all previous butcheries in the history of mankind. Revenge, enslavement, dispersion, large-scale slaughter of enemies, all are a commonplace of the past; but the physical elimination of a categorized segment of mankind was, both as idea and fact, new. "The destruction of Europe's Jews," Claude Lanzmann has written, "cannot be logically deduced from any . . . system of presuppositions. . . . Between the conditions that permitted extermination and the extermination itself—the *fact* of the extermination—there is a break in continuity, a hiatus, an abyss." That abyss forms the essence of the Holocaust.

2

I cannot think of another area of literary discourse in which a single writer has exerted so strong, if diffused, an influence as Theodore Adorno has on discussions of literature and the Holocaust. What Adorno offered in the early 1950s was not a complete text or even a fully developed argument. Yet his few scattered remarks had an immediate impact, evidently because they brought out feelings held by many people.

"After Auschwitz," wrote Adorno, "to write a poem is barbaric." It means to "squeeze aesthetic pleasure out of artistic representation of the naked bodily pain of those who have been knocked down by rifle butts. . . . Through aesthetic principles or stylization . . . the unimaginable ordeal still appears as if it had some ulterior purpose. It is transfigured and stripped of some of its horror, and with this, injustice is already done to the victims."

Adorno was by no means alone in expressing such sentiments, nor in recognizing that his sentiments, no matter how solemnly approved, were not likely

to keep anyone from trying to represent through fictions or evoke through poetic symbols the concentration and death camps. A Yiddish poet, Aaron Tsaytlin,
wrote in a similar vein after the Holocaust: "Were Jeremiah to sit by the ashes of
Israel today, he would not cry out a lamentation. . . . The Almighty Himself would
be powerless to open his well of tears. He would maintain a deep silence. For even
an outcry is now a lie, even tears are mere literature, even prayers are false."

Tsaytlin's concluding sentence anticipated the frequently asserted but as frequently ignored claim that all responses to the Holocaust are inadequate, including, and perhaps especially, those made with the most exalted sentiments and
language. Here, for instance, is Piotr Rawicz, a Jewish writer born in the Ukraine
who after his release from the camps wrote in French. In his novel *Blood from the
Sky*, Rawicz put down certain precepts that the very existence of his book seems
to violate: "The 'literary manner' is an obscenity. . . . Literature [is] the art, occasionally remunerative, of rummaging in vomit. And yet, it would appear, one has
to write. So as to trick loneliness, so as to trick other people."

Looking back at such remarks, we may wonder what these writers were struggling to express, what half-formed or hidden feelings prompted their outcries. I
will offer a few speculations, confining myself to Adorno.

Adorno was not so naive as to prescribe for writers a line of conduct that would
threaten their very future as writers. Through a dramatic outburst he probably
meant to focus upon the sheer difficulty—the literary risk, the moral peril—of
dealing with the Holocaust in literature. It was as if he were saying: Given the
absence of usable norms through which to grasp the meaning (if there is one)
of the scientific extermination of millions, given the intolerable gap between the
aesthetic conventions and the loathsome realities of the Holocaust, and given the
improbability of coming up with images and symbols that might serve as "objective correlatives" for events that the imagination can hardly take in, writers
in the post-Holocaust era might be wise to be silent. Silent, at least, about the
Holocaust.

This warning, if such it was, had a certain prophetic force. It anticipated, first,
the common but mistaken notion that literature somehow has an obligation to
encompass all areas of human experience, no matter how extreme or impenetrable they might be; and, second, the corruptions of the mass media that would
suppose itself equipped to master upon demand any theme or subject.

Adorno might have been rehearsing a traditional aesthetic idea: that the representation of a horrible event, especially if in drawing upon literary skills it
achieves a certain graphic power, could serve to domesticate it, rendering it familiar and in some sense even tolerable, and thereby shearing away part of the

horror. The comeliness of even the loosest literary forms is likely to soften the impact of what is being rendered, and in most renderings of imaginary situations we tacitly expect and welcome this. But with a historical event such as the Holocaust—an event regarding which the phrase "such as" cannot really be employed—the chastening aspects of literary mimesis can be felt to be misleading, a questionable way of reconciling us with the irreconcilable or of projecting a symbolic "transcendence" that in actuality is no more than a reflex of our baffled will.

Adorno might have had in mind the possibility of an insidious relation between the represented (or even the merely evoked) Holocaust and the spectator enthralled precisely as, or perhaps even because, he is appalled—a relation carrying a share of voyeuristic sadomasochism. Can we really say that in reading a memoir or novel about the Holocaust, or in seeing a film such as *Shoah*, we gain the pleasure, or catharsis, that is customarily associated with the aesthetic transaction? More disquieting, can we be sure that we do not gain a sort of illicit pleasure from our pained submission to such works? I do not know how to answer these questions, which threaten many of our usual assumptions about what constitutes an aesthetic experience; but I think that even the most disciplined scholar of the Holocaust ought every once in a while to reexamine the nature of his or her responses.

More speculative still is the thought that Adorno, perhaps with only a partial awareness, was turning back to a "primitive" religious feeling—the feeling that there are some things in our experience, or some aspects of the universe, that are too terrible to be looked at directly.

In ancient mythologies and religions there are things and beings that are not to be named. They may be the supremely good or supremely bad, but for mortals they are the unutterable, since there is felt to be a limit to what man may see or dare, certainly to what he may meet. Perseus would turn to stone if he were to look directly at the serpent-headed Medusa, though he would be safe if he looked at her only through a reflection in a mirror or a shield (this latter being, as I shall argue, the very strategy that the cannier writers have adopted in dealing with the Holocaust).

Perhaps dimly, Adorno wished to suggest that the Holocaust might be regarded as a secular equivalent—if there can be such a thing—of that which in the ancient myths could not be gazed at or named directly; that before which men had to avert their eyes; that which in the properly responsive witness would arouse the "holy dread" Freud saw as the essence of taboos. And in such taboos the prohibition was imposed not in order to enforce ignorance but to regulate, or guard against the consequences of, knowledge.

How this taboo might operate without the sanctions and structure of an organized religion and its linked mythology I cannot grasp: it would require a quantity of shared or communal discipline beyond anything we can suppose. Adorno must have known this as well as anyone else. He must have known that in our culture the concept of limit serves mostly as a barrier or hurdle to be overcome, not as a perimeter of respect. Perhaps his remarks are to be taken as a hopeless admonition, a plea for the improvisation of limit that he knew would not and indeed could not be heeded, but which it was necessary to make.

3

Holocaust writings make their primary claim, I would say, through facts recorded or remembered. About this most extreme of human experiences there cannot be too much documentation, and what matters most in such materials is exactitude: the sober number, the somber date. Beyond that, Holocaust writings often reveal the helplessness of the mind before an evil that cannot quite be imagined, or the helplessness of the imagination before an evil that cannot quite be understood. This shared helplessness is the major reason for placing so high a value on the memoir, a kind of writing in which the author has no obligation to do anything but, in accurate and sober terms, tell what he experienced and witnessed.

Can we so readily justify our feelings about the primary worth of reliable testimony? Prudential arguments seem increasingly dubious here, since it should by now be clear that remembering does not necessarily forestall repetition. The instinctive respect we accord honest testimony, regardless of whether it is "well written," may in part be due to a persuasion that the aesthetic is not the primary standard for judgments of human experience, and that there can be, indeed often enough have been, situations in which aesthetic and moral standards come into conflict. Our respect for testimony may also be due in part to an unspoken persuasion that we owe something to the survivors who expose themselves to the trauma of recollection: we feel that we should listen to them apart from whether it "does any good." As for the millions who did not survive, it would be mere indulgence to suppose that any ceremonies of recollection could "make up for" or "transcend" their destruction—all such chatter, too frequent in writings about the Holocaust, is at best a futility of eloquence. Still, there are pieties that civilized people want to confirm even if, sometimes because, these are no more than gestures.

Another piety is to be invoked here. We may feel that heeding the survivors' testimony contributes to the fund of shared consciousness, which also means to our own precarious sense of being, whether individual or collective, and that, somehow, this is good. Henry James speaks somewhere of an ideal observer upon whom nothing is lost, who witnesses the entirety of the human lot, and though James in his concerns is about as far from something like the Holocaust as any writer could be, I think it just to borrow his vision of consciousness for our very different ends. The past summoned by Holocaust memoirs not only tells us something unbearable, and therefore unforgettable, about the life of mankind; it is a crucial part of our own time, if not of our direct experience. To keep the testimony of Holocaust witnesses in the forefront of our consciousness may not make us "better" people, but it may at least bring a touch of accord with our sense of the time we have lived in and where we have come from.

There is still another use of this testimony, and that is to keep the Holocaust firmly within the bounds of history, so that it will not end up as a preface to apocalypse or eschatology, or, worse still, decline into being the legend of a small people. "Nobody," said the historian Ignacy Schipper in Majdanek, "will *want* to believe us, because our disaster is the disaster of the entire civilized world." Schipper's phrasing merits close attention. He does not say that the disaster was experienced by the entire civilized world, which might entail a sentimental "universalizing" of the Holocaust; he says that the disaster of the Jews was (or should have been) shared by the entire civilized world, so that what happened to "us" might form a weight upon the consciousness of that world, even as we may recognize that sooner or later the world will seek to transfer it to some realm "beyond" history, a realm at once more exalted and less accusatory. Yet history is exactly where the Holocaust must remain, and for that, there can never be enough testimony.

Chaim Kaplan's Warsaw diary, covering a bit less than a year from its opening date of September 1, 1938, is a document still recognizably within the main tradition of Western writing: a man observes crucial events and strives to grasp their significance. Kaplan's diary shows the discipline of a trained observer; his prose is lucid and restrained; he records the effort of Warsaw Jewry to keep a fragment of its culture alive even as it stumbles into death; and he reveals a torn soul wondering what premises of faith, or delusion, sustain his "need to record." Barely, precariously, we are still in the world of the human as we have understood it, for nothing can be more human than to keep operating with familiar categories of thought while discovering they will no longer suffice.

Elie Wiesel's first book, *Night*, written simply and without rhetorical indulgence, is a slightly fictionalized record of his sufferings as a boy in Auschwitz and
during a forced march together with his father and other prisoners through the
frozen countryside to Buchenwald. The father dies of dysentery in Buchenwald,
and the boy—or the writer remembering himself as a boy—reveals his guilty relief at feeling that the death of his father has left him "free at last," not as any son
might feel but in the sense that now he may be able to save himself without the
burden of an ailing father. No sensitive reader will feel an impulse to judgment
here. Indeed, that is one of the major effects of honest testimony about the Holocaust—it dissolves any impulse to judge what the victims did or did not do, since
there are situations so extreme that it seems immoral to make judgments about
those who must endure them. We are transported here into a subworld where
freedom and moral sensibility may survive in memory but cannot be exercised in
practice. Enforced degradation forms the penultimate step toward the ovens.

The ovens dominate the camps that the Nazis, not inaccurately, called *anus
mundi*. Filip Mueller's *Eyewitness Auschwitz* is the artless account of being transported from his native Slovakia in April 1942 to Auschwitz, where he worked for
two and a half years as a *Sonderkommando*, or assistant at the gas chambers. Somehow Mueller survived. His narrative is free of verbal embellishment or thematic
reflection; he indulges neither in self-apology nor self-attack; he writes neither
art nor history. His book is simply the story of a simple man who processed many
corpses. Even in this book, terrible beyond any that I have ever read, there are still
a few touches recalling what we take to be humanity: efforts at theodicy by men
who cannot justify their faith, a recital of the kaddish by doomed prisoners who
know that no one else will say it for them. In the world Mueller served, "the transformation of the person into flesh" and of flesh into dust "became complete." It
was a world for which, finally, we have no words.

But isn't there, a skeptical voice may interject, a touch of empiricist naiveté in
such high claims for Holocaust memoirs? Memory can be treacherous among
people who have suffered terribly and must feel a measure of guilt at being alive
at all. Nor can we be sure of the truth supplied by damaged and overwrought
witnesses, for whatever knowledge we may claim about these matters is likely
to come mainly from the very memoirs we find ourselves submitting, however
uneasily, to critical judgment.

The skeptical voice is cogent, and I would only say in reply that we are not helpless before the accumulated mass of recollection. Our awe before the suffering
and our respect for the sufferers does not disable us from making discriminations of value, tone, authority. There remain the usual historical tests, through

both external check and internal comparison; and there is still the reader's ear, bending toward credence or doubt.

The test of the ear is a delicate one, entailing a shift from testimony to witness—a shift that, except perhaps with regard to the scrappiest of chronicles, seems unavoidable. Reading Holocaust memoirs we respond not just to their accounts of what happened; we respond also to qualities of being, tremors of sensibility, as these emerge even from the bloodiest pages. We respond to the modesty or boastfulness, the candor or evasiveness, the self-effacement or self-promotion of the writers. We respond, most of all, to a quality that might be called moral poise, by which I mean a readiness to engage in a complete reckoning with the past, insofar as there can be one—a strength of remembrance that leads the writer into despair and then perhaps a little beyond it, so that he does not flinch from anything, neither shame nor degradation, yet refuses to indulge in those outbursts of self-pity, sometimes sliding into self-aggrandizement, that mar a fair number of Holocaust memoirs.

But is there not something shameful in subjecting the work of survivors to this kind of scrutiny? Perhaps so; yet in choosing to become writers, they have no choice but to accept this burden.

The Holocaust was structured to destroy the very idea of private being. It was a sequence of events entirely "out there," in the objective world, the world of force and power. Yet as we read Holocaust memoirs and reaffirm their value as evidence, we find ourselves veering—less by choice than necessity—from the brute external to the fragile subjective, from matter to voice, from story to storyteller. And this leaves us profoundly uneasy, signifying that our earlier stress upon the value of testimony has now been complicated, perhaps even compromised, by the introduction of aesthetic considerations. We may wish with all our hearts to yield entirely to the demands of memory and evidence, but simply by virtue of reading, we cannot forget that the diarist was a person formed before and the memoirist a person formed after the Holocaust. We are ensnared in the cruelty of remembering, a compounded cruelty, in which our need for truthful testimony lures us into tests of authenticity.

That, in any case, is how we read. I bring as a "negative" witness a memoirist not to be named: he puts his ordeal at the service of a familiar faith or ideology, and it comes to seem sad, for that faith or ideology cannot bear the explanatory and expiatory burdens he would place upon it. Another memoirist, also not to be named: he suborns his grief to public self-aggrandizement, and the grief he declares, surely sincere, is alloyed by streaks of publicity.

But Chaim Kaplan cares for nothing except the impossible effort to comprehend the incomprehensible; Filip Mueller for nothing except to recall happenings even he finds hard to credit; Primo Levi for nothing but to render his days in the camps through a language unadorned and chaste.

We are trapped. Our need for testimony that will forever place the Holocaust squarely within history requires that we respond to voice, nuance, personality. Our desire to see the Holocaust in weightier terms than the merely aesthetic lures us into a shy recognition of the moral reverberations of the aesthetic. This does not make us happy, but the only alternative is the silence we all remember, now and then, to praise.

4

"We became aware," writes Primo Levi, "that our language lacks words to express this offense, the demolition of man." Every serious writer approaching the Holocaust sooner or later says much the same. If there is a way of coping with this difficulty, it lies in a muted tactfulness recognizing that there are some things that can be said and some that cannot.

Let me cite a few sentences from T. S. Eliot: "Great simplicity is only won by an intense moment or by years of intelligent effort, or by both. It represents one of the most arduous conquests of the human spirit: the triumph of feeling and thought over the natural sin of language."

Exactly what Eliot meant by that astonishing phrase, "the natural sin of language," I cannot say with assurance, but that it applies to a fair portion of Holocaust writing, both memoir and fiction, seems to me indisputable. A "natural sin" might here signify the inclination to grow wanton over our deepest griefs, thereby making them the substance of public exploitation. Or a mistaken effort, sincere or grandiose, to whip language into doing more than it can possibly do, more than thought and imagination and prayer can do. Language as it seduces us into the comforting grandiose.

When, by now as a virtual cliché, we say that language cannot deal with the Holocaust, we really have in mind, or perhaps are covering up for, our inadequacies of thought and feeling. We succumb to that "natural sin of language" because anyone who tries seriously to engage with the implications of the Holocaust must come up against a wall of incomprehension: *How could it be?* Not the behavior, admirable or deplorable, of the victims, and not the ideologies the Nazis drew upon form the crux of our bewilderment, but—how could human beings, raised in the center of European civilization, do this? If we then fall back on intellectual shorthand, invoking the problem of radical evil, what are we really doing but expressing our helplessness in another vocabulary? Not only is this an impassable barrier for the thought of moralists and the recall of memoirists; it is, I think, the greatest thematic and psychological difficulty confronting writers of fiction who try to represent or evoke the Holocaust.

For the central question to be asked about these writings, a few of them distinguished and most decent failures, is this: What can the literary imagination, traditionally so proud of its self-generating capacities, add to—how can it go beyond—the intolerable matter cast up by memory? What could be the organizing categories, the implicit premises of perception and comprehension, through which the literary imagination might be able to render intelligible the gassing of twelve thousand people a day at Auschwitz? If, as Sidra DeKoven Ezrahi remarks, literature has traditionally called upon "the timeless archetypes of human experience" to structure and infer significance from its materials, how can this now be done with a sequence of events that radically breaks from those "timeless archetypes"? A novelist can rehearse what we have learned from the documentation of David Rousset and Filip Mueller, from Primo Levi and Eugen Kogon, but apart from some minor smoothing and shaping, what can the novelist *do* with all this? And if, through sheer lack of any other recourse, he does fall back upon the ideological or theological categories of Western thought, he faces the risk of producing a fiction with a severe fissure between rendered event and imposed category—so that even a sympathetic reader may be inclined to judge the work as resembling a failed allegory in which narrative and moral are, at best, chained together by decision.

Let us see all this concretely, as it might affect a novelist's job of work. Yes, the facts are there, fearful and oppressive, piled up endlessly in memoirs and histories. He has studied them, tried to "make sense" of them in his mind, submitted himself to the barrage of horror. But what he needs—and does not have—is something that for most ordinary fictions written about most ordinary themes would come to him spontaneously, without his even being aware that it figures crucially in the act of composition: namely, a structuring set of ethical premises, to which are subordinately linked aesthetic biases, through which he can integrate his materials. These ethical premises and aesthetic biases are likely to obtrude in consciousness only as a felt lack, only when a writer brooding over the endlessness of murder and torment asks how it can be turned or shaped into significant narrative. Nor, if he tries to escape from a confining realism and venture into symbolic or grotesque modes, can he find sufficiently used—you might say, sufficiently "broken in"—myths and metaphors that might serve as workable, publicly recognizable analogues for the Holocaust experience. Before this reality, the imagination comes to seem intimidated, helpless. It can rehearse, but neither enlarge nor escape; it can describe happenings, but not endow them with the autonomy and freedom of a complex fiction; it remains—and perhaps this may even figure as a moral obligation—the captive of its raw material.

The Holocaust memoirist, as writer, is in a far less difficult position. True, he needs to order his materials in the rudimentary sense of minimal chronology and reportorial selectivity (though anything he honestly remembers could prove to be significant, even if not part of his own story). Insofar as he remains a memoirist, he is not obliged to interpret what he remembers. But the novelist, even if he supposes he is merely "telling a story," must—precisely in order to tell a story—"make sense" of his materials, either through explicit theory or, what is better, absorbed assumptions. Otherwise, no matter how vivid his style or sincere his feelings, he will finally be at a loss. All he will then be able to do is to present a kind of "fictionalized memoir"—which means not to move very far beyond what the memoirist has already done.

To avoid this difficulty, some novelists have concentrated on those camps that were not just "corpse factories" and that allowed some faint simulacrum of human life; or, like Jorge Semprun in The Long Voyage, they have employed flashbacks of life before imprisonment, so as to allow for some of that interplay of character and extension of narrative that is essential to works of imaginative fiction. Once our focus is narrowed, however, to the death camps, the locale of what must be considered the essential Holocaust, the novelist's difficulties come to seem awesome. For then, apart from the lack of cognitive structures, he has to face a number of problems that are specifically, narrowly literary.

The Holocaust is not, essentially, a dramatic subject. Much before, much after, and much surrounding the mass exterminations may be open to dramatic rendering. But the exterminations, in which thousands of dazed and broken people were sent up each day in smoke, hardly knowing and often barely able to respond to their fate, have little of drama in them. Terribleness yes; drama no.

Of those conflicts between wills, those inner clashes of belief and wrenchings of desire, those enactments of passion, all of which make up our sense of the dramatic, there can be little in the course of a fiction focused mainly on the mass exterminations. A heroic figure here, a memorable outcry there—that is possible. But those soon to be dead are already half or almost dead; the gas chambers merely finish the job begun in the ghettos and continued on the trains. The basic minimum of freedom to choose and act that is a central postulate of drama had been taken from the victims.

The extermination process was so "brilliantly" organized that the life, and thereby the moral energy upon which drama ultimately depends, had largely been snuffed out of the victims before they entered the gas chambers. Here, in the death camps, the pitiful margin of space that had been allowed the human enterprise in the concentration camps was negated. Nor was it exactly death that reigned; it was annihilation. What then can the novelist make of this—what great clash or subtle inference—that a Filip Mueller has not already shown?

If the death camps and mass exterminations allow little opening for the dramatic, they also give little space for the tragic in any traditional sense of that term. In classical tragedy man is defeated; in the Holocaust man is destroyed. In tragedy man struggles against forces that overwhelm him, struggles against both the gods and his own nature; and the downfall that follows may have an aspect of grandeur. This struggle allows for the possibility of an enlargement of character through the purgation of suffering, which in turn may bring a measure of understanding and a kind of peace. But except for some religious Jews who were persuaded that the Holocaust was a reenactment of the great tradition of Jewish martyrdom, or for some secular Jews who lived out their ethic by choosing to die in solidarity with their fellows, or for those inmates who undertook doomed rebellions, the Jews destroyed in the camps were not martyrs continuing along the ways of their forefathers. They died, probably most of them, not because they chose at all costs to remain Jews, but because the Nazis chose to believe that being Jewish was an unchangeable, irredeemable condition. They were victims of a destruction that for many of them had little or only a fragmentary meaning—few of the victims, it seems, could even grasp the idea of total annihilation, let alone regard it as an act of high martyrdom. All of this does not make their death less terrible; it makes their death more terrible.

So much so that it becomes an almost irresistible temptation for Holocaust writers, whether discursive or fictional, to search for some redemptive token, some cry of retribution, some balancing of judgment against history's evil, some sign of ultimate spiritual triumph. It is as if, through the retrospect of language, they would lend a tragic aura. . . .

Many of the customary resources and conventions of the novel are unavailable to the writer dealing with the Holocaust. Small shifts in tone due to the surprises of freedom or caprice; the slow, rich development of character through testing and overcoming; the exertion of heroic energies by characters granted unexpect-

edly large opportunities; the slow emergence of moral flaws through an accumulation of seemingly trivial incidents; the withdrawal of characters into the recesses
of their selves; the yielding of characters to large social impulses, movements,
energies—these may not be entirely impossible in Holocaust fiction, but all must
prove to be painfully limited. Even so apparently simple a matter as how a work
of fiction is ended takes on a new and problematic aspect, for while a memoirist
can just stop, the novelist must think in terms of resolutions and completions.
But what, after having surrendered his characters to their fate, can he suppose
those resolutions and completions to be? Finally, all such literary problems come
down to the single inclusive problem of freedom. In the past even those writers
most inclined to determinism or naturalism have grasped that to animate their
narratives they must give at least a touch of freedom to their characters. And that,
as his characters inexorably approach the ovens, is precisely what the Holocaust
writer cannot do.

5

The Israeli critic Hannah Yaoz, reports Sidra Ezrahi, has "divided Holocaust
fiction into historical and transhistorical modes—the first representing a mimetic approach which incorporates the events into the continuum of history and
human experience, and the second transfiguring the events into a mythic reality where madness reigns and all historical loci are relinquished." At least with
regard to the Holocaust, the notion that there can be a "mythic reality" without
"historical loci" seems to me dubious—for where then could the imagination
find the materials for its act of "transfiguring"? Still, the division of Holocaust fiction proposed by the Israeli critic has some uses, if only to persuade us that finally
both the writers who submit to and those who rebel against the historical mode
must face pretty much the same problems.

The "mimetic approach" incorporating "events into the continuum of history" has been most strongly employed by the Polish writer Tadeusz Borowski
in his collection of stories This Way for the Gas, Ladies and Gentlemen. Himself an
Auschwitz survivor, Borowski writes in a cold, harsh, even coarse style, heavy
with flaunted cynicism, and offering no reliefs of the heroic. Kapo Tadeusz, the
narrator, works not only with but also on behalf of the death system. "Write," he
says, "that a portion of the sad fame of Auschwitz belongs to you as well." The
wretched truth is that here survival means the complete yielding of self.

Like Filip Mueller in his memoir, Borowski's narrator admits that he lives
because there is a steady flow of new "material" from the ghettos to the gas

chambers. "It is true, others may be dying, but one is somehow still alive, one has enough food, enough strength to work. . . ." Let the transports stop and Kapo Tadeusz, together with the other members of "Canada" (the labor gang that unloads the transports), will be liquidated.

Kapo Tadeusz lives in a world where mass murder is normal: it is there, it works, and it manages very well without moral justifications. The tone of detachment, which in a naturalistic novel would signal moral revulsion from represented ugliness, has here become a condition of survival. To lapse into what we might regard as human feeling—and sometimes Kapo Tadeusz and his fellow-prisoners do that—is to risk not only the ordeal of memory but the loss of life: a pointless loss, without record or rebellion.

Borowski's style conveys the rhythm of a hammering factuality, and in a way almost too complex to describe, one appreciates his absolute refusal to strike any note of redemptive nobility. Truthful and powerful as they are, Borowski's stories seem very close to those relentless Holocaust memoirs that show that there need be no limit to dehumanization. And that is just the point; for truthful and powerful as they are, Borowski's stories "work" mainly as testimony. Their authenticity makes us, I would say, all but indifferent to their status as art. We do not, perhaps cannot, read these stories as mediated fictions, imaginative versions of a human milieu in which men and women enter the usual range of relations. In Kapo Tadeusz's barrack there is simply no space for that complex interplay of action, emotion, dream, ambivalence, generosity, envy, and love that forms the basis of Western literature. The usual norms of human conduct—except for flashes of memory threatening survival—do not operate here. "We are not evoking evil irresponsibly," writes Borowski, "for we have now become part of it." Nor does it really matter whether Borowski was drawing upon personal memories or "making up" some of his stories. Composed in the fumes of destruction, even the stories he might have "made up" are not actually "made up": they are the substance of collective memory. *Hier ist kein warum.*

Inevitably, some Holocaust writers would try to escape from the vise of historical realism, and one of the most talented of these was the Ukrainian Jew Piotr Rawicz. Resting on a very thin narrative base, Rawicz's novel *Blood from the Sky* is a sustained, almost heroic rebellion against the demands of narrative—though in the end those demands reassert themselves, even providing the strongest parts of this wantonly brilliant book. What starts out as a traditional story soon turns into expressionist phantasmagoria seeking to project imagistic tokens for the Holocaust, or at least for the hallucinations it induces in the minds of witnesses. The story, often pressed far into the background, centers on a rich, highly educated, aristocratic Jew named Boris who saves himself from the Nazis through his expert command of German and Ukrainian—also through a disinclination to indulge in noble gestures. Upon this fragile strand of narrative Rawicz hangs a series of vignettes, excoriations, prose and verse poems, and mordant reflections of varying quality. The most effective are the ones visibly tied to some historical event, as in a brief sketch of a Nazi commander who orders the transport from Boris's town of all women named Goldberg because a woman of that name has infected him with a venereal disease. Symbolically freighted passages achieve their greatest force when they are also renderings of social reality, as in this description of a work party of prisoners sent by the Nazis to tear apart a Jewish cemetery:

> The party was demolishing some old tombstones. The blind, deafening hammer blows were scattering the sacred characters from inscriptions half a millennium old, and composed in praise of some holy man. . . . An *aleph* would go flying off to the left, while a *he* carved on another piece of stone dropped to the right. A *gimel* would bite the dust and a *nun* follow in its wake. . . . Several examples of *shin*, a letter symbolizing the miraculous intervention of God, had just been smashed and trampled on by the hammers and feet of these moribund workmen.

And then, several sentences later: "Death—that of their fellow men, of the stones, of their own—had become unimportant to them; but hunger hadn't."

The strength of this passage rests upon a fusion of event described and symbol evoked, but that fusion is successfully achieved because the realistic description is immediately persuasive in its own right. Mimesis remains the foundation. When Rawicz, however, abandons story and character in his straining after constructs of language that will in some sense "parallel" the Holocaust theme, the prose cracks under an intolerable pressure. We become aware of an excess of tension between the narrative (pushed into the background but through its sheer horror still dominant) and the virtuosity of language (too often willed and literary). Rawicz's outcroppings of expressionist rage and grief, no matter how graphic in their own right, can only seem puny when set against the events looming across the book.

Still, there are passages in which Rawicz succeeds in endowing his language with a kind of hallucinatory fury, and then it lures us into an autonomous realm of the horrifying and the absurd. But when that happens, virtuosity takes command, coming to seem self-sufficient, without fixed points of reference, as if floating off on its own. Losing the causal tie with the Holocaust that the writer evidently hopes to maintain, the language overflows as if a discharge of sheer nausea.

At least with regard to Holocaust fiction, I would say that efforts to employ "transhistorical modes" or "mythic reality" are likely to collapse into the very "continuum of history" they seek to escape—or else to come loose from the grounds of their creation.

6

M 'ken nisht, literally, Yiddish for "one cannot"—so the Israeli writer Aharon Applefeld once explained why in his fictions about the Holocaust he did not try to represent it directly, always ending before or starting after the exterminations. He spoke with the intuitive shrewdness of the writer who knows when to stop—a precious gift. But his remark also conveyed a certain ambiguity, as if m 'ken nisht had a way of becoming m 'tur nisht, "one must not," so that an acknowledgment of limit might serve as a warning of the forbidden.

In approaching the Holocaust, the canniest writers keep a distance. They know or sense that their subject cannot be met full-face. It must be taken on a tangent, with extreme wariness, through strategies of indirection and circuitous narratives that leave untouched the central horror—leave it untouched but always invoke or evoke it as hovering shadow. And this brings us to another of the ironies that recur in discussing this subject. We may begin with a suspicion that it is morally unseemly to submit Holocaust writings to fine critical discriminations, yet once we speak, as we must, about ways of approaching or apprehending this subject, we find ourselves going back to a fundamental concern of literary criticism, namely, how a writer validates his material.

Before. Aharon Applefeld's Badenheim 1939 is a novella that at first glance contains little more than a series of banal incidents in a Jewish resort near Vienna at the start of World War II. Each trivial event brings with it a drift of anxiety. A character feels "haunted by a hidden fear, not her own." Posters go up in the town: "The Air Is Fresher in Poland." Guests in the hotel fear that "some alien spirit [has] descended." A musician explains deportations of Jews as if he were the very spirit of the century: it is "Historical Necessity." Applefeld keeps accumulating nervous detail; the writing flows seamlessly, enticingly, until one notices that the logic of this quiet narrative is a logic of hallucination and its quietness mounts into a thick cloud of foreboding. At the end, the guests are being packed into "four filthy freight cars"—but here Applefeld abruptly stops, as if recognizing a limit to the sovereignty of words. Nothing is said or shown of what is to follow; the narrative is as furtive as the history it evokes; the unspeakable is not to be named.

During. Pierre Gascar, a Frenchman, not Jewish, who was a POW during World War II, has written in his long story "The Seasons of the Dead" one of the very few masterpieces of Holocaust fiction. Again, no accounts of torture or portrayal of concentration camps or imaginings of the gas chambers. All is evoked obliquely, through a haze of fearfulness and disbelief. The narrator makes no effort to hide his Parisian sophistication, but what he sees as a prisoner sent to a remote camp in Poland breaks down his categories of thought and leaves him almost beyond speech.

Gascar's narrator is assigned to a detail that takes care of a little cemetery molded with pick and shovel for French soldiers who have died: "We were a team of ghosts returning every morning to a green peaceful place, we were workers in death's garden." In a small way "death's garden" is also life's, for with solemn attentiveness the men who work there preserve the civilizing rituals of burial through which mankind has traditionally tried to give some dignity to death. Gradually signs of another kind of death assault these men, death cut off from either natural process or social ritual. The French prisoners working in their little graveyard cannot help seeing imprisoned Jews of a nearby village go about their wretched tasks. One morning they find "a man lying dead by the roadside on the way to the graveyard" who has "no distinguishing mark, save the armlet with the star of David"; and as they dig new graves for their French comrades, they discover "the arm of [a] corpse . . . pink . . . like certain roots." Their cemetery, with its carefully "idealized dead," is actually in "the middle of a charnel, a heap of corpses lying side by side. . . ." And then the trains come, with their stifled cries, "the human voice, hovering over the infinite expanse of suffering like a bird over the infinite sea." As in Claude Lanzmann's great film *Shoah*, the trains go back and forth, endlessly, in one direction filled with broken human creatures, and in the other empty. Death without coffins, without reasons, without rituals, without witnesses: the realization floods into the consciousness of the narrator and a few other prisoners. "Death can never appease this pain; this stream of black grief will flow forever"—so the narrator tells himself. No explanation follows, no consolation. There is only the enlarging grief of discovery, with the concluding sentence: "I went back to my dead"—both kinds, surely. And nothing else.

After. In a long story, "A Plaque on Via Mazzini," the Italian-Jewish writer Giorgio Bassani adopts as his narrative voice the amiable coarseness of a commonplace citizen of Ferrara, the north Italian town that before the war had four hundred Jews, one hundred eighty-three of whom were deported. One of them comes back, in August 1945: Geo Josz, bloated with the fat of endema starvation, with hands "callused beyond all belief, but with white backs where a registration

number, tattooed a bit over the right wrist . . . could be read distinctly, all five numbers, preceded by the letter J." Not unsympathetic but intent upon going about
their business, the citizens of Ferrara speak through the narrator: "What did he
want, now?" Ferrara does not know what to make of this survivor, unnerving in
his initial quiet, with his "obsessive, ill-omened face" and his bursts of sarcasm.
In his attic room Josz papers all four walls with pictures of his family, destroyed in
Buchenwald. When he meets an uncle who had fawned upon the fascists, he lets
out "a shrill cry, ridiculously, hysterically passionate, almost savage." Encountering a broken-down old count who had spied for the fascist police, he slaps him
twice—it's not so much his presence that Josz finds unbearable as his whistling
"Lili Marlene."

As if intent upon making everyone uncomfortable, Josz resumes "wearing the
same clothes he had been wearing when he came back from Germany . . . fur
hat and leather jerkin included." Even the warmhearted conclude: "It was impossible . . . to converse with a man in costume! And on the other hand, if they let him
do the talking, he immediately started telling about . . . the end of all his relatives;
and he went on like that for whole hours, until you didn't know how to get away
from him."

A few years later Josz disappears, forever, "leaving not the slightest trace after him." The Ferrarese, remembering him for a little while, "would shake their
heads good-naturedly," saying, "If he had only been a bit more patient." What
Geo Josz thinks or feels, what he remembers or wants, what boils up within him
after returning to his town, Bassani never tells. There is no need to. Bassani sees
this bit of human wreckage from a cool distance, charting the gap between Josz
and those who encounter him on the street or at a café, no doubt wishing him
well, but naturally, in their self-preoccupation, unable to enter his memories or
obsessions. His very presence is a reproach, and what, if anything, they can do to
reply or assuage they do not know. For they are ordinary people and he . . . The
rest seeps up between the words.

Aftermath. On the face of it, "My Quarrel with Hersh Rasseyner," by the Yiddish
writer Chaim Grade, is an ideological dialogue between a badly shaken skeptic,
evidently the writer himself, and a zealous believer, Hersh Rasseyner, who belongs to the Mussarist sect, "a movement that gives special importance to ethical
and ascetic elements in Judaism." But the voices of the two speakers—as they
meet across a span of years from 1937 to 1948—are so charged with passion and
sincerity that we come to feel close to both of them.

Like Grade himself, the narrator had been a Mussarist in his youth, only to
abandon the Yeshiva for a career as a secular writer. Yet something of the Yeshiva's

training in dialectic has stuck to the narrator, though Grade is shrewd enough to give the stronger voice to Hersh Rasseyner, his orthodox antagonist. What they are arguing about, presumably, are eternal questions of faith and skepticism—the possibility of divine benevolence amid the evil of His creation, the value of clinging to faith after a Holocaust that His hand did not stop. In another setting all this might seem an intellectual exercise, but here, as these two men confront one another, their dispute signifies nothing less than the terms upon which they might justify their lives. For Hersh Rasseyner the gas chambers are the inevitable outcome of a trivialized worldliness and an enfeebled morality that lacks the foundation of faith. For the narrator, the gas chambers provoke unanswerable questions about a God who has remained silent. Back and forth the argument rocks, with Hersh Rasseyner usually on the attack, for he is untroubled by doubt, while the narrator can only say: "You have a ready answer, while we have not silenced our doubts, and perhaps we will never be able to silence them." With "a cry of impotent anger against heaven"—a heaven in which he does not believe but to which he continues to speak—the narrator finally offers his hand to Hersh Rasseyner in a gesture of forlorn comradeship: "We are the remnant. . . ."

In its oppressive intensity and refusal to rest with any fixed "position," Grade's story makes us realize that even the most dreadful event in history has brought little change in the thought of mankind. History may spring endless surprises, but our responses are very limited. In the years after the Holocaust there was a certain amount of speculation that human consciousness could no longer be what it had previously been. Exactly what it might mean to say that after the Holocaust consciousness has been transformed is very hard to determine. Neither of Grade's figures—nor, to be honest, the rest of us—shows any significant sign of such a transformation. For good and bad, we remain the commonplace human stock, and whatever it is that we may do about the Holocaust we shall have to do with the worn historical consciousness received from mankind's past. In Grade's story, as in other serious fictions touching upon the Holocaust, there is neither throb of consolation nor peal of redemption, nothing but an anxious turning toward and away from what our century has left us.

7

The mind rebels against such conclusions. It yearns for compensations it knows cannot be found; it yearns for tokens of transcendence in the midst of torment. To suppose that some redemptive salvage can be eked out of the Holocaust is, as we like to say, only human. And that is one source of the falsity that seeps through a good many accounts of the Holocaust, whether fiction or memoir—as it seeps through the language of many high-minded commentators. "To talk of despair," writes Albert Camus, "is to conquer it." Is it now? "The destiny of the Jewish people, whom no earthly power has ever been able to defeat"—so speaks a character in Jean-François Steiner's novel about a revolt in Treblinka. Perhaps appropriate for someone urging fellow-prisoners into a doomed action, such sentiments, if allowed to determine the moral scheme of Holocaust writing, lead to self-delusion. The plain and bitter truth is that while Hitler did not manage to complete the "Final Solution," he did manage to destroy an entire Jewish world.

"It is foolish," writes Primo Levi, "to think that human justice can eradicate" the crimes of Auschwitz. Or that the human imagination can encompass and transfigure them. Some losses cannot be made up, neither in time nor in eternity. They can only be mourned. In a poem entitled "Written in Pencil in the Sealed Freight Car," the Israeli poet Don Pagis writes:

> Here in this transport
> I Eve
> and Abel my son
> if you should see my older son
> Cain son of man
> tell him that I

Cry to heaven or cry to earth: that sentence will never be completed.

Reaganism: The Spirit of the Times
{1986}

FRANKLIN ROOSEVELT'S NEW DEAL constituted, let us say, a quarter-revolution. It introduced the rudiments of a welfare state and made "the socialization of concern" into a national value. It signified not a society egalitarian or even just, but at least one that modulated the harshness of "rugged individualism." All later administrations, at least until that of Reagan, more or less accepted the New Deal legacy. Under Reagan, America experienced, let us say, a quarter-counterrevolution.

Segments of the American bourgeoisie had never accepted the general premise or sparse practice of what passed in America for a welfare state; they lived with it faute de mieux, waiting for a chance to shake off trade unions, social measures, and economic regulations. Ideological in a primitive way, they would have stared with incomprehension if you had suggested that their survival as a class might well have been due to the very social measures they despised. And then their moment came—with the inner disintegration of liberalism under Carter that opened the way for Reagan.

The more hard-bitten and fanatic Reaganites brought to office a maximum program: to undo the New Deal, which meant to demolish the fraction of a welfare state we have. When the limits of this perspective became clear to Reagan's

managers (most starkly after his administration's defeat in Congress when it
tried to tamper with Social Security), the Reaganites fell back, shrewdly enough,
on their minimum program. They would weaken, reduce, cripple, starve out the
welfare state. And in this they often succeeded. While leaving intact the external
structures of certain programs, they proceeded, with firm ideological malice, to
cut out and cut down a good many other programs. They brought about a measurable redistribution of income and wealth in behalf of the rich, and they repelled any attempt to pass further social legislation—not that the chickenhearted
Democrats made much of an attempt. Perhaps most important, the Reaganites
managed to create a political atmosphere in which the social forces favoring the
welfare state were forced onto the defensive. The very idea of a national health
act, for example, was no longer even mentioned by the few remaining liberals in
Congress.

Now there were sectarians—the right is blessed with them as well as the left—
who complained that Reagan did not go far enough. David Stockman judged Reagan to be "a consensus politician, not an ideologue." This was a dumb remark,
since it has been Reagan's peculiar skill to combine the two roles—consensus
politician and ideologue—just as he has put the politics of theater at the service of ideological politics. After all, to be an ideologue doesn't necessarily mean
to commit political suicide; as a Washington hand is quoted, "Reagan has never
been one to go over a cliff for a cause" (*Newsweek*, April 7, 1986). The shrewder
Reaganites understood that if they clung at all costs to their maximum program,
they might not even get their minimum. When it comes to political reality, Stockman has nothing to teach Reagan.

But the main achievement of the Reagan administration has not been institutional or programmatic. It has consisted of a spectacular transformation of popular attitudes, values, and styles, though how deep or durable this will prove to be
we cannot yet know. In a country where only two decades ago a sizable portion
of the population registered distrust of corporate America, the Reaganites have
largely succeeded in restoring popular confidence in the virtues of capitalism,
the mystical beneficence of "the free market," and the attractiveness of a "minimalist state," even though that state, faithfully attending to corporate needs, has
never been close to being minimalist. In the long run, the brilliant manipulation
of popular sentiment by Reagan and his men may turn out to be more important
than their economic and social enactments.

A certain worldview, not exactly fresh but with some clever decorations, has
come to dominate public discourse. Let me try briefly to sift out the main elements of the Reaganite vision.

The primacy of "success," the release of greed. For the segment of Reaganite operatives and backers that came from or represented the new rich of the West and Southwest—real estate developers, oil millionaires, movie magnates, in short, the arriviste bourgeoisie—the policies of the Reagan administration were immediately helpful. Still more important was the largesse with which these policies sanctioned appetites of acquisitiveness and greed that had been present, of course, before Reagan's presidency but not quite so blatantly or unashamedly. It was as if J.R. had found spiritual comrades in the White House, or even an office next door to, say, Michael Deaver. The inner circles of Reaganites and their managerial supporters throughout the country were sublimely untroubled by the cautions of certain skeptics (Felix Rohatyn, for one) in the Eastern financial establishment. Deaver's squalid story—his exploitation of White House connections in behalf of his lobbying firm—was just a minor instance of the by now commonplace shuttling between high governmental posts, especially in the Pentagon, and corporate boardrooms. It will take some years before we know the whole story of this jolly interpenetration between officialdom and corporations, but it takes no gifts of prophecy to foresee that, in its subservience to big money, the Reagan administration is likely to equal or surpass those of Grant and Harding.

The new rich, tasting power and light-headed with a whiff of ideology, could now have it both ways. They could persuade themselves that it was quite legitimate, indeed "the American way," to grab as much as they could, and "Screw you, Jack," if you suffered the consequences; while they were also morally comforted with the fairy tale that the sum of their selfishness would, through a sleight of "the invisible hand," come out as a public good. The corporate buccaneers who now felt free to act out the ethos of Social Darwinism could also preach that "the free market" brought plenty to all (which didn't, however, keep corporate America from pressing for every form of governmental handout that would further its economic interests). After all, few human experiences can be as satisfying as the simultaneous discharge of low desires and high sentiments.

The fever spread. While industrial America was being devastated and thousands of farmers trembled on the edge of bankruptcy, the corporate and financial "community" indulged in a spree of raids and mergers, almost all of them unproductive, sterile, asocial, but decidedly profitable. New terms entered our language: arbitrage, asset-shuffling, golden parachute, junk bonds, among others. New generations of profiteers, yuppies with clever brains and no minds, flourished in investment banking. A few may end in jail for "insider" trading. *Newsweek* (May 26, 1986) quotes a disillusioned Wall Streeter: "We have created two myths in the 1980s. One is that you need to be smart to be an investment banker. That's wrong. Finance is easy. Myth number two is that investment bankers somehow create value. They don't. They shuffle around value other people have created. It's a parasitical industry."

Reading about these young Wall Streeters, baby-faced creatures of the Reagan moment, one feels, almost, a kind of pity for them. Caught in illegal maneuvers, which in pleading guilty they now say were known to the top people in their firms, they seem like petty scapegoats, small fry who had not yet learned what the big fellows know: that you can evade the law without breaking it or can make yourself a bundle while remaining just this side of the law since, after all, it's your kind of law.

A psychiatrist, Samuel Klagsbrun, who treats "a lot of lawyers handling mergers and acquisitions," says that for these people "business is God" (Wall Street Journal, June 2, 1986). A young arbitrager reports that everyone "seems to want to make the quick buck. [They] move out into the left lane, put it into overdrive and hope the brakes don't fail when they hit the first curve" (Newsweek, May 26, 1986).

And more sedately, Ira Sorkin, the New York director of the Securities and Exchange Commission, says, "Greed knows no bounds. There's always someone who makes more than you do. Investment banking is the new gold mine" (New York Times, June 2, 1986).

Earning around a million dollars a year, some of these arbitragers and dealmakers live by a scale of values that can only repel Americans who still keep a fraction of the republic's animating values. Here is Hamilton James, thirty-five, of the firm Donaldson Lupkin, who shovels in over a million a year but says that "if we [his family] want a library and a room for an au pair girl, it could cost a couple million dollars. If it's anything fancy, four or five million" (Wall Street Journal, June 2, 1986). Any bets on what he'll pay the au pair girl?

None of this is new. There were Drew and Fisk, Morgan and Rockefeller in the days of and after the robber barons. There were the boys of Teapot Dome. There was Calvin Coolidge, who declared, "The business of America is business." There was Charlie Wilson, who said, "What's good for General Motors is good for the United States." Yet something is new, at least for the years since 1933, and that's the social and moral sanction that Reaganism has given to the ethos of greed. The Reagan administration did not "cause" the Wall Street shenanigans I've mentioned; Reagan himself need not say, like Richard Nixon, "I am not a crook," since no one supposes he is; but the bent of his policy, the tone of his rhetoric, the signals of his response have all enabled, indeed encouraged, the atmosphere of greed.

A few years ago our national heroes were men like Jonas Salk and Martin Luther King and Walter Reuther, but now it's an industrial manager like Lee Iacocca,
of Pinto fame, whose book is supposed to show even morons how to become
millionaires. Iacocca stars in a television commercial that wonderfully articulates
the spirit of the times: he strides through a factory in heroic style, blaring out the
virtues of his product, while behind him follows a group of autoworkers, mute
and cheerful, happy with the beneficence of Lee the First.

The lure of an earlier America, or the corruptions of nostalgia. Whether intuitively or by
calculation, the Reaganites grasped how deeply the collective imagination of this
country responded to "pictures" of an earlier, often mythic America—"pictures"
of small towns, rugged personal virtues, family stability, and sturdy yeomen cul-
tivating their own farms. The less such "pictures" correspond to social reality, the
greater their appeal, for it is obviously more pleasant to reflect upon the America
of Franklin and Jefferson than that of Exxon and IBM. And while much of this
pastoral nostalgia is manipulated by political hucksters, who have apparently
learned something from the commercials of Marlboro cigarettes and Busch beer,
there is still, it is important to remember, something authentic being exploited
here, a memory prettied up and sweetened but a genuine memory nonetheless.

Badly shaken by Watergate, the Vietnam War, and the countercultural excesses
of the late 1960s, many Americans have come to yearn for a return to "traditional
values," even if that return was being sponsored politically by a nouveau-riche
class which aspired most of all to conspicuous consumption. In any case, we are
paying now for the crude anti-Americanism, the feckless nose-thumbing and
flag-burning that marked a good part of the counterculture in the late 1960s. We
are paying for its insensitivity to native speech and sentiment, an insensitivity
that, strangely, is itself part of American tradition. Much of the Reaganite reaction, though eventuating in concrete socioeconomic policies, drew upon feelings
of hurt that were held by people not necessarily reactionaries or even conservatives. These feelings were exploited skillfully; many of us on the left quite under-
estimated the power of vague, incantatory appeals to "tradition"—just as we also
warned, to little avail, that the hijinks of "the young" in the late 1960s would be
paid for later by the workers, the poor, women, and minorities.

We live in a curiously mixed situation. On the one hand, a managed passivity,
submission to television captions, apparent indifference to social suffering, political chicanery, and a blundering president—the expected elements of a "mass
society." On the other hand, strong new popular movements that mobilize previously silent segments of the population to struggle over issues like abortion,
prayer in the schools, the death penalty, and so on. Such movements are hardly

symptoms of a "mass society"; they represent a shrewd appropriation by the right of methods and energies through which labor and liberals helped create a (sort of) welfare state.

Fundamentalism is familiar enough in American history, but the political energies and moral virulence characterizing it today may be rather new. When lined with religious passion and cast as agent of traditional values, right-wing politics takes on a formidable strength.

Pastoral nostalgia, individualist appeals, traditional values, religious fervor— it is the mixture of all these into one stream of collective sentiment that the Reaganites have managed. And up to a point it has worked: many Americans do "feel better about their country," if only because they have a president who says what they wish to hear. One reason this intellectual scam has worked is that so far, with perhaps the exception of Mario Cuomo, no political leader in the opposition has grasped emotionally the power of native speech and symbol. If, as I believe, we are paying for the irresponsibility of the countercultural left, we are also paying for the desiccation of liberalism, which in the figure of Jimmy Carter was reduced to a technological cipher.

It would be foolhardy in a few pages to try to sort out the many strands of American individualism, still one of the strongest components of national myth and belief. The Reaganites do have some claim upon this tradition: there is a clear line of descent from a corrupted late Emersonianism to the "rugged individualism" of Herbert Hoover to the "possessive individualism" of today (to possess: to grab). But the right has no historical ground for the *exclusiveness* of its claim within the American individualist tradition. There is, in reality, no single tradition; there is only an interweaving of many elements in complex, confused, and often contradictory ways. If individualism has often been used to justify economic depredation, it has also provided support to social critics standing alone, and independently, against government and mob, from the Mexican to the Vietnam wars. What is sad is that, through a default of will and imagination, the speech and symbols of individualism have been allowed to fall into the hands of the right.

The power of ideology (or: In America a little goes a long way). Reagan's most effective slogan has been "Get the government off our backs." It appeals to Americans who transfer their frustrations to "the bureaucrats." It appeals to Americans whose small businesses have been squeezed or destroyed by giant competitors. It appeals to Americans bewildered by the merger mania, known in earlier days as the concentration of capital. But above all, it appeals to the executives and managers of Big Business whose institutions were rescued from probable collapse by the welfare state but who never reconciled themselves to the agents of their rescue, and who now feel free to release their yearning for the good old days of "rugged individualism" and union busting.

Sensible people know that the talk about getting the government out of economic life has not led to a significant decline of government intervention in the economy. Indeed, it could not. It has only changed, in a reactionary direction, the social character and goals of government intervention. The policies of the Federal Reserve Board constitute a major intervention into economic life. The readiness of the federal government to bail out Lockheed, Chrysler, and Penn Central is quite as decisive an intervention as a program, if there were one, to help bankrupt farmers and create jobs for the unemployed. As John Kenneth Galbraith tartly observes, "Senator Jesse Helms stands staunchly and rhetorically for the free market and for a uniquely rigorous quota and licensing system for the tobacco producers (or landowners) who help to assure his election" (*New York Review of Books*, June 26, 1986).

About one thing we can be quite certain: the interpenetration of state and society, government and economy is an inescapable fact of modern life. Serious conservatives know this. Deputy Secretary of the Treasury Richard Darman says in a moment of candor: "We've been in the business of economic planning as long as we've been in the business of practical politics" (*New Republic*, May 5, 1986). The only question, but a big one, is whether the government's economic role will be progressive or regressive.

Exposing the cant about "getting the government off our backs," while necessary, is not likely to suffice. For the ideology behind such talk does speak to certain realities: the visible bureaucratization of large institutions, whether private corporations or segments of the state. But this ideology does not speak honestly or realistically to these facts of modern life. Nevertheless, especially when fused with nostalgia for American individualism, this ideological gambit is going to be effective, at least until put to the test of crisis—what can it say to the increasing poverty of even these boom years?—as well as to the test of deceitful practice— what credence does the "free market" rhetoric of a Jesse Helms merit when set against his insistence on government privileges for his tobacco constituency?

The ideology of a reclaimed laissez-faire is having a "run" in some parts of the industrialized world, especially because of social democratic and liberal inadequacies, though only in the United States and Great Britain has it had a modest economic success. The battle between advocates and opponents of the welfare state—which, like it or not, today has greater political urgency than an abstract counterposition between capitalism and socialism—will continue to the end of this century. But meanwhile there are some new ideological wrinkles.

The corporations have discovered the importance of ideas, or at least the manipulation of ideas. Some nine or ten years ago I noticed, in one of those institutional ads that corporations print on the *New York Times* op ed page, a quotation from the literary critic Lionel Trilling. This struck me as a turning point in intellectual life, or at least in our public relations, coming as it did only a few years after some writers had proclaimed "the end of ideology." In the last decade, under the shrewd guardianship of the neoconservative intellectuals—who offer their thoughts to the corporations, though not for free—corporate America has discovered the pragmatic uses of ideology, the importance of entering intellectual debate, and consequently has poured millions into foundations, magazines, conferences. Mobil and Exxon, borrowing apparently from the pages of *Public Interest*, offer solemn essays on political economy; the investment house of Shearson Lehman flashes snappy statements on television about the virtues of capitalism. Credit for enticing the corporations into ideological battle must go in part to Irving Kristol, who has made himself into a sort of back-room broker between the corporations and the Republican Party on one hand and available intellectuals on the other. He has taught American businessmen, at least some of them, the elementary lesson that social struggle takes place, perhaps most of all, in people's heads and that just as dropping some change into the cultural programs of public broadcasting helps create an "aura," so the interests of the business community may be served by subsidizing magazines like *New Criterion* and *Public Interest*, as well as the network of institutes, committees, foundations, and journals in which the neocons flourish.

There are times, however, when our corporate leaders forget all the babble about social responsibility and lapse into mere truth. Here is John Akers, chief executive of IBM, on divesting in South Africa: "If we elect to leave, it will be a business decision. . . . We are not in business to conduct moral activity. We are not in business to conduct socially responsible action. We are in business to conduct business" (*New York Times*, April 23, 1986). One can almost hear Kristol gently remonstrating: Yes, yes, John, but do you have to *say* it?

The war whoop of chauvinism. Shrewdly seizing upon a popular reaction against the often vulgar and mindless anti-Americanism of the late 1960s, the Reagan administration has succeeded partly in blotting out memories of the disastrous and destructive American intervention in Vietnam. A new national mood has been programmed. It's symbolized, half in myth, half in parody, by Rambo. It is released in the unsportsmanlike displays at the Los Angeles Olympics. It is embodied, more fiercely, in the indefensible Reaganite policy of intervening in Nicaragua. And it is raised to a pitch of madness in the Star Wars program (which E. P. Thompson has shrewdly described as an instance of American "individualism" gone berserk . . . the lone cowboy now ascending the heavens to clean up the rustlers). This new national mood draws upon two contradictory emotions held with about equal intensity: first, everybody has been kicking poor little America around; and second, we're the strongest country in the world (as was proved once and for all in Grenada) and we're going to straighten things out, even if we have to call in John Wayne to help out Ron.

2

A consequence of these transformations in public discourse has been a debasement in the social tone of American life, the texture of shared feelings, the unspoken impulses and biases. About such things one can only speak impressionistically, but we all recognize them. They strike upon our nerves. We are living in a moment of moral smallness, a curdling of generosity, a collapse of idealism. I don't mean to suggest that most ordinary Americans have become morally bad—of course not; only that the moral styles, the tones of speech and qualities of symbol which the Reagan administration and its journalistic and intellectual allies encourage are pinched and narrow-spirited, sometimes downright mean.

How else do you explain the readiness of a thirty-five-year-old arbitrager publicly to say that adding "a library and a room for the *au pair* girl" would come to four or five million dollars—and this at a time when thousands of New Yorkers had no homes last winter? This chap might have felt the same way at an earlier moment, but he would have been too cautious or ashamed to say it. Now, in the Reagan era, it's acceptable. Or, for that matter, how else do you explain that someone like Ed Koch can gain favor through a smirking double-talk that shows the folks in front of the tube how to put down blacks without quite saying so.

To live under an administration that featured such notables as James Watt and Rita Lavelle; in which the attorney general declares poverty in America to be merely "anecdotal," and the president himself (ignoring massive evidence, some of it accumulated by his own administration) announces that people go hungry in America only if they lack information on how to get help; in which the head of the Civil Rights Commission is part Uncle Tom and part, it seems, huckster; in which the president dares to compare the Somocista contras, some of them proven killers, with Washington and Jefferson—is to recall again the force of Brecht's sentence about another (still more) evil time: "He who laughs has not yet heard the terrible tidings."

The favored tone of worldly, or sometimes macho, indifference to the plight of the jobless and the homeless cuts through the whole range of the people in power and their intellectual allies. The sensibilities of the country's elites, all those who make policy and shape opinion, harden. We see it in the systematic refusal of the Reagan administration even to consider programs that would provide jobs for the unemployed; in the steady deterioration of OSHA-determined work safety regulations in factories; in the disdain lining even the surface of official policy toward blacks; in the steady efforts of the civil rights division of the Justice Department to sabotage affirmative action; in the surrender of the Koch administration in New York City to luxury developers; in the admiration shown a gun-toter like Bernhard Goetz; in the mere fact that a rag like the *New York Post* can survive.

3

How deep and durable is this shift in public sentiment? Will the rightward turn continue after Reagan? For that matter, is there a turn to the right? A not-very-profound article in the *Atlantic* (May 1986) argues that there has not been one. Its authors, Thomas Ferguson and Joel Rogers, produce an array of poll results showing that majorities of respondents still favor many of the programs associated with liberalism. How then, you may wonder, did Reagan manage to get reelected? Simple, conclude our authors: the economic situation got better and most people vote their pocketbooks.

This would be comforting if true, but at the very least it requires complication. If a majority of Americans favor liberal measures yet a majority of voters chose Reagan, doesn't this suggest that the appeal of the president and his slogans was deeper, more telling than any (perhaps fading or residual or formal) attachment to liberal programs? The polls do not measure *intensity* of commitment, or which of two conflicting sets of opinions held simultaneously may be the stronger. Evidently, for many Americans the appeal of Reagan and at least some of what he represents was stronger than the attachment to welfare-state measures. And that would seem to signify a shift to the right, would it not?

I don't claim to know how strong or lasting this shift will prove to be. One need only look at the dominant style of opinion within the Democratic Party to see that the rightward shift has all but overcome those who are supposed to resist it. (The code word is "pragmatic.") The very tone of the opposition, such as it is, which the leading Democrats adopt seems clear evidence that the Reaganites have come to set the terms of the debate. Liberal proposals are virtually invisible at the Democratic top. When was the last time that even Senator Ted Kennedy spoke out in favor of his once-featured project of a national health bill? Or that any of the leading Democrats remembered the Humphrey-Hawkins Full Employment Act? Except in their response to Reagan's outrageous feeler about canceling SALT II, the posture of the leading Democrats is defensive—or, worse still, acquiescent, as when Senator Bill Bradley votes for aid to the Nicaraguan contras.

4

Few things about the national condition are more depressing than the collapse of American liberalism. To recall Lionel Trilling's once-famous remark of the 1950s—that in America liberalism is the only viable political tradition—is to thrust oneself back into another world. In the face of the Reaganite victory, the organizational and ideological collapse of American liberalism has been astonishing. Hardly a politician dares acknowledge himself to be a liberal, the very word itself having come to seem a political handicap.

Of the older intellectual spokesmen for liberalism, Arthur Schlesinger, Jr. and John Kenneth Galbraith are still heard from on occasion, but they are understandably intent upon writing their own books and perhaps, again understandably, are weary of polemic. Schlesinger advances a consoling theory—consoling if true—about the periodicity of American politics, according to which the next swing of the pendulum will bring us happily back to liberalism (but why must the pendulum keep swinging?). Galbraith aims his neatly ironic shafts against Reaganomics, but with a world-weariness that seems to despair of ever again striking a blow that will tell. As for other social analysts who defend liberal measures and values—writers like Robert Kuttner, Barbara Ehrenreich, Michael Harrington, Robert Reich, Jeff Faux, among others—they are mostly spokesmen for the democratic left who have been forced, in these trying times, to pick up the slack of liberalism. What might be called mainstream liberalism seems quite unable to attract talented new advocates who can speak to audiences beyond the confines of the academy.

Why, one wonders, has American liberalism suffered so severe a decline? That there should have been losses; that the usual crew of opportunists should desert; that veterans would grow tired and step aside—all were to be expected. But so utter a rout? Is it possible, as some writers of the sectarian left have said, that liberalism in America has "exhausted itself"? A full answer to this question will have to wait for others, but here let me note a few possible causes for the unhappy state of American liberalism.

Fundamentally, I'd suggest, we have been witnessing the all-but-inevitable disintegration which affects every party or movement that has held power for a length of time. Success breeds complacency, obtuseness, and corruption, and these in turn make for an incapacity to see, let alone confront, the problems created by success. As long as the American economy was expanding and Keynesian prescriptions were more or less working, New Deal liberalism and its offshoots could retain vitality. But once they had to confront problems no longer soluble through the by now conventional New Deal measures—problems like the Vietnam War, third-world eruptions (Iran), the radical transformation of the world economy, new productive techniques, inflation, and so on—liberalism fell apart. The time had come for policies of a social-democratic slant but these an increasingly insecure liberalism would not approach. The comforts of office, the fears of yesterday's innovators before the risks of tomorrow's innovations—all disabled American liberalism.

Where in the 1930s liberalism was at least in part based on mass movements, notably the trade unions, and could claim a large popular suffrage, by the 1970s it had narrowed into an electoral apparatus or "political class" getting on in years and too much at ease with itself and its received ideas. By contrast, it should in honesty be said, at least some conservatives tried to engage in programmatic thought, speculating in their newly developed think tanks on the problems and contradictions, some contingent but others perhaps fundamental, of the welfare state in a capitalist economy. (That the welfare state might have inherent contradictions was an idea that rarely, if ever, surfaced in liberal thought.) After a time, the once-magical names of Roosevelt and Kennedy lost their glamour; new generations appeared that had little interest in the past and less capacity for memory. Liberalism, once at least occasionally linked with social insurgency, now came to be identified with a troubled status quo: a government that had dragged us into an indefensible war in Vietnam and by the mid-1970s was encountering economic difficulties (stagflation, unemployment) for which it knew no remedies.

The bureaucratization of liberalism, perhaps an unavoidable cost of its success, also meant that it came increasingly to depend on the intervention of the judiciary, especially on such difficult matters as school busing; and this too contributed to the decline of its popular base. As liberalism lost its charge of innovative energy, the conservative movement appropriated many of the techniques of liberalism's earlier, more heroic days. For what the conservatives now undertook to do, and in part succeeded in doing, was to build articulate popular constituencies.

With Jimmy Carter's victory in 1976, the disintegration of American liberalism quickened. A tradition that in the past had at least partly drawn upon social ideal-ism and popular commitment now dwindled into the outlook of an intelligent technocrat. As the political scientists celebrated the ascendency of "pragmatism" (a term that relieves many people of the need for thinking), another triumph was in preparation, that of the ideologically aroused Reaganites.

Well, then, is liberalism "exhausted"—not for the moment but historically, finally? Is it being swept off the historical stage, as dogmatists of right and left gleefully assert? If so, the situation of the American left, precarious enough al-ready, is far worse than we might suppose, for every lesson of American history teaches us that the left in America flourishes mostly during the times when liber-alism flourishes. In any case, it is clearly probable that a collapse of liberalism will benefit the right far more than the left.

We ought to be skeptical about theories of liberalism's "exhaustion," if only because they bear an embarrassing resemblance to earlier, dubious theories about capitalism's "inevitable collapse." American liberalism at its best has a rich tradition: a worldview devoted to political freedom, pluralist ways of life, and programs for social change. This liberalism has seen bad times, but found itself again; some of its leading figures have yielded to shoddy deals, others have stood firm by first principles. In bad shape right now, it could regain cogency if it were to confront socioeconomic problems more complex, and requiring more radical answers, than those of the New Deal era. Neither success nor failure is ordained: men and women still make their history, at least some of it.

5

Criticism and more criticism—that's the need of the moment, the need for tomorrow. Criticism of an administration that exalts greed and ignores need. Criticism of military chauvinism. Criticism of all those who, in the name of an abstract equality, would deny blacks a few steps toward equality through affirma-tive action. Criticism of every deal or accord with authoritarian dictatorships. And criticism of "our side" too, of the sluggishness of portions of the labor move-ment, of the collapse of the hopes raised by the French Socialists, of the intellec-tual drabness of much social democracy.

One needn't be a socialist to engage in such criticism. On some matters, such as the environment, not being a socialist may even render the criticism more ef-fective. But to scan our society from the perspective of democratic socialism of-fers at least this advantage: it enables a deep-going criticism of the imbalances of wealth and power in our corporate-dominated society, so that we can see those imbalances not as mere blemishes but as injustices built into the very structure of capitalist economy. Perhaps not an advantage in the immediate tactical sense, but very much so for serious intellectual work.

Even if the criticism is not as "fundamental" as we might like, let it be heard. Let people of determination, steady workers with some humor and no fanaticism, keep saying: "This is not what America is supposed to be, this is not how human beings should live."

The 1990s

Two Cheers for Utopia
{1993}

WE LIVE IN A TIME of diminished expectations. It's not exactly a time of conservative dominance, although the dominant politics in some countries is an unenthusiastic conservatism. Nor is it a time of liberal dominance, although in the United States the Clinton administration has given rise to some liberal hopes, by no means certain of realization. And it's certainly not a time of leftist domination, even though moderate social democratic parties hold office in some European countries.

It's tempting to compare this post–cold war moment to the postrevolutionary decades of early nineteenth-century England. But the comparison is of slight value, since what we are experiencing might better be called a postcounterrevolutionary moment. Idealistic visions, utopian hopes, desires for social renovation are all out of fashion — indeed, are regarded as dangerous illusions that set off memories of totalitarian disasters. Leftist bashing, in both newspaper editorials and learned books, is very much in. The current catchword is sobriety, which sometimes looks like a cover for depression.

This is true of the intellectual world, with the exception of a few mavericks like Günter Grass. It is also true for what remains of the European left—either solid,

315

decent social democrats with barely a touch of fire left in them or unrepentant communists masquerading as socialists in Eastern Europe.

There are, of course, many reasons for this mood indigo, only a few years after the enthusiasm raised by the "velvet revolution" in Czechoslovakia and the Gorbachev reforms in the former Soviet Union. But in this comment I want to focus on only one reason: the aftermath, or perhaps more accurately, the aftertaste of the collapse of communism.

Some years ago Theodore Draper made a remark in conversation that has stuck in my mind: the central experience of the twentieth century, he said, was communism, like it or hate it. To be sure, there was fascism and the end of colonialism, but fascism could be seen as essentially a ghastly reaction to the rise of radicalism and the end of colonialism as an all-but-inevitable cluster of events. In its years of influence and power, communism seized upon the imagination of millions of people throughout the world. Communist parties were powerful in most of the major European countries; a bit later, they appropriated the heritage of anticolonialism in Asian and African countries; and even in the United States, where the Communist party was never a major force, it has been reliably estimated that nearly a million people passed through the Stalinist milieu (not the party) between, say, 1920 and 1950.

Declaring itself the legatee of humanism and the bearer of good news, communism inspired thousands—no, hundreds of thousands—of workers, students, intellectuals, to feats of devotion and, sometimes, heroism. Seldom have so many good people sacrificed themselves for so bad a cause. There were of course careerists, hacks, and thugs in the communist movement; but for many ordinary people "the movement" burned with flames of hope. Those of us who were long-time anti-Stalinists, enclosed in our little groups and sects, found it hard to acknowledge the idealism—twisted, distorted, corrupted yet idealism nonetheless—that went into the communist movement. To be sure, in the East European countries the communist dictatorships attracted a large share of careerists (the kinds of people who in the United States might have been Republican officeholders). But there, too, the communists gained the support of decent, misguided followers. When the anti-Stalinist groups won over a handful of people from the Communist parties, it was almost always people who were intellectually and psychologically exhausted, their fanaticism burned out and their intellectual energies diminished.

The communist movement destroyed entire generations. The sheer waste of human resources, of the energies that might have been available for social renovation, is incalculable. With many rank-and-file militants, the sequel has been silence. With a good many former communist leaders, the sequel has been an ugly form of nationalism—as in Yugoslavia, where the leaders of both Serbia and Croatia are former prominent communists.

The results of this great historical disaster are staggering. Even those of us in the United States, insulated by our native mythologies, who were never tempted by Communism, are experiencing the consequences. New generations, new energies do not arrive overnight. There has first to be an interval of weariness, disillusionment, "pragmatism"—and diminished expectations.

You can see the signs of this exhaustion if you pick up any of the leading intellectual journals. Some are sour (usually edited by ex-radicals) and others are timid (usually edited by quasiliberals). Some subsist by mocking the hopes of their youth. Others avoid any long-range expectations or desires. Still others narrow their focus of concern to the daily routines of politics, sometimes saying useful things, though not much more.

What I've been saying here holds, I'm afraid, for large segments of the European social democracy. Let me be clear: if I lived in any of the major European countries, I would belong to or support the social democratic party. I might be critical, I might tilt a little toward whatever left wing it had. But I would be part of it.

Yet the truth is that, except in one or two countries, social democracy today has become a decent and honorable party that (rhetoric apart—and that even less and less) does not really aspire to move beyond the status quo. Little of the spirit of socialism remains in these parties. That much said, it's only fair to add that this isn't entirely their fault. For one thing, the constituencies of these parties, the people who vote for them, also share in their spiritual hesitation, their intellectual skepticism and bewilderment. It's not as if "the masses" are pressing the social democrats for a more radical outlook. Nor is it as if there were a clear socialist idea or vision that the parties reject. For the truth—as every *Dissent* reader learns from every issue we publish, perhaps to excess—is that the socialist idea is as precarious as the ideas of the conservatives and liberals, though the latter have the advantage of being at ease with the existing social and political order, while the social democrats presumably desire some change. The difficulty of formulating an attractive program is far more serious for the social democrats than for their opponents. Devoted to decency and democracy—no small matters—the social democrats cannot evoke the idealism and selflessness of the socialist yesterday. The memories of yesterday grow dimmer; one of the last to embody these was Willy Brandt, and now he is gone.

So there really is no point in the old-style leftist denunciation of social democracy. What we can and should criticize the social democrats for is not that they have failed to come up with the "answers"; it is for having largely abandoned the questions.

Well, we *Dissenters*, the handful of us, try to hold fast to the vision of social transformation, even as we have dropped many of the traditional proposals for how to reach it. Some of us call this belief socialism, out of a wish for historical continuity or for lack of a better label. It's not that we're smarter than most European social democrats; not at all. Our advantage, if that's what it is, consists in the fact that we are distant from power and therefore able or, indeed, driven to think in terms of long-range possibilities, the revival of the democratic left in what may turn out to be the not-very-near future. Of course we also respond to immediate issues, so that *Dissent* carries articles about taxes, health care, budget crises, and so on. But even if, at a given moment, the immediate issues loom large, at least some of us want to think in terms of long-range options. We want, that is, to avoid the provincialism of the immediate.

That's why in almost every issue of *Dissent* you'll find one or two articles about "market socialism" or allied topics. Some of our readers, I suspect, quietly skip past these articles. That's OK, as long as they see why we print them. Often enough, these articles are provisional, a little abstract, and inclined to disagreements with one another. They don't necessarily paint a picture of an actual future—who can? But they are efforts to indicate possibilities of renewal. They provide materials for developments some of us will never live to see. They are, if you please, sketches of utopia.

That word "utopia" has come into disrepute. In much intellectual discussion it tends to be used as a term of dismissal. And, of course, there are versions of utopia—based on force or terror or the will of a self-appointed "vanguard"—that are abhorrent. We have had enough of these.

But there are other utopias. There is the democratic utopianism that runs like a bright thread through American intellectual life—call it Emersonianism, call it republicanism, call it whatever you like. There is the utopia of community and egalitarianism.

In an essay Lewis Coser and I wrote some forty years ago in the second issue of *Dissent*, we quoted a passage from Ernst Cassirer that still speaks to our condition:

A Utopia is not a portrait of the real world, of the actual political or social order. It exists at no moment of time and at no point in space; it is a "nowhere." But just such a conception of a nowhere has stood the test and proved its strength in the development of the modern world. It follows from the nature and character of ethical thought that it can never condescend to the "given." The ethical world is never given; it is forever in the making.

In the sense that Cassirer speaks of it, utopianism is a necessity of the moral imagination. It doesn't necessarily entail a particular politics; it doesn't ensure wisdom about current affairs. What it does provide is a guiding perspective, a belief or hope for the future, an understanding that nothing is more mistaken than the common notion that what exists today will continue to exist tomorrow. This kind of utopianism is really another way of appreciating the variety and surprise that history makes possible—possible, nothing more. It is a testimony to the resourcefulness that humanity now and then displays (together with other, far less attractive characteristics). It is a claim for the value of desire, the practicality of yearning—as against the deadliness of acquiescing in the "given" simply because it is here.

With all due modesty, I think this version of utopianism speaks for us. So, to friend and foe, at a moment when the embers of utopianism seem very low, I'd say: You want to call us utopians? That's fine with me.

The Road Leads Far Away: Review
of A Surplus of Memory
{1993}

THIS UNFORGETTABLE BOOK contains the memoirs of Yitzhak Zuckerman, a leader of the Warsaw Ghetto uprising, which took place exactly
fifty years ago this April. Zuckerman, who used the pseudonym "Antek"
in the underground, was among the handful of Jewish fighters who survived the
rebellion. After the war he settled in Israel, and in the early 1970s he dictated his
memoirs while living in the Ghetto Fighters Kibbutz in the Galilee. He died in
1981 at the age of 66. His memoirs have now been translated and edited, superbly,
by Barbara Harshav, who provides almost all the auxiliary information a reader
might need. (The one thing missing is a map of Warsaw and its environs.)

A *Surplus of Memory* is an essential testimony. Zuckerman lacks the literary
skills of Nadezhda Mandelstam, but his memoirs can stand together with *Hope
Against Hope* as revelations of what it meant to live and to die in the totalitarian
age. Zuckerman speaks plainly, without verbal flourish or the wanton rhetoric
that has disfigured some writings about the Holocaust. He sometimes gets his
chronology entangled, he sometimes repeats himself, and he sometimes refers
to people and movements with which, despite the editor's excellent annotations,
an American reader is not likely to be familiar. No matter. His memoirs hold one

relentlessly. The dryness of his voice as he recalls terrible events comes to seem a sign of moral strength.

To supplement Zuckerman, I turned to Yisroel Gutman's *The Jews of Warsaw, 1939–1943*, a first-rate historical narrative that was published by Indiana University Press a few years ago. Because Gutman was able to use both German and Polish sources, his work has a completeness that Zuckerman cannot claim. If you have strong nerves, read the two together. Even if you don't have strong nerves . . .

When the Polish army collapsed before the Nazi attack in 1939, the Jews of Poland found themselves in a state of disarray and fear. Whoever could, fled. But the majority of Jews, who could not flee, hoped to survive—*iberlebn* in Yiddish—the Nazi occupation in the ways that Jews had survived in previous wars, through a mixture of submission and dogged persistence, and by trying to exploit the differences among the conquerors, specifically, between the S.S., intent above all upon exterminating Jews, and the Wehrmacht, intent primarily upon military victory. This latter strategy was effective only in a few instances, since most of the time the German army knuckled under to the S.S.

Neither the Polish Jews nor anyone else had any idea of what lay ahead. Historical precedents were of little use, and often they were completely misleading. When word began to filter through in later months about mass executions of Jews near Vilna and Chelmno, the messengers, according to Gutman, reported that "not a single person believed their stories about the outright exterminations." In any case, added some Warsaw Jews, such things simply could not happen in their city.

Though previously a well-organized community with strong secular parties, the Polish Jews were unable to develop a sustained strategy for resisting the Nazi occupation. Probably there was no strategy that could cope with terror on such an unprecedented scale. The mainstream Jewish organizations collapsed or tried to maintain themselves as a skeletal underground (which in practice often came to much the same thing). For a time the Jüdenrat, imposed by the Nazis, tried to act as a buffer, but all too soon it became primarily a vehicle for transmitting Nazi orders to the Jews. Half-starved, sometimes wholly starved, the masses of Jews were helpless.

It was the Jewish youth movements that managed best to pull themselves together. They concentrated their meager forces in underground cells in the main cities, while limiting themselves to cultural and educational activities in apartments, courtyards, and the soup kitchens. Though few were able to face up to so painful a reality, the youth movements in effect acknowledged that there was little they could do for the hundreds of thousands of Jews now packed into Warsaw. They could hope only to salvage a "saving remnant" of the young.

What held these movements together was not merely, or even mainly, their Zionist and socialist convictions: it was the systematic cultivation of fraternal ties. Friendship sustained morale and enabled these young people to take extraordinary risks. During the first year or so of the occupation, the Nazis seemed relatively indifferent to what was happening within the Jewish streets, perhaps because they dismissed the possibility of Jewish resistance. At least until word came of "the Final Solution," what the Nazi occupiers cared about was to steal Jewish property, to grab Jews off the streets for forced labor, and to indulge themselves in acts of random humiliation and violence against the Jews.

The Jewish youth groups set up a formal structure early in the occupation. They established committees, cells and leadership cadres. Now, from the distance of time, some of these organizational formalities may seem pathetic—and still more so their ideological discussions and debates that had lost all relevance. Mordecai Anielewicz, the future commander of the Warsaw uprising, would say that all the cultural activities—such as the more than ninety seminars in Warsaw that discussed the work of the Yiddish writer Mendele Mokher Sforim—were a waste of time. But they were not a waste of time. Anielewicz failed to understand, in his despairing impatience, that retaining some of the traditional interests was a way of preserving the humanity of the Jews. And he failed to consider the extent to which such seemingly innocuous activities, apart from their value as intellectual refreshment, could provide a basis in morale for the revolt that he was later to lead.

Similarly, Yitzhak Zuckerman, speaking in Israel after the war, would say that the Jews should have begun their revolt almost immediately after the Nazis entered Warsaw. He, too, was probably wrong—though who can be certain about such matters? In the early months of the occupation, the majority of Jews hoped to scrape through the war years; they would almost certainly have seen a call to armed revolt as a provocation. In fact, when the Jewish Fighting Organization, the unified youth structure, put up posters in early 1943 calling for armed revolt, Jews tore the posters down, and in a few instances even beat up the young people who had put them up. For the idea of armed revolt seemed not only impractical, it seemed suicidal.

Zuckerman has left a poignant description of his state of mind in the early months of the occupation, when he found himself for a brief time in the Soviet-occupied segment of Poland:

I had a great desire for life. I loved nothing more than life. I was 24 years old, in the prime of life. But I had no illusions. I was almost sure that they [the Soviet police] would catch me one day. . . . Sober consideration said we could go to Siberia. . . . But in comparison to the information we got from Warsaw we were really living in paradise! . . . I could move around. In this period, anyway. Whereas Warsaw under the Nazis scared me to death.

In order to join his comrades in Dror ("Freedom" in Hebrew), a Zionist-socialist youth movement, Zuckerman left the Soviet-occupied zone and tramped to Warsaw in early 1940. Anielewicz, a leader of Hashomer Ha'tsa'ir ("The Young Guardians" in Hebrew), another Zionist-socialist youth group but somewhat to the left of Dror, also came to Warsaw. These youth movements, together with one or two others and the youth of the Bund, the Jewish socialist party of Poland, cooperated in the limited day-to-day activities that were still possible (providing meager relief for starving friends, issuing underground papers, holding educational seminars), all with the aim, as Zuckerman puts it, of "preserving the ember."

A dark realism, not easily distinguished from a dark pessimism, came to underlie the work of Zuckerman and his friends in Nazi-occupied Warsaw. They came to realize, after a time, that "we are on a one-way road to Treblinka [the death camp near Warsaw], and there was no way back." Yet precisely this growing awareness steeled the ranks of the Jewish youth, enabling them to take the extraordinary risks that were necessary even for the modest tasks they set themselves. Sometimes even crossing a street could mean risking one's life.

Throughout the Holocaust years and into the immediate postwar period, Zuckerman held to a single idea, simple but powerful. He argued that the standard ideological divisions within the Jewish community of Poland—and there had been many of these!—should be put on hold. They had lost their relevance, though at some point they might regain it. In the face of unprecedented catastrophe, Zuckerman kept saying, it was necessary for Jews to hold, or to huddle, together, sometimes in doing what little could be done to alleviate their misery, sometimes in recognizing that their condition had become hopeless. This was not an "inspiring" idea, nor did it lend itself to exalted rhetoric. It was, at best, a last-ditch defense.

Within the politically conscious segments of the Warsaw Jewish youth, as well as among some adults, there were discussions as to whether to remain in the cities with the mass of terrorized Jews or try to join the Polish partisans in the woods. The Dror leadership, which often meant Zuckerman and his girlfriend, the indomitable Zivia Lubetkin, held to the view that they must remain in Warsaw with the other Jews, sharing their fate and perhaps being able to ease it a little. Only after the collapse of the Warsaw Ghetto uprising in 1943, when the Nazis burned the Jewish quarter to the ground, did Zuckerman and a few friends establish contact with the partisans.

On New Year's Eve 1939 in Lwow, Dror held what Zuckerman calls "a historic conference" that consolidated relations between the Warsaw center and the isolated groups in outlying areas. This was not easy to do, since the Nazis forbade Jews to ride on trains and summarily shot any who were caught. The youth groups adopted a policy of using female comrades to serve as couriers, since some could pass for gentiles. (One of them, Lonka Kozibrodska, described by a friend as "a tall girl who didn't look at all Jewish," was especially fearless; she was finally caught by the Nazis and died of typhus in Auschwitz at the age of 26.)

The youth movements, soon a single community, coiled themselves into a tight circle. Zuckerman speaks of his friends as "Puritans" who strictly subordinated personal interests to the needs of their cause. Still, it is good to learn that the young activists paired off rapidly into couples, as if to reach out for a little pleasure before encountering death.

One of the problems for Dror, Hashomer Ha'tsa'ir, and the smaller groups was the recurrent clash of opinion and feeling between them and their friends abroad, with whom, for a time, it was still possible to communicate. Zuckerman tells the story of Yosef Kaplan, a Hashomer activist, who received a solemn message from friends in Switzerland: "We are with you!" To which Kaplan, who must have been a delightful fellow, replied: "Better I should be with you!"

Kaplan's tone was jocular, but it pointed to a deeply troubled feeling among the young Warsaw activists that they had been virtually abandoned by the Yishuv, the Jewish community in Palestine. As Zuckerman, in his graver voice, puts it:

> We sent regular letters to Eretz Israel . . . we sent letters complaining bitterly that they weren't writing to us. . . . During the *aktsia* [the round-up of more than 250,000 Warsaw Jews in the summer of 1942] we sat with Yosef Kaplan making lists of who we're going to hang in Eretz Israel . . . we even talked about "gallows"; this was black humor, but it wasn't only joking: these things were very painful.

For some years now there has been a discussion among Israelis, with a self-lacerating edge, as to whether the Yishuv did all it could to help the Jews of Europe during the Holocaust. Zuckerman's comment touches upon this discussion, though probably without a full awareness of how complex were the problems facing the Yishuv during the war years and how sadly limited were its capacities to do much on behalf of the European Jews. There is now an authoritative study of the question by the Israeli scholar Dina Porat—an abridged translation called *The Blue and Yellow Star of David* was recently published by Harvard University Press— which argues that most leaders of the Yishuv, a community but not a state, were genuinely concerned about the fate of Europe's Jews, and undertook a range of projects to help and perhaps rescue them; that a lack of resources and still more, the indifference of the European states and the United States and especially the British mandatory power, crippled the efforts of the Yishuv; that the Palestinian Jews had their own severe anxieties regarding the possibility of a Nazi invasion through Syria that would destroy the future Jewish homeland. While there were numerous failures and some instances of ideological disdain for the European Jews, Porat argues, "the Yishuv in fact did more than it was ever given credit for— either then or now."

Still, between the Jews who suffered in the Holocaust and those who lived through the war in Palestine there were often acrid recriminations, perhaps best understood as a common helplessness in the most terrible moment of human history. Years later, in Israel, Zuckerman was asked by Chaim Guri, a well-known Israeli poet of the generation of the 1940s, "whether fighters from the Yishuv could have been of any help had they flown to Poland." (I take this from Porat's book.) Zuckerman replied:

> If 500 fighters had taken off, anti-aircraft fire would have brought 490 of them down on the way. And if you had been among the remaining ten, we would have had a problem hiding you—because of your native Hebrew accent, your Mediterranean eyes, the fact that you don't speak Yiddish or Polish. You could not have saved us. . . . Only a superpower could have saved us. A major power. But why didn't even one of you come? One! . . . It wouldn't have been a political or military question. It was only a question of ritual, of gesture, a sign, a hand extended, as a token of sharing our fate. Why didn't a single person come to Poland?

"Only a superpower could have saved us"—those are the decisive words. But the superpowers did not lift a finger.

A turning point in the Warsaw experience came with the establishment of a closed ghetto within the city; the Nazis did this through a series of steps that concluded in late 1940. Gutman writes that "according to German figures, 113,000 Poles and 138,000 Jews [would have to be] relocated" in order to shape the ghetto according to the Nazis' specifications. "The area of the ghetto was about 425 acres, of which 375 acres were residential space. This meant that 30 percent of the population of Warsaw was cramped into only 2.4 percent of the city." Zuckerman translates these figures into direct experience:

> The establishment of the ghetto meant a revolution in our life. Suddenly you saw poverty in a concentrated and harsh form. Every single day, the situation grew worse. Dead bodies rolled in the streets. Your senses did grow blunt in time. You got used to it, you moved a little and passed by. I was used to passing one family: two young people carrying a little girl. I recall the nobility in their stance and their silence. Every time I passed them, I would give them something. One day they disappeared and I knew they were no longer alive.

Now came the dark days. Zuckerman was arrested and sent to a labor camp. Dror had Lonka Kozibrodska nose about the camp to see if she could get some useful information. Meanwhile

> they started torturing me. Two of them stood and beat me, first on my head, with rubber clubs. When I felt blood flow, I tried to cover my head with my hands, and then they beat my hands and ears. . . . They went on like that, mercilessly, incessantly. At that stage, I didn't weep or whine. I took the blows in silence. And the more I got, the less pain I felt. . . . They wanted me to admit that [Lonka] was a Jew, but they didn't get that. . . . In time, I learned that if you want to endure an interrogation, choose what is important to you and don't retreat from that. I ordered myself to maintain [Lonka] was a Pole. I was wounded and very sick, but I kept my composure.

After a grueling week Zuckerman managed to get out of the labor camp, and for a while he became "the pampered child" of the Dror community. "They even gave me milk. . . . For the first time I had seen with my own eyes what a labor camp was. Before that, we used to distinguish between 'labor camps' and 'concentration camps,' but now I knew it was all the same."

Reports kept reaching Warsaw of mass deportations and slaughters, no longer a scattered few but hundreds, even thousands, across all of Poland. "The youth . . . accepted the interpretation that this was the beginning of the end. . . . A total death sentence for the Jews." Zuckerman fell into "a deep depression" that "went on all day and night." About his own state of mind during his years in the underground he is entirely candid: he has no use for the rhetoric of "heroism" that would later fill orations about the Holocaust. He reveals his vulnerability and several times admits that he—and no doubt the others—lived in constant fear. Several times he suffered a sort of breakdown accompanied by heavy drinking. Somehow—he was obviously a man of tremendous will—he recovered himself and went back to his tasks.

The largest of all the Warsaw *aktsias*, begun on July 22, 1942, lasted until September 12, 1942. During those seven weeks more than 250,000 Jews from Warsaw were shipped, or as the Nazis put it, "relocated," to Treblinka, where most were destroyed in the gas chambers. Two days after the *aktsia* began, Adam Czerniakow, the head of the Warsaw Jüdenrat, committed suicide. He had been feared and despised by the Jews of Warsaw, but in retrospect at least, Zuckerman is remarkably tolerant, seeing Czerniakow as a weak man, utterly unqualified for the post he had been forced to assume. At first he meant to shield some Jews by arranging their submission to the Nazis, and then, as their pressures on him steadily increased, he came to serve as their adjutant in the ghetto.

Only toward open traitors—some high in the Jüdenrat, many within the Jewish police and a number who spied for the Gestapo—does Zuckerman show hatred. It's as if he felt that all the Jews had been put into a situation of complete helplessness, and that it would be pointless and inhumane to condemn those who displayed weakness. For there are situations in which the passing of moral judgment becomes itself morally irrelevant, even morally cruel—or is to be undertaken, at least, only with the greatest reluctance.

Still, it cannot be denied that in these months, while there were some incidents of individual resistance by "wildcats" who tried to escape from the streets leading to the Umschlagplatz, the square from which they would be sent to Treblinka, most of the Jews went passively to their death. This remains one of the agonizing problems of the Holocaust. It is a problem that will never be solved to anyone's complete satisfaction.

Let us note, first of all, that there *were* Jewish revolts, in and out of the concentration camps—revolts that were suppressed at a high cost in blood. But these were mostly the desperate acts of militant minorities within the Jewish ranks. By the summer of 1942, the Warsaw Jews were worn down with hunger, suffering, and disease. They saw no possibility of resistance, or even survival. Perhaps there had come to many of them that numbness that follows a failed struggle to survive, a numbness by which the body signals its readiness for the end.

During the weeks of the *aktsia* the Nazi terror intensified enormously. It was reported by the Jüdenrat that 6,687 Jews were shot in the streets and houses of the ghetto between July and September 1942. The faintest sign of disobedience met with large-scale punishment, so that any Jew thinking of personal resistance had to be aware that he was endangering many other Jews. Nor was there yet an organized force capable of preparing even a token resistance. The Jews had no arms, nor any tradition of military action, with which to encounter the vastly superior forces of the German Nazis.

Gutman offers still another explanation for Jewish passivity:

> A profound faith in the Divine Will and a long-standing tradition of fatalism and submission prevented the Jews from resisting and made for a situation in which people being slaughtered by the thousands not only failed to respond but did not think to take revenge on their murderers.

This may explain the behavior of some Orthodox Jews, but it fails to explain the behavior of the many secular Jews who had, they often said, broken with the tradition of passivity. Perhaps that break did not cut as deeply into their consciousness as they liked to suppose; perhaps the abandoned old traditions lingered in the hearts of the Jewish socialists and Zionists.

And also, adds Gutman, the truth "simply could not be fully apprehended. Logic, emotion and the deep-seated convictions about man's basic humanity all dictated that what was going on at Treblinka was simply not possible." Genocide is, quite literally, incredible; and for that reason, I would add, passivity before genocide was hardly a uniquely Jewish trait. How, too, explain the passivity of the Cambodians slaughtered by the Khmer Rouge? Or the thousands of Africans slaughtered by their dictators? We had better acknowledge that there are things about this terrible century that resist explanation.

In March 1942 the Jewish secular parties and youth groups held an initial meeting to discuss forming an armed resistance. In his opening report Zuckerman urged that "a joint Jewish political representation" establish contact with "the civilian and military Polish underground" and "establish a general Jewish fighting force." At this point the representative of the Bund, Maurycy Orzech, argued vehemently that not only Jews were being killed by the Nazis, but also Poles; that the Bund rejected the idea of "Jewish unity" since major class divisions remained within the Jewish community; and that the Jews should wait for the Polish proletariat to rise up and then lend support to its rebellion.

Here, for once, Zuckerman loses his temper—and why not? The Bund statement could almost have been made in 1935; it ignored the fact that what was now at stake was not politics within the Jewish community, but the very survival of the Jews as a people. Still, even in his irritation with Bundist sectarianism, Zuckerman retains an understanding of why so many adult Jewish leaders clung to their old views: it seemed the one thing they could hang on to in a moment of despair. The position of the Bund, writes Zuckerman,

> was one of the contributing factors to our mood of great depression. It was also one of our delusions. Just as we believed that when the world learned of what was going on, something would happen, so I believed that when we found a common language with the Poles, with the help of the Bund, our salvation would come. But one day we did find a common language with the Poles, and it didn't change the Jewish fate. . . . Of course, this is said a long time later, in hindsight. But in those days I was ready to kill my Bundist comrades for their blindness.

Overcoming its ideological rigidity, the Bund soon changed its attitude and joined in creating the Jewish Fighting Organization (ZOB, Zydowska Organizacja Bojowa, in Polish) on July 28, 1942. Marek Edelman, then a young Bundist who would leave memoirs of the Warsaw Ghetto uprising as remarkable in their way as those of Zuckerman, soon became one of the leaders among the fighters. The ZOB cadres consisted of young people, mostly in their 20s, some still younger, and a few at the advanced age of 32 or 33, treated as old-timers. There was also another, smaller Jewish fighting organization, sponsored by the Revisionists, which, after failed negotiations with the ZOB, went its own way.

The remaining Jews of Warsaw—by September 1942, somewhere between 60,000 and 70,000—mostly demoralized and burrowing for places to hide, knew little or nothing about the formation of the ZOB; but the few remaining leaders of the Jewish parties did know, and they mostly approved or acquiesced. Zuckerman records a touching incident in which Rabbi Alexander-Zysza Friedman, a figure in the religious party Agudas Israel, explained why he could not go along with the formation of a fighting force. Rabbi Friedman "was weeping as he said words of love and respect to me: My son, the Lord gives and the Lord takes." (And where was God? Edelman, in his sardonic despair, had an answer: "God was on the side of the persecutors.") Perhaps, remarks Zuckerman, since the fighters couldn't really save anyone, Rabbi Friedman's attitude should also have been the attitude of the young militants; but at that time they still clung to the hope that a few might be saved.

Operating in conspiratorial fashion, the ZOB directed its initial efforts within the ghetto itself. It set fire to the houses from which Jews had been driven so as to prevent the Nazis from seizing Jewish property. It sent a trusted comrade to execute Josef Szerynski, head of the hated Jewish police, but the bullet merely grazed his cheek. Szerynski then went into hiding—a symbolic victory for the ZOB. His successor, Yaakov Lejkin, whose record was even worse—he took open delight in beating Jews—was executed by the ZOB in October 1942.

The ZOB set up an improvised prison in the ghetto, where it held a few informers. Zuckerman remarks that the Gestapo, by now keenly interested in what was happening within the ghetto, had succeeded in infiltrating several of the Jewish institutions, so that before any act of armed resistance could be undertaken it was necessary to remove the Jewish spies and informers. The ZOB also proclaimed penalties against "economic collaborators" within the ghetto, those who had grown wealthy by exploiting Jewish labor on behalf of the Germans. These penalties were for the most part financial, to provide funds with which to buy guns. All of these actions have an unpleasant ring, of the kind one associates with "vanguard" movements, but Zuckerman pleads necessity in desperate circumstances—and who is to gainsay him?

In one of the round-ups in September 1942 the much-loved Hashomer leader Yosef Kaplan was taken by the Nazis and murdered on a street near the Umschlagplatz. When his friend Shmuel Braslaw went out to see if Kaplan might be rescued, he too was captured and immediately killed because he had a knife in his possession. A few nights later the leading group of ZOB sat together mourning the loss of their comrades, and Kaplan's girlfriend, the courier Miriam Heinsdorf, sang a song in Russian, dry-eyed, "in a trembling voice":

> The road leads far away,
> Lead me, my beloved,
> I will part from you at the door,
> Perhaps—forever.

The ZOB leadership, now including Zuckerman, Lubetkin, Anielewicz, and Edelman, decided that whenever the Nazis would begin their next *aktsia*, they would rise up, ready or not. (What, after all, did "ready" mean in these circumstances?) The immediate task was to accumulate weapons, of which they had, literally, a handful. Emanuel Ringelblum, the archivist of the ghetto, would recall an incident in which two leaders of the Hashomer Ha'tsa'ir took him to a secret room to show him their arsenal—two revolvers.

One of the best Hashomer people, Aryeh Wilner—"he looked like a Polish *Sheygetz* [gentile man], spoke good, popular Polish [unlike Zuckerman, who had a

Vilna accent] and sometimes wore a hat with a feather like a well-to-do farmer"—
was sent to the "Aryan" side of the city to acquire arms. At first Wilner met with a
frigid response from the Home Army (A.K. in Polish), which possessed a considerable store of arms but refused to give any to the ZOB because the Poles did not
believe the Jews would ever put up an armed resistance. Only after January 1943,
when there was sporadic armed struggle in the ghetto during another *aktsia*—an
ill-coordinated struggle, with only a few ZOB units able to mobilize themselves,
yet still unnerving to the Germans—did the Home Army grant a small quantity
of arms to the Jewish fighters. There were sharply varying attitudes within the
Home Army to the very idea of Jewish resistance, with some leaders seeing it as a
Communist-inspired maneuver that might lead to a bloodbath of the Polish population and other leaders responding warmly to Wilner's appeals.

Until January 1943, according to Gutman, "the Home Army provided the ZOB
with a total of ten revolvers, while . . . an authorized representative of the Polish
government [in exile reported that] in the spring of 1943 the Home Army had
in its possession 25,000 rifles, 6,000 revolvers, 30,000 grenades and other types
of heavier weapons." The Home Army did not try even once to commit an act of
sabotage against the trains taking Jews from Warsaw to Treblinka.

After the Jewish resistance to the *aktsia* of January 1943, the ZOB heard from
the Home Army that they "saluted us," and the Poles sent fifty pistols, some
grenades, and a few kilograms of explosives. "Since we also got the recipe for
Molotov cocktails," writes Zuckerman, "we started collecting bottles. . . . There
were also the weapons our comrades bought on the Aryan side, as well as those
we bought from Jews [a few unscrupulous smugglers] in the ghetto." Once the
uprising began in April, there were about 500 organized fighters in the ranks of
the ZOB equipped with a motley collection of weapons, some of which, especially the revolvers, proved to be of limited or no use; but at no time were there
enough weapons for all the fighters. The armed forces of the Revisionists, num-
bering some 250, seem to have been somewhat better equipped; they fought
well during the first day of the uprising, but then, for unknown reasons, they left
the ghetto, making their way through a tunnel to the other side of the city and
from there to the countryside, where they were surprised by the Nazis and largely
wiped out.

In March, Aryeh Wilner fell into a Gestapo trap. Since he was a central figure
in negotiations with the ZOB and the two Polish forces, the Home Army and the
Communist-led guerrillas, there was a great fear that he might break under torture and reveal crucial facts. He was severely tortured ("they hung him up and put

white hot iron on the soles of his feet"), but he kept silent. Later, in a bold operation, he was rescued; he had to be carried, since he could not walk.

Meanwhile—we are now into early April—the ZOB had to find a replacement for Wilner. It was decided to send Zuckerman. In some of the most graphic pages of his memoirs, he tells how he slipped across to the "Aryan" side, was met by a young Jewish girl named Frania Beatus, "maybe 16 or 17 years old, blond, pretty," who "walked around in high-heeled shoes so she'd look taller and carried a woman's handbag, which she thought added maturity. So I had to smile when I saw her." (In May, Frania committed suicide upon learning the outcome of the uprising.)

Zuckerman now tramped through the streets of "Aryan" Warsaw, fearing that if he stayed during the daytime in the apartments that friends had provided, he might endanger their owners. He tried desperately to find more arms, seeking to persuade leaders of the Home Army to help the Jewish fighters, but had little success. He made contact with the Communist-led guerrilla force, from whom he got a little help. It is to Zuckerman's credit, I believe, that he does not allow later political arguments to keep him from saying that in these crucial weeks he found the underground Communists to be "fine people, aware, firm in their opinions. . . . They helped us with whatever little bit they could."

One evening Zuckerman was directed to the apartment of an "Armenian" woman where he would be safe. That night he woke to the sensation of a hand stroking his face. In his sleep he had been crying and shouting in Yiddish, and here was the "Armenian" woman sitting at his bedside, weeping and stroking him. "I had a vague memory of some nightmare, but I couldn't reconstruct anything. . . . I asked myself if the 'Armenian' woman was really Armenian, since she cried like a *Yiddishe mama*. I didn't ask because there was no need to ask."

About the uprising itself Zuckerman cannot provide a direct account, since he was stuck on the other side of Warsaw. Gutman, in his splendid book, has a classically restrained account, from which I borrow a few bits.

On April 19, 1943, as part of an *aktsia* that was to complete the Final Solution, a German military column came swaggering down the middle of Nalewki Street, a main thoroughfare in the ghetto. The Germans were singing loudly. This time, the ZOB was prepared. Chaim Frimmer, a ZOB fighter, describes their preparations:

> The windows were fortified with sandbags. People were assigned to their various positions [and] . . . received an order from Berl Braudo [the unit commander] to check the weapons and pass out ammunition to the men.

We filled baskets with Molotov cocktails. . . . Mordecai Anielewicz arrived and went into Yisrael [Kanal's] room. After consultation they came out and walked through the rooms and apartments, selecting appropriate spots for positions. . . . "Cjank" (doses of cyanide) was passed out to certain people, especially those whose tasks required them to be mobile and heightened their chances of being caught by the Germans and tortured.

The Germans, to their surprise, were attacked by ZOB units stationed in the upper stories of adjacent buildings, from which they threw grenades. The Germans panicked, retreating in disorder and leaving casualties in the street. A short while later the Germans returned, this time hugging the sides of the buildings for safety, but in order to fire they had to expose themselves. Again, a German retreat and no Jewish casualties.

Organized military resistance by the ZOB continued for several days. General Rowecki, head of the Home Army, reported to the Polish government in London: "The resistance of groups of Jewish fighters was far beyond all expectations." And once the ZOB units showed they could hold out, even destroying a few German tanks with Molotov cocktails, an unexpected reinforcement appeared. Ordinary Jews who had been hiding in elaborate bunkers that had been put up over the last few months now joined in the fighting with the ZOB units.

Zuckerman had shrewdly predicted that if Jewish resistance proved strong, the Nazis would resort to one measure the Jews would be unable to counter: they would set the entire ghetto on fire, forcing Jews out of the bunkers and exposing them to capture and death. General Stroop, the German expert in street fighting who had been rushed to Warsaw, reported that "scores of burning Jews—whole families—jumped from windows or tried to slide down sheets that had been tied together. We took pains to ensure that those Jews . . . were wiped out immediately." A few days later Stroop wrote in his report to Berlin: "Despite the terror of the raging fire, the Jews and the hooligans [Stroop's name for the ZOB] preferred to turn back into the flames rather than fall into our hands."

Organized combat could not be long sustained, since the Germans outnumbered the Jewish fighters and had far superior weapons. But sporadic resistance continued for at least a month. On April 23 Anielewicz, who would soon be killed in the fighting, sent a note to Zuckerman: "Things have surpassed our boldest dreams . . . the dream of my life has come true. I've lived to see a Jewish defense in the ghetto in all its greatness and glory." Edelman, by nature disinclined to boast, would later recall the struggle of a ZOB unit that fought until May 3: "It is difficult to speak of victory when people are fighting for their lives and so many are lost, but one thing can be said of this battle. We did not allow the Germans to execute their plans."

Once the resistance collapsed, one group of ZOB fighters led by Wilner committed suicide rather than fall into the hands of the Nazis. Another ZOB fighter, Lolek Rotblat, shot his mother and then himself. A small number of ZOB fighters escaped through the sewers to the "Aryan" side of the city, among them Lubetkin, who reunited with Zuckerman.

The remaining chapters of Zuckerman's memoirs deal with his efforts to help place survivors of the uprising in the safe places. About eighty of the ZOB people were rescued; many of them were later killed in clashes with German forces, and many, reports Gutman, were "murdered by Polish partisans." Only about a dozen lived to see the liberation. Zuckerman and Lubetkin fought in the Polish uprising of 1944, and again survived. From a military point of view, the Warsaw Ghetto uprising was of slight significance. From what I venture to call a human point of view, its significance is beyond calculation.

One of the many distinctions of Zuckerman's memoirs is that in two or three sentences he can bring to vivid life his comrades of the Jewish underground. One needs constantly to remind oneself that these were youngsters, what we would call "kids." For me, they have become an abiding part of consciousness, these boys and girls, these young men and women. Let me put down the names of a few of them: Mordecai Anielewicz, Zivia Lubetkin, Yitzhak Zuckerman, Frumka Plotnitska, Yosef Kaplan, Tosia Altman, Marek Edelman, Lonka Kozibrodska, Kazik (Simha Rotem). There were many others.

Mr. Bennett and Mrs. Woolf
{1994}

LITERARY POLEMICS COME AND GO, sparking a season of anger and gossip, and then turning to dust. A handful survive their moment: Dr. Johnson's demolition of Soame Jenyns, Hazlitt's attack on Coleridge. But few literary polemics can have been so damaging, or so lasting in consequences, as Virginia Woolf's 1924 essay "Mr. Bennett and Mrs. Brown," about the once widely read English novelists Arnold Bennett, H. G. Wells, and John Galsworthy.

For several literary generations now, Woolf's essay has been taken as the definitive word finishing off an old-fashioned school of fiction and thereby clearing the way for literary modernism. Writing with her glistening charm, and casting herself as the voice of the new (always a shrewd strategy in literary debate), Woolf quickly seized the high ground in her battle with Bennett. Against her needling thrusts, the old fellow never had a chance.

The debate has been nicely laid out by Samuel Hynes in his *Edwardian Occasions*, and I owe to him some of the following details. It all began in 1917 with Woolf's review of a collection of Bennett's literary pieces, a rather favorable review marred by the stylish snobbism that was becoming a trademark of the Bloomsbury circle. Bennett, wrote Woolf, had a materialistic view of the world; "he has been worrying himself to achieve infantile realisms." A catchy phrase, though exactly what "infantile realisms" meant Woolf did not trouble to say. During the next few years she kept returning to the attack, as if to prepare for "Mr. Bennett and Mrs. Brown." More than personal sensibilities or rivalries of status was involved here, though both were visible; Woolf was intent upon discrediting, if not simply dismissing, a group of literary predecessors who enjoyed a large readership.

In 1923 Bennett reviewed Woolf's novel *Jacob's Room*, praising its "originality" and "exquisite" prose, but concluding that "the characters do not vitally survive in the mind." For Bennett, this was a fatal flaw. And for his readers too—though not for the advanced literary public which by now was learning to suspect this kind of talk about "characters surviving" as a lazy apology for the shapeless and perhaps even mindless Victorian novel.

A year later Woolf published her famous essay, brilliantly sketching an imaginary old lady named Mrs. Brown whom she supplied with anecdotes and reflections as tokens of inner being. These released the sort of insights, suggested Woolf, that would not occur to someone like Bennett, a writer obsessed with dull particulars of setting (weather, town, clothing, furniture, etc.). Were Bennett to write about a Mrs. Brown, he would describe her house in conscientious detail but never penetrate her essential life, for—what a keen polemicist!—"he is trying to hypnotize us into the belief that, because he has made a house, there must be a person living there."* In a quiet put-down of Bennett's novel *Hilda Lessways* (not one of his best), Woolf gave a turn of the knife: "One line of insight would have done more than all those lines of description. . . ."

From the suave but deadly attack of "Mr. Bennett and Mrs. Brown," Bennett's literary reputation would never quite recover. He remained popular with the general public, but among literary readers, the sort that would become the public for the emerging modernists, the standard view has long been that he was a middling, plodding sort of Edwardian novelist whose work has been pushed aside by the revolutionary achievements of Lawrence, Joyce, and, to a smaller extent, Woolf herself. When Bennett died in 1930, Woolf noted in her diary that "he had some real understanding power, as well as a gigantic absorbing power [and] direct contact with life"—all attributes, you might suppose, handy for a novelist but, for her, evidently not sufficient. In saying this, remarks Hynes, Woolf gave Bennett, "perhaps, the 'reality gift' that [she] doubted in herself, the gift that she despised and envied." Yes; in much of her fiction Woolf resembles Stevens' man

---

* Herself sensitive to the need for a room of her own, Woolf seemed indifferent to what a house might mean for people who had risen somewhat in the world. For a writer like Bennett, however, imagining a house was part of the way to locate "a person living there."

with the blue guitar who "cannot bring a world quite round, / Although I patch it as I can."

Still, none of this kept Woolf from steadily sniping at Bennett's "shopkeeping view of literature." Bennett was a provincial from the Five Towns; Bennett was commercially successful; Bennett was an elder to be pulled down, as elders must always be pulled down even if they are also admired a little.

Through more than a decade of their guerrilla encounters, Bennett tried to parry Woolf's attacks, but as a polemicist he was sadly outclassed. (Hynes writes in a personal letter that Bennett was a poor polemicist "because he was simply too nice.") In 1920 Bennett made a fatal tactical blunder: he wrote in the *Evening Standard*, a London paper, that Woolf is "the queen of the high brows; and I am a low brow." Now this may have tickled his readers, but among the literary people who would be making and unmaking reputations, it was the equivalent of shooting himself in the foot. For one mark of the modern era has been a ready celebration of the high against the low brow—though Bennett wasn't really a low brow, he had been baited by Woolf into a truculent misrepresentation of himself. Years earlier he had already written in his journal that "we have absorbed from France that passion for artistic shapely presentation of truth, and that feeling for words as words, which animated Flaubert, the de Goncourts, and de Maupassant." Hardly the sentiments of a low brow. And in one or two of his novels Bennett would himself write in accord with the word "from France."

Feelings of class, always abrasive in England, also figured in this dispute, and again Bennett was outmaneuvered. Woolf attacked from both sides, first as a patrician looking down a prominent nose at the grubby lower middle class of the provinces and then as a free spirit elegantly bohemian and contemptuous of shopkeeper mentality. Bennett couldn't even salvage for himself the doubtful advantage of claiming he was a sturdy proletarian—his father had been a solicitor in the Five Towns. And in the 1920s to be called a "shopkeeper's novelist" meant being thrust into philistine darkness.

Bennett and Woolf, writes Hynes, were "not antithetical in their views of their common art." After all, Bennett had shown respect for new writing, had praised Dostoevsky and Chekhov when the Russians were translated into English, had declared admiration for the "conscious art." What had actually happened, I think, was that Bennett had allowed feelings of class inferiority—they persisted despite his success, his yacht, his mistress—to shift to the arena of cultural judgment, and Woolf had been quick to take advantage of this confusion. Yet Hynes may be overstating the case a little when he sees nothing "antithetical in their views of their common art." There really was a serious clash regarding "their common art," and at one point in "Mr. Bennett and Mrs. Brown" Woolf made clear what the issue was. Older writers like Bennett and Wells were using one set of "conventions"—that's the key word—while younger writers found these to be "ruin . . . death." The "Edwardian tools," she said, "have laid an enormous stress on the fabric of things. They have given us a house in the hope that we may be able to deduce the human beings who live there." Or to put it in other words: the Edwardian novelists believed that human nature could be revealed by rendering conduct and circumstance—"from the outside," as some critics would say.★

In one of her objective moments, Woolf admitted that "the tools of one generation are useless for the next." What was consequently involved in her clash with Bennett was not the superiority of one set of fictional conventions over another—for it is very doubtful that such superiority can ever be demonstrated—but, rather, that two generations had reached a fundamental division over the kinds of novels to be written. Outside/inside, objective/subjective, social/psychological: let these stand as rough tokens of the division. Where Woolf gained a polemical advantage was in claiming, or at least arguing as if, there was something inherently better about the novel of sensibility as against the novel of circumstance. She didn't yet have to consider that in a while the new becomes old, giving way soon enough to the still newer new.

What I have just said is not, however, the most important point. True, Woolf was using her self-chosen role as advocate of the new in order to undermine Bennett, but she was also doing something else. She was writing in behalf of a great new cultural impulse, that of literary modernism. By 1924, if it had not yet entirely triumphed, this impulse was certainly well on the way to triumph, and in retrospect Woolf's essay seems less the outcry of a beleaguered minority than evidence that this minority was consolidating its cultural power. An attendant irony is that while Woolf spoke for the new and had a certain right to do so, she was unfriendly to, indeed rather obtuse about, the great modernists: she found Joyce "indecent" and Eliot "obscure."

So Woolf won the battle, if not perhaps the argument. I remember several decades ago being informed by authoritative literary persons that Woolf, *once and for all*, had demolished Bennett. Growing older, I have come to recognize that "once and for all" often means no more than a few decades. By the end of our century,

---

★ A memorable expression of this view is provided by a character in Henry James's *The Portrait of a Lady*. Madame Merle says, ". . . every human being has his shell. . . . By the shell I mean the whole envelope of circumstances. There is no such thing as an isolated man or woman. . . . What do you call one's self? Where does it begin? Where does it end? It overflows into everything that belongs to us—and then it flows back again."

literary modernism has settled comfortably into the academy; there is no longer a
need to defend it against detractors, and one might even look back upon it with a
critical eye. The deeper issue, then, wasn't really, as both Woolf and Bennett said,
which writer could create more persuasive characters; it was a clash over competing versions of the novel as a form. Such clashes are never fully settled; they keep
recurring in new ways.

Matters become still more complicated if we glance at the novels Bennett and
Woolf wrote. At least one of Woolf's novels is greatly to be admired, and that is
To the Lighthouse, where in her own fragile and iridescent way she does command
"the reality gift." But Woolf's reputation needs no defense these days; it has been
inflated for reasons having little to do with her work as a novelist. What does
need to be said is that Bennett still merits attention as a fine, largely traditional
novelist in a few of his books (he wrote too many): Anna of the Five Towns, The Old
Wives' Tale, Clayhanger, and Riceyman Steps. His prose is often slapdash and flavorless, quite without Woolf's felicity of phrasing; his psychology is intuitively bluff
rather than precisely nuanced; and in technique he often stumbles. Yet he had
the true novelist's gift, what Woolf called "a gigantic absorbing power" or what
the Russian critic M. Bakhtin meant when he wrote that "for the prose artist the
world is full of the words of other people." Listening to those words, Bennett recorded through them the lives of ordinary people with what he once marvelously
called a "crushed tenderness."

In his novels there is a strongly realized sense of place—those cramped dingy
towns of provincial England, bristling with high aspirations, streaked with mean-
ness of spirit. Place, not as a Hardyesque rising to spiritual transcendence, but
confined, local, the narrow corner of a province. In Clayhanger, a modest classic in the subgenre of the Bildungsroman, Bennett faithfully charts the yearnings
for emotional articulation of a printer's son in the Five Towns ("a new conception of himself"). He depicts the homely, almost speechless love of middle-aged,
middle-class men and women with a stolid respect, if not the flair of a Woolf or
the depth of a Lawrence. Bennett is a master of the middle range of life and literature, neither soarings of sublimity nor plunges into the soul. He is indeed the
prosing poet of the shopkeepers (who may also deserve a poet of their own).

Riceyman Steps, published in 1923, late in Bennett's career, is something else
again, a tour de force Flaubertian in its stringent organization but with moments
of Balzacian power. In a style somewhat unnervingly detached, this short novel
depicts the lives of shopkeepers trapped in miserliness, showing not only the
predictable psychic costs but also how self-denial can become a twisted expression of the life-force. Here is the kind of passage that leads one to invoke Balzac;

it describes a moment when the shopkeeper protagonist is at the height of his obsession:

> He took a third drawer out of the safe, lifting it with both hands because of its weight, and put it on the table. It was full of gold sovereigns. Violet [his wife] had never seen this gold before nor suspected its existence. She was astounded, frightened, ravished. He must have kept it throughout the war, defying the government's appeal to patriots not to hoard. He was a superman, the most mysterious of supermen. And he was a fortress, impregnable.

Finally, however, even an admirer of Bennett must admit that there is something in his work—some strand of feeling or aspiration—that is thwarted, unfulfilled. In all his novels except *Riceyman Steps* the life of the narrative has a way of gradually draining out, as if creation were also a mode of exhaustion. A costive heaviness sets in. Why should this be? Perhaps because there is some truth in the idea that the kind of Victorian novel inherited by Bennett and the other Edwardians had reached a point of exhaustion, what might be called the routinization of realism. And Bennett, a latecomer in the development of the English novel, lacked those mad outpourings of energy which mark the greatest of the Victorians. At moments a touch of modern sadness seeps into his soul, some grim deprivation bred in provincial life.

Something like this may have been what D. H. Lawrence had in mind when he wrote: "I hate Bennett's resignation. Tragedy ought really to be a great kick at misery." Bennett himself seems occasionally to have had similar responses to his own work, though in a fine essay about George Gissing he provided a justification for its grayness of tone. Gissing, he said, "is . . . just, sober, calm, and proud against the gods; he has seen, he knows, he is unmoved; he defeats fate by accepting it." Whether this quite disposes of Lawrence's criticism is a question, though I would venture the opinion that Lawrence's attack cut more deeply and painfully than Woolf's, even though it is Woolf's that has been remembered.

The years pass, and by now the dispute between Bennett and Woolf has settled into history. It may be time for a spot of justice for Arnold Bennett, not a great but at times a very good novelist. But I doubt that it will come, since it is a delusion to suppose that the passage of time is an aid to justice, and, in any case, there hovers over Bennett's work and reputation the shadow of the formidable Mrs. Brown, called into being by the silkily ferocious Mrs. Woolf.

Dickens: Three Notes
{1994}

Absolute Goodness and the Limits of Fiction

It is a truism frequently acknowledged that few things are more difficult for the novelist than to portray an absolutely good person—indeed, the greater the goodness, the greater the difficulty. I see no reason to challenge this judgment, but propose here to glance at a few instances that may yield attractive complications.

Let's start with the approximation that unalloyed goodness may take the form of a ready submission of selfhood to the needs, even the desires of others. Such behavior can excite our admiration almost as much as it may violate our sense of probability. The truly good person, whether we seek him in ourselves or in others, seems mostly a figment of hope. And this persuasion as to how things really are, this moral realism—it need not be engraved as a dogma of original sin—serves as a powerful controlling presence in our responses to works of fiction, including those written in nonrealistic modes.

The effort to portray, even the ability to imagine, a state of absolute goodness takes the mind into realms—misty, speculative, transcendent—which the novel as a genre finds hard to accommodate. Grubbing along in the low vistas of actuality, or at least simulated versions of actuality, the novel is not usually hospitable to elves, fairies, ghosts, angels, devils, and gods. Many novels show God as a figure keenly desired, but only rarely does He make an appearance, whether as voice or sheet of flame; and as for devils, they have the decency, when they do make an occasional entry, to dress as gentlemen. Now it is true that such hypothetical beings are not unconditionally excluded from novels, since of all modern genres the novel is best able to put up with alien matter; but God and the angels, especially the unfallen ones, are clearly not as comfortable with Balzac as with Milton.

When we think about the problem of rendering goodness in fiction, we are likely to turn, first of all, to Don Quixote. It's not at all clear, however, that "goodness" is the most accurate description of the Knight of the Mournful Countenance. He lives by a chivalric code of good works, he sees himself as a man of action, and when in the grip of his mania, which is throughout the richest parts of the book, he is completely serious about his intention to bring justice to earth: "I am the valorous Don Quixote de la Mancha, righter of wrongs and injustices," he says. And "What are we to do? Favor and aid the weak and needy." Precisely his exalted aims, bringing him to the threshold of grace, are what unhinge the poor fellow, as each act in quest of justice leads to an absurd pratfall.

We are not invited by Cervantes to disparage Don Quixote's intentions, but we cannot avoid recognizing that, more often than not, he either does unwitting harm or turns out to be ineffectual. An insatiable hunger for *purpose*, for a goal beyond the mere exercise or gratification of ego, drives him into recurrent states of agitation—and this, while surely admirable, is rather different from a pure goodness. Once "the idealism of [Don Quixote's] idée fixe takes hold of him," remarks Erich Auerbach, "everything he does in that state is completely senseless and so incompatible with the existing world that it produces only comic confusion there." It also produces intense pathos, though the confusion and the pathos must both be distinguished from the visible presence of goodness.

Don Quixote wishes to release an *active* principle in the workings of the world, which is one reason he must always be on the move. His behavior, sometimes heroism and sometimes a parody of heroism, seems to confirm or shadow the idea, similar perhaps to the quietist element in Christianity, that action, as it locks into the fallen world, carries within itself the seeds of destruction. Between actor and act there is a chasm not to be bridged—not, at least, in this world. Only when Don Quixote turns his back on the windmills, the giants, and other phantasms of his sublime delusion, only when he ceases to be Don Quixote can he revert—we are now at the end of Cervantes's book—to his decent, flawed, commonplace self, Alonso el Bueno, Alonso the Good. This return to familiar sanity and alloyed goodness is purchased at the price of spiritual and, soon enough, physical death, so that the book may be read as implying—or is this a modernist misreading prompted by the ethic of striving?—that the return to sanity should be taken as a kind of fall. Throughout most of the book Don Quixote is too exalted or too deluded—he is always too busy—to live by the norms of absolute goodness, whatever those might be, indeed, to live by any norms but the chivalry of madness.

Dostoevsky, struggling with *The Idiot*, wrote a letter to his niece in 1868 speculating on the problem of positive goodness in fiction:

> The chief idea of the novel [the one he is writing] is to portray the positively good man. There is nothing in the world more difficult to do, and especially now. All writers, and not only ours, but even all Europeans who have tried to portray the *positively* good man have always failed. . . . There is only one positively good man in the world—Christ (so that the appearance of this immeasurably, infinitely good person is, of course, an infinite miracle in itself). . . . Of the good figures in Christian literature, the most perfect is Don Quixote. But he is good only because at the same time he is ridiculous [comic]. Dickens' Pickwick (an infinitely weaker conception than Don Quixote, but nevertheless immense) is also ridiculous [comic] and succeeds only by virtue of that fact. Compassion appears toward the good that is mocked and does not know its own value. . . .*

Why does Dostoevsky believe "positive goodness" to be credible, or more credible, when presented as "comic" or "ridiculous"? Because our compassion is stirred when we see a virtue "that does not know its own value," a virtue neither proud nor self-conscious that is being mocked. (This, by the way, may echo Turgenev's remark in his 1860 lecture "Don Quixote and Hamlet": "we are ready to love someone whom we have laughed at.") It is, then, the innocence or naivete of the good person, the refusal to take affront at the world's mockery, that wins our love.

Let me suggest another reason for thinking that goodness is credible, or more credible, when presented through the lens of the comic. Goodness so regarded

---

* There are problems of translation here. I have used the version in Ernest Simmons's biography of Dostoevsky, since it seems the clearest, but in the English translation of Konstantin Mochulsky's study of Dostoevsky, the key phrase is rendered as "a positively beautiful individual." I think it all but certain that, given Dostoevsky's cast of mind, he would have been referring to moral qualities. Simmons translates Dostoevsky's description of Don Quixote and Pickwick as "ridiculous"; the translator of Mochulsky prefers "comic." Both convey Dostoevsky's point, but for my purposes "comic" seems preferable.

tends to shrink to something life-size or smaller than life; it does not disconcert us or fill us with a despairing awe as might a "positive goodness" of large scope.

Mulling over this matter in his notebooks for The Idiot, Dostoevsky writes about Prince Myshkin, the character he hoped to establish as an exemplar of "positive goodness": "How to make the hero's character sympathetic to readers? If Don Quixote and Pickwick, as virtuous types, are sympathetic to the reader . . . it is because they are comic."

But in The Idiot, Dostoevsky instructs himself, he will try for something much more difficult. "The hero of the novel, if not comical, then possesses another sympathetic trait—*he is innocent.*" Rather than gain the effect of innocence through the oblique devices of comedy, as Cervantes and Dickens did, Dostoevsky would now try to represent innocence directly, full-face, without comic aids or embellishments.

But is this what he actually did in The Idiot? I think not, and, what's more, I think he could not. His intention has been shrewdly inferred by Harold Rosenberg: "Myshkin's function is not to alter the course of the action but to disseminate the aura of a new state of being, let events occur as they will." Yes; but simply because it *is* a novel and not an idyll or allegory, the book Dostoevsky wrote demonstrates that despite Myshkin's marvelous qualities he cannot long remain a figure emanating "a new state of being." Very quickly he is drawn into the Dostoevskian chaos, the typical ambience of this writer (some might add, of the world), and there Myshkin must, alas, become a force of disorder, altering events in ways he had not anticipated, perhaps even in ways Dostoevsky had not planned. Myshkin has no choice. In his own lovable way he turns out to be almost as destructive as the worldly and malevolent figures Dostoevsky sets off against him. A searcher who cannot remain at rest, Myshkin strains, a little like Don Quixote, to negotiate radical transformations of consciousness and thereby reach a universal state of goodness. But for this, in the Russia within which he must act, he has little capacity and less time. It seems to be a "rule" in fictions devoted to such characters that they cannot be granted long stretches of time—a keen intuition shared by greatly different writers about both the nature of reality and the limits of fiction.

Myshkin is a deeply affecting creature, at times even magnificent, but he is hardly innocent. Good Dostoevskian character that he is, Myshkin admits that "it is terribly difficult to fight against these *double* thoughts. I've tried. Goodness only knows how they come and how they arise." They sound, these "double thoughts," very much like the afflictions suffered by the rest of humanity, and perhaps to make certain that even the slowest reader will get the point, Dostoevsky makes Myshkin into an epileptic, a sufficiently gross sign of imperfection.

One of Dostoevsky's notebooks contains this remarkable sentence: "*Meekness is the most powerful force that exists in the world.*" If this remark helps explain the power of goodness in Christ and Buddha, it may also explain the power of destruction in Christ and Buddha. "What is so destructive in [Myshkin]," writes Murray Krieger, "is the sense others must get from his infinite meekness that they are being judged. Of course, Myshkin knows the sin of pride that is involved in judging and so carefully refrains, condemning himself instead. But this very inversion of the process constitutes a form of judgment too for the guilty. . . ." Aglaya, the acute young woman with whom Myshkin becomes involved, says to him: "You have no tenderness, nothing but the truth, and so you judge unjustly." A remark at once astonishing and profound—and worth remembering with regard to Melville's Captain Vere. I see it as clear evidence that Dostoevsky knew that, whatever else, he had not succeeded in his stated intention regarding Myshkin.

What he did succeed in doing was to write a wonderful novel, in good part because he moved past his stated intention. He complicated the portrayal of goodness with mental imbroglios, murderous attacks, epileptic seizures, and sexual disasters. The road to great fiction is strewn with the collapse of high intentions.

From Prince Myshkin to Milly Theale, the fragile heroine of Henry James's *Wings of the Dove*, there is an enormous distance, but there is also one crucial similarity: neither character can find a place in common life; the very distinction of each constitutes a sentence of doom. Each displays loveliness of soul, but both Dostoevsky and James refuse to grant them, perhaps because they cannot locate, the ground for a sustained exercise of goodness. Myshkin, suffering from a surplus of consciousness, cannot manage the circumstances of the Russia into which he is thrust; Milly, radiating generosity of spirit, cannot deal with the ways of London society.

Exquisite, dove-like, Milly Theale rises, as the novel continues, to heights of the angelic. Forgiving all who have betrayed her and casting the shadow of her luminous wings over their lives, Milly suggests something of the cold purity, but also the sheer terror, of angelic being. The more she seems to rise above the comfortably human, the more she is unable to gain the small pleasures and fulfillments of the human—and, as if in recognition that this does not permit of any sustained representation, James sees that he must rapidly withdraw his angelic creature from the shabby milieu into which, as a novelist, he felt obliged to put her. Milly's loveliness is signaled by her fatality: at least on earth, the angelic has no prospect of duration. So Milly barely lingers with the actualities of goodness:

she passes beyond these, into a tremor of sublimity, now hovering, as the mildest of rebukes, over the mortals who survive her.

Dickens, in a few of his novels, also struggles with the problem of rendering absolute goodness. He succeeds with Pickwick, though on a smaller scale than Cervantes with Don Quixote, because he does not strain to make Pickwick into an archetype. A good-hearted, sweet-souled petty bourgeois, Pickwick serves as a "local deity" of Olde England, created to lull readers into a persuasion that benevolence can smooth away the difficulties of life. Pickwick does not try to rise above his class position; he realizes himself through limited social definition and inherited bias, occasionally stretching but never breaking these. He is always on the move, but never moves very far. He cannot be imagined as existing anywhere but in stagecoach England, indeed, anywhere but in his own neighborhood, as an ornament of the provincial imagination. Precisely this historical specificity makes him so greatly loved by the English reading public, and sometimes bewildering to those who know him only through translation. For a moment, with Pickwick and his bumbling troupe, the clock of history stands still: that is the pleasure of it.

Everyone knows how numerous are the tests of goodness that would be beyond Pickwick, and everyone feels glad that Dickens has shielded him from them. Brought low through comic plotting, Pickwick finds himself briefly in prison, from which Dickens contrives through some appropriately silly business to rescue him. It is a traditional strategy of the comic to glance just a little beyond its limits, into stretches of experience that comedy is ill-equipped to cope with. Pickwick's goodness, insofar as we agree to suspend disbelief for a while, can thrive only in the spaces of a comedy that history has made irretrievable.

A deeper conception informs Dickens's treatment of Little Dorrit. Mild, unassertive, and selfless, she neither represents the virtues of local custom, like Pickwick, nor strains toward universality of value, like Myshkin. She is a figure at rest, in a setting where everything else is turbulent and false; she is sufficient unto herself, harmonious in nature, unqualifiedly responsive to others. She has no need to think about, nor in responding to her do we feel obliged to invoke, the categorical imperative or any universalization of Christian values. Her goodness is a quality of being without any pressure to invoke whatever might be "higher" than or "beyond" goodness. The imaginative realization of this figure is so pure and lucid, mere ideas fade away.

Little Dorrit is not innocent and rarely, if ever, sentimental. No one who has grown up in the Marshalsea prison could be innocent; no one who has had to put up with all those wretched Dorrits could long be sentimental. She knows quite enough about the varieties of selfishness; that is why Dickens has provided her with the family she has, to educate her in the ways of the world. And though she exists entirely within the world, she has no designs upon it, neither to transform nor transcend it. She has no designs of any kind; she is simply a possibility, very rare, of our existence.

What seems to have inspired the creation of Little Dorrit was Dickens's residual sentiment of Christianity, a sense or memory of a faith unalloyed by dogma, aggression, or institution. This is a "religion," if religion at all, of affection, or an ethic without prescription or formula. Dickens himself, as he knew quite well, was far from embodying anything of the sort, but his imagination cherished the possibility, arousing in him the sort of upwelling emotions that the vision of Billy Budd must have aroused in Melville. The religious experience had largely been lost to Dickens, except insofar as it might leave a sediment of purity.

Little Dorrit is not at all a "Christ figure." She does not ask anyone to abandon the world's goods and follow her; she could not drive the money changers from the temple; nor can one imagine her on a cross, though she might be among those mourning near it. Nothing even requires that we see her as a distinctively Christian figure, though nothing prevents us either. The great demand upon the reader of Little Dorrit—it can bring on a virtual moral crisis—is to see her quite as she is, unhaloed, not at all "symbolic," perhaps sublime but in no way transcendent. She makes no demands upon anyone, nor does she try to distinguish herself in any respect. Her behavior is geared entirely to the needs and feelings of those who are near her. She is a great comforter, which may be all that goodness can be in this world. No one could possibly say of Little Dorrit, as Aglaya says of Prince Myshkin, that she lacks tenderness and "has nothing but the truth." What can truth be to her, who lives by the grace of daily obligation?

Little Dorrit is an astonishing conception, perhaps the sole entirely persuasive figure of "positive goodness" in modern fiction. (The only possible rival is the grandmother in Proust's great novel.) As against Dostoevsky's prescription, she is drawn neither in the comic mode nor as an innocent. For modern readers she constitutes a severe problem. Some dismiss her as insipid; others find it difficult to credit her reality and perhaps difficult to live with that reality if they do credit it. Finally, as with all literary judgments, we reach a point where exegesis, persuasion, and eloquence break down, and fundamental differences of perception have to be acknowledged. I myself feel that a failure to respond to the shy magnificence of what Dickens has done here signifies a depletion of life.

How does he manage it? I wish there were some great clinching formula but do not believe there is—a part of critical wisdom is to recognize the limits of critical reach. Part of the answer, a fairly small part, may be due to what some critics have seen as Dickens's limitation: his inability to conceptualize in a style persuasive to modern readers, or, still more to the point, his lack of interest in trying to conceptualize. Dickens makes no claim for Little Dorrit, he fits her into no theological or theoretical system, he cares little if at all about her symbolic resonance. He simply *sees* her, a gleam of imagination. He trusts to the sufficiency of his depiction, a feat of discipline by a writer not always disciplined.

Quite deliberately Dickens shrinks Little Dorrit in size, voice, will, and gesture. Though clearly an adult, she seems almost childlike. She loves Arthur Clennam, the thoughtful, melancholy man worn down by failure. They marry, not in a rush of sensuality but as a pact of "making do," two people bruised into tenderness. Other writers seeking to validate goodness have fixed upon their characters' revealing flaws in order to retain some plausibility. Dickens, however, presents goodness not through the persuasiveness of a flaw but through the realism of a price. The price of Little Dorrit's goodness, as of her marriage to Clennam, is a sadly reduced sexuality—an equivalent perhaps to Billy Budd's stammer. It is as if Dickens had an unspoken belief that a precondition for goodness is the removal of that aggression which may well be intrinsic to the sexual life.

Impresario of Minor Characters

The picaresque novel sets in motion a line of episodes, which in principle is open to indefinite extension, the sole limitations being the protagonist's energy and the reader's patience. The picaro moves from adventure to adventure, and each cluster of incidents brings him into relation with a new set of minor characters whose task it is to speed the action and then fade away (also to entertain a bit). Within the picaro (assuming he has a "within"), nothing much happens: he simply moves along to the next episode. What counts here is not experience but energy—which may explain why a mode of fiction in which the central figure keeps rushing through events comes finally to seem quite static. It is a little like running in place.

Dickens, in his last great novels, takes the picaresque line of action and bends it into a sphere or circle enclosing the modern city. The picaro's seemingly endless dash through linear space now becomes a claustral repetitiveness of set pieces, with each cluster of incidents bringing back an ensemble of minor characters. But now, especially in *Bleak House*, the most original of Dickens's formal innovations, the "minor characters" come to occupy or to appropriate the forefront of the action. In Dickens's hands, the novel draws upon a large number of interlocking and juxtaposed social groups, in their sum constituting what has been called a polyphonic structure. Simultaneously, the novel appears to acquire a voice of its own, the collective voice of the city, for which Dickens's virtuoso rhetoric serves as stand-in. In this atmosphere of bewildering appearances and shifting phantasms, the city comes to seem an enormous, spreading, and threatening creature, a fearsome Other apart from the men and women inhabiting it. London, by the time Dickens wrote his last complete novel, *Our Mutual Friend*, struck him as a hopeless city "where the whole metropolis was a heap of vapour charged with muffled sounds of wheels, and enfolding a gigantic catarrh." This sense of the city will spread through large parts of European literature, from Döblin to Céline, Beckett to Kafka. If by now it seems familiar, an effort of the historical imagination can recapture its revolutionary character.

Revolutionary too is Dickens's treatment of minor characters in the late novels, especially *Bleak House* and *Little Dorrit*. In Smollett's picaresque fictions, obviously an important influence on the early Dickens, it barely matters whether his figures are reasonable facsimiles of human beings, let alone whether they have finely demarcated selves. Like the physicist Laplace dismissing God as an unneeded hypothesis, Smollett can dispense with the hypothesis of selfhood (supposing, which is unlikely, that he was even aware of it), and thereby gain freedom for play with incident and language. But Dickens, in massing his minor characters, is very much aware, even negatively obsessed, with the problem of self or identity. He is making a discovery of very large consequence: that most of the urban figures whom he renders as caricature or grotesque have no souls. In a valid artistic exaggeration, he "totalizes" their soullessness.

Some new and barely identifiable power in the world, destructive and crushing, has annulled whatever souls these figures might have had. For Dickens this comes as a great shock—walk through our cities today and it can still be a great shock. Dickens wheels in his Chadbands, Guppeys, and Smallweeds not just for entertainment, nor just to populate the "Dickens theater"—it is the soullessness of these figures that, through a demonic comedy, provides the ground for the entertainment. Dickens is also testing a hypothesis, in the one certain way a novelist can: through representation. Can he find in these creatures anything but soullessness? Occasionally, as with Snagsby in *Bleak House*, there is a shred of soul, but most of these minor characters turn out to be quite as he had feared, the waste of the city.

In the great novels of Dickens's last years, the minor characters may be slotted as mere accessories to the action, but they soon break out of these limits, so that in *Bleak House* and to a lesser extent in *Little Dorrit* and *Our Mutual Friend* they often become the center of interest while the ostensible heroes and heroines, too often paste figures, have to carry the plot.

Why should the minor characters come to seem so much more memorable than the major ones, indeed, come to be what the Dickens novel "is all about"? I offer a few speculations:

While formally enlisted in Dickens's elephantine plots, the minor characters are allowed repeatedly to step forward on their own, like performers in a skit, so that the plot can do little or no damage to their vitality.

The fine sentiments which the official Dickens feels obliged to drape about his major characters are largely abandoned when the authentic Dickens, fierce and corrosive, allows his minor characters freedom to exhibit or, as we now say, to do their own thing.

The minor characters are not burdened with an excess of civilized qualities; they act out of a direct and "primitive" (often really a socially decadent) energy, quite as if the "humor" were a basic truth about mankind.

With most of the minor characters there is no pretense of individuality; they can be uninhibited in their generic or even reductive traits, making of the type a monolithic, unshaded force. Indifference to subtlety brings enormous gains in graphic representativeness.

In their grouping and regroupings, their repeated appearances, the minor characters are truly of the city, inconceivable in any other setting, while a good number of Dickens's major characters seem to be transplanted to the city, alien there and unhappy. The minor characters are utterly at home.

In Little Dorrit, it is true, one major character, Arthur Clennam, is full-scale and persuasively subtle, but even there the gallery of the soulless, those on top who make things go and those on the bottom who do the going, occupies a large part of the book's foreground. Lacking a ready vocabulary with which to describe or place such figures, we call them grotesques. What Dickens is actually doing with these minor characters—more abundantly in Bleak House, with diminished fervor in Our Mutual Friend—is akin to what his literary cousin, Gogol, evoked with the phrase "dead souls." Evil is no surprise for Dickens; he has plenty of it in his early books. But by the late novels, evil has been somewhat subordinated as an active principle. Soullessness—that for Dickens is now more terrifying and familiar, the discovery of creatures formed in the image of man but operating as mere functions of the city.

This is a radically new vision of things. Notwithstanding some connections and similarities with Ben Jonson's "humors," it is also a radically new way of presenting characters, for Dickens sees them in their social specificity, as Jonson did not. Chadband and his monumental cant, the Smallweeds in their smoldering venality, the Barnacles in their sublime presumption—all are transfigured into varieties of comedy but embodying an increasingly acute sense of class and an utterly grim sense of the world. These are the antimen of greed, commerce, repression, the paltry carriers of the cash nexus. Entering the novel individually as minor characters, they mass together as a major presence.

Becoming Dostoevsky

To be true to one's self: this modern yearning takes the form of hoping, first of all, to discover what that self might be. Among writers it figures as a search for an authentic voice, which is to say, a public or literary voice, an outward simulation of self. But then, as the years pass, writers, fearing the humiliation that comes when fading of energy leads to self-imitation, want to break away from their true self. They want a second chance, another start. They want a new self won through transcending the old one. At the very moment of his death, Henry James, in his unfinished novel *The Ivory Tower*, was on the verge of creating a new Henry James, fiercely satirical in his view of society as he had seldom been before. Similar things could be said about Melville, George Eliot, Fitzgerald. But the most striking instance seems to me that of Dickens, who was only fifty-eight when he died, but who in his late great work—the four novels from *Bleak House* to *Our Mutual Friend*—was steadily becoming "another" writer.

In *Little Dorrit* there is a passage likely to excite the curiosity of any serious reader. It occurs in Book the First, Chapter 14. Little Dorrit, having been locked out of the Marshalsea Prison, walks with her weak-minded friend Maggy through the cold London night. They have no shelter. They meet an unnamed prostitute who at first takes Little Dorrit to be a child.

> The supposed child kept her head drooped down, and kept her form close at Maggy's side.
>
> "Poor thing!" said the woman. "Have you no feeling, that you keep her out in the cruel streets at such a time as this? Have you no eyes, that you don't see how delicate and slender she is? Have you no sense (you don't look as if you had much) that you don't take more pity on this cold and trembling little hand?"
>
> She had stepped across to that side, and held the hand between her own two, chafing it. "Kiss a poor lost creature, dear," she said, bending her face, "and tell me where she's taking you."
>
> Little Dorrit turned toward her.
>
> "Why, my God!" she said, recoiling, "you're a woman!"

"Don't mind that!" said Little Dorrit, clasping one of her hands that had suddenly released hers. "I am not afraid of you."

"Then you had better be," she answered. "Have you no mother?"

"No."

"No father?"

"Yes, a very dear one."

"Go home to him, and be afraid of me. Let me go. Good night!"

"I must thank you first; let me speak to you as if I really were a child."

"You can't do it," said the woman. "You are kind and innocent; but you can't look at me out of a child's eyes. I never should have touched you, but I thought that you were a child."

And with a strange, wild cry, she went away.

The prostitute assumes Little Dorrit is safe to approach because she is a child, since a child will not rebuff her. Actually, being quite indifferent to the world's judgments about "fallen women," Little Dorrit would welcome her with kindness. But the prostitute, even while recognizing that Little Dorrit is "kind and innocent," cannot really credit her essential goodness, for all experience dictates that such goodness in an adult is beyond credence.

Dickens offers no explanation of why he included this passage, nor does he bring back the prostitute on a later page, as is his usual way with minor figures.

Now there is a way of "absorbing" this passage into the scheme of the novel, and that is to suggest that the prostitute's response to Little Dorrit is an extreme refraction of the worldliness which, in this book as no doubt in the actual world, denies the possibility of the kind of goodness represented by Little Dorrit. This would seem to be a fairly plausible reading, at least thematically, but it quite fails to account for what is most striking about the passage—its intense, even overwrought tone, the vibration of the prose. It is overwrought and pulsing even for Dickens, with an excess of emotion beyond any cause that we can plausibly locate in the story itself.

Our natural desire to find a harmonious relation between a local passage and the novel's dominant theme can easily lead us into the error—rather frequent in academic criticism—which takes it for granted that everything in a novel has a necessary function. If it's there, there must be a good reason for it, and the critic's job is to find the reason. The error consists in a failure to recognize the frequency with which, in extended works of fiction, there are and perhaps need to be loose ends, cues not taken up, false starts. No writer, not even the most self-conscious craftsman, is likely to keep every line under entire control.

Let me then propose a speculation. Dickens was the kind of novelist who kept looking past the work on which he was engaged, straining toward new insights and devices, retuning moral premises which, it might be, he had not yet fully developed in the book he was composing. None of his novels was quite like either its predecessors or successors: there is constant restlessness, movement forward and sometimes backward.

In the passage I have quoted, Dickens was anticipating that late in his career he might become Dostoevsky. There is a powerful urge, never completed, to enact a transition from the Dickens who was using his early comic grotesques in behalf of a stringent moral-social criticism to a dimly envisaged Dickens who would penetrate, as no English novelist had yet done, mixed psychological states, extreme versions of human personality and its disorders, and perhaps even negotiate the Dostoevskian vision of redemption through sin. The prostitute seems more like a character out of *Crime and Punishment* than out of any of Dickens's novels: there is really no urgent "need" for her in *Little Dorrit*, although the tone of the passage suggests that in ways we will never quite grasp Dickens felt a need to imagine her. And perhaps—I continue to speculate—if Dickens had gone ahead to "become" Dostoevsky, the figures of Little Dorrit and the prostitute, here briefly crossing, would have been conflated.

By the time Dickens came to write *Our Mutual Friend*, his last completed novel, he was struggling toward a view of the human psyche and, still more important, a prospect of salvation not realized in any of his earlier books, though anticipated in the chapter about Miss Wade in *Little Dorrit* and in the portrayal of Bradley Headstone in *Our Mutual Friend*. Done with a caustic innerness unique in Dickens's fiction, Bradley Headstone represents a fusion of class *ressentiment* and psychological malaise. Earnest, sweaty, rigid, Headstone suffers the exquisite pain of a plebeian risen, through costly exertions, to the status of respectability—he is a schoolmaster—but constantly aware of his clumsiness of person and speech. His dark-suited outer presence barely masks a seething mass of anger, frustration, self-hatred, and he knows that no exertions on his part will ever bring him the ease and polish of a gentleman. In this truly Dostoevskian portrait, Dickens projected both a sense of lingering plebeian rage and an equally powerful wish to subject his memories to punitive rebuke. The result is a great piece of work, even if ill-adjusted to other parts of *Our Mutual Friend*. We respond to such elements or strands in the late novels as to a musical composition which contains a phrase that will be fully developed only in a later work—which in the life of Dickens never materialized. So there is little point in asking what light the passage I have quoted from *Little Dorrit* sheds on the novel as a whole, for the passage really belongs, as it were, to another novel, one that might have brought Dickens to a triumph of self-transcendence but was, alas, never to be written.

That Dickens greatly influenced Dostoevsky is common knowledge (see Angus Wilson's "Dickens and Dostoevsky" in his book *Diversity and Depth in Fiction*). That Dickens knew only a story or two by Dostoevsky seems also well established—it is quite impossible that he could have been significantly influenced by Dostoevsky. What was at work were parallel developments and inclinations within two writers profoundly troubled by the life of nineteenth-century Europe and, more important still, profoundly moved by the possibilities evoked in the story of Christ. To become Dostoevsky could, I venture, have been Dickens's literary fate had he lived another seven or eight years. Or to phrase this notion more modestly, let us say that Dostoevsky is a name we give to the glimpsed desires of the late Dickens.

Tolstoy: Did Anna Have to Die?

{1994}

IN HIS BOOK *Personal Impressions* Isaiah Berlin prints an account of a lengthy conversation he had in 1945 with Anna Akhmatova, the great Russian poet. Why, Akhmatova asks him,

Why did Anna Karenina have to be killed? . . . As soon as she leaves Karenin, everything changes; she suddenly becomes a fallen woman in Tolstoy's eyes. . . . Of course there are pages of genius, but the basic morality is disgusting. Who punishes Anna? God? No, society; that same society the hypocrisy of which Tolstoy is never tired of denouncing. In the end he tells us that she repels even Vronsky. Tolstoy is lying: he knew better than that. The morality of *Anna Karenina* is the morality of Tolstoy's wife, of his Moscow aunts; he knew the truth, yet he forced himself, shamefully, to conform to philistine convention. Tolstoy's morality is a direct expression of his own private life, his personal vicissitudes. When he was happily married he wrote *War and Peace*, which celebrates family life. After he started hating Sofia Andreevna, but was not prepared to divorce her because divorce is condemned by society, and perhaps by the peasants too, he wrote *Anna Karenina* and punished her for leaving Karenin. When he was old and no longer lusted so violently for peasant girls, he wrote *The Kreutzer Sonata*, and forbade sex altogether.

To this vivid account Berlin adds the remark, "Perhaps this summing up was not meant too seriously: but Akhmatova's dislike of Tolstoy's sermons was genuine. She regarded him as an egocentric of immense vanity, and an enemy of love and freedom." Just how seriously Akhmatova meant her attack on Tolstoy we will never know, but it is interesting that D. H. Lawrence, a writer utterly different from her, had a similar view of Tolstoy's novel, though in somewhat cruder form. Lawrence wrote:

> Why, when you look at it, all the tragedy comes from Vronsky's and Anna's fear of society. . . . They couldn't live in the pride of their sincere passion, and spit in Mother Grundy's eye. And that, that cowardice, was the real "sin." The novel makes it obvious, and knocks old Leo's teeth out.

Well, old Leo's teeth are not so easily knocked out. Provocative as the remarks of Akhmatova and Lawrence may be, they suffer from a common fault: they fail to consider Anna Karenina as a character in a novel, as she actually appears in Tolstoy's pages.

Anna is so sexually vibrant, so striking in her beauty and charm, that one can easily forget how limited are her social views and circumstances. The wife of a high czarist official, Anna is a woman completely part of the Russian upper classes. At no point does she express any explicit criticism of the values that inform her society and her class, let alone any rebellious sentiments. She is not a George Sand or a Frieda Lawrence, not even a George Eliot. Tolstoy is quite clear about this in a passage that comes shortly after Anna has told Karenin about her affair with Vronsky:

> She felt that the position she enjoyed in society, which had seemed of so little consequence that morning, was precious to her after all, and that she would not have the strength to exchange it for the shameful one of a woman who has deserted her husband and child to join her lover; that, however she might struggle, she could not be stronger than herself. She would never know freedom in love. . . .

Especially telling are the words, "she could not be stronger than herself"— something that a self-declared rebel might be supposed to be. Until this point Tolstoy has shrewdly, with what might be called his sexual cunning, persuaded us of Anna's attractiveness. He relies very little on direct statement, knowing that it is seldom effective in this respect, but instead registers the impressions Anna makes on other characters, most strikingly in the incident toward the end of the novel where the upright Levin, meeting her, with his disposition toward righteousness, succumbs to her completely. Anna's power of attraction clearly rests on a strong, increasingly asserted sexuality, especially of course for Vronsky; when he first pursues her, she experiences "a feeling of joyful pride," the pride of a beautiful woman. Her sexuality is not aggressive, except a little toward the end, when unhappiness prods her to an exercise of her powers; but in the main, it is a sexuality that is simply part of her splendid being. Yet even though she is able to rise above, or, if you prefer, sink below, the norms and customs of her social milieu, she makes no effort to deny or reject these. Her passion is neither sustained nor spoiled by an idea.

And that is precisely what makes Anna so interesting. An intellectual rebel against the norms of nineteenth-century Russian society might well engage our sympathies, but in a way less dramatic, less internalized than by the situation Tolstoy creates. Anna Karenina is not struggling for a new mode or path in life, either for herself or for her sex; she cares only about being with the man she loves, quite apart from any larger social or moral issues. Yet this soon becomes the root of her dilemma. The love between Anna and Vronsky, based as it is on a fine mixture of sexual attraction and personal sympathies, brings her into a deadly clash with society, a clash she never desires nor quite understands. Indeed, I would say that the power of the novel depends on the fact that Anna remains a conventional woman—intelligent, sensitive, even bold—but still a conventional woman driven by the strength of her feelings into an unconventional role she cannot in principle defend. She feels her love to be good, she believes her behavior is bad.

If my account, so far, has any merit, then the question to be asked is not Why must Anna be killed? A real-life Anna would probably not kill herself, but would drag out her years unhappily, with or without Vronsky. For certain kinds of readers, her death is to be seen as a mere novelistic convention, a device for rounding out the plot. But I think the real question, drawing upon the entirety of the action provided by Tolstoy, is not the death of Anna; it is the impossibility of the life she has chosen with Vronsky—an impossibility that finds its final realization in her suicide. In saying this, I should add that, as drawn by Tolstoy, Vronsky is a decent and honorable man who loves Anna and suffers because of her suffering. The two are trapped simply because it is impossible for people like them—which is to say, almost everyone—to live "outside" society. Portrayed as it is with a protective tenderness, the love of Anna and Vronsky seems deeply affecting: Tolstoy offers no judgment, either for himself or on behalf of his aunts; but this love remains unsupported by any principle (or delusion) strong enough to enable them to resist the judgments of the society in which they must continue to live.

There is a revealing incident when Anna and Vronsky go off to live comfortably in Venice. Cut off from his usual pursuits, Vronsky decides to take up painting, perhaps with some hope for self-fulfillment, perhaps simply to pass the time. ("Soon he felt a desire spring up in his heart for desires.") Anna and Vronsky meet a Russian painter named Mikhailov, an irritable fellow but a serious artist, and through his unspoken but harsh judgment of Vronsky's painting we recognize a dismissal of artistic dilettantism. Vronsky himself, acknowledging as much, abandons his painting and returns with Anna to Russia. He is a nobleman, an officer and sportsman, unable to live for long apart from his "natural" milieu. Meanwhile Mikhailov's view of Vronsky's painting has a certain impact on Anna's passing notion that she will write children's books. Art and literature cannot provide a sanctuary; step by step Tolstoy tightens the noose of their isolation.

Unlike Vronsky, Anna can for a time live by love alone ("To have him entirely to herself was a continual joy"). Now I suppose this might be taken as evidence of Tolstoy's sexual bias—the belief that while personal relations suffice for women, men need a larger arena of public life. But it is also possible—I think, plausible—to conclude that Tolstoy is showing that, for all their individuality, Anna and Vronsky cannot wrench themselves away from the mores of their historical moment. Even Anna comes to feel that a life devoted entirely to love can be stifling and that, like everyone else, she needs the comforts of sociability, so that when her sister-in-law Dolly comes to visit the house she shares with Vronsky, Anna is delighted.

Just how does society press down on the two lovers? Not through a lack of money. Not through social cuts, though they suffer a few. It is the verdict of society that deprives Anna of her son, Seryozha, and Vronsky, with the best will in the world, cannot quite grasp, let alone share, the pain this brings her. The most severe pressures, however, are internal, within Anna and Vronsky themselves. They introject society's judgments, they feel uneasy in the presence of others, they make others feel uneasy in their presence. The very atmosphere of their life forms a kind of social pressure. Without normal social relations, Anna and Vronsky, even while deeply in love, begin to get on each other's nerves, become suspicious and hurt, start protecting themselves from the wounds each feels the other is inflicting even while aware that neither intends to. It is all insidious, terrible, part of the destructiveness so often interwoven with a great love. Society manifests itself in the most painful way: through their self-consciousness. All this Tolstoy understood with an intuitive exactness, and nothing he ever wrote matches in honesty his portrait of the disintegration of their love.

No, Anna does not have to be killed. She had only to be defeated in the central adventure of her life; after that, the killing hardly matters.

Personal Reflections

Reflection on the
Death of My Father
{1982}

THE DAY MY FATHER DIED I felt almost nothing. I stood near the hospital bed and stared at the shrunken body of this man who never again would greet me with an ironic rebuke. I saw nothing but inert flesh, a transformation beyond understanding. Then came a sequence of absurd tasks—notifying my father's *landsmanshaft* (fraternal society) to arrange for a grave; deciding whether to buy the more expensive coffin, ornately carved, or the bare wooden coffin that my father would have chosen, sullenly, while preferring the expensive one. These rituals which, honor them or not, I had to get through, served at least to blunt grief.

Even before my father died I had made him into a myth. Myths are wonderfully convenient for blocking the passage between yourself and your feelings. Now into his mid-eighties, my father steadily grew feebler and complained, even whined, a good deal—I judged this to be a "weakness," partly out of fear that I shared it with him. To see your father lose masculine force is an experience profoundly unnerving, like watching your own body disintegrate. To see him fall because he could no longer walk was unbearable, and then I would berate myself for the cowardice that kept me from bearing it. Had my father become senile it might have been easier. But his mind grew keener as his body decayed, and he would describe his plight with a self-pitying exactitude.

What did he want from me? To move in with him, yielding entirely to his needs? No, he said, he didn't want that at all. He wanted nothing from me, there was nothing I could do for him, his complaint was not directed to me or indeed to anyone. He sat there in his apartment in Co-Op City, staring at the walls but still—I knew him as I knew myself—fearful of death. Had my father used my kind of language, he would have said all this is simply in the nature of things and there is nothing to do but submit. Submit, yes, but not without some noise.

When I took him to the hospital, he still had enough strength to argue against my proposal that we hire a private nurse. He didn't need one. And what could a nurse do, make him young again? His eyes glinted as he said this, waiting to see if I would record his last stab at paternal irony.

Oh, the unmeasurable willfulness of these immigrant Jews, exerted to their last moment in the service of self-denial! My father had saved, literally from years of sweat, some forty thousand dollars, but that had to be kept . . . for what? He didn't say, but didn't have to. I understood: *the night cometh when no man can work.* The last dike against helplessness is a bankbook.

So he was right again, my sardonic Pop, as so often he had been about my ways, my women, my life. I hired a private nurse and, to no one's surprise, my father accepted her without protest. His obligation had been to argue against hiring her, mine to hire her. It was my turn to pay. He had never before allowed it, but now it was all right—no, it was right.

I did my duty. I ran up to Co-Op City in the northeast Bronx, to Montefiore Hospital in the northwest Bronx. I did all a son is supposed to do, but without generosity, without grace. It would take me three hours to get to and from the hospital, but in the hospital itself I could not bear to stay more than twenty minutes. I spoke to the doctors, scheduled the nurses, brought my father food, and all the while could not look at his wasted body, for I knew myself to be unworthy, a son with a chilled heart.

I could not speak words of love because I did not love my father as a man. I had discovered, long ago, that he was "weak," too dependent on women—an affliction that seems to run in our family. Yet I was overwhelmed with emotion at the thought of his decades of suffering and endurance. Even while still breathing he had become for me a representative figure of the world from which I came, and I suppose a good part of *World of Our Fathers* is no more than an extension of what I knew about him.

Close to the end he told my son that finally I had been a good son. He did not say a loving son. Was there a difference in his mind? Could I doubt his gift for discriminations? Whereas he, perhaps not such a good father, had been a loving one, always ready, after his opening sarcasm, to accept my foolishness and chaos. The words he spoke in praising me, which I knew to be deeply ambiguous, finally brought the tears long blocked by my hateful addiction to judgment.

I knew the end was close when one day I came to his room and saw he no longer troubled to cover his genitals. Like most immigrant Jews, he had been a severely respectable man, shy about his body, even wearing a tie and jacket in the August heat. Now it no longer mattered. I could pay for the nurse, he could leave himself exposed.

In death he seemed terribly small, and I kept thinking back to all those years he had spent over the press iron, the weariness, the blisters, the fears, the subways. In the space that circumstances had thrown up between us there still remained a glimmer of understanding, a tie of the sardonic. To make a myth of the man I should have mourned as a father, to cast him at the center of the only story I had to tell, was to reach a kind of peace between generations.

From the Thirties to the Rise of Neoconservatism: Interview with Stephen Lewis

{1983}

RVING HOWE IS NOT JUST ONE of the leading intellectuals of the twentieth century; he is the complete eclectic. He is rooted in the East European Jewish tradition, which migrated to the United States, and in particular, to New York City at the end of the nineteenth century and which put its roots in scholarship and the trade union movement. The amalgam produced a tremendous literary and social culture of which Irving Howe became one of the chief exponents. His migration, the pattern of migration of his people, was mirrored in his wonderful book, *World of Our Fathers*, a cultural and social history of East European Jewry, which covers from the end of the nineteenth century to the mid-twentieth. It won the National Book Award in 1977.

The high points of his career, Howe's trade union experience, the Socialist experience, the Jewish experience, came together in active politics, anti-Stalinist, anti-Soviet, Trotskyite in nature particularly in the late 1930s and 1940s. He spent his life in passionate scholastic, dialectical debate. And then, as he developed his political arts, he became more and more academic, and more and more literary. And in the latter forties and early fifties he became part of that intellectual community that surrounded the journal *Partisan Review*, part of the most vibrant intellectual community that the United States produced in the postwar period, which has since largely disintegrated. When Socialism itself dismembered, he became founder and editor of a quarterly journal called *Dissent* in 1954.

Howe is better known as a literary critic and a political commentator. The two were inseparable for him. He is a great Yiddishist in the sense that he translates a lot of Yiddish into English that gives Socialist culture an almost folklore view of history. He is an apostle, in a way, of Trotsky and has published the selected works of Trotsky. He is a literary critic of extraordinary dimensions. He's written critical biographies of Thomas Hardy, Sherwood Anderson, William Faulkner. He brought together the literary and the political in a fashion that has rarely been achieved in the United States.

Howe is cherubic, gentle, and principled. He speaks with anecdotal passion and in the reverberation of the voice is a constant intellectual depth.

Q [LEWIS]: Tell me about your strong early Jewish working class antecedents.

A [HOWE]: I cannot walk by a small store in any city in America or Canada without asking myself, "How does he remain in business?" Because it reminds me of my own father's experiences. He ran a little grocery store and he lost it during the early years of the Depression. And to me a small store is immediately a focus of anxiety.

And this, I'm sure, is characteristic of many people who come out of a Jewish background. Whenever I hear somebody, a professor at a faculty occasion, start ranting against trade unions, it immediately arouses in me an absolute uncontainable fury. Because I remember that after my folks lost their little store, they both became garment workers in the New York garment district. My mother's first job was for $12 a week, my father became a presser, and in 1933 the International Ladies Garment Workers Union called a strike, which was then a very risky business, and suddenly my mother's wages, when the strike was successful, went up to $27 a week. Now that was a significant change. And suddenly there was meat on the table and I could have a shirt for a birthday present and things of that sort.

My parents were not political people. They were like the ordinary people, what we call in Yiddish the "folksmassen," they were neither religious nor political. They always voted for Franklin D. Roosevelt, but that was just part of being Jewish, and they were good trade unionists, but they never went to a meeting. They paid their dues. If there was a strike called, you went on strike. To scab was equivalent to apostasy, and the idea of the value of a trade union was sort of built into my life as a result of that.

Q [LEWIS]: In your own terms, the genesis of your Socialism was rooted in the Jewish community of New York and its internationalist background. It wasn't sectarian in that sense. It was almost universalist.

A [HOWE]: Well, I grew up in the East Bronx, now called the South Bronx. And, at that time this was an entirely Jewish neighborhood. You could get by, almost completely, with Yiddish. And the Socialists at that point were the second party in local elections behind the Democrats. Radicalism of one or another sort was very pervasive in the immigrant Jewish community. The Communists were very strong, probably the best organized group, and so this was simply accepted as part of the secular inheritance of the immigrant Jewish community.

The trouble was we could never get beyond certain ethnic boundaries. We couldn't break into other kinds of communities. We couldn't break into, for example, the Irish neighborhoods. When I grew up, the Roman Catholic Church was looked upon as a bastion of reaction. And one of the most astonishing experiences of my life and from my point of view, very encouraging, has been to see the way the Catholic Church in America has opened itself up, has become much more liberal. In fact, at the moment, decidedly more liberal than the Jewish community. The milieu in which I grew up, the immigrant Jewish milieu, which was largely secular, leftist, etc., has almost entirely disappeared. There are only a few old-timers. You can imagine [how old] that is if I am still considered one of the young ones.

Q [LEWIS]: I can imagine. I am an expression of it myself, because although I understand a great deal of Yiddish, I don't speak it. And one of the things that almost brings tears to one's eyes is to go and speak to a meeting of the Workman's Circle, and there are loving remnants. There are fifteen or twenty people now, very old, who ask you questions in Yiddish, which you answer in English. In your own life, in the latter thirties, the inability to break into the broader community, to some extent I take it, resulted in the—retreat perhaps isn't a fair word, but I'll use it—an intense scholastic internal anti-Stalinist but post-Trotskyist debate.

A [HOWE]: Yes. Well, you see, in the American intellectual community, and in the Left in general, Trotsky played a role, which he did not play, I think, in any other country. The intellectual world in America in the thirties was very heavily under Communist, or as we called it then Stalinist, domination. The majority of American leftist intellectuals, for example, supported the Moscow trials and believed that the trials were legitimate. Those of us who were anti-Stalinist and who were beginning to see the terrible things going on in the Soviet Union, tended to gravitate to the image of Trotsky because he was so eloquent and so forceful and so forthright, and unyielding, uncompromising in his opposition to Stalinism.

The negative side was that, as it regarded American politics, it led us into a dead end from which some of us extracted ourselves only after a certain number of years. And indeed the formation of *Dissent* began as part of that process of pulling out of that sectarianism. But the appeal that Trotsky had, for a little while, for a few years, has to be understood in terms of the special situation of American intellectual cultural life in the late thirties. He was the counterforce against the deceit and the mediocrity of Stalinist influence.

Q [LEWIS]: Before *Dissent* came, you had this minor and inconsequential aberration of writing briefly for *Time* magazine and then you went on to become part of that wonderful greatness of the *Partisan Review*. Can you nostalgically reflect on those days?

A [HOWE]: Yes. In those days, *Partisan Review*, though it had a circulation of no more than six or seven thousand copies, was surely the most influential cultural magazine. You see, we won the intellectual war against the Stalinists and fellow travelers by the early forties. In France, presumably a much more advanced country, this took at least another thirty years. We won it because there was a greater spirit of independence, the tradition that goes back to Emerson and Thoreau of standing on your own feet among American intellectuals, and people like Edmund Wilson, James T. Farrell, Lionel Trilling, Meyer Schapiro, many others, broke away from the Stalinist influence during the thirties and they gravitated around this small magazine.

It was a magazine which tried—not I think with entire success but for the moment very interestingly—to combine two impulses, anti-Stalinist leftism and the defense of cultural and literary modernism. Two avant-gardes. As it turned out, the avant-gardes were moving in opposite or different directions. Nevertheless, for a short while, the union of these two things had a great impact. It also developed a style of its own. Freelance, polemical, aggressive, with a great concentration on bravura and brilliance. It perfected the essay as a literary mode. It didn't do so terribly much in regard to fiction [or] poetry, but for the combative brilliant display essay, it really was an extraordinary phenomenon.

Well, I came along in the late 1940s. I was born in 1920, so when I got out of the war in 1946, and I began looking around and to develop literary ambitions, and I decided that the revolution was not going to come in America, and I had no particular place in organizing it, since it wasn't going to come, I developed more literary interests and I made contact with the editors of *Partisan Review*. In typical leftist fashion, you'll surely appreciate this, my first overture to them was to send them an attack on their magazine. And Philip Rahv, who was the editor, also knowing something about the psychology of this, roared with laughter and said, "You don't think we're going to print this?" I guess I really didn't expect him to. But it began a friendship. You begin a friendship on the left by attacking somebody. It began a friendship and then it continued.

Q [LEWIS]: Are you good at thumbnail sketches? Let me throw some names at you. Edmund Wilson.

A [HOWE]: I first met Wilson in 1951 or 1952. I was doing a book on Sherwood Anderson. Wilson had known Anderson when he was younger. I went up to Cape Cod to talk to him about Anderson. He was then younger than I am now, but I thought of him as [a] great man, he was a great man in a way. He was fat. He looked like a mixture of Herbert Hoover and W. C. Fields, and little bit of Henry James thrown in physically. And we sat down to talk presumably about Anderson.

But Wilson had this omnivorous hunger for information. He found out that during the war I had been stationed in Alaska. Instead of my learning about Anderson, he learned about Alaska. I left him about one in the morning, and he was a tremendous drinker. And from the background that I come from, you don't really learn to drink. And he was terribly scornful. He was greatly amused at my inability to match him in scotch. Now the truth is, most of the gentile intellectuals couldn't match him either.

Q [LEWIS]: What about the essayist Dwight Macdonald?

A [HOWE]: Dwight Macdonald was this gangling skinny chap who afterward developed a potbelly. When I first knew him he was a member of the small left-wing group that I belonged to for a time. A group led by a man named Max Shachtman, and then he [Macdonald] dropped out. And he started putting out a magazine called *politics*, a very brilliant left-wing magazine . . . very open, lively. I came out of the army and needed work, and Dwight hired me as a part-time assistant on *politics* for the munificent salary of $15 a week. I used to do a magazine chronicle for Macdonald and he gave me a pen name of Theodore Dryden, who he said raised ferrets on Staten Island! I suppose some future historian is going to be searching the population of Staten Island for this ferret breeder.

And afterwards we tended to drift apart, not so much because of political differences, but the notion that there was this intellectual community in New York was at one time true. But by the time word got out about it, it was no longer true. In general, I think that you can make that as a useful summary. When the word is out about something in *Newsweek*, it no longer is true.

Q [LEWIS]: When did you meet Saul Bellow and collaborate with him?

A [HOWE]: Saul Bellow I met in the late forties at the house of a friend of his. By the time I met Bellow, he was an aspiring novelist, terribly thin-skinned, very handsome, and rather rude in manner. And then I knew him for a time when I was living in Princeton in the late forties and early fifties when he was part of a quite brilliant little group, [including] Delmore Schwartz, John Berryman, and some other young writers.

My first close relationship of a literary kind with Bellow came in the middle fifties, it must have been 1955, the year isn't exact in my mind. I was then working on a volume called *A Treasury of Yiddish Stories*, together with a Yiddish poet, Eliezer Greenberg, and we were doing translations, or editing translations of Yiddish fiction, the first such serious volume in the English language.

We came across an extraordinary story by a writer who was then totally unknown, Isaac Bashevis Singer, called "Gimpel the Fool" and we tried to think— you see, translation is like matchmaking, you try to find the translator who will fit the writer. And the one who seemed best to fit Singer was Bellow, and at that time he was not yet the great man that he'd become, and he was delighted with the opportunity to do this.

Bellow has a pretty good command of Yiddish. We sat him down in Greenberg's apartment on East 17th Street and he banged out this translation at enormous speed in a couple of hours. Greenberg would read the Yiddish to him; Saul would type it out in English. Once in a while Bellow didn't know a word and Greenberg would translate it for him and I just sat watching the whole thing completely entranced. And then he took it and fixed it up a little bit. And that was it. And it turned out to really be a classical translation, and it was the beginning of Singer's career in the English language.

Q [LEWIS]: To hear you talk of this period, of the 1940s and 1950s, is to hear about a period of renaissance in intellectual and literary thought which one does not feel in the late 1970s, early 1980s.

A [HOWE]: It may be that there are young people around who have groups and are doing exciting things and we don't know about them yet. I suspect that what you say is true in this sense. If you look at the cultural situation in America today, there is an enormous amount of talent. A lot of gifted younger writers,

I could name some. Raymond Carver, Ann Beattie, a whole host of others. But somehow it doesn't add up to an interesting literary situation.

There is another reason for this. A lot of us have gotten into the academy, who never thought we would end up as professors. That is good from one point of view, because even intellectuals have to eat, and we eat more regularly when we have regular jobs. But for intellectual life there have been some disadvantages to this.

At that point, if you were a young writer, you naturally thought of coming to New York, getting a little place in the Village, and eking out a livelihood by doing book reviews and odd chores. Now, in a more affluent society, it is impossible to live the life of what Paul Goodman once called "respectable poverty." So writers have to get jobs, often in universities. There was a mass expansion of higher education in America after the war with largely good, some bad results, and as a consequence, the universities were willing to hire oddballs like us who didn't have Ph.D.s. The intellectual community is now scattered across the country.

This may be good for some regional culture, though it makes for a great deal of loneliness. But there no longer is that concentration, that focusing of energy, that makes for an intense creative life, so that you learn the situation today, where you can pick up a book of short stories—for some reason the short story is especially thriving in America—by this or that writer, and it really is very good writing. But you cannot say that you feel you are living in an intense and vivid and exciting cultural moment.

[LEWIS]: It must seem quaint, strange, curious, surreal to some of the audience to hear all of these references to Stalinism and fellow travelerism and Trotskyism and these arcane ideological truths which possessed the lives of intellectual and literary figures in the thirties, forties, and early fifties. And yet it was tremendously real for them. And it honed an analytic skill, writing skills, argumentative skills, which served people like Irving Howe wondrously in the years that followed.

We also today think of the fifties as the era of McCarthyism. McCarthy was representative of two truths. One, the shift to the right in American society, which made a lot of these people uncomfortable, and the other, the gradual deterioration of those schizophrenic, left-wing commitments. What did Howe call it? "Extracting himself from the dead end." And so he established, as part of another community, of those who were creating something new, he established the magazine Dissent.

If I can be personal for a moment, in my day, in the university days of the late fifties and early sixties, Dissent to many of us on the Left was everything, it was a Bible. When we wanted to learn about NATO, we read Dissent. Or German rearmament, the civil rights movement, Vietnam, we read *Dissent*. It was central to the development of our own ideology on the Left both in Canada and in the U.S., and I suspect for a lot of British Socialists as well. And it was a growing counterpoint to the right-wing emphasis of *Commentary* and *Encounter*, and people like Irving Kristol and Norman Podhoretz, because *Dissent* had Richard Wright, C. Wright Mills, Erich Fromm, etc. It was developing psychoanalytic views of human behavior as well as Marxist views of human behavior.

So there was a whole Socialist framework on the one hand that Howe created and sustained against the gradual right-wing development. The Socialist group was partial, tentative, ever more modest in numbers. And that was very distressing for some of the literary figures whom Irving Howe enumerates. They simply lost their political commitment entirely and went off to pursue cultural and literary careers.

Q [LEWIS]: We constantly hear right now comparisons with the fifties. I think that there are cyclical realities that keep repeating. And the beauty of your life is that it encompassed all of it and speaks strongly and feelingly with discernment, which is essentially that we have been moving steadily to the right for some time.

A [HOWE]: I think that the dominant secular line in the postwar years has been toward the right. I don't like it but I must admit it to be a fact. But this was interrupted during the sixties by the early Kennedy period, then interrupted by the Vietnam War, which split the country right down the middle, and also split the intellectual community and some of my old friends were now new enemies or new opponents. And then of course there were certain unfortunate incidents during the administration of Mr. Nixon which caused a certain amount of shame on the right, something called Watergate and things like that. But the basic drive, the dominant energy in American intellectual life, has been that of the conservatives. I don't think the best thinking—but there is a difference between the best thinking and the dominant energy.

Q [LEWIS]: Do you see a fairly straight line between the emergence of the Right in the fifties and the neoconservativism of today? I remember you saying at one point that what occurred in the fifties was as though it were a restoring of the balance, that for the first half of the century, certainly since 1917, that we had been preoccupied with left-wing analysis and thought, and that it was only natural that civilization would make that shift.

A [HOWE]: I think that is largely true. Now this again may be nostalgia; it may be that I like old conservatives better than young ones, or dead ones better than living ones. The fifties, as it seems to me now, had a conservatism that was much more qualified. Much more reflective than the neoconservatism of people today. The conservatism of the fifties, for example, was not breathing fire to push the cold war. The conservatism of the fifties would have felt embarrassed at the thought of supporting someone like Ronald Reagan.

Today, neoconservatism is much more crude and blatant and ideological. One of the interesting things, and surely you've encountered this in your own experience, about ideological politics is the way it takes on a life and a rhythm of its own. In, for example, *Commentary* magazine, which is one of the centers of neo-conservativism, it is as if each month that magazine has to take a more extreme position in order to justify itself to itself because it exists on its own excitation. Just the way the New Left did in the late sixties. And so Norman Podhoretz comes out for sending American troops to Central America, an utterly disastrous idea, which even the Reagan Administration hesitates to say in public.

I think that what is going to happen is that this is going to burn itself out. There is something about ideological politics which leads to self-immolation, to going up in smoke and flame. With one significant difference between this experience and that of the New Left, and that is, that in America today, I don't know if this is true in Canada, the big corporations have discovered the uses of ideology. And they are pouring a lot of money into the magazines, and the institutions, and the think tanks of the neoconservatives. Until about ten years ago, most American corporations thought all this intellectual talk was just nonsense and of no importance, and they simply went about their business of making money. But they discovered that in the welfare state, or the truncated version of the welfare state that we have in America, there is a conflict of ideas which is of crucial importance to them. It is just as important to Exxon as it is to the AFL-CIO.

So you have a new interpenetration between the corporate world and the intelligentsia. And you have this comic spectacle of someone like Irving Kristol, whom I recruited into the Young People's Socialist League in 1939, one of my biggest mistakes, who now sits on many corporate boards. He is a very nice and amiable fellow, but the thought of him now being a spokesman for Republicanism really raises whatever few hairs I have left. Therefore, it is possible that the neoconservatives, even if they burn themselves out intellectually, will have an institutional base that will enable them to persist.

Q [LEWIS]: You surely don't engage in self-flagellation over Kristol. One never knows in this world how quickly people will move from left to right, incorporating the new fanaticism.

A [HOWE]: As a matter of fact I sometimes think that my own intellectual career consists of constantly turning my head from left to right, watching people who had attacked me from the left as they move toward the right.

Q [LEWIS]: About ten years ago on the left in Canada there was the emergence of something called the Waffle Group, which was intensely nationalistic and ideological and left-wing and given to all of the traditional nationalization and other programs. Now of course many of them are respectable junior executives for the equivalents of IBM, and one sees in a mere decade a most remarkable shift.

A [HOWE]: If you can't nationalize the industries, you join them.

Q [LEWIS]: They would say, in a spasm of self-defense, that you bore from within. I take it that the description that you have of the current neoconservatives and their extremism was really the kind of feeling that you had of the excesses of the New Left in the 1960s. Fundamentally, that is, what divided the Old Left, if I may put it that way, and the New Left, were the terrible authoritarian touches.

A [HOWE]: With an important emotional difference: when I see what is going on now with neoconservatives, it raises an impulse to combat. I want to go in and start fighting. But, with the New Left in the late sixties, I had feelings of sadness and frustration because I saw once again the waste of energy which has been characteristic of American left-wing experience. I felt at the time that once again there was a terrible waste on our side. Now, about some of the New Leftists, I no longer felt that there was any real connection between them and me. They had gone too far and become Maoists and terrorists, and I felt that some of them, the Weathermen, were semi-fascists. But there were a lot of people within the New Left, who, driven crazy by the madness and the evil of the Vietnam War, pushed themselves into sectarian positions from which they could not retreat. Some of them have since come around and become relatively friendly with the kind of politics that I espouse, but there was a terrible waste, so that emotionally—I don't know if you've felt this in your own experience—I still find it harder to argue with people to my left than people on the right.

Q [LEWIS]: That's really interesting. I must admit I don't. But then it isn't the same experience because we've had an active political party in Canada, and so [I] resent the people on the left and the impact they have in undermining what [I] think to be the legitimacy of social democracy.

A [HOWE]: You know the story, the wonderful story, I think it is a wonderful story, about Cohen. I was at Stanford in California in 1969. I was not at the university, but I was near it. My wife at the time was teaching, was working on the campus, and I would come for lunch. And there was a gang of New Left kids who would follow me shouting slogans, harassing me in the most absurd way, a childish kind of thing. And I should have known better, and not let it get to me but of course it did get to me, since I am only human. For a number of days I kept quiet, and tried to pretend that I was above it all, but finally I lost my temper and I turned around to this very bright boy named Cohen, who was the leader of this gang.

And I said to him, "Cohen, you know what you are going to be when you grow up, when you get older, you are going to turn out to be a dentist." And he turned pale, because you know, for some reason that is not entirely clear to me, the idea of a dentist around the radical world has always been associated with philistinism and petit-bourgeois life. He felt that this was the most dreadful insult that I could have given him.

Well, I got two or three letters from various people claiming that they knew who this Cohen was and what had happened to him. One report had him as an assistant professor at Cornell, another report said he was a corporation lawyer in Los Angeles, none of them made him quite literally a dentist, but all of them suggested that he had found a very comfortable place in the world of the status quo. And so it was very hard because it was like seeing your own children going off the deep end and rebelling.

Now the point you made before is absolutely right. If there really were a structured, coherent social democratic party in America, such as the New Democratic Party here in Canada, then one could feel that these people were doing it terrible damage by destroying its possibilities to win an election or to rule a provincial government or whatever the case may be. But with us, where left-wing politics has a much more chaotic, abstract form, it was sort of like a free-for-all. It was very hard in the late sixties, very hard.

Q [LEWIS]: Your most recent publication is the editing of a collection of essays on Orwell. We are doing this interview in the latter part of 1983; 1984 is upon us. I take it that this is quite visceral with you. That for many, many years Orwell has been central for you. I even recall that at one point you attempted to model your literary writing on Orwell, some of your journalistic writing.

A [HOWE]: Yes, Orwell has been for me a very important figure. *Nineteen Eighty-Four* is a work of admonition, a work of warning and as such, it has played an enormous role. I now think that the greatest contribution that it made was toward the cleansing of the English language. When, for example, I hear Ronald Reagan say, "We are going to go into Central America in order to defend democracy" and in none of the countries that he wishes to go into is there any democracy, then the first adjective that comes to mind is that this is an Orwellian expression. It is a version of Newspeak.

Now fortunately, when one lives in a democracy, one can criticize this, and I think that the people who say that we have reached a condition at all like that of *Nineteen Eighty-Four* are being very foolish. Because the mere fact that they can say it proves that it isn't true. The whole thing of Newspeak and doublethink—this was such an extraordinarily brilliant innovation. When you read for example that in the Soviet Union, subscribers to the official encyclopedia get sets of new pages from page 428–32 to replace the existing entry with another one which changes it entirely, and they are supposed to cut out the pages and paste in the new ones, you say to yourself, Orwell was simply describing common reality.

You know the famous essay, "Politics and the English Language," which every politician should be made to read at least once a year on a day of penance, I think on Yom Kippur. All the Jewish and the goyische intellectuals and politicians should be made to read "Politics and the English Language." Would you introduce a bill like that if you were in the provincial parliament again?

Q [LEWIS]: We will make it mandatory in 1984 [laughter]. It seems to be appropriate.

Indeed, after 1984, I imagine we can expect from Irving Howe exactly what we've had until now. He'll be writing and fighting and arguing and believing, making a magnificent intellectual and literary contribution. I think one expects from him his own phrase, I noted it down: "Living the intense creative life."

Sources

"This Age of Conformity." From *Partisan Review* 21 (January–February 1954): 1.

"The Country of the Pointed Firs." From *The New Republic* 130 (May 17, 1954), 24.

"The Stories of Bernard Malamud." From *Midstream* (Summer 1958): 97–99.

"Doris Lessing: No Compromise, No Happiness." From *The New Republic* 148 (December 15, 1963).

"Life Never Let Up," review of *Call It Sleep* by Henry Roth, with an afterword by Walter Allen (New York: Avon, 1964). From *The New York Times*, October 25, 1964.

"New Styles in 'Leftism.'" From *Dissent* 13 (Summer 1965): 3.

George Orwell: "As the Bones Know." From *The Collected Essays, Journalism and Letters of George Orwell* (New York: Harcourt, Brace & World, 1968).

"The New York Intellectuals." From *Commentary* (October 1969): 4.

"A Grave and Solitary Voice: An Appreciation of Edwin Arlington Robinson." First published as "Tribute to an American Poet," *Harper's* (June 1970).

"What's the Trouble?: Social Crisis, Crisis of Civilization, or Both." From *Dissent* 18 (October 1971).

"The City in Literature." From *Commentary* 51 (May 1971): 5.

"Tribune of Socialism." From *New York Times Book Review* (November 7, 1976), SM35.

"Strangers." From *Yale Review* 66 (Summer 1977): 4.

"Introduction: Twenty-five Years of Dissent." From *Twenty-five Years of Dissent: An American Tradition*, compiled by Irving Howe (New York: Methuen, 1979).

"Introduction to *The Best of Sholom Aleichem*." From *The Best of Sholom Aleichem*, edited by Irving Howe and Ruth Wisse (Washington: New Republic Books, 1979).

"Mission from Japan," review of *The Samurai* by Shusako Endo, translated by Van C. Gessel (New York: Harper & Row, 1982). From *The New York Review of Books* 29 (November 4, 1982): 17. © 1982 by Irving Howe.

"Absalom in Israel." From *The New York Review of Books* 32 (October 10, 1985): 5.

"Why Has Socialism Failed in America?" From *Socialism and America* (New York: Harcourt Brace Jovanovich, 1985).

"Writing and the Holocaust." From *The New Republic* 195 (October 27, 1986): 17.

"Reaganism: The Spirit of the Times." From *Dissent* 33 (Fall 1986): 4.

"Two Cheers for Utopia." From *Dissent* 40 (Spring 1993): 131.

"The Road Leads Far Away," review of *A Surplus of Memory: Chronicle of the Warsaw Ghetto Uprising* by Yitzhak Zuckerman, translated by Barbara Harshav (Berkeley: University of California Press, 1993). From *The New Republic* 208 (May 3, 1993): 18.

"Mr. Bennett and Mrs. Woolf." From *A Critic's Notebook* (New York: Harcourt Brace, 1994).

"Dickens: Three Notes." From *A Critic's Notebook* (New York: Harcourt Brace, 1994).

"Tolstoy: Did Anna Have to Die?" From *A Critic's Notebook* (New York: Harcourt Brace, 1994).

"Reflection on the Death of My Father." From *A Margin of Hope: An Intellectual Autobiography* (New York: Harcourt Brace Jovanovich, 1982).

Stephen Lewis, "From the Thirties to the Rise of Neoconservatism: Politics and Intellectual Life Across a Half-Century," radio interview with the Canadian Broadcasting Company, December 1983.